D1223564

The North of England

The North of England

A History from Roman Times to the Present

FRANK MUSGROVE

Basil Blackwell

Copyright © Frank Musgrove 1990

First published 1990

Basil Blackwell Ltd
108 Cowley Road, Oxford, OX4 1JF, UK

Basil Blackwell, Inc.
3 Cambridge Center
Cambridge, Massachusetts 02142, USA

British Library Cataloguing in Publication Data

A CIP catalogue record for this book is available from the British Library.

Library of Congress Cataloging in Publication Data

Musgrove. Frank.
The north of England: a history from Roman times to the present/Frank
Musgrove.
p. cm.
ISBN 0–631–16273–9
1. England. Northern —History. I. Title.
DA670.N73M87 1990
942.7—dc20
90–416
CIP

Typeset in 11 on 13pt Caslon
by Hope Services (Abingdon) Ltd., Oxon
Printed in Great Britain by
T. J. Press Ltd, Padstow, Cornwall

Contents

Maps

Tables

I

Two Northern Millenniums

This book tells the story of the north of England over a period of some 2,000 years. During that time, between the arrival of the Romans at the Trent and the Humber in the middle of the first century AD, and the miners' strike in the mid-1980s, there have been four periods of particular northern distinction, importance and power. The first spanned the third century AD, when the imperial house of Severus established a separate northern province, 'Britannia Inferior', from south of Lincoln to the recently established (and even more recently re-established) Hadrian's Wall. At both the beginning and the end of this period Roman emperors (Septimius Severus and Constantius 'Chlorus') ruled the Roman empire from York. The second was the spectacular 'age of Bede'. It extended from the early seventh century to the end of the eighth, when Northumbria enjoyed cultural and religious influence and renown on a truly international scale, culminating in the mission of Alcuin to the court of Charlemagne. The third was the military age of the Nevilles and Percies, from the mid-fourteenth to the late fifteenth centuries; the North was then the site of great political power, enjoyed for a short period colonialist exploitation of the South, and provided England with its first and only northerner king. The fourth period of pre-eminence was the age of the industrial revolution, from the later eighteenth century to the end of the nineteenth, when northern England was the site not only of a powerful new system of industrial production, but of a great burgher civilization and a successful bourgeois revolution. The seventeenth-century bourgeois revolution that was based in London and the eastern counties, 'the great rebellion', had received only subsidiary, although by no means negligible, support from the industrial and commercial West Riding, south-east Lancashire and Cheshire; it was at last brought to a successful conclusion after 1846, with the overthrow of landed and aristocratic power, in the commercial and industrial North. Each of these periods of northern distinction lasted for about a century and a half; each was followed by a time of relative decline. What was decisive in the rise of the North on all four occasions was external circumstances. Context was of critical importance; decline followed when the context changed.

Historians have usually seen northern England as undistinguished, backward and impotent, at least before the nineteenth century. Macaulay expressed this view in graphic terms; Paul Johnson has more recently painted a similar picture; even the distinguished medievalist, G. W. S. Barrow, claims that northern England has typically, over the centuries, been little more than 'an agglomeration of intensely conservative and relatively poor communities'. He concedes only two periods of some distinction, both extremely brief, and both 'accidental': seventh-century Northumbria and the nineteenth-century industrial North. But 'The pre-eminence of the North in the century from Aethelfrith to Aldfrith is quite untypical'; it was indeed an anomaly, an aberration, and it would be another thousand years before anything of great note occurred in the North. When northern society was transformed by industrialization in the nineteenth century, it was a 'paradox' that anything so momentous should occur in such a backward region. In any event, says Barrow, it has been accorded an undue importance because it has loomed so large in the national consciousness. It was a freak: 'an extraordinary phase . . . a development which could take place only in the most unusual combination of circumstances'.[1] They could never be repeated, and northern England was predestined to revert to its normal mediocrity, obscurity and impotence.

Paul Johnson sees an inexorable and unvarying tendency to south-eastern supremacy and the political unimportance of the North. Such distinction as the North achieved in the nineteenth century was merely 'a deluding aberration', highly transitory and never of really great account. For a very brief period 'it seemed possible that the English fulcrum was shifting to the north and the west', but the wealth generated in the North tended to flow to the South and by the end of the nineteenth century 'the historic pattern was re-establishing itself'. The North was again taking on the character of a 'distressed area' exactly as the logic and pattern of history required.[2]

Macaulay, writing in 1848, quite correctly saw northern greatness in the first half of the nineteenth century arising principally from coal: from the discovery that 'the regions north of the Trent possessed in their coal beds a source of wealth far more precious than the gold mines of Peru.' But before this discovery and exploitation of coal, all was barbarism and backwardness in the North: 'Physical and moral causes had occurred to prevent civilization from spreading to that region.' Poor soil and climate played their part, but crucially the problem was centuries of armed conflict with the Scots, which continued informally, said Macaulay, into the eighteenth century. This was a region which, 'even when there was nominal peace, was constantly desolated by bands of Scottish marauders'. As late as the seventeenth and early eighteenth centuries, at least in the border counties, 'The inmates slept with arms at their sides. No traveller ventured into that country without making his will.' In the seventeenth century people on the upper Tyne were 'scarcely less savage than The Indians of California . . . half naked women chaunting a wild measure while the men with brandished dirks danced a war dance'.[3]

The accounts of supposed northern backwardness are often couched in very simple terms of geographical determinism. Highland-zone theories have been intermittently popular since Haverfield, more than eighty years ago, claimed that during the Roman occupation northern Britain was scarcely Romanized principally because of its upland and mountainous terrain.[4] Cyril Fox developed this into an 'absorption theory' to account for the abrupt cut-off of religious and political influences originating in Ireland from the seventh to the tenth centuries. Patently this influence was not repelled, as Roman influence was allegedly repelled, but it was soon absorbed by this highly resistant region and could not spread further south: 'It would appear that whenever culture centred on Ireland expands, its force is spent in the Highland Zone . . . It does not effectively reach across the mountain barriers to southern England.'[5] Highland-zone theory still emerges to explain alleged northern conservatism.[6] Paul Johnson also invokes geography in a simple, deterministic way: it is 'the constant and remorseless force of geography' that in some unexplained fashion ensures that wealth and power find no permanent home in the North and always 'gravitate' to the South-east.[7] Geography is crucially important to any grasp of northern history, but this highly dubious, pseudo-scientific geographical determinism does a grave disservice to both history and geography and any serious understanding of the North.

What is immensely damaging is isolation. But isolation is not a simple fact of geography, an automatic consequence of distance from the 'centre'. It may indeed be this – the conservatism, backwardness, and generally undistinguished history of Cornwall is a clear example. But Durham, like Truro, is 270 miles from London, and Durham was the home of outrageously powerful prince-bishops. Northern history has been enacted in shifting contexts of significance, and it is these contexts to which the story must constantly refer. It is true that they have been more helpful to some parts of northern England than others, and the region on the east of the Pennines has stood at the crossroads of influence more often than regions on the west. But in all four periods of pre-eminence involvement in a wider world has been of crucial significance.

The first period of pre-eminence, from the late second century to the early fourth century AD, arose on a strategic and highly vulnerable sector of the Roman empire's frontier. The seventy-mile stretch that Hadrian decided should be magnificently fortified, without equal in any other province, was 1 per cent of the empire's 7,000-mile land frontier; it was a relatively confined area, seen in sharp focus, a theatre where military careers and reputations and political gestures could be made. Its importance in the third century arose from its geograhical location, its proven military importance, and imperial policy which favoured the Roman army and poured money into highly militarized zones (see chapter 2).

The second period of pre-eminence, in the seventh and eighth centuries, arose from Northumbria's strategic location at the crossroads of cultural influence in north-western Europe, lying between the German and Irish seas. Northumbria lay between two great centres of influence, one religious and cultural, in Ireland, the other political and commercial, in Scandinavia: it rose to eminence and international repute astride a strong east–west flow of men, artifacts, and ideas (see chapter 3).

The period of great military and political importance in the later Middle Ages arose from northerners' dual and strikingly symmetrical involvement in war with both Scotland and France. In this period even historically isolated Derbyshire and Lancashire were pulled centre-stage in a vast imperial enterprise. This was the age not only of Percies and Nevilles but of John of Gaunt, duke of Lancaster and king of Castile, and of Edward of Woodstock, the Black Prince, earl of Chester and prince of Aquitaine. It was an age when modernity came early to the North, as the exigencies of border defence called for flexible social and military institutions based not on tenure and homage but on contracts and cash. Modernity was forged in the crucible of frontier warfare in the North and was the basis of military triumph in France (see chapter 6).

The fourth era of northern pre-eminence rose, as Macaulay said, on coal; but it rose also on cotton, and this is an essential part of the story. Raw cotton came from abroad and finished cotton material was marketed abroad: this international framework of supply and markets was quite basic to the industrial revolution's take-off and sustained development. The advance of Manchester and Liverpool in the nineteenth century to great cities of European stature was made possible by the productivity of the upland soil of the southern United States of America.[8] Finding supplies of raw cotton and selling finished cotton products abroad pulled Lancashire out of more than two centuries of deep isolation and backwardness (see chapter 10).

These were the high points in the history of the North. But for 1,000 of the past 2,000 years, northern England has been an exposed frontier province under frequent and sometimes sustained and remorseless attack: by the Caledonians and the Picts for the four centuries of Roman rule; by the Scots for six centuries from the battle of Carham in 1018 to the union of Scottish and English crowns in 1603. This ensured continuing political importance and high privilege for the North. In between these two long periods of military and consequently political importance, an independent kingdom of Northumbria, which extended from the Humber to the Forth and Clyde, solved the problem of the Hadrianic frontier by obliterating it and reconstituting the frontier, in effect, at the Antonine Wall. This natural kingdom between the Humber and the Clyde was dismembered to ease its incorporation into a unified English state (see chapter 3). This was an enormous price to pay for a unified kingdom. A high price continued to be paid for the next 600 years, but the North, paradoxically, in spite of sometimes ferocious devastation, was a principal beneficiary. This is one of the central themes of this book.

Periods of particular importance are identified and highlighted in the following chapters, but this book is not written simply in terms of four epochs of pre-eminence. Indeed the periods which follow the high points are often of considerable cultural or political importance. Decline is relative. But 1603 must be seen as a major demotion for the North: the foundations of its power extending back for a millennium and a half were undermined by the union of the Scottish and English crowns. Similarly, the seventeenth century, although by no means without significant northern contribution to great affairs, was one of its least distinguished periods. London and the eastern counties, without serious challenge, held the centre of the stage (see chapter 9).

The twelfth and thirteenth centuries, like the sixteenth and seventeenth centuries, fall between high peaks of northern importance; but they saw great cultural and economic developments and notable political initiatives in defence of the realm and in opposition to the politics of King John. Eastern Yorkshire in particular rose in wealth and power: in the twelfth century it saw monastic and urban development on a spectacular scale and Walter l'Espec, lord of Holmsley, along with the archbishop of York, took responsibility for withstanding the enormous ambitions of the very advanced, sophisticated, and expansionist kingdom of the Scots. The same part of eastern Yorkshire saw the mobilization of resistance to King John in the early thirteenth century (see chapter 5). It was also the base for resistance to the revival of feudalism by the first two Tudor kings in the Pilgrimage of Grace in 1536. This was a complex movement, basically to protect northern England as a viable society capable of continuing its historic defensive role against the Scots; but it was also a protest against the de-modernizing policies of the Tudor kings which revived feudal tenures and taxes and reinstated the rule of male primogeniture. East Yorkshire gentry – led by Robert Aske and Sir Robert Constable – stood firm for modernity when the English parliament had been bullied by Henry VIII into abandoning it (see chapter 8).

Power shifted from east Yorkshire to south Yorkshire in the early seventeenth century. It was now heavily concentrated in the Wentworth connection. This followed the dissolution of the monasteries in 1539 and the downfall of the Percies, essentially east Yorkshire magnates, in 1569; but it finally followed the shift in economic productivity and power which had been occurring over the previous three centuries. In the twelfth and thirteenth centuries Beverley, Hedon and other east Yorkshire towns were important centres for the manufacture of high-quality cloth; as they declined in the later Middle Ages the textile industry of the less restrictive West Riding rose. But it was the priors and abbots of west and south Yorkshire who became rich: their sheep-runs supplied the rising textile industry with wool, and while ecclesiastical wealth in England generally declined as a proportion of all wealth, in the West Riding it rose steeply between 1334 and 1515 (see chapter 8). It was only after the dissolution that the rising economic fortunes of the West Riding of Yorkshire were reflected in the wealth and power of West Riding squires: they had bought up the monastic lands and were now as rich as the priors had formerly been. On the royalist side Thomas Wentworth, earl of Strafford, George Savile, earl of Halifax and Thomas Osborne, earl of Danby, were part of a closely interconnected circle of rich and ambitious south Yorkshire squires who made their mark at the highest levels of the nation's political life. On the parliamentary side was Sir Thomas Fairfax of the West

Riding, who led an army of Bradford and Dewsbury clothiers to military glory and shared in the triumph of Marston Moor. The seventeenth century was London's century; but in a minor key it was also south Yorkshire's century.

The relative decline of northern England in the twentieth century seems clear enough. It has been marked by contracting heavy industry, disproportionate levels of unemployment, class war and urban decay. It reinforces the theories of geographical inevitability which have been popular; perhaps it inspired them in the first place. And yet the rise of the new Labour party (with its principal strength in the North) as one of the two parties of government would have seemed virtually impossible in 1914; and the dramatic rise in the political power of the Yorkshire coal-fields by 1974 would have seemed highly unlikely even in 1960. But the political power of Yorkshire coal has terrified recent Conservative governments and pushed them into an enormously expensive programme for developing nuclear power which would never have arisen from market forces and considerations of profit. At the same time, a half-baked theory of geographical inevitability, as expounded by Paul Johnson, justifies the actions of the same governments in abandoning programmes of regional aid because they are against nature. The crude simplicities of Johnson's predestinarian geography led him to advocate leaving northern England as a vast leisure park.[9] The conclusion of this book is that the interplay of regional history and geography is hugely complex and subtle, and the future is much more open than Paul Johnson knows. But I must confess that I have been driven to a small predestinarian theory of my own. It is outlined at the end of this chapter.

THE NORTH

John Le Patourel confessed that he was never quite sure whether 'the North' comprised four, six or even eight counties. In this book it comprises seven: the four border counties of Northumberland, Durham, Cumberland and Westmorland, and Lancashire, Yorkshire and Cheshire. Cheshire is something of a problem; but there is no doubt about the other six. Nevertheless, John Le Patourel was quite right to insist: 'We must not be too rigid in setting our territorial limits.'[10] For some purposes and for some periods the Trent may be the southern limit, and the Forth–Clyde isthmus, rather than the Tees, Tyne or Tweed, the boundary in the north. But both northern and southern boundaries are rivers – in effect moats – and for most purposes the North begins at the Don.

The North has been a kingdom but has never been a principality or a province. It has never been encompassed by a single administrative authority, and even the sixteenth-century King's Council in the North had no jurisdiction over Lancashire and Cheshire (Cheshire was for a time under the jurisdiction of the Ludlow-based council of the marches in Wales); the wardenships of the marches towards Scotland were also outside its authority; and for most purposes it was little more than the King's Council in Yorkshire. The North has always been marked by cultural and administrative pluralism; the counties have remained basic and separate administrative and social units; duchies, palatinates and regalities have remained deeply embedded in it; and yet it has always had, and still in some measure retains, a strong sense of separateness and of its own distinctive identity.

Pragmatically the North began at the point of no return – as did other distinctively perimeter zones like the Welsh march. From London you could get to Doncaster on horseback in a day – as Sir Robert Carey did on 24 March 1603 when he rode to take the news of Elizabeth's death to James at Holyrood. Doncaster (like Ludlow) is 170 miles from London; on the second day you could travel the next 170 miles to Berwick-upon-Tweed. At Doncaster you were committed: there could be no turning back that day. But at Doncaster you could command the North. It was there that you established your new forward base.

Doncaster was the gateway to the North – as it had been for the Romans, who drove a road there from Lincoln as an alternative to crossing the Humber to Brough. The Roman highway from the South was not to Nottingham and through Nottinghamshire, but to Lincoln and thence to Doncaster and northwards to Piercebridge, Corbridge, and Hadrian's Wall.

The earl of Surrey made his first administrative stop at Doncaster on his way to victory at Flodden on 1 August 1513. He was ten days out from London, which he had left with 500 infantry on 22 July. At Doncaster he mobilized the North, issuing instructions to the sheriffs and nobility of the northern shires to assemble their forces at Newcastle-upon-Tyne on 1 September. Pay and victuals of foot-soldiers assumed twenty miles a day; the earl of Surrey was a little slower than that. But one day on horseback (very hard riding) or a week on foot (very hard marching) marked the effective perimeter from which forward operations could be staged. Ludlow (170 miles) or Shrewsbury (160 miles) were similar forward administrative bases for operations in Wales.

Doncaster was where the gentlemen of the northern counties assembled in 1399 to proclaim the usurper Bolingbroke not only duke of Lancaster but King Henry IV. It was where the North met to negotiate with the 'centre' during the Pilgrimage of Grace in 1536. (In fact it was precisely on the bridge over the Don.) This great northern rising, which carried the banner of St Cuthbert as well as the badge of the five wounds of Christ, spread throughout the northern counties but never extended south of the Don. On 27 October royal representatives met four delegates of the 'pilgrims' on the bridge; the pilgrims were massed on the plain behind. On 6 December ten northern knights, ten esquires and ten commoners met the duke of Norfolk on the bridge. The duke never got north of the river and the pilgrims imagined they had won.

Early medieval royal officials like escheators and foresters were appointed *citra et ultra Trentam* (justices of the forest were so appointed until 1831) and in these civil service terms the North might be seen to begin at the Trent. In fact when terms of appointment were set out this geographical distinction was not always invariable or precise.[11] An even more southerly line of demarcation made sense when the king and his officers had little business and less interest in the palatinates and regalities beyond the Tees and the Tyne in which the king's writ did not run; still more southerly lines were drawn at times.

It was only in the middle of the thirteenth century that English kings began to show as much interest and spend as much time in their lands beyond the Humber as in their cross-channel domains.[12] Before this time royal officials might be appointed to a northern division which began in Buckinghamshire, Oxfordshire, Essex or Northamptonshire. This was the case with the justice of forests appointed in 1229. But serious attention was being given a few years later to problems of the far North and in particular to clarifying and confirming the Anglo-Scottish border which had existed somewhat informally since 1157. This was done in the treaty of York of 1237. It was as attention was turning towards the far North – in fact in 1236 – that the justice of forests was appointed not beyond Buckinghamshire but beyond Trent.[13] But there was still no great business for him beyond the Tees: the palatine county of Durham was of course excluded from the royal justice's remit. And so was Westmorland. *Ultra Trentam* was a division arrived at by administrative trial and error: it did not define or express a political or social reality and it did not create one. A sense of political community began not at the Trent but at the Don.

It was expressed not in royal officials appointed 'beyond Trent', but in a long line of warrior-bishops, warrior-archbishops, and indeed warrior-priests. In these the two defining traditions of northern England met, and both traditions reached down from the Tweed to the Humber, the Aire and the Don. The powerful defining religious tradition extended back to St Cuthbert of Tweedale, Durham and Lindisfarne, St John of Beverley and St Wilfrid of Ripon; the frontier tradition of military obligation and indeed exposure to Scottish attack also extended to south Yorkshire. It was on the plain of York at Northallerton, 100 miles south of the Scottish border, that Archbishop Thurstan confronted the Scottish army of invasion in 1138. In almost the same place, at Myton-on-Swale, Archbishop Melton confronted another invading army in 1319. These were the experiences that gave the North its sense of separateness and distinctive identity.

The bishopric of Durham was in an exposed frontier zone and the bishopric's high privileges were confirmed and further extended in return for its role in defence. Bishop Bek, friend of Edward I, valiant and perhaps over-zealous at fifty-eight in the battle of Falkirk, is the outstanding example of the northern bishop as commander in the field (his successor in 1388 failed to get to the battle of Otterburn on time). The archbishops of York as warriors are a little more surprising: Zouche in arms with Sir William Rokeby at Neville's Cross in 1346; Bowet at sixty, leading his priests from Yorkshire to defend Berwick-upon-Tweed in 1417, old, sick, and carried into battle on a litter (exactly like the septuagenarian Thurstan at the battle of the Standard in 1138). The church was closely bound up in defence: the dean of York, the abbots of Selby and St Mary's, all fought at Myton in 1319, and among the dead at the end of the day were 300 priests in full canonicals.[14] When archbishops and abbots were not fighting the wars they were financing them: Melton, the abbots of Fountains and St Mary's, were war financiers on a grand scale (especially the archbishop), lending money not only to the king but investing in northern knights whose profits were usually respectable and sometimes huge.

There were no warrior-bishops in Lancashire; indeed, there were no bishops at all (the Chester bishopric was established in 1541). This is indicative of the traditional separateness (and low profile) of Lancashire down to our own times. It also underscores the great variability within the 25 per cent of England defined here as 'the North'. There are major historic differences between northern England on the east and the west of the Pennines, and north and south of the Tees.

Yorkshire, bigger than any other northern county, and richer at least down to the nineteenth century, was always more central, less isolated: tied tightly into a great mercantile North Sea civilization; on the highway from London to Scotland and the great immunities and privileged 'peculiars' beyond the Tees. The historic highroad to Scotland skirted Lancashire: from Stamford to Doncaster, seventy miles through the vale of York to Scotch Corner, then turning north-west through the Stainmore pass to Appleby, Penrith and Carlisle. It carried knights, traders and monks from east Yorkshire to the sister abbeys in Cumbria and southern Scotland. Lancashire was bypassed. It has been the most intensely isolated county in the North.

It was involved in the frontier defence against Scotland, its levies were regularly called to the border (they fought with notable distinction at Nevill's Cross), and Clitheroe was a particular target for Scottish attack. Lancashire's distinctive institutions, no less than its geographical position, however, have been deeply isolating. The separateness (and 'softness') of Lancashire has been noted by historians and variously explained. John Le Patourel thought it originated in four centuries of settlement by (relatively peaceful) Norsemen coming over from Ireland before 1066, as distinct from settlement by Danes in Yorkshire who came in from across the North Sea. A. J. P. Taylor ascribed it to some mystical quality of cotton combined with a soft climate.[15] These explanations are not very convincing and perhaps not entirely serious.

The creation of the duchy and palatine county of Lancaster in the mid-fourteenth century, with its separate jurisdiction, intensified an already considerable isolation, although for a time it brought military leaders in Lancashire and Derbyshire into prominence in the Hundred Years War. The sixteenth-century power of the earls of Derby on their great Lancashire estates and as lords lieutenant of the shire, a great convenience to Tudor kings, had a similar effect; and the large post-Reformation Catholic residue in western Lancashire – the largest in England – reinforced from the late eighteenth century by large-scale Irish immigration, accentuated Lancashire's separateness. Lancashire was little involved in the great northern insurrection, the Pilgrimage of Grace; it was not involved at all in the northern rebellion of 1569; it was outside the jurisdiction of the King's Council in the North; it was Jacobite in the eighteenth century when the Stuart pretenders found little favour generally in the North. It turned towards the Liberal party eventually, in 1906, nearly half a century after it had been expected to renounce Conservatism in the wake of the second Reform Act and the introduction of the secret ballot.[16] It turned to the Labour party only after the rest of the industrial North had done so, and never so completely (see chapter 12). Even its strong nonconformity along its border with Yorkshire never led to the level of support for the Liberal party that was a feature of strong nonconformist areas elsewhere.

Cheshire was always ambiguous. Its early medieval importance, indeed its Roman importance, lay in its military relevance to Wales. But it was also linked to the frontier province of the North and often made a disproportionate contribution to Scottish campaigns. The Chester diocese of 1541, which embraced Lancashire and even large areas of north Yorkshire and Westmorland, both expressed and further reinforced Cheshire's northern links.

Its ambiguity was painfully highlighted in 1399 when the northern triumph of the Lancastrian usurpation was accomplished through the overthrow of Cheshire's indulgent royal patron, Richard of Bordeaux. Richard had only recently promoted Cheshire to the status of a principality and his power rested heavily – too heavily – on his Cheshire guard. Cheshire was often uneasily yoked with Lancashire, with which it was conflated in the Domesday survey. The rich and powerful early medieval earls of Chester also held the honour of Lancaster, and the sixteenth-century earls of Derby were lords lieutenant of both counties. In spite of its palatine status (which certainly did not help), however, Cheshire was never as isolated as Lancashire, and never as poor. It was a rich source of supply for the Black Prince in his ambitious continental campaigns. Chester was a flourishing medieval port, involved in trade with Ireland and troop movements to Scotland, but also with a significant participation in the wine trade with Bordeaux. Cheshire was never as poverty-stricken as some historians have supposed.[17] Rich abbeys, especially the great Benedictine house of St Werburgh, reflect something of the county's wealth: at the dissolution they were a third richer than the monasteries of Lancashire and even those of Durham. This monastic wealth was 'released' at the dissolution, rather like the wealth of south and west Yorkshire, to enrich a gentry class which turned to a wider world of London and the court.[18] The county was more puritan and more radical than Lancashire, which produced no parliamentary military commander in the seventeenth-century civil war, while the West Riding of Yorkshire produced Fairfax and Cheshire produced the redoubtable, widely connected, Brereton (see chapter 9). It is still a serious error to conflate Cheshire with Lancashire.

The variability among northern England's county communities is at odds with any notion of a general northern character. And yet powerful and interrelated religious and military traditions within a remote frontier society gave northern England a sense of common identity. But by the seventeenth and eighteenth centuries this heritage was far in the past. Religion continued to distinguish northern society, but it also promoted differences within it: the strong concentration of Catholics in Lancashire and, by the mid-nineteenth century, England's largest concentration of Wesleyan Methodists in west and south Yorkshire. By 1851 religion was in any event a minority activity in the industrial northern counties: less than in most of England, roughly the same as in London (see chapter 11). In 1639 the least militarily competent and inclined society in England was Yorkshire (see chapter 9).

Attempts to identify and explain regional character have often referred to the alleged 'racial' characteristics of early settlers, especially the Vikings and Danes. The historian H. R. Loyn has most recently speculated along these lines, drawing attention to the 'sheer addition in genetic terms' that the Scandinavians made to England. In north Lancashire, west Yorkshire, Cumberland and Westmorland, 'a vital new element was added to the ethnic pattern in the early decades of the tenth century' by Vikings who came over from Dublin and the Isle of Man.[19] Havelock Ellis was likewise very interested in genetics and Danes, but his elaborate regional studies were wholly inconclusive, at least on the subject of 'race'. They are of considerable value nonetheless. Ellis, like another late-Victorian medical man, Conan Doyle, examined the geographical origins of men who had made a distinguished contribution to the various 'intellectual' walks of life, broadly conceived, ranging from literature and music to engineering, politics and law. Certain of his conclusions are clear: serious poetry begins south of Lincoln, and serious engineering north of the Tees; Suffolk, Hampshire and Somerset have been England's most distinguished counties, Derbyshire and Lancashire the least. There are only two other comparable intellectual deserts: Cornwall and Sussex.

Conan Doyle's study was confined to the nineteenth century; Havelock Ellis reviewed thirteen centuries of English history; both drew their samples from dictionaries and directories of leading men and women in different fields, Havelock Ellis principally from the Dictionary of National Biography. They expressed the level of a county's distinction as a ratio based on area for earlier times, and on population for the nineteenth century. Conan Doyle located his distinguished men simply in terms of birthplace; Havelock Ellis saw this as somewhat 'accidental' and tried to establish the roots of his subjects by taking their parents' place of birth into account. In this rather complicated way he scored England's counties for intellectual productivity. Conan Doyle published his study in 1888, Havelock Ellis published his in 1904.[20] There is substantial agreement between them: in both studies East Anglia and Southampton's hinterland are pre-eminent; the north Midlands and northern counties generally the least productive of intellectual eminence. The hinterland of the Cinque Ports, especially on Havelock Ellis's longer perspective, make a very poor showing too.

In Havelock Ellis's review of thirteen centuries East Anglia occupied a place of high distinction, producing not only eminent ecclesiastics and scholars but half of the country's foremost musical composers and one-third of the painters. The following 'wholly belonged' to East Anglia: the Bacons, Thomas Cavendish, Constable, Cowper, Cranmer, Gainsborough, the Newmans, Pusey, Walpole, Wolsey, and some notable men of action like Nelson. The other centre of great distinction was the South-west, with Somerset over the centuries being strikingly productive, Hampshire and Wiltshire too. This area had produced daring thinkers and intellectual innovators: Roger Bacon, Coleridge. Hobbes, Hooker and Locke. But northern England generally was an intellectual desert. Ellis, pursuing his genetic theories, was particularly interested in that part of northern England from Lincolnshire to Northumberland that had been heavily settled by the Danes. He concluded that the men of this area had been 'more remarkable for force of character than force of intellect': they were practical, forceful, unimaginative, capable administrators, even applied scientists. They had an aptitude for martyrdom and little taste or natural bent for abstract thought. Newton was the supreme if rather solitary example of an inclination towards exact science.

Conan Doyle's nineteenth-century sample also showed concentrations of eminent men in East Anglia and the South-west. This was unexpected in view of the massive geographical redistribution of the country's wealth. Hampshire was pre-eminent: 'There were few more surprising results elicited in the preparation of these lists than the brilliant position taken by Hampshire.' The East Anglian counties were also very distinguished, but the north Midlands and the northern counties generally were not. Yorkshire was more distinguished than Lancashire, but 'In both counties, the proportion of celebrities to the total population is low compared with many other districts of England.' Derbyshire was at the same low level as Lancashire and Northumberland was only redeemed by its engineers: 'There are no poets and few authors in her records, but *en revanche* there is in the past the great Robert Stephenson, and the present Lord Armstrong and Sir Daniel Gooch, engineers, with Burdon Sanderson, Sir G. Airy and Birket Foster.' The ratio of eminent men to total population in Northumberland was 1:22,000, lower than Suffolk and Hampshire (1:14,000 and 1:13,000 respectively) but significantly better than Derbyshire (1:75,000) and Lancashire (1:74,000). 'It is', said Conan Doyle, 'a relief to turn from the sterile midlands to the eastern counties, which are remarkably productive of successful men.'

One circumstance above all others appears historically to have been associated with a region's intellectual eminence: landed wealth. Havelock Ellis examined various correlates – class, 'race', wealth, and various personal and psychological characteristics – and concluded that the most powerful correlate was 'the amount of real property per head of population.' Certainly Derbyshire and Lancashire before the nineteenth century were among the poorest counties in England, measured by personal property assessed for tax. In 1334 Lancashire was thirty-eighth out of thirty-eight counties assessed, and was still thirty-eighth in 1515; Derbyshire was thirty-third at the first date, thirty-fourth at the second; Sussex was twenty-seventh, improving slightly to twenty-fifth. Somerset, by contrast, rose from twenty-third in 1334 to second in 1515. It was then almost thirty times richer than Lancashire: personal property was worth £104 per thousand acres in Somerset and only £3.8 in Lancashire.[21]

This book will show in its early chapters how great power and even great wealth came to northern England because of its importance as a militarized frontier zone. There is little doubt, however, that this military commitment, along with the poverty of some, but by no means all, of its land, shaped its practical, pragmatic character. (Even the monks, predominantly Cistercians, were notable not for scholarship or even prayer but pragmatic and efficient development of difficult land.) It is in many ways similar to Sussex (but unlike Hampshire, rich in itself and the gateway through Southampton to Bordeaux). Sussex is a relatively poor county and was under sustained attack by the French throughout the Middle Ages, with especial ferocity in the late fourteenth century. The prior of Lewes had an active role in military defence; Rye and Hastings had something of the character of Berwick-upon-Tweed. It is not surprising that such frontier regions, whether in the North or the South, were unremarkable for intellectual excellence or any inclination to abstract thought. It was not only northern bishops who were perforce military men; the parish priest of northern England as far south as north Yorkshire slept for five centuries with swords beneath their beds.

Only two circumstances are as disastrous for intellectual life as low levels of landed wealth and being a militarized frontier zone: one is isolation, the other is mining and manufacturing industry. (Banking and high commerce are an entirely different matter: traditionally connected with the landed gentry, they are also associated with artistic and intellectual life.) High intellectual creativity is associated with cosmopolitan communities on the crossroads of international communications networks, peace, and landed and mercantile wealth. All four conditions were met in Northumbria in the age of Bede. (Landed wealth was very considerable in this kingdom which included not only eastern Yorkshire but Lothian and Galloway, the rich and fertile lands which later supported great abbeys and now constitutes southern Scotland. Indeed, on the evidence of both Havelock Ellis and Conan Doyle, Dumfriesshire, Haddingtonshire, Lanarkshire and Midlothian have enjoyed a ratio of eminent men over the centuries comparable to Suffolk, Hampshire and Somerset.) Highly productive contexts for the intellectual life do not include militarized frontiers or heavily industrialized towns (see chapter 11). It was the misfortune of northern England after the age of Bede that its greatness was based on both.

CENTRE AND CIRCUMFERENCE: DECENTRALIZATION EVERY 400 YEARS

The north of England is an outer province, a sector of England's perimeter. It has enjoyed, especially throughout the Middle Ages, a high degree of independence of the 'centre'. It had come into a unified kingdom in the first place through bribery and cajolery which included granting new privileges or confirming and enhancing old ones in anciently independent communities like Beverley and Ripon in Yorkshire and especially St Cuthbert land beyond the Tees. Northern England's quasi-independence and separatism were reinforced by its strategic role in the long conflict with the Scots. Full integration within a unitary state was delayed by five centuries. This medieval separatism has been seen by historians as the essential 'problem of the North' which the Tudors went some way toward solving.[22] But the strong assertion of distinctively northern interests did not end in the sixteenth century. In the eighteenth century there was a particularly powerful and remarkably successful reassertion of the privileged tax position of northern landed estates (see chapter 10).

A history of northern England must constantly refer to the relationship with the 'centre', broadly conceived as a complex of key political, social and economic institutions based on London. This history is one of both conflict and co-operation. Conflict has often been highly dramatic, but some of northern England's greatest achievements, like Magna Carta and the Labour party, have in fact been bipolar accomplishments. But always there is a degree of tension between centre and circumference. The hold of the centre on the circumference is tightened up every 400 years.

The centre of any nation may be variously defined in terms of dominant influence: of central values, of a ruling class, of a power elite. In this book it is geographic: the place where central government is based and where key initiatives in all the major areas of national life tend to originate. For a thousand years this has been London. Only York in the Middle Ages and Manchester in the nineteenth century have presented anything like a challenge to London's centrality. Insofar as there has been a serious competitor it has been in the North: Norwich, Bristol or Exeter, for example, have never offered the same challenge.

London already had formidable wealth and power in 1066 and William the Conqueror wisely placated it and built fortifications there. There was as yet no concept of a 'capital' anywhere in Europe, but London was pre-eminent among England's cities. It had great military and financial power, and in the twelfth century Londoners claimed the right to choose England's king.[23] In the early thirteenth century, at a crucial moment, London threw in its lot with the barons against King John. While the North initiated the rebellion, it was, in the end, the power of London that brought John to submission at Runnymede.

The power of the centre is not necessarily at the perimeter's expense. London has sometimes pulled northern England into wealth and power in its wake. Thus, its phenomenal expansion and demand for coal in the sixteenth century pulled Newcastle-upon-Tyne into unprecedented prosperity. But the enormous wealth of the city of London as a financial institution had in some sense subverted the north of England as a manufacturing base by the early years of this century.[24]

The centre is a constellation of institutions and powers and may be deeply divided within itself. London was often a source of great strength to the crown; it was also a constant threat. The power of London in the reign of Richard II seemed likely to drive the king permanently on to the perimeter, perhaps at Chester, even in Ireland, or possibly York (to which the exchequer was removed as a precaution in 1392). London's financial backing was vital to the first Yorkist king, Edward IV, after 1461. Froissart was very impressed by the military might of London. The height of its political power, however, came in the seventeenth century when it did in effect make and unmake kings.

It is the enormous power of the centre that any account of perimeter England must keep constantly in view. Geographically the centre extended to an arc seventy-five miles beyond London: key points on this arc were Northampton, Southampton and, by the later Middle Ages, Dover. At seventy-five miles, roughly half the distance from London to Doncaster, a man on a horse could return to base the same day, and if he did not he could keep in easy contact. It was at Northampton that representatives of the centre met hostile deputations from the North, just as it was at the Don that representatives of the North met emissaries from the centre. It was at Northampton that the North negotiated with the South, as it did in 1065 when the northern nobles who had expelled the northern viceroy, Tostig, went south to deal with the king. The rebels met the king's ambassador, Harold, at Northampton. In the spring of 1138, when the North tried to negotiate support for dealing with the military crisis that was imminent, the archbishop of York went down to Northampton to meet the government's representatives and discuss possible arrangements. In the spring of 1215 the northern and eastern barons came together to deal with King John and negotiate an alliance with London: they did so at Stamford and Northampton before moving to Brackley. When Richard of Gloucester came down from Middleham in north Yorkshire in 1483 to seize the throne he went straight to Northampton. From this base he moved to intercept the young king and his uncles at Stony Stratford. It was seventy-five miles out of London that northern England in defiant or demanding mood intersected with the South.

Southampton, in a different way, was of even greater importance on the centre's outer rim. Norman and Angevin England has been described as a channel state.[25] English kings in the later Middle Ages were even more deeply involved in their cross-channel conquests and inheritance. Henry V regarded Normandy as an integral possession of the English crown, held in full sovereignty; and in the treaty of Troyes of 1420 a dual monarchy between England and France was proposed. The duchy of Aquitaine remained a highly prized inheritance of English kings from 1154 to 1453. The deep involvement of England's rulers in cross-channel affairs down to 1453 was not really optional; and at the heart of England as a channel state was a line that ran from London through Southampton to Bordeaux.

The rich and strategic London–Southampton axis, the 'centre-south', was the real polar antithesis of the northern perimeter before the sixteenth century. Paul Johnson has made extravagant claims for the historic power and importance of the South-east,[26] but it was of relatively little account, especially poor and embattled Sussex. (In 1483 Richard III wisely planted his northern followers preponderantly in the rich and important centre-south.) The developed condition and political weight of the centre-south is reflected in its highly disproportionate representation in later thirteenth- and early fourteenth-century parliaments. When sheriffs were asked to nominate boroughs of sufficient importance to send burgesses to parliament they could nominate none in Buckinghamshire, Hertfordshire and Middlesex; but ten were nominated in Hampshire, thirteen in Wiltshire, and a further nine in Dorset and Somerset. (In 1295 114 towns were nominated throughout England.) The only comparable cluster was eleven boroughs in eastern Yorkshire.[27]

The capture of Calais in 1347 and its growing military and commercial status was the beginning of greater importance for south-eastern England, but it was the loss of Normandy and Gascony in the mid-fifteenth century that diminished Southampton and pulled Calais and the South-east into prominence. The Tudors confirmed and consolidated the South-east as England's 'centre'. The royal forests from Windsor to the New Forest still took the king's hunting parties to the outskirts of Southampton, but important men, goods and ideas flowed increasingly along the London–Dover road.

The shifting wealth and power of England's regions is part of the dynamic of English history. Indeed, 'the provinces' (never adequately identified or defined) have been seen as a main engine of political change in the eighteenth and nineteenth centuries.[28] It has also been claimed that provinces rather than 'classes' may be the prime units in social conflict and that 'geographical sectionalism' is a major factor in historical change: 'a region as well as a class may feel itself aggrieved.'[29] There is nothing in this book that would run counter to this emphasis on regional fortunes and identity in shaping national history, but the analogy with class conflict is seriously defective. An aggrieved class fights another class; an aggrieved region does not fight another region – it invariably fights the centre.

Regions have felt aggrieved over a wide range of issues but principally over their contribution to defence, their inadequate representation in national institutions, especially parliament – an important issue in the north of England in the early nineteenth century; their exclusion from royal justice on account of some special local jurisdiction; and above all over taxes. In medieval and early modern England they were aggrieved if the taxes they paid were for a purpose of no direct benefit to themselves. In 1489 Yorkshiremen rose in rebellion against a tax for a distant Breton war; in 1497 Cornishmen rose against taxation for an equally distant war in Scotland.[30] The West Riding of Yorkshire, like other inland areas but with particular vehemence, was strongly opposed to paying the 'ship-money' tax which financed naval defences and brought prosperity principally, it was said, to coastal towns. It was left to John Hampden to discover legal–constitutional grounds for opposing it.[31]

Northern England was in fact an immensely privileged zone for 600 years, from the early tenth to the early sixteenth century: a region of great immunities, regalian franchises and palatinates. These areas of privilege and immunity were greatly extended in the fourteenth century. On the negative side, however, some privileged areas were excluded from royal justice, and this was a growing concern in the North. Another related problem was lawlessness. Northern England stands out nonetheless as a privileged province, and it enjoyed tax concessions, reductions and abatements down to the early seventeenth century.

But there have been occasions when the special interests of northern England seemed to be disregarded. One was the run-down of the monasteries in 1536, another was the run-down of coal-mines in the 1970s and 1980s. The first led to the Pilgrimage of Grace; the second to the great miners' strike of 1984–5. The miners' leaders used all the rhetoric of class war, but neither revolt was a class revolt. Both were revolts against the centre.

The most frequently aggrieved region of medieval England was the seriously disadvantaged South-east. It paid taxes but got inadequate defence against the French, an issue that was behind the Peasants' Revolt of 1381.[32] Moreover, the South-east paid *de facto* higher taxes than the North, even when the rate was the same, because tax evasion there was much more difficult. Evasion of late fourteenth-century poll taxes was between 50 and 70 per cent in Lancashire and Yorkshire: this was evident from the reduced numbers paying on successive occasions. In Middlesex evasion was only about 10 per cent; in Kent 20 per cent.[33] The home counties lived in the shadow of the apparatus of central government; exchequer officials were omnipresent; collectors and commissioners bombarded the South-east.[34] The pervasiveness (and corruption) of royal officials was an issue behind Jack Cade's rebellion in Kent in 1450 (as well as dismay at the imminent loss of England's protective empire in France).[35] Northern England was not necessarily disadvantaged or aggrieved by its remoteness from the centre.

Regional grievances have led to attacks on the centre rather than on other regions for a simple reason: the action that caused the imbalance was often originated by central government itself, and in any event the remedy was in central government's hands. There was little point in attacking a more favoured region which was powerless to supply a remedy.

The relationship between centre and perimeter seems to change every 200 years. For 200 years the relationship is close and the influence of the centre is pervasive; then for 200 years central control is relaxed and the provinces take more responsibility for their own affairs. Centralization alternates with decentralization. Since the Romans invaded in AD 43 we have had five periods of highly centralized government which have alternated with four periods of relative provincial autonomy. A fifth is imminent. Since 1830 we have experienced a period of accelerating central control which has squeezed out provincial initiatives. A period of decentralization is palpably at hand. The privatization of nationalized enterprises is the principal sign of its beginning.

The purpose of this book is simply to tell a story: the history of a region. But in the course of writing it there was, every 150 to 200 years, a strong sense of *déjà vu*. The centralization engineered by the Tudors in the sixteenth century after a long period of great provincial power was strongly reminiscent of the Angevin kings, especially King John, nearly 400 years before (both severely provoked the North), while Benthamite measures began a new phase of centralization nearly 400 years later (especially in the shape of the new Poor Law which sorely provoked northern England again). The periods of decentralization tend to release initiatives and generate creative energies in perimeter zones. It is true they can also be experienced as neglect, when the centre seems to withdraw support. The inner cities of northern England today, no less than the northern frontier defences of the early twelfth century, may feel abandoned by the centre. But the early twelfth century in northern England was an age of spectacular monastic development as well as desperate military improvization, and northern landowners took the initiative in collaboration with Scotland's King David to create a brilliant 'second age of Bede' (see chapter 3).

The 400 years of Roman Britain divide tidily into an initial 200-year period of highly centralized rule (during which the conquest was firmly established and culminating in the rebellion of the Governor Clodius Albinus in AD 197) followed by 200 years with a greatly weakened centre. Possibly soon after AD 197, and certainly by AD 212, 'Britannia Inferior' had been created: a devolutionary move severely curtailing centralized power.

Roman rule was followed in the North by the highly centralized kingdom of Northumbria which enjoyed stability under its powerful royal house from the seventh to the ninth centuries. Ecclesiastical policy and organization proceeded by royal decree. The extensive network of Northumbrian monasteries was possible only with effective central co-ordination and control and a ubiquitous royal family in key appointments.

The sheer size and diversity of the unified kingdom of England that followed made strong regionalism inevitable. For two centuries after Athelstan, Edmund and Edgar, from the early tenth to the mid-twelfth century, it was marked by great concentrations of regional power. William of Normandy prevented the extreme devolution that some, especially the northern earls, had hoped for, but what is remarkable is the extent to which he accepted and in some respects reinforced great blocks of regional power.[36] England beyond the Tees was not included in the Domesday survey and retained a high degree of autonomy. The arch-bishop of York was indeed subordinated to Canterbury, but the bishops of Durham became earls and enjoyed viceregal powers. By the early twelfth century the semi-independence of northern England was such, and its social and cultural ties with southern Scotland so strong, that it seemed likely to secede and, united with southern Scotland, reconstitute the Northumbria of the age of Bede.

It was during this period of relatively undeveloped central power that provincial England showed spectacular initiatives. Regional 'capitals' like Exeter, Norwich, Lincoln, Bristol and York were now firmly established (York recovered its position of national importance in the reign of Stephen). Most remarkable, however, was the founding of monasteries, one of the glories of the English provinces. New foundations were especially numerous in the North. The founders were Norman landowners like Walter l'Espec of Helmsley, Robert de Brus of Cleveland, and Henry de Lacy of Pontefract. Through their endowments these Norman families expressed their growing rootedness in the English regions: they became closely allied to provincial life.[37] They were making not only a gesture of piety but an expression of provincial importance and power.[38]

The first half of the twelfth century, when this monastic movement was at its height, was a period of massive administrative decentralization: as monasteries grew in numbers (at least 115 were founded between 1135 and 1154), so did the number of earls (from seven to twenty-two in the same period). They carried heavy regional responsibilities, especially in defence.[39] Sheriffs too were men of highly independent power, often great landowners of baronial rank. The most remarkable devolutionary step was taken in 1139 when the earldom of Northumbria (embracing Northumberland, Durham, Cumberland, Westmorland and Lancashire north of the Ribble) was revived for the son of King David of Scotland, to whom the barons of these counties would do homage. This step was taken not out of weakness but strength: an Anglo-Norman army had recently triumphed over the Scots at the battle of the Standard.

The Angevin kings after 1154 took a much tighter hold on provincial affairs. Under the interventionist and centralizing regime of Henry II the exuberant monastic movement of the early twelfth century came to an abrupt end. Power was gathered to the centre: the justiciar now emerged as a great officer of state. In 1166 Henry II checked up on the service obligations of his great landowners (John did the same in 1212); in 1170 he checked up on the powers and conduct of his sheriffs and dismissed all but four of them. William the Conqueror would never have dared to do that.[40] An innovatory tax on personal property ('movables') was introduced which taxed men not as anybody's tenants but as the king's subjects. In the thirteenth century the distraint of knighthood (on the basis of wealth rather than tenure) produced a cadre of local administrators under direct central control. This period reached its peak in the great centralizing statutes of Edward I, especially the statutes *quia emptores* and *quo warranto* in 1290. Intended to reinforce the power of the centre by discouraging the re-granting of land ('subinfeudation') the statute *quia emptores* had the long-term effect of subverting it (see chapter 7).

The highly decentralized period which followed began in the early fourteenth century and came to an end in the late fifteenth century. This was the age of bastard feudalism and the creation of 'unnecessary' palatinates; of a perimeter awash with power from Calais through Normandy and Gascony to the marches of Wales and the frontier province towards Scotland. It culminated in the 'golden age of the North'.

Members of Parliament were highly responsive to local communities and regional interests before they were disciplined by party organization in the later nineteenth century: the frequency with which Parliament met in the fourteenth and fifteenth centuries, although closely connected with the exigencies of war finance, was both a reflection of and contribution to regional power. Its relatively infrequent assembly in Tudor and early Stuart England was one aspect of the new age of tighter central control. This period was a relatively low ebb in the history of the North. (see chapters 8 and 9).

The late seventeenth to the early nineteenth centuries was again a great age of decentralized power (and highly independent members of Parliament with a strong sense of obligation to their regions). The Webbs characterized the period 1688 to the Municipal Reform Act of 1835 as one virtually devoid of central government influence over the conduct of local affairs. But the eighteenth century saw what has been called an 'urban renaissance' throughout provincial England, not least in the North. Thus, twenty-five towns established permanent, purpose-built theatres around the middle of the century, and 40 per cent of the towns were in the northern counties of Yorkshire and Lancashire.[41] By 1780 political radicalism was no longer simply Wilkite and metropolitan: under the leadership of the Revd Christopher Wyvill of Richmondshire it was quasi-revolutionary and nothern-provincial.[42] The growth of the industrial revolution in the late eighteenth century was closely bound up with economic and social adjustments which redressed the imbalance of an overblown London (see chapter 10).

The latest age of centralization began in the 1830s.[43] The Factory Act of 1833 is a major landmark: it initiated the age of the government inspector. There were 140 of them by the middle of the century, all fervent believers in individualism and Adam Smith pioneering the creation of a new centralized state.[44] The management of the social consequences of the industrial revolution called for new agencies of central control.[45] This has been called the 'nineteenth-century revolution in government'.[46] It is strikingly like the revolution in government inaugurated nearly 400 years before by the early Tudors; and 400 years before that by the Angevin kings. These centralizing revolutions in government at approximately 400-year intervals all provoked resistance in the North: under the Angevins it culminated in the Magna Carta; under the Tudors in the Pilgrimage of Grace; in early Victorian England in insurrection and protracted civil disobedience, such as that at Todmorden, led by the factory owner, John Fielden. All three centralizing revolutions had the effect of squeezing initiative out of provincial life.

This last phase of centralization moved towards its high point in the welfare legislation after 1906 and reached it in the central planning of the Second World War and the programmes of the Labour government that followed it. During the course of the twentieth century the proportion of people at work who are employed by government (central, local, and nationalized industries and services) rose steeply from 3.6 per cent in 1891 to 6.9 per cent in 1911, 9.7 per cent in 1931, and 24.3 per cent in 1950.[47] The reaction against this latest build-up of power at the centre began not only with the Thatcher government in 1979 but when trade unions began to lead assaults not on capitalists but on central government – partly because government was now England's principal employer.

This book has not been structured around these great 200-year rhythms and alternations of powerful centres and powerful perimeters, partly because they were not very clear until it had almost been written. But in the writing of it there seemed, quite palpably, to be underlying self-correcting processes, semi-automatic adjustments which redressed the imbalances of over-powerful centres and over-powerful perimeters. The build-up of power seemed to take between 150 and 200 years to reach its peak. It was then creating more problems than it solved. (It is also relevant that the periods of centralization occurred with great upswings in population and their attendant problems. Relative provincial autonomy arose in the intervals when population was falling or at least static. This was probably true of the Roman period; it is certainly true of the past millennium.) These 200-year rythms in provincial life are implicit in this story of the north of England – and sometimes quite explicit.

Northern England's periods of distinction have occurred in times of extreme decentralization: the third century AD; the late eleventh- and early twelfth-century era of exuberant monastic development and rising provincial 'capitals'; the 'golden age' of the fifteenth century, culminating in the reign of Richard III; the take-off of the industrial revolution in the eighteenth century which arose in some measure out of reaction to an economically over-dominant centre. The exception seems to be the age of Bede. But the North at that time was certainly not constrained by any 'centre'. It was itself a centre. Northumbria in the age of Bede was both centre and circumference.

Under Roman Rule AD 43–410

FRONTIER PROBLEMS: SOME MEDIEVAL COMPARISONS

The Emperor Septimius Severus ruled the Roman empire from Eboracum for four years, AD 208–11; a thousand years later King Edward I ruled England from York for six years, 1298–1304. The Roman emperor and the English king based themselves in York for the same purpose: to confront personally and directly urgent problems on the military frontier in the North. For a millennium and a half the military threat from unconquered peoples beyond the Tyne, Tweed and Forth was the main reason for the high importance placed on the lands beyond the Trent.

The solution to the problem of the northern frontier was quite straightforward: the conquest of Scotland. What is remarkable is that this was achieved neither by the Roman empire at its height nor by the powerful medieval English state that accomplished Crécy and Agincourt. Often what was lacking was political consistency and will. But the conquest of Scotland should have been achieved by four men: Agricola in AD 81–3; Emperor Septimius Severus in AD 211; Edward I after 1298; Edward III in 1335. Whereas the medieval kings of England were facing an evenly matched enemy directly across the Tweed, however, Roman generals were dealing with hardy and courageous, though relatively unsophisticated, Caledonian tribes from beyond the Firth of Forth. And indeed, Rome could always intervene and decide within very broad limits precisely where the frontier should be – perhaps at the Tyne or the Forth or even at both – in a way that was quite impossible for medieval English kings. [1]

Agricola was the governor of Britain from AD 78 to 85 and during that time established control over the island as far as the Forth and the Clyde. He had reached the Tay in AD 80 but the following year fell back to the Forth–Clyde isthmus which his son-in-law, the historian Tacitus, said he regarded as a natural frontier. He almost certainly intended to make it the permanent boundary of the province of Britain and of the Roman world.[2] The isthmus was an ancient cultural and linguistic divide;[3] but its main virtue as a military and political frontier was that it was short. Agricola was much more interested in proceeding to occupy Ireland than the highlands. Under imperial orders, however, he turned north and defeated the Caledonians at *Mons Graupius*.[4] It is possible that he imagined that he had now effectively conquered the entire island (Tacitus said that he had), but all the more northerly areas were very insecurely held. Forty years later, when Hadrian's Wall was built from the Solway to the Tyne, it was in fact 'a monument to failure'.[5]

Emperor Septimius Severus might well have conquered the whole of Scotland after AD 211 if he had lived. He had been alerted by the governor of Britain to a great emergency in the North and had come with his two sons, Geta and Caracalla, a staff of high ranking senators, and substantial military reinforcements in AD 208. There is no doubt that his intention was to conquer the whole of Scotland and immense resources were assembled for this task. The largest granaries in the Roman empire were developed at South Shields to supply by sea the Severan armies beyond the Tay[6] But Severus was an old man in his sixties and ill: he was carried on a litter on his northern campaigns. After initial military victories he retired to York and was preparing to return to his northern wars when he died. Rome was never again in a position to take the offensive against the northern tribes and incorporate into the empire the lands beyond the Forth.[7]

Edward I was also an old man when he turned his undivided attention to Scotland and, in 1298, effectively transferred England's capital to York (see chapter 6). He was facing a highly organized military society under formidable leaders; but he, too, was formidable, very able, and very determined. He had great resources at his command. Falkirk was a great victory, but Edward was now sixty, and when he died in Cumberland in 1307 he was sixty-eight. His grandson, Edward III, did not even have the excuse of advanced age. He was twenty-three at the time of the Roxburgh campaign in 1335: a tremendous military effort on the scale of the Calais–Crécy campaign ten years later. It did not end like Bannockburn in England's defeat, but it was no great triumph either.

The military failure in 1335 guaranteed the importance of the north of England for another two centuries and a half.

There were important differences between northern frontier conditions and problems in Roman and medieval times. The policies of imperial Rome and the political and personal problems of emperors could cut across local decisions grounded in local knowledge. The decisions to build Hadrian's Wall between the Solway and the Tyne in AD 122 and the Antonine Wall across the Forth–Clyde isthmus in AD 143 owe more to imperial politics of prestige than any immediate military need.[8] The Romans in Britain were never so consistently hard pressed from the North as was the medieval English state, and Hadrian's Wall with its customs officers (*beneficiarii consularis*) was probably of considerable commercial importance in regulating cross-border trade, but often of doubtful military relevance. The enemy in Roman times was a hundred miles north of Hadrian's Wall and 200 miles north of the military headquarters at York. In the Middle Ages the enemy was directly across the Tweed and often pressing hard upon the Tyne.

The land between the Tyne and the Forth was the land of the highly cultivated Votadini tribe with its opulent Romanized (and unfortified) capital in Lothian at Traprain Law. Neither the building of Hadrian's Wall in AD 122 nor the retreat from the Antonine Wall (probably in AD 163) severed the commercial and amicable political ties between the Romans and the Votadini and related Selgovae tribes.[9] The purpose of Hadrian's Wall was to regulate contact with these tribes, not to prevent it. Lothian in fact was a Roman protectorate, and in striking contrast to the fifteenth and sixteenth centuries, when this area was thick with pele towers, castles and tower-houses for defence against English attack, there were in the second century scores of undefended settlements of stone dwellings, many on sites which had been fortified in an earlier, pre-Roman age. Undefended settlements extended westwards beyond Votadini territory: in the region of lowland Scotland where there were some 180 pele towers by the sixteenth century, there were in Roman times 225 undefended settlements of stone huts.[10] Even the Novantae tribe in south-west Scotland appears never to have been a threat, and the Roman fortifications along the Cumbrian coast are evidence more of bureaucratic central planning than attacks by tribes from Galloway across the Solway Firth.[11]

Throughout the Middle Ages cross-border attacks by Scottish forces occurred predictably and promptly in response to England's internal political crises or weakened home defences during cross-channel campaigns.

This was especially so during the 300-year war (1296–1586) but it was a feature of earlier centuries, too. Scottish invasion following hard on the heels of internal crisis occurred in 1069–70 in the reign of William I when northern England was in revolt; in 1138 (the battle of the Standard) when there was particularly acute crisis in Stephen's reign; in 1215–16 in the post-Magna Carta civil war in the reign of John; in 1388 (the battle of Otterburn) at a critical time in the reign of King Richard II. When England's expeditionary forces left for the Crécy campaign there was prompt invasion in 1346, halted at the battle of Neville's Cross; after Agincourt the 'foul raid' of 1416; after Henry VIII's cross-channel military venture in 1513 the invasion which was halted, catastrophically for Scotland, at Flodden.

The northern defences of Roman Britain were denuded on four occasions, when governors or generals in Britain made a bid to usurp the imperial throne. This happened in AD 197, 296, 383 and 407. There is no evidence whatsoever that the northern tribes saw their opportunity and decided to invade.

The first large-scale withdrawal of troops from Hadrian's Wall was by the governor of Britain, Clodius Albinus, in AD 197 when he proceeded with his army to Gaul. The second was by Allectus in AD 296: a naval commander in the channel, he had declared himself emperor, based himself in Britain, and was waiting in Berkshire for long-heralded retaliation by the Emperor Constantius. Historians until quite recently have claimed with an impressive certitude, in spite of the enormous and admitted difficulties of archaeological evidence, that on both occasions the northern barbarians swept through the frontier defences: in AD 197, said Collingwood, Hadrian's Wall was 'wrecked with astonishing thoroughness' and 'a flood of destruction swept over northern Britain as far south as Chester and York.'[12] The historian of Roman Britain, Peter Salway, said the same in 1965 but by 1981 had somewhat grudgingly recanted: there was no evidence of any destruction at Housesteads on Hadrian's Wall, he now conceded, and there was no literary report of serious frontier trouble in AD 197.[13] Other historians have now reached the same conclusion: 'there is no evidence that the frontier was cast into disarray in 197.'[14] There was undoubtedly a tendency until recently to read into Roman times the frontier experiences of the Middle Ages.

Earlier versions of the events of AD 296 have now been similarly revised. Collingwood's view was of catastrophe on a giant scale: 'For the first time since Clodius Albinus crossed to Gaul, the frontier was left undefended. The northern tribes took their opportunity: they broke in, and along the Wall we can trace the destruction they left behind them.'[15] There may, perhaps, have been a little looting, but we are now warned against regarding this alleged barbarian invasion as 'a major landmark in the chronology of Roman Britain'.[16]

Curiously, both the usurpers of AD 197 and AD 296 were stopped and killed by ruling emperors who some ten years afterwards came to York (and both of them died there): Septimius Severus defeated Clodius Albinus at Lugdunum near Lyons; the Emperor Constantius Chlorus, after three years of preparation and a campaign of great complexity based on Boulogne, invaded Britain, defeated Allectus, and was received in triumph in London. Septimus Severus went to York eleven years after defeating Clodius Albinus because there was a crisis on the northern frontier; Constantius Chlorus went to York nine years after defeating Allectus for the same reason. Neither emperor proceeded to York after defeating the usurpers and would undoubtedly have done so if there had been any serious trouble in the North.[17]

There was undoubtedly serious trouble from time to time on the northern frontier during the four centuries of Roman rule; but 'internal' trouble from the warlike Brigantes who lived in the plain of York and across the southern Pennines partly explains the military importance of the relatively southerly York.[18] South Shields survived and prospered over the centuries of Roman occupation without suffering a serious attack:[19] a busy and important port and supply depot near the terminus of Hadrian's Wall, it was comparable in many ways to Berwick-upon-Tweed on the new frontier a thousand years later. But Berwick had a stormy history: constantly besieged, it often changed hands. The immunity of South Shields in a broadly comparable situation must bring into question any notion of sustained and persistent barbarian attack.

The two Roman military commanders based in Britain who next claimed the imperial throne with army support did not cause havoc on the northern frontier either. Magnus Maximus in AD 383 and Constantine in AD 407, like Clodius Albinus and Allectus before them, denuded the Hadrianic defences of troops. There is no evidence whatsoever that the Picts, who had now evolved from the Caledonians and other far-northern tribes, thereupon swept down on an exposed frontier.[20] But in AD 408 barbarian attacks came from a different quarter: Saxons invaded the defences of the 'Saxon shore'.

There were major problems on the northern frontier but they seem to have occurred at quite long intervals. Some were so grave that Roman emperors came to York to deal with them. Hadrian's visit, which led to the building of the wall, was not a response to a military emergency: it was more in the nature of a routine inspection. But crisis brought Septimius Severus to York in AD 208, Constantius in AD 305, and Constans in AD 341. Constantius was drawn into the far north of Scotland where he gained a victory over the Picts; Constans came partly on account of the south coast defences against the Saxons (he was particularly interested in the development of Pevensey as a fort and naval base), but Pictish troubles were probably his major concern.[21] His crossing the channel in mid-winter suggests some considerable urgency. The rise of the Picts in the fourth century undoubtedly constituted a considerable threat in the North; but it was not only the northern frontier that was now of major strategic significance.

The history of the northern frontier in medieval England was not simply a rerun of the history of the Hadrianic frontier in Roman Britain. Nevertheless, there were broad correspondences between the two periods. In both the military importance of the North was a source of political power. The great military leaders of northern England in the later Middle Ages, the Percies and Nevilles, were kingmakers over a period of nearly two hundred years (see chapter 7); the Roman armies in Britain were emperor-makers for two hundred years (AD 197–407). Clodius Albinus and his army from Britain were quickly annihilated in AD 197, but later usurpers sponsored by the Roman army in Britain met with greater success. Army influence was brought to bear in York over two disputed successions: it prevented Caracalla from excluding his brother and becoming sole emperor in AD 211; in more complex and controversial legal and political circumstances it proclaimed Constantine as augustus in York in AD 306. Two other emperors were entirely the army's creation. Magnus Maximus, the *dux Britanniarum* based in York, was a successful general against the Picts: he was backed by the army in his bid for the imperial throne in AD 383 and ruled effectively from Gaul for the next five years. In AD 407 it was the army in Britain that elevated a soldier, Constantine, to emperor to combat the rising tide of barbarian invasions. The army's judgment was good: in these last days of imperial Rome Emperor Constantine III had considerable success in holding back the barbarians from Gaul.

LUXURY VILLAS AND HIGHLAND ZONES

Northern Britain under Roman rule was of great military importance, but some thirty miles to the east of York it was also the site of a particularly strong concentration of highly developed country estates or 'villas', one of the glories of the civilization of Rome. Civilian urban development also achieved considerable vitality in the North, although less formally planned and sponsored than in the South; and grain was almost certainly produced on a sufficient scale for regular export. Military importance and some mountainous terrain did not preclude development on other fronts.

It is seriously over-simple to divide England sharply and tidily into a highland and a lowland zone. That is what Haverfield did in a classic paper on Roman Britain in 1905: it has shaped the assumptions and perspectives of historians and archaeologists down to our own time.[22] Some highly influential scholars (Piggott, Rivet) have given their full weight to its simplicities, with all its undertones of naive geographical determinism.

The highland zone (on this view) was simply military, with forts, soldiers and ponies; the lowland zone was civilian, with cities and civilization. 'The two were marked off', said Haverfield, 'not in law but in practical fact, almost as fully as if one had been *domi* and the other *militiae*. We shall not seek for traces of Romanization in the military area.'[23] One area was occupied by troops, while the other 'contained nothing but purely civilian life'. Within this perspective it was possible to give credence to the astonishing idea that the fenland of eastern England was developed (from a plan by Hadrian) as a great grain growing area for supplying the troops in the North via the Cardyke canal system, the Trent and the Ouse. The North was a consumption area; the South a supply area.[24] This dependence of the military North on the civilian and corn-growing South had obvious political consequences: 'While the army of the North remained dependent on the South for its food, he who controlled the South could ultimately dictate the policy.'[25] The highland zone, for all its military might, was thus merely an appendage of the South. This view of Roman Britain is, quite simply, an absurdity.

Even the sharp distinction between the urban South and the rural North has its problems. Haverfield emphasized it and others have followed him claiming, for instance, 'free-standing, locally based towns in the South' which were 'a totally different thing' from the settlements of traders and camp followers alongside occupied forts in the North.[26] It is true that the score of 'official' towns laid out by Roman surveyors were mainly south of York – apart from York itself only the *civitas*-capitals at Brough-on-Humber, Aldborough (near modern Boroughbridge) and Carlisle were in the North. But only five of these towns (or six including

London) were ever of great significance, and they include Lincoln and York (the other three were Colchester, St Albans and Gloucester).[27] It is also true that after about AD 130 there was little or no new planned urban development anywhere in Roman Britain. Official towns did indeed reflect the wealth of a region: they were largely parasitic and only rich regions could afford to subsidize them;[28] but prosperous civilian towns which were genuinely 'free-standing' and marked by great cultural vitality grew under the stimulus of the richly-endowed war economy of the North.

Northern Britain was a high-consumption area if only because the soldiers, especially in the third century, were remarkably well paid. (A strikingly similar relationship between a prosperous military society and overall economic regional development emerged again in the fourteenth-century North.) The civilian towns that developed near the military forts were cosmopolitan and highly sophisticated: Bearsden has yielded evidence of a very varied and sophisticated diet on the Antonine wall (near modern Glasgow). There was an advanced urban, civilian society along Hadrian's Wall: 'It is not easy to think of places less comfortable to live in than Housesteads or Corvoran, yet civilians flocked to both settlements.'[29] Catterick and Norton (outside Malton), as well as Corbridge and Carlisle, the great ports at South Shields and Brough-on-Humber, were organic urban developments of great wealth and vitality. Brough had its theatre after the forum and bath-houses had been built. When the towns of southern Britain entered into sustained if not cataclysmic decline in the third century, the urban centres of northern Britain prospered as never before.[30]

There are two principal respects in which the highland zone was allegedly inferior to the South: in its production of grain and in its degree of 'Romanization'. In fact extensive grain production in the vast river basin of the Yorkshire Ouse was probably a major reason for the Claudian invasion of Britain in the first place:[31] the first Roman road system, which carried the Fosse beyond Leicester to Newark and Lincoln and the Ermine street from Lincoln to the Humber, shadowed the Trent to its confluence with the Ouse. Grain from this region was probably a principal British export throughout the period of Roman rule, and the high concentration of Roman villas on and around the Yorkshire wolds was an ornament of Roman Britain. These northern villas shared fully in the renaissance of villa development in the late third and early fourth centuries and continued to flourish into the fifth when this supreme expression of Roman civilization had faded in the South.

Salway has defined the North (or highland zone) in such a way as to exclude not only the plain of York but the north Yorkshire moors, the southern Pennines and the Yorkshire wolds, restricted in effect to the Cumbrian and Durham backdrop to Hadrian's Wall.[32] On such a definition the Roman villas beyond the Humber are outside the military complex of highland Britain. But marking their southern limit there was the naval station at Brough-on-Humber, immediately to the east the legionary headquarters at York, and immediately to the north the fort and grain depot at Malton. It is true that this was the land of the pacific and highly cultivated Parisi, but the villas of the Yorkshire wolds were embedded in the military framework of the highland zone.

The geographical distribution of medieval monasteries and of Roman villas is broadly the same. The reason is quite simple: both were manifestations of landed wealth and reflect its areas of concentration. A great belt of twelfth- and thirteenth-century monasteries extended diagonally from south-west England across the south Midlands into the eastern counties. A great belt of Roman villas likewise extended from Dorset, Wiltshire and Hampshire across Oxfordshire, Berkshire and Hertfordshire into East Anglia. In northern England on the west of the Pennines there were relatively few monasteries and there were no Roman villas; on the east of the Pennines monasteries were relatively numerous with a particularly marked concentration in eastern Yorkshire (see chapter 5). There were no Roman villas beyond the Tees but there was a heavy concentration in the east Yorkshire wolds.

There were 553 monasteries in medieval England; a thousand years earlier there were 604 villas in Roman Britain.[33] Of the monasteries, 4 per cent (twenty) were in a quite limited area of eastern Yorkshire around the wolds; of the villas, 4 per cent (twenty-four) were in the same area.[34] In a region comprising scarcely 2 per cent of England's area there were 4 per cent of all the medieval monasteries and 4 per cent of all the Roman villas. (In Yorkshire on the east of the Pennines, including the vale of York, there were thirty-six Roman villas; in this more widely defined 'eastern Yorkshire' there were thirty-nine monasteries.)

The monasteries in and around the Yorkshire wolds (they were scattered more widely than the villas) included some major and wealthy foundations such as the Cistercian abbeys at Meaux near Hull and Byland, the Augustinian priory at Kirkham near Malton, and a particularly rich priory at Bridlington. But there were half a dozen relatively poor priories of Augustinian canons in or near the wolds: North

Ferriby, Warter, Drax, Newburgh (near Coxwold), Healaugh, and Haltemprice near Hull.

A thousand years earlier the Roman villas in and near the wolds included some of striking opulence, rich and highly developed by continental standards, but also a number on a much more modest scale. The 'winged corridor house', the very pinnacle of villa development, was perhaps less common, even debased, in this highland zone,[35] but half a dozen villas were of high sophistication, with bath-houses and superior mosaic pavements. The luxurious villas at Harpham and Rudston (near modern Bridlington) would stand comparison with any in the land.

There were three main clusters of wolds villas: in the north of the region a group of ten, centred on the *vicus* – a civilian settlement outside but associated with a fort – and fort at Malton (including the opulent Beadlam and Langton villas); in the south of the region a group of nine, centred on the *civitas*-capital and naval base at Brough (including notable villas at North Cave, South Cave, Newbald, and Brantingham which had particularly fine mosaic pavements); a smaller, much more luxurious group of four, centred on what was probably the town and port of Bridlington (including Harpham and Rudston). (Two more villas, Drax and Millington, were more isolated.) It has been estimated that about a hundred Roman villas were 'luxury' or 'class A' villas; six of these were in the wolds area of east Yorkshire – 6 per cent in less than 2 per cent of the area of Roman Britain.[36]

Although most of these villas were near a major Roman fort and undoubtedly flourished under its protection (especially in the later period of Saxon attacks from the North Sea), the military–civilian, highland–lowland, division of Britain is basically an irrelevance. There were other 'thin spots' (in Haverfield's terminology) as well as north-west Britain beyond the Pennines: these included Sussex and Cornwall. What counted in 'Romanization' is what counted in monastic development a thousand years later: landed wealth. It accounts for the developed civilization of the Parisi in eastern Yorkshire between the Humber and the Tees before the Romans came, and it accounts for the luxury villas which adorned the region into the fifth century.

The distinction between highland and lowland zones has led to some startling assumptions: the most notable being, perhaps, that virtually no grain was grown in the North, certainly not a surplus, and not even a sufficiency. Stuart Piggott saw the Fosse Way as a sharp divide between economic zones, and 'What was to take shape as the civil portion of the

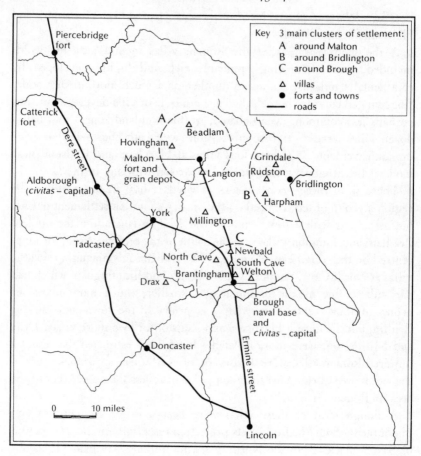

MAP 2.1   Principal Roman villas in northern Britain
Source: adapted from H. Ramm, *The Parisi* (Duckworth, 1978).

Roman Province was in fact its granary.'[37] There was little grain grown beyond the Humber, said Piggott: it was a land of ponies. Roman Britain was divided into grain-growing and horse-breeding zones.

Rivet has done considerable calculation to show what a strain on food resources the military garrisons would be: 106,000 acres under grain would be needed to support them.[38] This was undoubtedly the case, but 106,000 acres is about one-tenth of an average English county; perhaps 0.3 per cent of the area being farmed in second century Britain, equivalent to a dozen medium-sized farms of today. The needs of Roman forts could almost certainly be met locally, without some improbably grandiose development in the Fens, even around the highest military sites in the highland zone.

Fenland surveys have failed to support the view that this was the source of grain for Roman legions in the North or, indeed, anywhere else.[39] The productivity of upland sites has been well attested, even 700 feet above sea-level in upper Wharfedale at Grassington. Valleys and sheltered slopes in the highland zone produced more than enough grain for the army.[40] Highland forts were commonly in fertile river valleys: even along the Stainmore pass from Scotch Corner to Carlisle, while Bowes was high above the valley floor; in the east Greta Bridge and Piercebridge were in the rich grain-growing lower valley of the Tees; in the west, Brough was near the Cumbrian plain and Kirkby Thore while Brougham and Carlisle were in the fertile Eden valley. Malton was in Rydale with easy communications with the vale of Pickering and Catterick was in the vale of York. Ilkley is in middle Wharfedale, and both Ilkley and Bainbridge could be supplied from the remarkable grain-growing area in upper Wharfedale at Grassington, comprising hundreds of acres of Romano-British development, an extension of an earlier Celtic agricultural site.[41] Even the forts on Hadrian's Wall often had adjacent grain-growing areas (even Housesteads). The great granary at South Shields did not supply Hadrian's Wall – it did not need to – but was a major depot for grain exports, storing grain grown in the North-east. The large granary at Rudchester, the fourth fort from the eastern end of Hadrian's Wall, certainly stored more grain than the garrison would need and was probably used in part 'for storage pending export'.[42]

The Roman geographer Strabo, who died twenty years before the Claudian invasion in AD 43, listed grain as Britain's principal export (ahead of hides, silver, iron and hunting dogs). The production of grain throughout Britain greatly increased under Roman rule and was undoubtedly the main reason for Rome's concern to keep Britain in the empire in the fourth century, and maintain its elaborate defences, when far less peripheral parts of the empire were abandoned or suffered comparative neglect.[43] Certainly after the first century there was a surplus of grain for export which was shipped regularly to Europe, and not only in times of crisis like the famine of AD 361.[44] As the empire's crowded southern cities devoured the corn of Egypt and the Black Sea, the prairies of Britain were a vital source of supply.

Of the two great grain-growing river basins, the Thames and the Yorkshire Ouse, the latter was undoubtedly the more productive and important. This, it has been argued, was the true basis of the third-century importance of York, making it a serious rival to London and in many ways overshadowing the 'capital'.[45] The great crisis of Emperor Julian's reign in AD 361, when the Roman army in the Rhineland was able to receive massive emergency supplies of grain from Britain transported in 600 ships, has a striking parallel a thousand years later in the Crécy campaign of 1346. Victuals were required for England's vast expeditionary force in France. The bulk of the corn came from the basin of the Yorkshire Ouse, assembled at collecting points on the tributary rivers: at Boroughbridge on the Ure, Tadcaster on the Wharfe, Wansford on the river Hull, Selby on the Ouse, and Newark, Torksey and Gainsborough on the Trent. The grain was ground into flour in mills near Hull. This northern source provided 217 tons of flour which was 56 per cent of the total achieved by the receiver of the king's victuals for shipment to France. Another 30 per cent came from the eastern counties and was shipped from Lynn; The Thames basin provided the remaining 14 per cent which was shipped from London and Maldon.[46] Emperor Julian's Rhine army probably received its supplies in similar proportions from the same areas in AD 361.

THIRD CENTURY AD: THE HIGH POINT FOR BRITANNIA INFERIOR

The third century saw a massive decentralization of power in Roman Britain and a long period of prosperity and importance for the northern region with its capital at York. The first 180 years of Roman rule, which had seen a successful province established under powerful governors, ended in the Caracallan restructuring of government and administration in AD 212. This radically reduced the power of the 'centre' and gave independent power to the North.

There were two reasons other than decentralization for the 'high point' enjoyed by northern Britain in the third century: the first was an internal matter, the effective reorganization of border defences with heavy reliance on forward forts five to forty miles beyond Hadrian's Wall, which ensured peace for almost a century (this was a reversal of the forward policy of Emperor Septimius Severus by his son Caracalla); the second arose from empire-wide policies which favoured the Roman army largely at the expense of towns and townsmen. The relatively more militarized and less urban north prospered under such policies while southern Britain experienced a century of decline.

The Claudian invasion of AD 43 had been rapidly successful to the east of the broad frontier zone which ran from Exeter through Cirencester to Leicester, Newark-upon-Trent, Lincoln, and the Humber. After the first twenty years in which this area was consolidated, the province was extended northwards to control the troublesome Brigantes and afford protection against the 'Caledonian tribes'. The road system was established and a score of towns were centrally planned and built. The powerful centralized machinery of government that achieved this produced powerful governors. The culmination was Governor Clodius Albinus who, with the backing of the army, in AD 197 felt strong enough to make a bid for the imperial throne. The Caracallan reforms of AD 212 were a reaction against an over-powerful centre: measures to curtail central power and prevent any recurrence of AD 197.[47]

Northern Britain had become important in the first and second centuries as a military frontier; the arrival of Emperor Septimius Severus with his sons in York in AD 208 set the seal of importance on the northern province.[48] York was promoted to a *colonia* – one of only four in Britain – probably in AD 212. In the peace of the third century northern Britain consolidated its position and enjoyed strong economic growth, mainly though not only through the extension and development of agricultural estates, after more than a century of front-line involvement in very high-profile frontier defence:[49] a situation rather like the fourteenth-century consolidation and development of the Welsh march (see chapter 7).

In AD 212 Britain was divided into an upper province, Britannia Superior, (because it was nearer to Rome) with its capital almost certainly in London, and a lower province, Britannia Inferior, with its capital at York. The boundaries did not mark off a tidily delimited highland or military zone. The northern province, Britannia Inferior, included Lincoln and Lincolnshire and extended from a line from the Wash to a point on the west coast above Chester and northwards to the Hadrianic defences on the Tyne–Solway line.[50] Thus its civilian (and lowland) area was considerable and it included two of Britain's four legally privileged, high-status *coloniae*, Lincoln and York. The extent and character of any subordination of the northern to the southern province are unclear. The governor of Britannia Superior was usually of consular rank while the governor of Britannia Inferior was only accorded praetorian status. This was a difference with no necessary or automatic implications of subordinate power: the administrative or financial dependency of the northern on the southern province was probably quite minor. Much has been made by some historians of the supervisory and communications officials, the *consularis singulares*, on the governor's staff. Some from London may just conceivably have been posted to the far North.[51] The London-based governor had probably 1,000 *singulares* on his staff; but the York-based governor had 1,000 too.[52] There is no doubt that after AD 212 the northern province enjoyed a high degree of independent power.

This was the outcome of the Caracallan reorganization of the government and administration of the province of Britain; the Caracallan reorganization of northern defences was also highly important for the development of the third-century North. The number of troops on Hadrian's Wall was increased from around 9,000 in Hadrian's day to 12,000, and forward forts were now a key feature of defence: Risingham, High Rochester, Bewcastle, Netherby and Cappuck were all up to forty miles beyond Hadrian's Wall. This outpost system clearly took the strain from forts in the rear and the garrisons were withdrawn from the forts on the Stainmore pass (except Piercebridge). Bainbridge in Wensleydate was also evacuated (but not Ilkley in Wharfedale).[53] The Brigantes always remained a potential danger from within.

The effectiveness of the third-century frontier was not only a matter of the disposition of forts and the use of forward patrols: the new legal right of Roman soldiers to marry local women, and increasing local recruitment to auxiliary military units, gave the army a greater sense of commitment to the frontier society in which they were based. But this did not spell immobility, a major problem of early medieval frontier defence (see chapter 4): in the third century a unit of 'British volunteers', probably from the Scottish lowlands, was stationed on the German frontier.[54] And Roman soldiers did not acquire land in either the third or fourth centuries and become farmer-soldiers, a peasant-militia, as some historians, extrapolating from developments elsewhere in the empire, have supposed.[55] They remained full-time professionals to the end.[56] This was not the beginning of feudalism, of the military obligations of land tenure: the knight and his fee. Roman military commanders did not become territorial magnates: they did not pre-figure the Percies and Nevilles of a later date. The defence of the third-century frontier was not in the hands of a landowning military aristocracy, embryonic wardens of the march.

The third century was also, throughout the empire, a time of inflation, economic stagnation and urban decline. One important contributary factor was that emperors now often came to power with army support and remained heavily dependent on army goodwill; they taxed cities and urban elites to fund the highly favoured conditions of a military life. The house of Severus was a supreme example and it has been claimed that 'To corrupt the soldiers Caracalla needed enormous sums . . . It was mostly derived from systematic draining of the wealth of the propertied classes.'[57] More openly than his father Septimus, Caracalla squeezed the intellectual classes and the bourgeoisie. This policy produced not only urban decline but contributed to rising inflation. High army pay and retired soldiers' pensions were a major factor in the economic problems of these times.

They were also a principal reason for boom conditions in Britannia Inferior. There was now a new era of prosperity in the urban *vici* which had grown up outside the forts in the North and they were now often three or four times as extensive as the forts themselves.[58] Carlisle became a considerable trading centre with a flourishing civilian population; Corbridge was a boom town; Piercebridge grew into a small town; York was no longer primarily a legionary fortress, but an expanding administrative and trading centre. Military wealth and urban expansion were a great stimulus to northern agriculture: 'The high, and improving, economic status of Roman soldiers in frontier provinces is of major importance for an understanding of developments within Romano-British society in the third century.'[59] The first stone buildings of a thoroughly Roman type now appeared at the villas on the Yorkshire wolds and sophisticated villa farming was notable in the very heartland of the Brigantes, the vale of York.[60] This era of peace in northern Britain made fertile regions like the vale of York attractive to those with money to invest like veterans and rich traders.

Britannia Superior had now entered on a period of steep decline. It was not only the great towns of the South that were in trouble: agriculture was in a state of decay and villas throughout the South were being abandoned. This was an age of violence in the South. The plight of towns was probably not quite as catastrophic as Collingwood once supposed. On the basis of excavations at one site, Verulam (St Albans), and extrapolation from studies of the wider empire, Collingwood concluded that 'the cities, which until now had stood for Romanization and enjoyed a privilege of civilized life, suffered a blow of a most devastating kind.'[61] The towns of Britain, like those throughout the empire, were the victims of 'a predatory financial policy which found in their accumulated wealth an easily tapped source of revenue'.[62] It was probably not quite as devastating as that, at least in Britain, but all the indications are that there was at least stagnation: the construction of shops and houses declined and public building was virtually at a standstill.[63] In the meantime prosperity was high and rising in the North.[64]

EPILOGUE: THE SAXON SHORE

The northern province rose again in military importance in the course of the fourth century as the Pictish nation emerged as a powerful and formidable foe. Two more Roman emperors came to York to direct military campaigns on the threatened northern frontier: Constantius Chlorus in AD 306 and Constans in AD 342. But other frontiers were now seriously under threat; the Hadrianic defensive system was progressively less important than the 'Saxon shore'.

The channel and the south-east of Britain were of increasing strategic significance from the later third century. The appointment of Carausius in AD 285 as admiral of a fleet based at Boulogne to counter the Franks and the Saxons who were now infesting the seas marks the emergence of a major military command. (Indeed, it was so important that Carausius, when challenged over his financial management, felt he had the power to declare himself emperor; his lieutenant Allectus who later murdered him, did likewise.) The command had the same high importance for essentially the same reasons as the captaincy of the English base at Calais after the mid-fifteenth century: it too had a vital role in protecting the South-east from attack and provided a powerful southern military and political springboard for the northerner Richard Neville, earl of Warwick, when he was captain of Calais between 1456 and 1461 (see chapter 7). At this time too danger from the channel tipped the balance of strategic importance to the South-east, away from the wardens of the northern march. The military and political importance of the Calais command was a crucial factor in the overthrow of the Lancastrian dynasty in 1461.

After the middle of the fourth century there was a progressive withdrawal of troops from the forward forts to the north of Hadrian's Wall. Any refurbishing of northern forts like Piercebridge was now old-style, with none of the technical sophistication now appearing in fortifications on the south-east coast. No doubt this contributed to the debacle on Hadrian's Wall in AD 367 when it fell victim to the 'barbarian conspiracy', an 'unnatural alliance' of Picts, Scots and Saxons who attacked widely with devastating effect. The coast of Gaul suffered extensive damage as well as northern Britain where, for the first time,

Hadrian's Wall fell while fully garrisoned.[65] But lowland Britain was now perforce a militarized province on an even far more formidable scale than the highland zone.

Eastern Yorkshire (the region of the Humber, of Malton and the wolds), however, remained of great strategic importance with relevance to the defences of the Saxon shore as well as the frontier to the north. The naval base at Brough-on-Humber, important since the late first century in northern defence, was now an element in the defensive system facing the North Sea. The ten main forts of the Saxon shore extended from Portchester along the coastline of Sussex, Kent and Norfolk to Brancaster on the Wash, but an important line of signalling stations was also built along the Yorkshire coast from Filey and Scarborough to Ravenscar and Goldsborough, probably linked to the fort at Malton. It was eastern Yorkshire's significance on this new strategic perimeter, and the protection afforded by this new eastern and south-eastern system of defence, that enabled its luxurious villas to thrive into the fifth century when in the South there was only desolation and decay.

3

The Lost Kingdom

There is a natural and perfectly viable kingdom of the North between the Humber and the Forth–Clyde isthmus. It probably had a prehistoric existence in a rudimentary form, and Agricola seemed to recognize and acknowledge its boundary when in AD 81 he halted his northern march, built forts between the Clyde and the Firth of Forth (and turned his attention to its historic partner, Ireland). In post-Roman times it enjoyed an independent existence for 400 years, from the middle of the sixth to the mid-tenth century; although it was seriously de-stabilized by Viking raids and settlement at the end of the ninth century and consequently diminished in geographical extent and political power.

It was annexed by England in the mid-tenth century (albeit very loosely, retaining extensive liberties and immunities); but its individuality was latent for a further two centuries. The great kingdom of the North from the Humber to the Clyde lay just below the surface of political life, scarcely concealed, ready to emerge. The heavy settlement of Danes, politically supine, depressed rather than encouraged its separatism. But its re-emergence as at least a quasi-independent kingdom of the North was a real possibility until the battle of the Standard in 1138. A victory for King David of Scotland, which even his enemies expected, would have meant the rebirth of the Northumbria of the age of Bede.

The year 1138 saw the end of any realistic chance to renew the historic kingdom of the North, but Greater Northumbria had a subterranean existence until 1296. In that year Edward I abruptly, finally and decisively ended its life as a prelude to his war against the Scots. Its latent separatism had been a major problem earlier in the century for King John. Edward I cut through the network of relationships which transcended the boundary along the Tweed by identifying fifty-two north-of-England landowners with estates in southern Scotland and doubtful allegiance to the English crown, and depriving them of their lands.[1] There now began a war, 'one of whose consequences was to make English settlement in Scotland, or for that matter Scots settlement in England, almost impossible for three hundred years'.[2]

FACING EAST AND WEST: THE AGE OF BEDE

The post-Roman kingdom of Northumbria gave political expression to a geographical complex, the key elements of which were the Humber and the Clyde. These were highways to wider worlds: to the east, north-western Europe and to the west, Ireland. It was its position at the crossroads of northern Europe that contributed to Northumbria's wealth and the immense cultural vitality which found full expression in the age of Bede.

Bede said that King Ida founded Northumbria's ruling house. His twelve-year reign began in AD 547. He established a base at Bamburgh and brought Bernicia, the land beyond the Tyne where the Votadini lived, under his rule. His grandson Ethelfrid ruled not only Deira, the territory between the Humber and Hadrian's Wall, and Bernicia, the territory beyond it: he extended his rule into south-west Scotland. He defeated an army of highland Scots from Argyll at Degaston in Liddesdale in AD 603. Since that time, wrote Bede more than a century later, 'no King of the Scots has dared to do battle with the English.'[3] Spiritual authority over the Northumbrian monasteries and bishoprics was exercised in the mid-seventh century by Iona: but it was the political stability of the kingdom of Northumbria that made their foundation possible and ensured their survival. The wide scatter of monastic houses from Lastingham in the Yorkshire moors (near Helmsley) to Coldingham in Lothian (between Edinburgh and Berwick-upon-Tweed) suggests a considerable degree of political security and indicates that the authority of the Northumbrian kings extended to the Firth of Forth by AD 650.

Northumbria pushed towards the valley of the Clyde and the west (its authority probably extended to Dumbarton by the mid-eighth century); but it had a profound sense of its heritage from the east. This was kept alive in poetry and histories. The monkish historians Glidas and Bede wrote of Anglo-Saxon soldiers coming by invitation from north Germany to defend the Britons against the Picts and the Scots. Bede was very precise: they arrived, he said, in AD 449 in three long ships. Both the chronology and the organization were certainly more complex than that; and indeed Bede spoke of subsequent Anglo-Saxon invaders who came to seize and settle on the fertile land. But 'all the Northumbrian stock (that is, those people living north of the river Humber)', were descended from these Angles, and the Northumbrian missionaries of Bede's day went to north Germany to convert their own kinsfolk. They faced danger and even martyrdom, but they had a strong sense that they were returning home.

Northern England throughout the Dark Ages looked to the east and the west. From the east came raiders and settlers from north Germany and Scandinavia; from the west came first Christian missionaries and then Vikings from Ireland. Northern England was caught up for six centuries in this east–west traffic of men and ideas.

The first fruit of these east–west influences was the spectacular Northumbrian Christian civilization of the late seventh and eighth centuries, remarkable for its monasteries, missionaries, scholarship and Hiberno-Saxon art; the second was the linked Viking kingdoms of Dublin and York in the ninth and tenth centuries. There were, indeed, strong influences which pulled towards the South, notably the 'Roman' victory at the synod of Whitby in AD 663, when the king of Northumbria gave judgement against the Celtic method of Easter-reckoning and so promoted the authority of Rome over the saints and traditions of the Irish church. But in AD 735 the archbishopric of York was created, in no way subordinate to Canterbury. All the weight of Northumbria's ecclesiastical power and authority in the early eighth century marched east to west: only York of the four bishoprics was south of the Tyne. In the far east there was Lindisfarne, in the centre Hexham, and Whithorn was in the far west.

William of Normandy re-aligned his new kingdom on a north–south axis. 'The Conquest marks the point at which the integration of the North into the kingdom of England really began.'[4] Although William's coronation, like that of Harold before him, was for technical–legal reasons (the pope had not recognized Stigand) conducted by the archbishop of York, in 1070 Thomas of Bayeux became the new archbishop only after a profession of obedience to Lanfranc. This break with tradition after more than three centuries was a calculated political move.[5] Northumbria had been a North Sea kingdom, but Norman and especially Angevin England was a channel state. Seen in the long perspective of history and prehistory, this was a seismic change from the

North's age-old east–west orientation which had been culturally highly productive over a period of more than 3,000 years.

The dense clusters of neolithic long barrows and chamfered cairns on the Yorkshire wolds and in north-eastern Ireland point to a close connection between these rich and favoured lowland zones some 3,000 years ago; a similar geographical patterning of Bronze Age 'food vessels' points to a close connection a thousand years later.[6] The seventh and eighth century connection between the monasteries and minsters at Melrose, Coldingham, Lindisfarne, Lastingham, Whitby, Ripon and York and Ireland falls into the same pattern; so does the ninth- and tenth-century link between the Viking kingdoms of Dublin and York.[7] The flow of men, ideas and artefacts was predominantly east–west, from northern Europe to the Humber and thence by sea, circumventing the Pennines and the Cumbrian mountains, via the Forth and the Clyde to eastern Ireland. The journey from York to Dublin involved only twenty miles of land travel, between the Forth and the Clyde. (During the Bronze Age, when the Forth–Clyde lowlands were densely forested, the route was probably from York by sea to the Tweed and thence via Lauderdale, Eddleston and Biggar Waters to the upper Clyde.) What is now southern Scotland was an integral part of a great east–west cultural and communications arc.

Bede never left Jarrow, but in his *History of the English Church and People*, written around AD 730, there is a sense of wide horizons. He was born ten years after the synod of Whitby and Jarrow was a 'Roman' monastery; but Bede looks westward to Ireland with unqualified affection and approval as the source of Christian religion in Northumbria; he looks eastward with no less affection to the north German land of his kinsfolk, the Angles, from whom the post-Roman settlers in Northumbria came. But his horizons were even wider, for Jarrow in the early eighth century was a truly cosmopolitan centre of learning where Celtic and European traditions met.

It is not enough for an international centre of learning to stand at the crossroads of Europe: it must stand there with appropriate facilities. At Wearmouth there was the great library built up by a high-born Northumbrian, Benedict Biscop, in the later seventh century. He had made five journeys to Rome during which he had made extensive collections of books. It was precisely because Benedict Biscop had been five times to Rome that Bede could spend a highly productive life as a scholar without ever leaving Northumbria.

Celtic Christianity was in the ascendant in Northumbria for only thirty

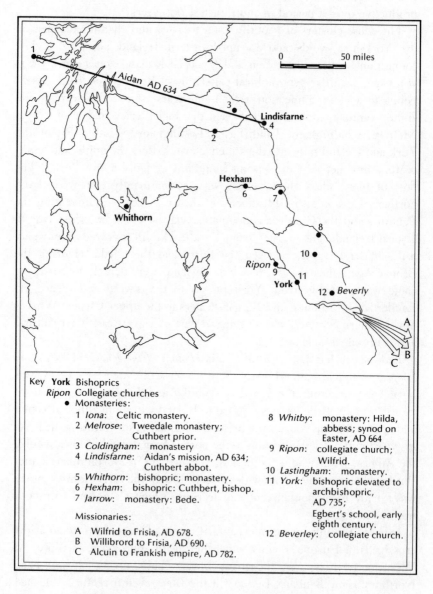

Key **York** Bishoprics
Ripon Collegiate churches
● Monasteries:

1 *Iona*:   Celtic monastery.
2 *Melrose*:   Tweedale monastery;
                    Cuthbert prior.
3 *Coldingham*:   monastery
4 *Lindisfarne*:   Aidan's mission, AD 634;
                    Cuthbert abbot.
5 *Whithorn*:   bishopric; monastery.
6 *Hexham*:   bishopric: Cuthbert, bishop.
7 *Jarrow*:   monastery: Bede.

Missionaries:

A   Wilfrid to Frisia, AD 678.
B   Willibrord to Frisia, AD 690.
C   Alcuin to Frankish empire, AD 782.

8 *Whitby*:   monastery: Hilda,
                    abbess; synod on
                    Easter, AD 664
9 *Ripon*:   collegiate church;
                    Wilfrid.
10 *Lastingham*:   monastery.
11 *York*:   bishopric elevated to
                    archbishopric,
                    AD 735;
                    Egbert's school, early
                    eighth century.
12 *Beverley*:   collegiate church.

MAP 3.1   Main religious centres of the kingdom of Northumbria in the seventh and eighth centuries

Source: author

years; from AD 634 when Aidan came, at the king's invitation, from Iona to Lindisfarne, to AD 663, the year of the synod of Whitby, after which many Irish priests returned home. But its influence remained strong. Cuthbert embodied its values and sustained its influence for another twenty years. This Teviotdale shepherd entered the abbey at Melrose, became prior of Lindisfarne and (reluctantly) bishop of Hexham, and died as a hermit on the Farne Islands in AD 687. His life was a powerful statement of the ascetic, other-worldly values of the Irish church. It was Cuthbert who would remain the great cultural hero of the north of England for a thousand years.

After AD 663 Northumbria was firmly in Europe, its church leaders in close contact with Rome; but Celtic values were still pervasive: a deep love of learning, belief in self-exile for Christ, a contemplative, other-worldly style of religious life. The great Northumbrian missionary enterprise to north Germany did not begin in earnest until thirty years after the synod of Whitby – and it did so only after receiving the blessing of the pope – but the impulse of an evangelizing Celtic church is evident from the outset. Willibrord, the most eminent of the missionaries, was a protege of Wilfrid and had been educated at Ripon; but he had spent twelve years in Ireland after that. A century later, when Northumbria's most eminent cultural emissary, Alcuin, was resident as Europe's spiritual overlord at the court of Charlemagne, the Celtic influence had receded. In the late seventh century, however, this influence was a potent ingredient in the missionary work in northern Europe which has been called with some justice 'one of the most remarkable achievements in the whole history of the Church in England'.[8]

After the death of Bede in AD 735 York became Northumbria's international centre of learning. Egbert, a brother of the Northumbrian king, was head of the cloister school and became the first archbishop of York. The school was a centre for the study of the liberal arts and the authors studied included Aristotle, Cicero and Virgil. 'Scholars flocked to York from all over Europe.'[9] Albert, who became archbishop after Egbert's death in AD 766, was a distinguished teacher of astronomy and geometry. Alcuin was the school's most famous pupil and for the last two decades of the century, first as Charlemagne's director of studies at the court at Aachen, and then as abbot of Tours, he presided over a revival of interest in literature which permeated the entire Frankish empire.

The religious and intellectual creativity and international influence of Northumbria lasted for a century and a half. It virtually ended with the death of Alcuin in AD 804. It has been explained by historians mainly in terms of accident: the 'accident' of a handful of personalities, and of somewhat fortuitous events. Thus the first step towards the mission to Frisia was taken in AD 678 when Wilfrid, en route to Rome, was prevented from crossing the channel and forced to make landfall at the mouth of the Rhine. Wilfrid took the opportunity to begin evangelizing work, and Willibrord more than a dozen years later simply continued a tradition 'which had been accidentally created by Wilfrid'.[10] This trivializes a great movement which was in fact the outcome of the history, social structure and geographical context and configuration of the ancient kingdom of Northumbria.

The late seventh-century and eighth-century religious and cultural achievements of Northumbria occurred in a kingdom which was strong and relatively peaceful, which was rich and aristocratic, and in which the king was powerful. It was a supremely self-confident society (it was also very self-satisfied and a little naive). The leading figures in the church, both the men and especially the women, tended to be high-born, often of royal blood. Egbert, the first archbishop of York and master of the cloister school, the missionary Willibrord, and the cultural emissary Alcuin were all related to Northumbria's ruling house. So was Hilda, abbess of Whitby. They could associate easily and correspond freely with the crowned heads of Europe. Willibrord owed much of his success to his friendship with Pippin, the 'duke of the Franks'. When Alcuin encountered Charlemagne in Parma in AD 781 their conversation developed easily and the emperor pressed the Northumbrian cleric to take up residence with his family in the imperial palace. Alcuin moved confidently in the highest circles and his voluminous correspondence with abbots, bishops and kings is familiar and very assured.

Major initiatives were usually royal initiatives. It was the king of Northumbria who invited Aidan from Iona; it was a royal decision that was the climax of the synod of Whitby; even the great Wilfrid of Ripon was deprived of his bishopric when he offended the king. Northumbria was royal, aristocratic, and rich. Monasticism is closely associated with great landed wealth. There is sufficient surplus wealth to endow monasteries and support a monastic life. Indeed, monasteries in eighth-century Northumbria tended to be regarded as the private property of their patrons and even as a way of providing for kinsfolk. Monasteries could easily become – as Bede complained – aristocratic enclaves of wealth and privilege.

Above all Northumbria was a perimeter kingdom at the point of intersection between different cultural traditions: the line from Iona through Melrose to Lindisfarne lies at right-angles to the line from Ripon and York. Other parts of England were aristocratic, royal and rich; only Wessex was comparable in both wealth and marginality. Kent and Sussex were the natural springboard to Europe, but only the two rich outer kingdoms sent missionaries: Wessex produced in Boniface a religious leader and missionary who, in the mid-eighth century, stands comparison with Wilfrid, Willibrord and Alcuin. Boniface was raised in the monastery at Exeter and entered the house at Nursling in Hampshire from which he embarked on his mission to Germany. The church in Dorset and Hampshire was also a centre of great learning (where once again well-born women made an important contribution). Dorset and Hampshire, like eastern Northumbria, would be singled out for attack by the Danes at the end of the eighth century: they knew not only that there was wealth, but that a sophisticated social organization had the machinery to assess and collect it. The two perimeter kingdoms have striking and relevant similarities.

There can be great energy and creative tension in perimeters, margins and intersections. This is perhaps especially clear in the turbulent career of Wilfrid and quite explicit in his speech to the synod at Whitby in AD 663. When he argued the case for the Roman method of reckoning the date of Easter he spoke from first-hand knowledge of the customs and practices of Italy and Gaul; he made informed references to Egypt, Asia and Greece; and he spoke with some contempt of the practices of some of those in Ireland and northern England who were living in what he called 'the two uttermost islands of the ocean'. This widely travelled, cosmopolitan churchman referred the outer circumference of his world to the centre. It was the tension between centre and perimeter that provided the dynamic of the Northumbrian church.

And yet these widely travelled churchmen who were at home in the great affairs of a wider world had a curious naivete born of a secure and settled society which had been free for the past two centuries from external attack. There was comparative peace within Northumbria, and in Bede's writing there is a strong sense of stability.[11] But Bede also had a feeling that perhaps life in Northumbria was too easy, leading to a neglect of civil and military obligations and over-full monasteries: 'As such peace and prosperity prevail in these days, many of the Northumbrians, both noble and simple, together with their children, have laid aside their weapons, preferring to receive the tonsure and take monastic vows rather than study the arts of war. What the results of this will be the future will show.'[12] This was indeed prophetic. When the Danes attacked Lindisfarne some

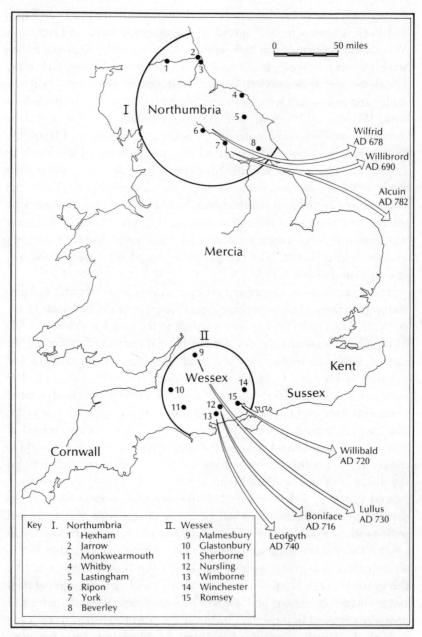

0   50 miles

I   Northumbria

1 Hexham
2 Jarrow
3 Monkwearmouth
4 Whitby
5 Lastingham
6 Ripon
7 York
8 Beverley

Wilfrid
AD 678

Willibrord
AD 690

Alcuin
AD 782

Mercia

II

Wessex

Kent

Sussex

Cornwall

9 Malmesbury
10 Glastonbury
11 Sherborne
12 Nursling
13 Wimborne
14 Winchester
15 Romsey

Willibald
AD 720

Lullus
AD 730

Boniface
AD 716

Leofgyth
AD 740

Key I. Northumbria   II. Wessex
     1 Hexham   9 Malmesbury
     2 Jarrow   10 Glastonbury
     3 Monkwearmouth   11 Sherborne
     4 Whitby   12 Nursling
     5 Lastingham   13 Wimborne
     6 Ripon   14 Winchester
     7 York   15 Romsey
     8 Beverley

MAP 3.2 Two off-centre foci of seventh- and eighth-century missionary initiative

Source: adapted from M. Falkus and J. Gillingham, *Historical Atlas of Britain* (Kingfisher Books, 1987).

sixty years later, in AD 793, the outrage of Alcuin was matched only by his innocence: he was astonished that this exposed, highly vulnerable and undefended island should be attacked at all. In a letter of condolence and advice to the bishop of Lindisfarne he spoke of 'nearly 350 years that we and our fathers have inhabited this most lovely land, and never before has such terror appeared in Britain as we have now suffered from a pagan race'. His recipe for future safety was not defensive ramparts but repentance: 'Do not glory in the vanity of raiment . . . Do not go after the luxuries of the flesh and worldly avarice'.[13] When the Danes attacked Lindisfarne again some eighty years later, the island and the monastery were still wholly unprepared, and the monks now left the island, first for Chester-le-Street and finally for Durham. Holy Island was not in fact fortified for nearly another seven centuries. In 1550 a castle was built for defence against the Scots.

THE DISASTER OF THE DANES

Two disasters befell the kingdom of Northumbria after 'the age of Bede': settlement by Danes and absorption into England. The first extinguished not only monasteries but any real life of the mind for almost three centuries; the price of the second was that Northumbria was beheaded – its wealthiest region, Lothian, and indeed all the rich lands beyond the Eamont and Tweed, were now lost.

A unified kingdom of England which was Winchester- or London-based was incapable of retaining effective control of these far-northern lands. Cumbria, Galloway and Strathclyde had always been precariously and intermittently held. In the middle and towards the end of the tenth century these territories were ceded by English kings to the king of the Scots, though the poorest part, Cumbria between Stainmore and the river Esk, would be regained, eventually, after 200 years. The north-western region was ceded to the king of the Scots in AD 945 and partially regained in 1157.[14]

The ninth century was the century when the Danes settled in the North; the tenth was the century when the North was annexed by England. The Danes began to settle on the land as well as sailing away with the proceeds of their raids; in AD 867 they took York, but it was nine years later according to the *Anglo-Saxon Chronicle*, that 'Hafdan [their leader] shared out the land of the Northumbrians and proceeded to plough and support themselves.' There were probably about a thousand Danish warriors involved in this land settlement around York.

Other Scandinavian raiders, Norwegians (or 'Vikings'), also came and settled in the North. They came from the pirates' base they had established in Ireland, from the Isle of Man and from Norway. This wave of Vikings came later than the Danes, mainly in the early tenth century: it penetrated high up the remoter Yorkshire dales like Dentdale; it also spread through the plains and valleys on the west of the Pennines. Vikings came over from Ireland via the Wirral and the Ribble and settled from Lancashire to Westmorland and Cumberland and beyond. This new wave of immigrants in the North did not promote a generalized Scandinavian social or political solidarity: it subverted it. (Cumberland, Westmorland and indeed Northumberland were never included in the so-called 'Danelaw'.) There was much internecine warfare between the Norwegians and the Danes in the north of England especially after AD 919 when the Norwegians took York.[15]

The great weight of Scandinavian influence in northern England was Danish rather than Norwegian. There was a spectacular but very brief interlude of Viking political power centred quite narrowly in practice on York; but it was the heavy Danish settlement between the Welland and the Tees that was of particular long-term social and cultural influence. This was 'the essential Danelaw'.[16] Its political consciousness and impact were in fact virtually nil; its social and cultural consequences were catastrophic.

The Danes obliterated monasticism in the North. The area of most intensive Scandinavian settlement from the Welland to beyond the Tees remained a monastery-free zone for 200 years. When the great tenth-century revival of monasticism occurred across the south Midlands, notably through the vale of Evesham across to the Fens, there was no significant stirring of religious life in the North. The archbishopric of York declined catastrophically in wealth and power and for long periods was held in plurality with the rich bishopric of Worcester. A richly endowed and intellectually vital religious life now extended north-east from Glastonbury through more than thirty houses to Ramsey and Ely. Worcestershire was especially notable for its monastic vitality and a quarter of all monasteries were in Dorset and Somerset. Only Sussex and Cornwall, among southern counties, were as barren as the North.

When the monastic revival began in the North in the late eleventh century it owed nothing whatsoever to the Anglo-Danish landowners of the North. The initiative came wholly from the South. Monks from

Evesham set out for Wearmouth and Whitby in 1074 quite explicitly to recover some of the lost glory of the age of Bede. Among them was Reinfrid, a former Norman knight, and the endowments he secured for the restoration of Whitby came from a fellow Norman, William de Percy, who now held land in north Yorkshire. It was Norman aristocrats, and not Anglo-Danish smallholders, on whom monastic renewal would depend.

The Danes were not especially anti-Christian; they attacked monasteries at first as regional safe-deposits. They later became Christian themselves and even endowed parish churches, and the minsters at Beverley, Ripon and Southwell began to look like quite wealthy ecclesiastical corporations. But this was negligible compared with the splendour of Glastonbury, Pershore, Evesham and Worcester.

The Danes, it has been said, made two important contributions to the North: a numerous free peasantry and a concern for law. Both have been seen as having some kind of wider, long-term consequence, making in some unspecified manner 'a mark which time has not erased'.[17] Neither, in fact, had any long-term consequence of note. The 'masses of independent peasants'[18] coexisted with downright slavery and there is no evidence whatsoever that either Danish sokemen or Danish law made any particular contribution to English liberties. The laws of the Danelaw were mainly the detailed regulation of agricultural life; and the Danish heritage never amounted to much more than the division of the rent-paying year, in Yorkshire, at Whitsun and Martinmas.

The free peasantry never rose for freedom. They are most charitably described as accommodating. It is precisely because the north of England was a land of independent peasant smallholders that institutions supporting a vital literary, artistic and spiritual life were extinguished. In the Dark Ages, as in the Middle Ages, the endowment of monasteries and institutions of learning was associated with great landed wealth unequally distributed in a highly hierarchical society.[19] Danish sokemen were small-scale farmers, pragmatic men of the soil, with a grasp of detail and a total lack of imagination. Competent, acquisitive men of practical good sense, they increased the productivity of the land and developed iron-smelting, pottery and cloth-making, notably at Stamford.[20] They were wholly without vision or ideas.

The tenth century saw northern England finally dislodged from its age-old east–west axis, and the beginning of domination by the South. The last product of the North's location between the Irish and German seas was the Viking empire centred on Dublin and York which had a shadowy existence for a few years after AD 919. Ragnall, a Viking leader from Ireland based himself at York after invading via the Clyde and marching south after military victories at Corbridge and Dunblane. The result has been called 'a Scandinavian empire of impressive proportions';[21] an older judgment is probably nearer the truth: that a succession of Norwegian adventurers now ruled in a highly precarious fashion from York.[22]

The importance of York to the tenth-century Vikings was still its geographical location between east and west: a staging post between Ireland and Scandinavia. Ireland was a great source of wealth to the Vikings but its resources were not cultivated but pillaged. The booty was still most easily and safely transported first to York via the Isle of Man and the waterways of southern Scotland before shipment to Scandinavia. 'Hence the constant expeditions of Dublin Viking kings to conquer York, and York Viking kings to conquer Dublin.'[23]

The Vikings' Hiberno-Northumbrian empire lasted for precisely thirty-five years, from AD 919 to 954, and suffered a major though not decisive defeat at the hands of the Wessex king, Athelstan, at Brunanburh (probably in south Yorkshire; perhaps on the Don) in AD 937. At least eight Viking leaders ruled in York during that time. The last Norwegian out of Dublin who ruled in York was Eric Bloodaxe, driven out not by the kings of Wessex but by the Northumbrians themselves and killed in battle on Stainmore in AD 954.

NORTHERN SEPARATISM

There was nothing either inevitable or intrinsically desirable in Northumbria's absorption into a unified kingdom of England, while the price of this absorption was immense: the loss of its richest lands beyond Eamont and Tweed. It was precisely this loss, however, that made the absorption irreversible.

Only the most general overlordships were established by the kings of Wessex in the later tenth century. It was only by confirming and granting extensive franchises and liberties that their overlordship was possible at all. Athelstan was lavish on his visits to the North in his grants of privileges to religious communities, notably at Beverley and Ripon. The kings of all England in fact ruled the North through viceroys who were members of the house of Bamburgh: previously kings, they were now earls of Northumbria, with scarcely diminished powers. It was the earls of Northumbria and not the kings of England who determined who would be bishops of Durham. They were not appointed earls of Northumbria by the king of England: they succeeded by hereditary right. And they appear to have paid no tribute to the English king.[24]

Northumbria survived into the medieval English state as a land honeycombed with palatinates and liberties where the King's writ did not run. Their independence was jealously guarded and in some instances actually increased, especially in the fourteenth century when their strategic importance in the war against Scotland was at its height. In fact the first great encroachment on their legal immunities was not until the parliamentary statute of 1536 'for Resuming Liberties to the Crown'. The 'regalities' defined the north of England as a land of privilege for a period of six centuries.

The most important of these privileged enclaves were Tynedale, Redesdale and the liberty of Durham. In the tenth century the future palatinate of Durham was still an integral part of the earldom of Northumbria. They were not lands and lordships granted after 1066 by Anglo-Norman kings: they had an anterior legitimacy as remnants or residues of the ancient kingdom and earldom of Northumbria.[25]

This is one side of the coin; the other is the loss of northern lands which decisively altered the balance of power between northern England and the South. In AD 945 Edmund the Elder, king of England, ceded the extensive territory of Cumbria (which included much of what is now south-west Scotland) to Malcolm, king of the Scots; in AD 975 King Edgar ceded Lothian to Malcolm's son, Kenneth, and the boundary of Northumbria receded from the Forth to the Tweed. This transference of territory was one of the great turning points in the history of the North, utterly transforming its relationship with the South.[26]

It was the regalities and liberties that underpinned the separatist posture of the North within a unified English state; the Danish settlers, albeit with distinctive customs and social structure, were an irrelevance. The regality of the ancient earldom of Northumbria was still intact in 1086 north of the Tees and these lands were excluded from the Domesday survey: since nothing went from them to the royal exchequer, 'there was no need to survey them'.[27] Yorkshire was surveyed, however, and was in fact more fully integrated. Earl Morcar had divided his Northumbrian earldom into two in 1065 and had retained for himself the earldom of York. He forfeited this in 1071 when he joined the Conqueror's enemies at Ely. He was not replaced. Yorkshire was brought more directly into the Anglo-Norman state, although great honours and liberties like Pontefract and Holderness were established and consolidated as quasi-

principalities for purposes of defence. It was these that kept Yorkshire
somewhat apart, although much less apart than Northumberland and
Durham.

Danish settlers in northern England made no significant contribution
to northern separatism. Even historians highly sympathetic to the Anglo-
Danes concede their lack of political initiative. They may, conceivably,
have hoped that northern England would become part of a Greater
Denmark, but they were willing only to wait on events, 'never prepared
to take their destinies into their own hands'.[28]

There were three points in the eleventh century when, it has been said,
the Anglo-Danes in northern England did show a separatist tendency –
when Scandinavians invaded via the Humber in 1014, 1066 and 1069.
The argument is based wholly on negative evidence: the separatism of the
Anglo-Danes is claimed not because they rose to support the invaders
(they did not), but because they did nothing at all.

In 1014 the Danish king, Swein, established a base at Gainsborough on
the Trent where the Anglo-Danish population 'submitted with suspicious
readiness';[29] in 1066 King Harold Hadrada of Norway gained a military
victory over northern defenders at Fulford but made no attempt to molest
the inhabitants of York, moving upstream to make his base at Stamford
Bridge. This has been invested with great significance.[30] In 1069 the
king of Denmark sent a great armada of some 300 ships up the Humber
under the command of his brother and three sons. When this invasion
failed William of Normandy 'harried the North' in order, it is said, to
punish his rebellious subjects. But any serious rebellion by Yorkshire's
Anglo-Danes in support of the Danish invaders would have ended
Norman rule in the North before it had fairly begun.

The Norman plantation in Yorkshire in 1069 was remarkably light, as
it would be seventeen years later when the Domesday survey was made.[31]
If the Normans were an army of occupation it was on a very small scale
(their true significance was as a small but strategically deployed frontier
defence force concerned less with the enemy within than the enemy
without). The invading Danes succeeded in taking York and leading
Normans, including the sheriff, William Malet, were made prisoner.
William of Normandy eventually arrived only after three weeks' delay at
the river crossing at Pontefract. By this time Norman rule in Yorkshire
should have been extinct. When William made contact with the invaders
he was unable to inflict military defeat: they were now prepared to be
bought off but were able to insist that they remain throughout the winter
in occupation of an area of east Yorkshire near the Humber. William was

already destroying the countryside to make a more protracted stay unattractive. This is the key to his famous 'harrying of the North' which is usually described as 'punitive'. It was not to punish his rebellious Anglo-Danish subjects who had not rebelled on any significant scale; it was a scorched-earth policy to make the land unappetizing for future would-be Scandinavian settlers.

It was not in Anglo-Danish Yorkshire that northerners took the initiative and seriously rebelled after 1066, but in Durham. In 1069 they killed the Norman Robert de Commine who had been given the title of earl and sent by the Conqueror to rule north of the Tees; in 1080 they killed Bishop Walcher, a cleric from Lorraine who had been made bishop of Durham in 1071. The heart of northern resistance and separatism was in St Cuthbert land.

'Northern separatism was Northumbrian separatism.'[32] It was not Danish separatism. It had been evident in the appointment and conduct of the earls of Northumbria in 1065 and 1066. 'Separatism' is perhaps an overstatement. What was evident in the northerners' treatment of Earl Tostig and in the conduct of his successor Earl Morcar was strong regionalism.

Tostig, Earl Godwin's son, a southerner without experience or connections in the North, had been made earl of Northumbria in 1055. A complete outsider had been appointed in preference to a member of the house of Bamburgh.[33] The northern nobility expelled him ten years later, partly because he had disregarded northern customs, but undoubtedly because he represented the dominance of the South.

The northern nobles appointed Morcar in his stead, and then invaded the South. They bargained at Northampton with Harold, the future king, now King Edward's emissary. They resisted all attempts to have Tostig reinstated. The conference of Northampton was a triumph for the North. But it also shows the northerners' essential acceptance of a centralized kingdom: they had marched south not to declare an independent kingdom of the North but to secure the king's approval of their action and ratification of Morcar's appointment. They were claiming strong regional power but within the framework of the English state.

Events of the following year, in the prelude to the battle of Hastings, have been seen as a bid for a separate kingdom of the North: Earl Morcar of Northumbria and his ally Edwin, earl of Mercia, hung back from supporting Harold in the Hastings campaign, entertaining hopes of 'bringing about their darling scheme of a divided kingdom'.[34] But in fact Morcar and Edwin promptly submitted to the victorious William.

Regionalism was rampant in 1065 and 1066; but full-blooded separatism was virtually dead.

Northern separatism received a powerful impetus from unlikely quarters in the early twelfth century – the new Norman aristocracy and a Scottish king – and four centuries after Jarrow was at the height of its international fame Norman abbots, bishops and landowners to the north and south of the river Tweed re-created the age of Bede. This was the last chance to establish an independent kingdom of the North between the Humber and the Forth–Clyde isthmus and beyond. It only failed by a whisker, but after the battle of the Standard in 1138 full-blown northern separatism was dead.

Two men with a strong sense of history played a major part in recreating a tight-knit religious and upper-class community extending from south and east Yorkshire to southern Scotland: Thurstan, a Norman born at Bayeux who was archbishop of York from 1114 to 1140; and David, earl of Huntingdon and lord of Hallamshire in south Yorkshire, who was king of Scotland from 1124 to 1153. Thurstan had a powerful sense of the history of the Northumbrian church (he re-established the bishopric of Whithorn in south-west Scotland in 1125); David had a strong sense of ancient political boundaries as far south as the Humber; he made his capital at Carlisle. Their attempt to re-create the essence of eighth-century Northumbria – David's ambitions undoubtedly went somewhat beyond Thurstan's – was a deliberate and self-conscious policy.

David and Thurstan had been close associates at the court of Henry I where the former served his apprenticeship as a knight and the latter was a royal clerk. With David's help Thurstan would later extend his ecclesiastical jurisdiction far beyond the Solway and the Tweed, even claiming spiritual lordship over St Andrews. (Bishop Thomas was consecrated by Thurstan at York in 1127.) He established a bishopric at Carlisle in 1133. They would also collaborate in promoting monasticism and establishing close links between the great abbeys north of the Tweed and those in south and east Yorkshire. King David's great fee of Hallamshire was within the spiritual lordship of the archbishop of York.

Secular interconnections between southern Scotland and northern England, especially Yorkshire, were just as strong and multifarious. They were principally the outcome of King David's deliberate Normanization

of his kingdom and his introduction of the tenurial and military relation-
ships known as 'feudalism'.[35] This was as deliberate and self-conscious as
Thurstan's re-creation of Northumbrian diocesan administration. It
brought Norman officials and Norman landholders into southern
Scotland on a considerable scale: some were brought in directly from
Normandy, some from David's Huntingdon estates scattered over the east
Midlands, but principally they were drawn from Norman families settled
in Yorkshire. Walter of Rydale went from the North Riding to serve
David I and founded the Scottish family of Riddell; Ranulf son of Walter
of Lowthorpe in the East Riding became the king's falconer and founded
another great Scottish dynasty. This migration of Normans from
Yorkshire was a major contribution to the feudal plantation north of
the border and involved the great families of Brus, Balliol and Mowbray
as well as many Anglo-Norman families of humbler standing. What
was happening was a redistribution of population from one part
of ancient Northumbria to another, with a consequently greater
inter-locking and strengthening of 'Northumbria's' internal social
bonds.[36]

There was a growing sense of solidarity among the Norman ruling
class of this renascent Northumbria. When King David of Scotland was
under threat in 1134 from the rebellious earl of Moray in the highlands,
he asked his Yorkshire-Norman friends for military support and they
assembled under Walter l'Espec of Helmsley at Carlisle. They agreed to
send a force north overland and a fleet from the Tees or the Tyne to the
Moray Firth. The earl of Moray ceased to rebel when he heard of this
Yorkshire alliance.[37]

Secular and religious interests came together in the foundation of
monasteries, in which the Norman aristocracy and King David were
deeply involved. The founding of four great monasteries in southern
Scotland, in the valley of the Tweed and Teviotdale, and half a dozen in
east Yorkshire in the thirty-eight years between Thurstan's preferment in
1114 and King David's death in 1152, reflects the great wealth of these
two regions; it also reflects a great co-operative enterprise between the
Norman landowners of Yorkshire and Scotland.

The houses established in Scotland were Kelso (1128), Melrose
(1136), Jedburgh (1138) and Dryburgh (1150). They were closely
connected through their founders and the appointment of priors and
abbots with the great houses of Yorkshire. There were particularly close
links with Nostell priory near Wakefield (endowed by the Lacy family,
lords of the honour of Pontefract) and Rievaulx abbey and Kirkham

priory near Helmsley (both founded by Walter l'Espec). The great abbey
at Melrose, founded by King David, received its first monks from
Rievaulx, and the abbot of Rievaulx, Ailred, came from King David's
court. David's stepson, Waltheof, entered Nostell priory and later
became prior of Kirkham. The Nostell canons had established an
Augustinian house at Scotland's hallowed centre, Scone; and in 1124
Robert, prior of Nostell, was promoted to Scotland's premier bishopric,
St Andrew's.[38]

These complex secular and ecclesiastical interconnections are well
illustrated in the life and work of the Norman Hugue de Morville who
came from a family near Cherbourg to enter King David's service and
became his constable in 1150. He received extensive lands from David in
Lauderdale and in Westmorland around Appleby; he also held fees in the
Lacy honour of Pontefract at Seacroft and Thorner near Leeds. He
founded the great abbey at Dryburgh in 1150. This house was established
by monks who came from the monastery at Alnwick.

Thus Norman abbots, bishops and landowners and a Scottish king were
creating a tight network of family, ecclesiastical and tenurial bonds within
the boundaries of the ancient kingdom of Northumbria. They looked
back quite consciously over four centuries to the age of Bede. There was at
this time extensive writing about Irish saints: thus, Laurence of Durham
wrote a life of Bridget, the Irish saint, which he dedicated to Ailred, later
abbot of Rievaulx, then a layman at King David's court. New monasteries
were founded quite deliberately, where possible, where hermits were or
had been living: Nostell, Bridlington and Kirkstall, for example. The
building of the new abbey at Melrose began piously but ill-advisedly on
the site of Cuthbert's old monastery but had to be moved to a more
satisfactory site two miles to the west.

The ancient kingdom of the North had been virtually re-created: it was
a kingdom-in-waiting for a definitive political act. King David took
advantage of the political difficulties in England, arising from a disputed
succession to the throne, to make a bid to achieve this in 1138. This was
one of the decisive years of English history: the last chance for a great
kingdom of the North. It was a chance lost in battle at Northallerton on
22 August. What is even more surprising than David's defeat is that a
battle was necessary at all.

David's intentions were well known at the beginning of the year. They
were discussed at an Easter conference at Northampton, where the North
and the centre intersect and the problems of their relationship have
traditionally been discussed. Archbishop Thurstan presided. But the

problem was not defined as England's problem: it was Yorkshire's. There was never any question of the king's raising a national, feudal army to defend his kingdom; it was whether the sixty-eight-year-old archbishop would raise an army to defend Yorkshire. It was not entirely clear that Yorkshire wished to be defended, however, and a negotiated settlement was envisaged which would concede to King David virtually everything he claimed.

David's march south into Yorkshire was opposed only with great reluctance. Two emissaries met him to negotiate peace: Bernard Balliol and Robert de Brus. Both held land in Yorkshire and in Scotland; they were friends and vassals of David and reminded him that Yorkshire Normans had come to his aid against Malcolm of Moray only four years before. When these overtures failed Thurstan felt it expedient to call on Yorkshire's Norman knights to pledge their loyalty to the king of England. Some took up arms against David with deep misgivings, notoriously William of Aumale, lord of Holderness. Alain de Percy, who held a little land in Scotland and a great deal in Yorkshire, decided to fight for David. But the Normans of Yorkshire generally stood firm under the leadership of David's two elderly friends, Archbishop Thurstan and Walter l'Espec.

Why did they fight at all? One reason was that a political conflict was converted into a holy war and on these terms a formidable popular army could be raised. (In this way an initially reluctant north of England was repeatedly mobilized down to 1642.) One column of David's army had earlier attacked Clitheroe with a ferocity that dismayed even this violent age: holy places were desecrated. Elsewhere recent monastic foundations were destroyed. It was possible, in these circumstances, for Thurstan to mount a crusade composed of parishioners led by parish priests. The militia of Beverley and Ripon were important military units. This was the popular 'fyrd' in action. Ailred, the abbot of Rievaulx, in his account of the armed opposition to David, emphasized its Norman character; but it was not a feudal host and Norman knights were a minor part of it. In fact David's invading army was much more feudal and much more Norman: the prior of Hexham wrote that the *Normanni* numbered 200 – a large body of knights for any medieval army.

The battle of the Standard was a very Yorkshire affair. The contribution to defence from north of the Tees was minimal. The battle was fought near Northallerton which was a parcel of the liberty of Durham, a 'peculiar' of St Cuthbert land. Both contemporary chroniclers and modern historians have made much of this: the prior of Hexham ascribed the victory over the sacriligious Scots to Cuthbert's divine intervention; one modern historian has claimed (on very indirect evidence) that the army that fought David was recruited in Durham.[39] But Cuthbert's was not even one of the standards planted on the field of battle: two were those of Yorkshire's late seventh-century saints, Wilfrid of Ripon and John of Beverley and the third was of St Peter of York. In fact defenders north of the Tees had failed to defend and had often joined the invaders. The bishop of Durham's fortress at Norham offered no resistance at all; Eustace Fitz John, a prominent Norman in Northumberland, surrendered Bamburgh and offered to surrender Malton, more than a hundred miles to the south, in due course. (Fitz John had indeed recently been relieved of his northern command by King Stephen but this was precisely because his loyalty was suspect.) As David marched south deep into Yorkshire there was no trouble at his rear.[40]

The Normans who opposed King David at the battle of the Standard were Yorkshire landowners; reinforcements came not from further north but a little further south – William Peverel brought a contingent up from Nottinghamshire, and Robert de Ferrers a contingent from Derbyshire. The principal Norman defenders were men from eight Yorkshire landowning families: William de Percy, Richard de Stuteville, William Fossard, Roger de Mowbray, Robert de Brus, Walter de Gant, Ilbert de Lacy, lord of the honour of Pontefract, and William of Aumale, lord of the liberty of Holderness.

Seventy-five years later these eight Yorkshire families would supply the principal opposition to King John of England (four would be included in the twenty-five 'charter barons' appointed to enforce Magna Carta: Lacy, Mowbray, Percy and Aumale). In 1138 they were opposing King David of Scotland. On both occasions they were resisting capable, centralizing administrators who would seriously threaten their local power and independence. David was a ruthless modernizer and highly efficient: his fuedalism was meticulously regulated and his introduction of *Vicecomes* as military, judicial and financial royal officials – sheriffs without shires – was a powerful weapon of central control.[41] When his Norman friends fought against him at Northallerton in 1138 they were not fighting for England or for their king: they were fighting to retain their highly autonomous position in Yorkshire.

England north of the Tees would have accepted and even welcomed reincorporation by David into the ancient kingdom of the North. Indeed, a year after David's defeat, it did so, in effect, in the treaty of Durham. But a difference in posture between Yorkshire and England north of the

Tees and the Tyne – between ancient Diera and Bernicia – was always latent; it had become increasingly manifest after 1065 when Morcar divided his earldom of Northumbria into two earldoms, and especially after 1071 when the earldom of York, which Morcar had retained for himself, was forfeited, fell into the king's hands and was not renewed. North of the Tees the earldom of Northumberland continued, severely truncated, but still conscious of its ancient ties with Lothian; and the bishop of Durham, lord of the liberty of St Cuthbert and also of the liberty of Norham on the border, held, in effect, a second powerful earldom. (At times he was in fact also the earl of Northumberland.) The liberties of Durham and Norham looked with traditional piety to Cuthbert's homeland in Teviotdale beyond the Tweed.

David lost the battle of the Standard against all expectation, but his rewards were appropriate to a great victory. He had strong support from south as well as north of the Tweed and he commanded a large army. The bishop of Orkney (a Norman who had never actually been to the Orkneys) absolved the Yorkshire Normans of their sins before the battle in which they confidently expected to die. But David fought his battle as he organized his feudalism, punctiliously. The Yorkshire Norman knights were prepared to dismount and fight on foot; David's knights were not. They charged, were carried beyond their enemy, and were cut down when they tried to rejoin the main force. But the victorious Yorkshire army made no attempt to pursue David's retreating troops and eject them from English land further north. David was secure in his capital at Carlisle and in his control of Cumbria and Northumberland.

By the treaty of Durham concluded the following year David's son Henry became the earl of Northumberland with jurisdiction over the whole region beyond the Tyne, excluding Newcastle, Bamburgh and the priory lands of Hexham. David himself received part of the honour of Lancaster and was left in possession of Carlisle and Cumbria. The frontier stood at the Derwent and the Tyne.

The restoration of the ancient kingdom of Northumbria was still seen as a possibility. David's European reputation was high and his ambitions still had wide support, even in Yorkshire. When Thurstan died in 1140 William of Aumale proposed David's stepson Waltheof, now prior of Kirkham, as archbishop of York. (Waltheof declined.) In 1149 Henry of Anjou, the future king of England, now sixteen years old, left Normandy to make his way through England to be knighted by David at Carlisle. He swore that if he became king of England he would give Newcastle to David and confirm him and his heirs for ever in possession of the lands between the Tyne and the Tweed. He was prepared to go even beyond that and with David made plans for an attack on York. When Henry became king of England in 1154, however, he made Malcolm, who was now king of Scotland, surrender the northern counties and in 1157 he effectively established, the Anglo-Scottish border where it is today.

But the real reason for the defeat of this twelfth-century attempt to re-establish the eighth-century kingdom of the North as it had existed at the time of Bede was much deeper. Greater northern regionalism had foundered on Yorkshire localism. There was never again any real possibility of a kingdom of the north between the Humber and perhaps the Ribble and the Forth–Clyde isthmus. The tragedy of King David's defeat at Northallerton on 22 August 1138 has bedevilled the North for almost a thousand years.

4

A Frontier Province

The most striking feature of the management of England's northern military frontier in the early Middle Ages was its ineptitude. The attitude of central government was often extraordinarily detached and disengaged. In times of crisis – which were frequent in the twelfth century and often of catastrophic proportions in the early fourteenth – central government usually abandoned the northern frontier province to fend for itself: to buy off the Scots as best it could and make its own local treaties and deals. (It was quick to rebuke collusion and arrangements that looked like treason, however.) It was left to a remarkable collection of somewhat elderly warrior-bishops to stiffen resolve and, more importantly, mobilize troops, at some of the crisis points in these turbulent and often demoralized days.

The history of the northern province throughout the Middle Ages is generally one of military failure. It is strikingly different from the history of English arms in Wales and France. Over almost five centuries of virtually continuous warfare there was never any real prospect of a military solution in the North. There were indeed some notable but isolated victories: the battle of the Standard in 1138, Falkirk in 1298, Halidon Hill in 1333, Neville's Cross in 1346, Homildon Hill in 1402, and Flodden in 1513. Three of these were essentially defensive (the Standard, Neville's Cross and Flodden) and merely held a precarious status quo. And against the more sustained and highly organized and at times successful campaigns of the fourteenth century must be set the monumental disasters of Bannockburn in 1314 and Otterburn in 1388.

Bannockburn was probably the greatest defeat of an English army in the entire history of England; and in the thirteen years between Bannockburn and Edward III's abortive Weardale campaign in 1327 England experienced a protracted period of military helplessness and national humiliation. The northern province was not only humiliated: it was devastated. The southern limit of this devastation affords one of the best definitions that we have of 'the North': it was a crucible of a northern sense of identity and it extended as far south as the Humber and the Aire. The most loyal communities as far south as Beverley were driven to making private treaties with the Scots and, at enormous cost, attempting to buy them off.

The reasons for this dismal record over half a millennium are not simply military inadequacy and inappropriate organization. There was often a lack of political commitment in northern England to war against the Scots, and central government was often, but by no means invariably, preoccupied with wars on other fronts. (Edward I was totally committed and his war effort was sustained and formidable.) The most important reason, however, was probably the wealth and advanced civilization of populous lowland Scotland. England's border counties were poor, sparsely populated and remote from the centre; Scotland's border regions were rich, thickly populated, suburban and cosmopolitan. France as a long-standing ally gave Scotland's struggle not only a European dimension but advanced military technology; border fortresses were a couple of hours on horseback from Edinburgh and less than a day's ride from Perth. This was a region of great landed wealth where younger sons of the Norman aristocracy found a land of promise and, later, powerful lairds developed great estates. For England's border counties it was an unequal struggle from the start. They found a more satisfactory answer to the problem of border defence in the early fourteenth century in the invention of a new institution, the wardenship of the march. This brought greater rationality and co-ordination to border defence. But it was no special advantage to the English: the Scots established wardenships too.

Northern England's natural disadvantages were compounded by military institutions and traditions which were chronically disabling. These were border tenures, privileges and immunities which had an apparently direct relevance to border defence; this no doubt explains their survival from the remote Northumbrian past into the Anglo-Norman state. But their effect was that the forward areas of the northern province were locked in immobility which made them virtually powerless in the face of rapid cross-border strikes and deep-penetration guerrilla raids. The form that the new institution of feudalism took in the border counties did little to help: the obligations of feudal service that were very lightly superimposed on these forward areas was principally in the form of 'castle-guard'. Knights immobilized in border castles were no answer to the frontier problems of the North, however.

There were four quite distinct institutions that furnished soldiers for operations on the northern frontier: 'regalities' (notably Tynedale and Redesdale) which gave sanctuary to felons in return for military service; ancient northern tenures (notably 'cornage') which carried an obligation (non-commutable) for strictly limited military service in border areas;[1] the new and generally very light knight-service obligations of border barons; and the ancient citizen-levies, composed of all men between sixteen and sixty, raised by the sheriff in the shires.[2] Of these four the last was potentially the most important: it was a flexible instrument and very powerful from the mid-thirteenth century onwards when it was stiffened with distrained (non-feudal) knights.

In border counties, however, shire organization was relatively weak: the sheriff had no right of entry into the regalian franchises, where the king's writ did not run, for example, and in Durham the sheriff was not the king's but the bishop's. Private sheriffs and exclusion zones weakened the shire system in the North, and 'shire' as in Hexhamshire and Islandshire connoted a castle-based rather than sheriff-based form of local administration. Shire authority was also overshadowed by powerful northern traditions of geographically delimited military service, so that the shire levies – no less than the cornage tenants – fighting for Bishop Bek in 1299 began to claim that they need not serve beyond the Tyne or the Tees. (This was a wholly different issue from the arguments about who should pay them from which point, which were common enough.) This refusal was more than a political embarrassment to the great warrior-bishop and friend of the king: it was a military catastrophe. Even when Edward I personally intervened in April 1303 they still refused to serve, invoking an ancient tradition of 'haliwerfolk' which restricted local military obligation to guarding St Cuthbert's remains.[3] The border counties were thus entombed in traditions which isolated and immobilized them and were deeply damaging.

For over a century after the Norman Conquest there was an over-reliance on castles in border operations. The king's new castle on the Tyne was begun in 1080 and when an 'aid' (a royal impost on feudal estates, usually when the king's eldest son was knighted and his eldest daughter married) was paid in the year 1212 Hugh Balliol, lord of Bywell in Northumberland, had a barony of five fees but provided thirty knights for castle-guard duty there.[4] Twelfth-century kings of Scotland in pursuit of their claims to Northumbria crossed and re-crossed the border with consummate ease and conducted effective military campaigns deep into Lancashire and Yorkshire, with resounding success at Clitheroe in 1138. In this the peak of military feudalism in England, northern defences were catastrophic. One historian concludes from the dismal record of almost a century that 'No attempt at organized resistance to these repeated invasions had been made.'[5] Feudal castles were singularly ineffective, easily isolated, surrounded and bypassed. The invasions of King David I (1136–39) and William the Lion (1173–4) were ferocious and met with resounding success (short of total conquest). All the border castles except Bamburgh were soon outflanked and quickly surrendered in the first invasion, and many did so in the second. The custodian of Appleby castle was later heavily fined for failing to hold out.

The most instructive event of this period was the battle of the Standard fought in 1138 (see also chapter 3). It was remarkable not because it was a great (and wholly unexpected) English victory, but because it was an action to defend the northern frontier fought a hundred miles to its rear. It was not fought by a defending army that had been pushed back and finally, at Northallerton, been able to stand and fight: a defensive strategy had been planned five months earlier at a council at Northampton and there had never been any intention, because there was no serious possibility, of making a stand further north. Only one feature of this action was more remarkable than its southerly location: the abandonment by the king and central government of any serious involvement, military or otherwise, in this northern defence of the realm. The king had in effect abdicated responsibility to the septuagenarian archbishop of York. The action fought in August had been expected since March. No military forces were involved from further south than the Trent. Only one thing was more strikingly inadequate than the defensive system beyond the Tees, and that was the support of the centre.

It was not until the early fourteenth century that northern defences acquired an appropriate degree of mobility. Two developments were necessary for this, one institutional, the other technical: the answer was the 'hobelar', a lightly armed but mounted infantryman in the service of the shire. The range of operations of shire levies was limited by considerations neither of tenure nor tradition: men served not because they were anybody's tenants and owed service or homage but simply because they were the king's subjects and owed him allegiance.[6] Now, as hobelars, they could be rapidly deployed with devastating effect.

The hobelar was a military innovation of a northern knight and sheriff of Cumberland, Sir Andrew Harclay. The effectiveness of these highly mobile shire forces was dramatically demonstrated in 1322 when the king called on his sheriffs to mobilize against his Lancastrian enemies who were engaged in treasonable dealings with the Scots and moving north from the Midlands towards the border. The king made his appeal on 12 March; by 16 March Harclay had come south with the shire levies of Westmorland and Cumberland to confront the king's enemies at Boroughbridge, twenty miles north-west of York, where his hobelars dismounted, routed the Lancastrians and captured more than a hundred knights.[7]

A second advance was made in the mounting of archers. These now became the mainstay of county forces and accounted for the spectacular victory at Neville's Cross in 1346. In the space of thirteen days shire contingents of Lancashire and Yorkshire had been mobilized to counter a Scottish invasion, moved up to Durham, achieved a great victory, been paid at the king's wages and returned home. There were 900 mounted archers in the Lancashire contingent, and no less than 3,020 in the contingent from Yorkshire. For their rapid and effective deployment the Lancashire troops were awarded an increase in pay.[8] (These innovations pioneered on the northern frontier would later be used with telling effect in France.)

By contrast with the now highly mobile shire levies, effectively led by non-feudal shire knights (four from Lancashire received special rewards after Neville's Cross), the feudal host was as disastrous as the feudal castle. It has often been seen as a peculiarly northern institution, enjoying a particularly long lease of life in northern warfare when it was no longer used in France.[9] Indeed, it has been said that 'The North remained feudal longer than the South. It had to because it was a frontier society.'[10] In fact feudal forces called by the king to meet their obligations of tenure were used very sparingly and highly selectively in the North. Edward I had a feudal element in all the armies he used in Wales and Scotland;[11] but after the early fourteenth century it is doubtful how far formally feudal contingents were really feudal at all. The last technically feudal host was raised for war against Scotland in 1385; there had not been one previously since 1327. When Flodden was fought in 1513 the feudal host had been extinct for 128 years.

The difficulty with feudal hosts in northern campaigns was that they drew key military personnel from the rear and left strong points critically exposed. This was no problem when feudal forces had a large element drawn from ecclesiastical estates, because the military obligation of land held by the church north of the Humber was minuscule. No northern monastery had any obligation at all, but twenty-four houses in the South had *servitia debita* of 293 knights; fourteen southern bishops had an obligation of 440 knights; the archbishop of York and the bishop of Durham had a total obligation of 17.[12] The north of England contributed 2 per cent of the church's feudal service.

William I took the first feudal army to Scotland in 1072 and it was largely composed of knights provided by southern abbots whose service had recently been fixed. It is significant that the last feudal host, which assembled at Newcastle-upon-Tyne in June 1385, was also heavily recruited from ecclesiastical estates. There were nearly 3,000 tenants-in-chief in England; between 100 and 150 might receive a writ to provide service in a host. In 1385 ninety-two received writs; of these 40 per cent (thirty-six) were tenants-in-chief of ecclesiastical estates.[13] Of course the call-up of county levies from Yorkshire and Lancashire also left an exposed rear (which often caused troops to desert); but to strip southern Yorkshire of its greater tenants-in-chief was an invitation to the enemy which they found hard to resist. It was much safer to keep feudalism alive in Dorset and draw service for Scotland from there.

Armies based on feudal service were deployed in the North with apparent reluctance. When Henry II went to Carlisle in 1186 to mount an attack on Roland of Galloway he raised neither the northern shires nor the feudal host. The expedition had been planned well in advance (as part of a marriage agreement with the king of the Scots) and Henry had time to do either or both. But instead of calling a feudal host he took a scutage – 'the great scutage of Galloway'; and instead of raising northern frontier defence forces he took a great force of light cavalry (*servientes*) from Wales.[14] No northern military personnel were pulled away from their local responsibilities for service at Carlisle and beyond.

This happened with disastrous consequences in 1319 and well illustrates the danger of calling feudal service from the North for frontier campaigns. The king had summoned his feudal forces to Newcastle-upon-Tyne in June 1319 in order to attack and recapture Berwick-upon-Tweed. Yorkshire tenants-in-chief who had been summoned to the frontier included the earl of Lancaster, who proceeded north with his followers from his castle at Pontefract. Yorkshire was left fatally exposed and a Scottish contingent moved south to attack Pontefract and York.

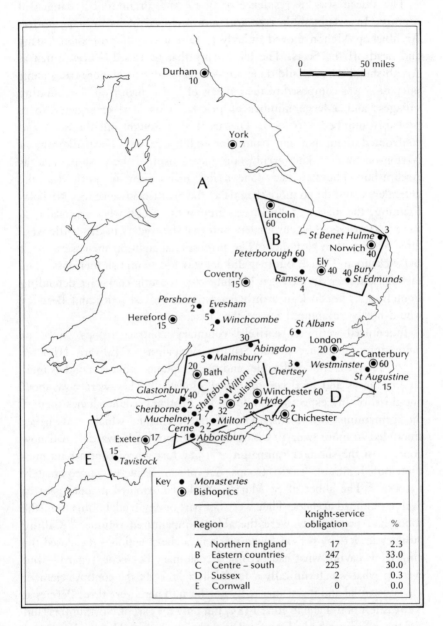

Key
● Monasteries
◉ Bishoprics

Region	Knight-service obligation	%
A Northern England	17	2.3
B Eastern countries	247	33.0
C Centre – south	225	30.0
D Sussex	2	0.3
E Cornwall	0	0.0

MAP 4.1 Feudal (knight-service) obligations of monasteries and bishoprics in 1166 (total knights: 753)

Source: adapted from H. M. Chew, *English Ecclesiastical Tenants-in-Chief and Knight Service* (Oxford University Press, 1932).

The queen was in residence at York and in imminent danger of capture. In a vulnerable rear area now stripped of its military leaders Archbishop Melton moved quickly to raise a very unprofessional army and head off the Scots. The local army that he raised – very much as Archbishop Scrope would do eighty-six years later for a more treasonable purpose – was composed of the citizens of York, men from surrounding villages, and a large number of priests. This local emergency force probably numbered 10,000. The archbishop sought out the Scots and confronted them not far from Boroughbridge and Northallerton, at Myton-on-Swale. The archbishop gave inspired leadership, just as Archbishop Thurstan had done a few miles away in 1138, but the defenders could do no more than delay the Scottish advance. Sir Nicholas Fleming, the mayor of York, was among the 3,000 who were slain; so were 300 priests. The chroniclers said that the leaders in this battle were fitter to pray than to fight.[15] The professional fighting men were up at Berwick-upon-Tweed, but they did not stay to accomplish their task. The earl of Lancaster decided that his duty was in south Yorkshire defending Pontefract. The Yorkshire military captains moved south and Berwick would not be recaptured for another fourteen years.

Indentured retinues, entirely voluntary contract troops, were of increasing importance in the Scottish campaigns of Edward III after 1330. They were more flexible, and their captains could respond as their circumstances and local commitments allowed.[16] They were now about one-third of any expeditionary force for Scotland; county levies formed the remaining two-thirds. The feudal element, which had never amounted to more than 375 knights in the wars of Edward I, had now gone.[17] In the summer campaign of 1335 forty-three contract retinues contributed almost 4,000 troops out of an army of approximately 13,000.[18] The abbot of St Mary's, York, contributed a contingent of twelve mounted archers. They were not part of any feudal obligation (the abbot had none): they were the abbot's indentured retinue.[19] Calling military leaders by personal writ was now a cheap option – it excused the king from paying what had become a customary bonus or 'regard' – but even in what was technically a feudal host in 1385 the contract element was substantial and it was markedly northern. There were three Percies at Newcastle-upon-Tyne in June 1385, but only the earl of Northumberland was there because he had received an individual writ. Thomas Percy and Henry Percy were great landowners, too, but they were there simply as captains of paid, contract troops. More than a hundred other military captains were present in this technically feudal host as leaders of indentured retinues.[20] Feudalism had in fact been long superseded; and it had been superseded in fourteenth-century wars against Scotland precisely because it was so detrimental to the defence of the North.

It could survive much more profitably in the South, which seems to have received a disproportionate call for feudal service for the Scottish campaigns of Edward I. The cavalry forces of Edward I were a mix of mercenary, contractual and feudal elements,[21] but certainly the feudal element for the Dunbar campaign of 1296 came wholly from south of the Trent. Thirty-five barons and two earls received personal writs: they were mostly from Dorset and Somerset, with a few from Berkshire and Buckinghamshire. None was from the North: the most northerly was Ranulph de Rye who held land in Derbyshire and Nottinghamshire. For the Falkirk campaign of 1298, when resources were more fully stretched, thirty-six lesser landowners were summoned in addition to eighty greater tenants-in-chief: their lands were mainly in Suffolk, Sussex and Kent. 'The lessening of the French danger and the resultant relaxing of the coastal defences probably accounted for the Kentish block.'[22] Feudal service in the North was a danger to northern defence. It was not the feudalism of the North that supported the wars against Scotland, but the feudalism of the South.

OUTER PERIMETER AND INNER CORE

The northern frontier province had a basic structure of outer perimeter and inner core. The outer perimeter consisted of the four border counties; the inner core was Yorkshire. Lancashire had some of the characteristics of both: although for the most part geographically in the rear, it was at the low economic level of the outer perimeter, and its lands beyond Clitheroe and the Ribble, and especially in Furness, were an exposed and disputed frontier zone. Clitheroe castle, no less than Appleby, stood as a forward frontier fortress (for a long time in the hands of the powerful Lacy lords of Pontefract) at least until the early thirteenth century.

The outer perimeter was poor and sparsely populated; the core was comparatively rich and eventually became a great reservoir of military manpower and resources (victuals and horses, for instance). The core was located on the direct line between London and the forward zone and its position brought enormous power to the lands flanking the highway that crossed a succession of strategic rivers as it ran north through the vale of York. This power was concentrated primarily in the honours of

Richmond and Pontefract (so named because of their importance). Of
these the southern honour centred on the river Aire had the longer period
of power. Indeed, southern Yorkshire between the Aire and the Don was
the geographical and political pivot of England for eight and a half
centuries, from the battle of Brunanburh in AD 937 to the death of
Charles Watson-Wentworth, marquis of Rockingham, in 1782.

The outer perimeter began where the Domesday survey ended: at the
river Tees. Beyond it were blocks of highly independent power which
were held by their lords *per regalem potestatem*. They were not grants of
William the Conqueror. Their powers and privileges had a more
venerable origin: they were remnants or residues of the ancient kingdom
of Northumbria. England's northern frontier was not an especially thick
and reinforced line of royal power and authority: it was a region of gaps,
discontinuities and lacunae in which the king's writ did not run. The
greatest of these lacunae was the 'liberty' of Durham. The pre-Conquest
church of St Cuthbert had land, men and immunities (from royal
taxation, for instance): 'Thus at the period of the Conquest the bishopric
of Durham was, and had been for some time, a great franchise or
immunity.'[23] William recognized this by not including it in his
Domesday survey: there was no point since it was exempt from his taxes
and would provide no revenue.

Durham and the other regalities – of which the largest and most
important were Tynedale and Redesdale – have a frontier significance
similar to that of the Welsh marcher lordships: they were a highly
decentralized form of border defence and their role in maintaining the
frontier was the basis of their privileges. In the scale of 'liberties', as seen
by medieval lawyers, the Welsh march stood at the apex. Norman barons
had conquered and settled the frontiers of Wales as the king's subjects and
with his general support and approval; but the march remained outside
the institutional and legal structure of England until the mid-sixteenth
century.[24] The Welsh marcher lords claimed that they held their
lordships, which had never been a 'parcel' of England, by right of
conquest and exercised power which was in no way conditional. 'The
Marcher lord was indeed "soveraigne governor" in his lordship; its
inhabitants were not only his tenants; they were also his subjects.'[25]

The northern regalities were a little less powerful, a little less outside
the normal institutional and legal framework of England: thus a subject of
a marcher lord had no right of appeal beyond his lord's court; but a
'subject' of the bishop of Durham had a theoretical right to appeal to the
king's bench. In practice this was very difficult and very rare. In his

northern principality the bishop of Durham 'exercised an authority equal in its scope to that of the king elsewhere in the realm'.[26] The northern regalities were in fact more insulated and isolating than the Welsh marcher lordships for a simple reason: Welsh marcher lords held great estates in 'mainland' England; the lords of the far-northern regalities did not. The Welsh marcher lordships were enormously rich and their (untaxed) wealth underpinned the power of England's top nobility.[27] The Welsh marcher lords can be compared with the Nevilles and Percies in the fourteenth and fifteenth centuries, but that is quite a different matter.

The regalities were the distinctive features of the outer perimeter beyond the Tees, but the honours south of the Tees were also blocks of highly independent power, similarly arising from frontier conditions. The regalities had an exterior and prior origin in the kingdom of Northumbria; the honours were post-Conquest grants of the Anglo-Norman kings. In the last analysis, the regalities north of the Tees, in spite of their impeccable pedigree, continued on royal sufferance (and in the crisis year 1302–3 the Durham estates were taken into the king's hands);[28] but like the Welsh marcher lordships they claimed an 'external' legitimacy. The bishops of Durham never invoked any grant of the Conqueror when their regalian powers were challenged.[29] But the honours were fiefs granted by William I, centred on castles in strategic areas near Pennine passes and at other vulnerable points (for instance the Humber estuary) when the *de facto* border was much further south than the Tweed or even the Tyne.[30] The power and authority of lords of honours were tenurial and feudal; those of lords of regalities were quite different: they were 'franchisal'.[31] The lord of an honour was a tenant of the king, but the lord of a regality was a viceroy.

There were political consequences of these different principles and origins of honours and regalities: the honours were much more involved with the centre. The privileges of the far-northern regalities were independent of feudal relationships and obligations and were more politically isolating. Honours, like the regalian franchises, had private sheriffs, but they were not outside the jurisdiction of royal escheators who dealt with matters of succession and inheritance. Honours, although they retained their integrity, could fall back into the hands of the crown and be re-granted, perhaps within the context of larger, more complex estates. The regalities were isolated by their fiscal, military and judicial immunities. The Umfraville lords of Redesdale, for all their great power and privilege would never be deeply involved in either co-operation or conflict with the centre and would never move politically centre-stage.

The power that the Percies and the Nevilles eventually found on the outer perimeter was not as lords of regalities, or even as great tenants-in-chief of the king (the Nevilles held much of their land as tenants of the bishop of Durham), but as royal, fee-paid officers at the head of very modern, military–bureaucratic superstructures.

The forward area of the northern frontier province had no entirely 'normal' shire wholly under the authority of a royal sheriff. On the other hand, the king had twenty-two tenants-in-chief in these counties: eighteen in Northumberland, four in Cumberland and Westmorland. Against this feudal establishment, however, should be set 296 tenants-in-chief in Yorkshire at the inquest of service in 1166. In three counties which collectively made up 75 per cent of the area of Yorkshire there were only 7 per cent of Yorkshire's number of tenants-in-chief. Cumberland was the border county which was nearest to southern 'normality'; but even there the extensive liberty of Cockermouth was outside the jurisdiction of the royal sheriff. In Westmorland sheriffs were hereditary, members of the Clifford family from the fourteenth century. The effective sheriff was a deputy appointed by the Cliffords and could not be removed by the king. Northumberland had a sheriff appointed by the king, but huge regalian franchises throughout the county were outside his authority.

The distinguishing feature of the perimeter zone was in fact eight islands of regalian power and immunity, the largest being the future palatine county of Durham, the 'lordship of the blessed Cuthbert'. The others were Redesdale and Tynedale; Hexhamshire, which was a 'peculiar' of the archbishop of York; Tynemouth which was held by the prior; and Islandshire, Norhamshire and Bedlington, which were held by the bishop of Durham. (The bishop also had three franchises in Yorkshire: Allertonshire, Howdenshire and the manor of Crayke.)[32] Norham on the Tweed had an important frontier castle and was a centre of international diplomacy.

Whatever their origin and legal status as seen by medieval lawyers, these far-northern regalities continued because they had a contribution to make to northern defence (and might hopefully be left to take care of it by themselves). By the early fourteenth century the theory had taken shape that the bishop of Durham derived his franchise and privileges not from a remote regal past but in return for currently defending the borders. It was then, too, that the term 'palatinate' was first used and the bishop began to claim his privileges as *comes palatinus*. The bishop was sole landlord in his palatinate just as the king was sole landlord in his kingdom; in Durham it was not 'the king's peace' but the bishop's peace. As the gentry of Durham rose in wealth, power and importance they deeply resented these isolating and insulating regal powers. The bishops were in touch with the centre as military leaders; the gentry were increasingly in touch with royal commissions and with Parliament (in which Durham was not represented) in order to challenge the bishop's regal authority. Regalian power on the far-northern perimeter increasingly isolated and eroded the power of the North.

By contrast the great honours in the northern province south of the Tees were embedded in all the crucial political issues and power struggles of the Middle Ages. To quite a remarkable extent they created them. But they were not monoliths and they were involved in national power structures at different levels. Although their tenants did not hold land 'in-chief' of the king – they were honourial barons – this did not isolate them or diminish them in national affairs; and many received personal writs to attend the embryonic House of Lords. The inner core of the northern frontier province was not a single political and military society: it was a constellation of competing, sometimes co-operating, but invariably centripetal powers.

There were seven principal honours: Richmond, Pontefract, Tickhill and Holderness in Yorkshire; Tutbury in Derbyshire; Lancaster and Chester. (The last two would acquire palatinate status at a later date and would be considerably isolated by doing so, but they were a parcel of England when William the Conqueror came, and Cheshire and Lancashire as far north as the Ribble were included in the Domesday survey.) Politics, inheritance and diplomacy would lead to regrouping and Pontefract (in 1311) along with its south Yorkshire neighbour Tickhill (in 1372) would become the heart of the Lancastrian estates. Rich Tutbury in Derbyshire likewise became part of the Lancastrian inheritance and helped to deflect its orientation away from the 'true North'.

Holderness was a relatively minor honour: the Humber lost its historic military significance. Chester fell back to the crown in 1237. But Pontefract (within the earldom and later the duchy of Lancaster) and Richmond would dominate the history of the later Middle Ages: they would be of major significance in the 'Wars of the Roses' in the fifteenth century when the principal Lancastrian power base was in south Yorkshire between Doncaster and Pontefract and the main basis of Yorkist power was between Middleham and Sheriff Hutton in Richmondshire. When Richard of Gloucester had both Pontefract and Richmond in his hands after 1471 he was virtually omnipotent on the

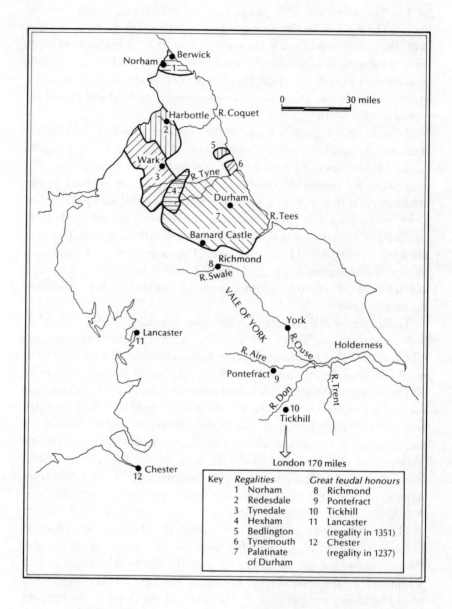

MAP 4.2 Medieval regalities beyond the Tees in which the king's writ did not run

Source: adapted from R. R. Reid, *The King's Council in the North* (Longmans, Green & Co., 1921).

national political stage. Richmond and Pontefract were the twin poles of northern England, always the foci of great power, partly because they had the resources for great independence, but also because they had close relationships, feudal and otherwise, with the centre.

The greatest of these northern honours in the early Middle Ages was Richmond. It consisted of about 160 fees, some sixty in Yorkshire, mostly in lower Swaledale and Wensleydale. At the time of the Domesday survey it was the third richest of all the estates held by over a thousand tenants-in-chief. Forty-five lay and ecclesiastical tenants-in-chief had estates worth between £200 and £1,750 a year; Richmond was worth £1,200.[33] The honour of Lancaster would eventually overtake it in the extent and wealth of its lands, but it would take two and a half centuries to do so. It had not done so when Edmund, the first earl of Lancaster, died in 1296 when its total revenues were only £1,193.[34] Through additional grants by the king, strategic marriages and inheritance, however, the Lancaster estates enjoyed a phenomenal increase in wealth in the fourteenth century. The first duke of Lancaster's gross revenues amounted to over £8,000 in 1361;[35] John of Gaunt's to around £12,000.[36] In the early fifteenth century the Lancastrian revenues were around £15,000.[37] Lancashire itself never contributed more than around 10 per cent of the total gross income.

Unlike the far-northern regalities, the honours were not geographically compact: thus the honours of Chester, Lancaster and Richmond derived only a minority of their total income from land in Cheshire, Lancashire and Yorkshire respectively. Their geographical extent also promoted their wider political involvement. More than half of the land of the honour of Richmond was in Nottinghamshire, Lincolnshire, Cambridge-shire, Norfolk and Hertfordshire: the honour extended in a south-easterly direction from the borders of Durham to the vicinity of London and so was of strategic military and political significance.[38] The honour of Lancaster was always a predominantly Midlands estate and its lords (and later earls) had strong Midlands rather than northern interests. (Its very detached Dunstanburgh estate on the Northumberland coast gave it a somewhat illusory significance in relation to Scottish affairs.) In terms of fees, when the honour was held by Edmund, the first earl of Lancaster in the later thirteenth century, more than 50 per cent were in Derbyshire, Lincolnshire, Leicestershire and Northamptonshire, with only 7 per cent in Lancashire.[39] This was before Pontefract became part of the Lancastrian estates in 1311. In the middle of the fourteenth century Yorkshire contributed around 15 per cent of the Lancastrian revenues,

Lancashire around 10 per cent.[40] It was not only sentiment, therefore, that made John of Gaunt regard Pontefract as the heart of his Lancastrian domain in the later fourteenth century.

The northern honours were not monoliths with all-powerful lords and insulated, powerless tenants. Many honourial barons were men of consequence not only locally but on a wider political stage. Thus the Grelleys of Lancashire were active in the military and administrative service of the crown: one served in the mid-thirteenth century as warden of the king's forests south of the Trent. The Grelleys had nine military tenants. The barony of Montbegon was of similar size, with eight military tenants holding fractional fees. The Montbegon barony would provide one of the twenty-five 'charter barons' in 1215. The greatest tenant of the Lancaster honour was in fact Lacy, lord of Pontefract, whose estates in Lancashire included Clitheroe which had sixteen military tenants.[41] Honourial barons in Richmond were likewise often men of substance and standing. The Middleham estate was particularly valuable, consisting of a total of fifteen fees, six in Yorkshire, six in Norfolk and three elsewhere.

The honours were centripetal, turning towards the centre in both co-operation and conflict. This was only partly because they were of sufficient importance to provide lordships for kings' sons. John, the future king, was lord of the honour of Lancaster and used it as a base for rebellion against his brother, Richard I; Edmund, son of Henry III, used the honour to support his brother Edward I in wars against Wales and Scotland; Thomas, second earl of Lancaster, used it along with the honour of Pontefract to rebel against his cousin Edward II. The Richmond honour was held by Edward III's son, John of Gaunt, for thirty years, and for the last ten he also held (through his wife) the honour of Lancaster. When he relinquished Richmond for political and diplomatic reasons in 1372, various Yorkshire estates including the honour of Tickhill were granted to him in compensation. John of Gaunt used his northern lordship to support his father Edward III and his nephew Richard II in their wars against Scotland and France. (He also used his northern estates, especially Pontefract, as a refuge from his immense unpopularity in London.) It was from this northern honourial base, and in particular from its Yorkshire estates, that John of Gaunt's son was able to seize the crown from Richard II. It was at Pontefract and Doncaster that the notables of northern England confirmed him in his bid for the throne.

Pontefract in the hands of the Lacy family was for long an important honour before it was added to the Lancastrian estates. It did not lose its identity and increased in importance as a centre of Lancastrian power. The castle at Pontefract was expensively extended by John of Gaunt; Earl Thomas had been executed there for treason, in the courtyard of his own castle, in 1322; Richard II would be murdered there in 1400. The castle at Pontefract was the symbol of supreme power in the North. It was a suitable place to house the most distinguished prisoners of war. Dunstanburgh castle could suffice for Scottish notables after Homildon Hill, but the duke of Orleans was imprisoned at Pontefract after Agincourt at a cost to the estate of twenty shillings a day.

The isolation of the perimeter was reinforced by both its privilege and its poverty. The border counties were often granted exemption from taxes and from sending members to Parliament because they were so poor. Their poverty was the main reason for their very low levels of feudal knight-service obligation, which had fiscal as much as military significance. Though linked with real or notional military quotas, knight service obligations were probably even in origin a form of tax assessment on which land taxes in the form of scutages and aids could be based. (The exclusion of northern monasteries from providing quotas of knights was essentially a tax privilege.) Knight-service obligations were not quite as arbitrarily imposed as is sometimes claimed. Thus Norfolk, Suffolk, Essex and Hertfordshire, 10 per cent of England's area, had 20 per cent of England's personal wealth in the early fourteenth century, and 20 per cent if its knight-service obligation. (These four counties owed the service of some 1,400 knights out of some 7,000 for the whole of England and their wealth was assessed at around £7,000 out of some £34,000 in 1307 for the entire country.) Lincolnshire and Kent had light obligations in relation to their rising wealth in the early fourteenth century, but in Hampshire and in Worcestershire, as in East Anglia, the correspondence was exact. 'Personal wealth' is not, at least directly, landed wealth, but it is a general index of affluence and the ability to pay.

In northern England the level of knight-service obligation was below even the low level of wealth, and markedly so in the border counties. Northumberland, 4 per cent of England's area, had 2 per cent of England's wealth but only 1.3 per cent of its military obligation. (Its wealth was assessed at £685 in 1307 and its knight-service obligation in 1298 was ninety-three.) The discrepancy between wealth and obligation in Cumberland and Westmorland was even greater: nearly 5 per cent of England's area, they had a little over 2 per cent of England's wealth (£722) but a total obligation of only ten knights (0.14 per cent of the total). Yorkshire's obligation was more closely in line with its wealth. It had 7 per cent of the total knight-service obligation, but made up 10 per cent of England's area and had nearly 10 per cent of the country's assessed wealth. (Including Richmond, it owed the service of 486 knights and its assessed wealth in 1307 was £3,429.) These shortfalls in knight-service obligation were in effect tax concessions for the North. A similar pattern of privilege with regard to taxes on land would prevail in northern England until the late eighteenth century (see chapter 10): moderate privilege in Yorkshire, high privilege in the border counties. Yorkshire, like the rest of northern England, had relatively light taxes on its landed estates, but was more nearly in line in both obligations and wealth with East Anglia and the more prosperous Midlands and South.

Yorkshire had made good progress from the low ebb of its fortunes at the time of the Domesday survey. It had pulled significantly ahead of the border counties. In 1086 Yorkshire was 17 per cent of the area of England surveyed but had only approximately 2 per cent of the population, 2 per cent of the landed wealth and 2 per cent of the tenants-in-chief. By the end of the thirteenth century – and probably long before – Yorkshire had population, personal wealth and tenants-in-chief in accordance with its size (it had the 'appropriate' number of tenants-in-chief at the inquest of 1166).

The first satisfactory comparative information on the state of all the northern counties comes only with the tax assessments of the early

TABLE 4.1   Resources: England and Yorkshire 1066–1307

	Area (m²)	Tenants-in-chief (1166)	Value of personal property (1307)	Population (1377)
England	50,330	2,864	£33,910	2,232,370
Yorkshire	6,120	296	£3,429	196,560
Yorkshire %	10	10	10	9

Sources: J. Schlight, Monarchy and Mercenaries (New York University Press, 1968).
    J. C. Russell, British Medieval Population (University of New Mexico Press, 1948).
    J. H. Ramsay, 'Statistics from subsidy rolls of Edward II', English Historical Review, 24 (1909), pp. 317–19.

fourteenth century; even then the picture is distorted by the effects of intensive and protracted Scottish raids. Northern counties had generally stabilized by 1352 and the relative positions of core and perimeter show Yorkshire's wholly disproportionate share of resources. Occupying 46 per cent of the area of northern England, Yorkshire had 64 per cent of all the personal wealth.

TABLE 4.2   Resources: core and perimeter 1352

	Area (m^2)	Value of personal property (1352)	Population (1377)
Six northern counties	13,320	£3,637	310,000
Yorkshire	6,120	£2,408	196,560
Yorkshire %	46	65	64

Sources: J. C. Russell, British Medieval Population (University of New Mexico Press, 1948).
    J. F. Willard, 'Taxes upon movables in the reign of Edward III', English Historical Review, 30 (1915), pp. 69–74.

From the later fourteenth century the differentiation was accentuated in purely military terms. Defensive battles were no longer fought as far south as the Ribble, the lower Ure, the lower Swale, or even the Wear. Otterburn (1388) is nearly fifty miles north of Neville's Cross; Flodden (1513) is thirty miles north of Otterburn, virtually on the Tweed. Yorkshire and even Durham south of the Wear, by the end of the fourteenth century, were not even intermittently in the front line; the inner core now extended as far north as Chester-le-Street. The inner core and the now heavily militarized outer perimeter were closely related at a more personal level, however. The new leaders in the war against Scotland were not border barons but the Nevilles from south Durham and the Percies from east Yorkshire. The far North was now commanded and led by men who moved up from the rear.

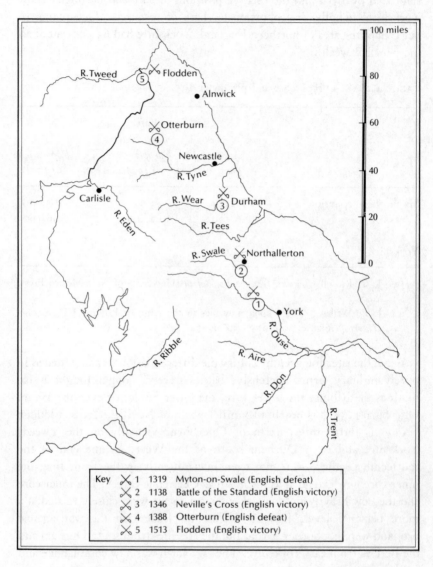

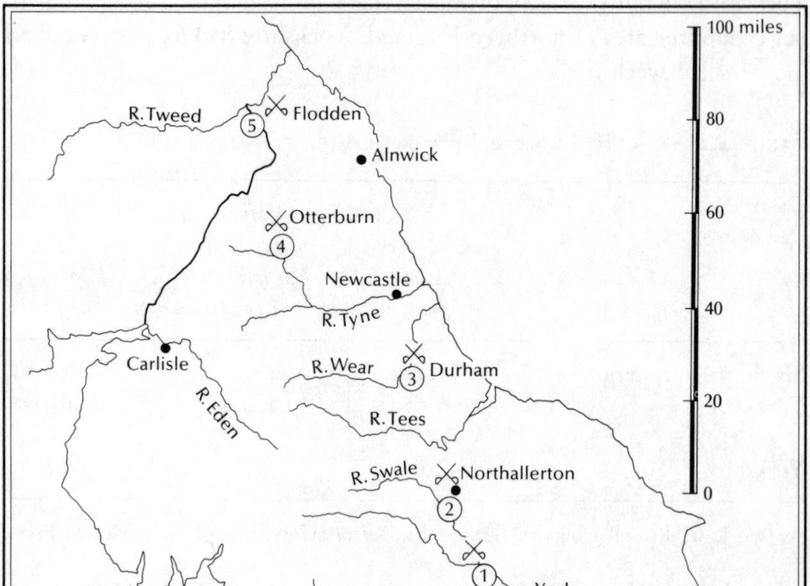
100 miles
80
60
40
20
0
R. Tweed
Flodden
5
Alnwick
Otterburn
4
Newcastle
R. Tyne
Carlisle
R. Wear
3
Durham
R. Eden
R. Tees
R. Swale
Northallerton
2
1
York
R. Ouse
R. Ribble
R. Aire
R. Don
R. Trent
Key
1 1319 Myton-on-Swale (English defeat)
2 1138 Battle of the Standard (English victory)
3 1346 Neville's Cross (English victory)
4 1388 Otterburn (English defeat)
5 1513 Flodden (English victory)

MAP 4.3 Major defensive battles with Scottish invaders, 1138–1513
Source: author

LORDS AND TENANTS

The northern province in the early Middle Ages was not top-heavy with a great landowning aristocracy (that did not happen till the nineteenth century). There were some 190 barons throughout England; forty might be described as men of real substance; no more than five or six of these were northerners. The North had a sufficiency of knights for administrative purposes, but northern barons who had great estates and wealth by southern standards were very few.[42] Barons were still not formally distinguished from knights: it was the rise of parliament later on, and not feudal tenures, that defined them and set them apart; but in the years of crisis between 1204 and 1215 they came to the fore in the North as leaders in opposing, or in a few cases supporting, King John. Eleven or twelve came out against him, three or four in his support. Of this total only four (Lacy, Mowbray, Vesci and Aumale) – apart from the very rich loyalist Earl Ranulf of Chester – would be ranked (towards the bottom) among England's forty or so top landowners.

Northern England did not have a large and elaborate aristocratic superstructure in the early Middle Ages partly because it could not afford one. But there were other important reasons for a wider distribution of power in the North. There had been a famine of tenants in post-Conquest northern England. This was true of both under-tenants and tenants-in-chief (whose wealth and status should not be overstated: only a small proportion would rank as barons; over 90 per cent of the 1,400 tenants-in-chief in 1086 had land worth less than £10 a year while only 40 had land worth over £200).[43] The crisis of estate management and development, no less than military emergencies, called for the urgent colonization of these exposed and often devastated northern lands. It was not great barons who were in short supply, but under-tenants and tenants-in-chief who would develop and manage land worth between £2 and £10 a year. There were 251 tenants (29 holding land in-chief and 222 under-tenants) in Yorkshire in 1086; in Essex, Norfolk and Lincolnshire, which together are almost as big as Yorkshire, there were 1,620. It was the famine of lower and middling tenants in northern England that ensured them secure tenancies and positions of some independence and power. Security, independence and power were more difficult to come by among the superabundant lesser tenantry of eastern England.

It has been said that the social landscape of thirteenth-century England was dominated by 'skyscrapers': men of enormous and wholly dispro-

TABLE 4.3 Tenants and land values in 1086 (Yorkshire and eastern counties)

	Area (m²)	Tenants-in-chief and undertenants	Land values (£/p.a.)
Yorkshire	7,024	251	1,084
Lincolnshire	2,646	506	3,253
Norfolk	2,037	498	4,094
Essex	1,515	615	5,047
England	44,118	9,270	71,573
Yorkshire %	17	2.7	1.5
Eastern counties %	14	17.4	17.3

Sources: H. C. Darby, Domesday England (Cambridge University Press, 1977), Appendix 12, p. 359.
H. Ellis, A General Introduction to Domesday Book (Commissioners on Public Records, 1833), vol. 2.

portionate wealth. 'The aristocratic hierarchy was no pyramid. It would be better likened to a collection of skyscrapers towering above the plain where dwelt the great mass of petty lords of hamlet and village.'[44] There was only one such 'skyscraper' in the North: the bishop of Durham.

The bishop had an income from land of £809 in 1130, £2,650 in 1212, and £2,666 in 1312.[45] (The archbishop of York had only about half this income.) Ranulf of Chester in the early thirteenth century, the lord of the Lancaster honour at the end, and the lord of the honour of Richmond throughout the thirteenth century all had incomes below this level but were nevertheless in this league. In all three cases, however, by far the greater part of the income came from lands outside the North. The lord of the honour of Pontefract was more truly and exclusively northern, but his income was not at their level (he has been described as a 'class-C baron').[46] The bishop of Durham derived some of his income from land in Lincolnshire, but the greater part of it came from the North. His principal estates extended from the Humber to the Tweed. In both the source of his wealth and the region in which he exercised his power he was unequivocally of the North.

Northern England in the early Middle Ages was not a land of great barons; it was pre-eminently a land of knights. They dominated the social, administrative and military landscape of the North, holding a variety of royal appointments (such as tax assessors and collectors, for example) and management posts in the great honourial estates. They were men of consequence, but they were typically men with £20 to £40 a year – they were not barons with £200 to £2,000.[47]

The status of knights throughout England had undergone a revolution since the twelfth century. Then they had often been little more than somewhat superior peasant farmers;[48] they were now a new class in terms of their wealth, public service duties and powers.[49] It has been suggested that barons increased their estates at the expense of knights in the course of the thirteenth century,[50] but this as a general trend is very doubtful. What especially increased the power of knights *vis-à-vis* the greater baronage was their direct connection with the centre which was established by the king's distrainment of local gentry to become knights and by the positions they increasingly held in their localities as paid officials of central government.[51] They also had highly independent power as administrators of great honourial estates. When Sir Adam Banaster and Sir William Bradshaw were aggrieved by the running of the Lancastrian estates and took up arms in 1315 to secure a remedy, their adversary was another knight of enormous power, Sir Robert Holland, the estates' chief officer. What was remarkable about these events – which effectively amounted to civil war in Lancashire – was the extent to which the earl was outside them and had no control over them.[52]

While the status of knights improved in the thirteenth century their numbers almost certainly declined, principally through extensive sub-infeudation: the fragmentation of estates. This decline was reflected in a realistic and drastic (but informal) reduction of the knight-service obligation of feudal estates to around one-sixth of the 6,500 or so knights fees.[53] The reduction was very uneven, with large estates undergoing disproportionately large reductions. The obligation of the large, scattered honour of Richmond, which contained about 160 fees, was reduced in 1241 to the service of five knights.[54] While the obligation was reduced to 15 per cent, the actual call-up for any particular campaign was no more than 5 per cent: 300 to 400 knights.[55]

It has been said that there was an acute shortage of knights in the thirteenth century.[56] This is largely mythical. There was certainly no shortage in northern England in relation to the administrative and military jobs that had to be done. It has also been claimed that in at least fourteen counties, around the year 1312, it would have been impossible to get a jury of twelve knights.[57] This would be true of Cumberland and

Westmorland. It was certainly not true of Yorkshire. The total number of knights fees in Yorkshire at the scutage of 1279 was 486:[58] a reduction to one-sixth suggests that Yorkshire might have 80 knights. In fact at an enrolment of knights in the county court on 9 May 1324 there were 127.[59] This was 10 per cent of the probable 1,250 knights in England at this time,[60] a figure fully in line with Yorkshire's size, population and wealth.

There was no shortage of knights in Northumberland. The knights fees at the scutage of 1279 numbered ninety-three; one-sixth indicates fifteen knights. In fact there were twenty-one in 1324. At no time throughout the thirteenth century would it have been impossible to get a jury of twelve knights. There was no difficulty in 1245 in obtaining twenty-four for the physically exacting and dangerous task of surveying the borders. There were eighteen knights in Northumberland at the inquest of 1166, twenty-seven at the aid of 1212, twenty-seven also at the inquest of 1242, and forty when gentlemen with an income from land of £20 a year were distrained into knighthood in 1278.[61] This was the peak in Northumberland and it occurred eighteen years before Edward I mounted his great offensive against the Scots. The varying number of knights in Northumberland between 1166 and 1324 mirrored (in a remarkably exact fashion) both the rising economic fortunes of the county and the subsequent catastrophic devastation in the years after Bannockburn. In 1324 the number of knights was exactly half of what it had been in 1278. Over a period of almost fifty years, which broadly corresponds with this period before and after Bannockburn, personal wealth in Northumberland was also halved: at the assessment for tax in 1307 personal wealth in Northumberland amounted to £685; at the assessment of 1352 it was £333.[62]

Northern England was not remarkable for 'skyscrapers': it was at much lower levels of society that power and authority lodged. The need to attract and retain an adequate population on the land in a frontier province ensured liberal terms for middling and lesser tenants. Ancient border tenures with a high degree of security and military service as 'rent' were retained and reinforced. Cornage tenants were secure in the thirteenth century from being distrained as knights: that would have meant their availability for service elsewhere. In 1224 the sheriff of Cumberland was unable to distrain Richard of Levinton for military service which would have taken him to the seige of Bedford:[63] he held his land by cornage and was protected from any such general availability.

The security and liberality of northern tenures were well established by the thirteenth century. This was evident at the level of peasant farmers (villeins). In Suffolk, 42 per cent of the rent of peasant farmers was in the relatively servile form of labour rent (as distinct from rent paid in money or kind); in Yorkshire the figure was 8 per cent; throughout the eastern counties (East Anglia and Lincolnshire) it was 40 per cent; but in Northumberland, Westmorland and Cumberland it was only 10 per cent.[64]

This strikingly lower level of servility and higher level of modernity in the northern counties was certainly not because they were more economically developed than East Anglia: on the contrary, they were a good deal less. They were also much less populous. At the time of the Domesday survey the discrepancy was huge; even at the end of the fourteenth century, in the tax year 1377 (when some reasonable population estimates can be made), the six northern counties, which occupy 26 per cent of England's area, had only about 14 per cent of the total population. Essex, Norfolk and Lincolnshire, by contrast, which together occupy 12 per cent of England's area, had 16 per cent of the population.[65]

It is the conjunction of population shortage and continuing military need in the northern frontier province that accounts for favourable tenurial conditions and more generally for a wider diffusion of power and privilege. It helps to explain the paradox of 'modernization' that was earlier and more extensive in the remote northern province than in advanced areas like East Anglia. This modernization process would be enormously speeded up in the fourteenth century under the impetus of the huge war effort that began in 1296.

THE WEALTH OF SCOTLAND'S FRONTIER ZONE

The English border area was poor; the Scottish border zone beyond the Tweed and the Esk was rich – it was also breathlessly up to date in its religious institutions, feudal organization and military architecture. There was a certain symmetry between the two border areas in some respects: administrative and judicial institutions developed in parallel; there were even joint arrangements for dealing with border disputes and infringements of border custom and law. In economic terms, however, the Scottish and English frontier areas were markedly asymmetrical. High quality wool was produced in the hill country of southern Scotland and exported through Berwick and Leith, especially to Flanders, and the

Cistercian monasteries, established in Scotland's border region in the early twelfth century, were both a symptom of great landed wealth and a means of increasing it. This was also a region of considerable urban wealth, as the mendicant orders were fully aware when they established their friaries in the thirteenth century.

In the absence of tax assessments and accounts books of monasteries and other landed estates, there are three principal indicators of wealth: the number and distribution of monasteries in the twelfth century; of friaries in the thirteenth century; and of pele towers and pele houses in the fourteenth and fifteenth centuries. Another indicator is the extent and character of the feudal obligations that southern Scotland was able to meet at the behest of King David I and his immediate successors. Feudalism and the new monasticism were simultaneous developments in twelfth-century Scotland and both show a remarkable awareness of a sophisticated, wider world. Both were somewhat mannered, posturing, with a slight air of artifice;[66] neither was possible without a firm basis of wealth.

The feudal superstructure imposed on southern Scotland in the course of the twelfth century would not have produced a body of knights capable of withstanding a major cavalry force from England (although this body of knights was too important to border defence to be deployed in campaigns in the turbulent highlands and William the Lion recruited mercenaries in England instead) but it was at least comparable to the feudal establishment of England's border counties. The Brus overlordship of Annandale was held for the service of ten knights.[67] This was exactly the same as the total obligation to the king of England of all the landed estates in Cumberland and Westmorland. After the rapid development of a feudal system by David I, further obligations of more than forty knights service were imposed in the border region in the reigns of Malcolm IV and William I.[68] Feudal obligations meant taxes (aids and reliefs) charged by the fee and, in Scotland, military service without the option of paying scutages in lieu. This was the expensive form of feudalism: by the early thirteenth century it was four times as expensive as the commutation now widespread in England. Scutage was a convenience for kings and a saving for landowners: a scutage (in England) was £1; the cost of a knight (quite apart from equipment) was two shillings a day for forty days – £4. It was this particularly expensive variant of feudalism, on a significant scale, that Scotland's border regions were able to bear.

Monastic endowments and foundations are more straightforward indicators of wealth than feudal obligations. Twenty-four monasteries were established south of the Forth–Clyde isthmus mainly in the early twelfth century. They represented all the great European orders although the only Benedictine house was at Coldingham; the Cistercians had five, so had the Premonstratensians, and the Augustinian canons had four. (The total of twenty-four was just one short of the twenty-five in England's four border counties). There was a cluster in Galloway: Whithorn was a Premonstratensian house and a monastic cathedral, Glenluce and Sweetheart abbeys were Cistercian. But the most important cluster was in the valley of the Teviot and the middle Tweed: Jedburgh, Melrose, Kelso and Dryburgh. The counts of Flanders gave protection to the Cistercian abbey at Melrose to safeguard their wool supplies. The wealth of these great abbeys nurtured a vigorous intellectual life and Dryburgh was the house of the late fourteenth century philosopher Ralph Strode who was sent to Merton College, Oxford, by King David II and is referred to by Chaucer as his friend in his inscription to the conclusion of *Troilus and Cressida*.

What is more remarkable than the twelfth-century foundation of these monasteries is their subsequent re-foundation, on an ever more opulent scale, after being repeatedly destroyed by English armies. Dryburgh was destroyed and rebuilt eight times. The most extensive damage was done by Edward II's armies in 1322, by Richard II's in 1385, and by Henry VIII's astonishing 'rough wooing' of the infant princess Mary in 1544–5. Dryburgh was never rebuilt after that.

The wealth of Scotland's monasteries was assessed in 1561 and some of the border houses were among the richest. (One English pound at this time was worth ten Scottish pounds and the estimated annual incomes of Scottish houses have been divided by ten in the details given below.) Out of twenty-four monasteries in southern Scotland seven had incomes over £200 a year;[69] out of the twenty-five in England's four border counties only four had incomes over £200 a year at the dissolution in 1536.[70] None of the monasteries in southern Scotland could match Durham priory (£1,366), but no other monastery in the English border counties could match Melrose (£518), Kelso (£483) or Holyrood (£560). The income of Tynemouth priory was £397, Holmcultram in Cumberland (which had been founded as a colony of Melrose) was £477 and Carlisle was £418. No other English house had an income over £200 (St Bees and Hexham were roughly the English average with £143 and £122 respectively). In southern Scotland Coldingham had £260, Whithorn £254, Jedburgh £248 and Dryburgh £221.

The friaries established north of the border in the thirteenth century

identify centres of significant and worthwhile urban wealth. There were
ten towns south of the Forth–Clyde line which had either a Dominican or
Franciscan friary: Ayr, Berwick-upon-Tweed, Dumfries, Edinburgh,
Glasgow, Haddington, Kirkcudbright, Lanark, Roxburgh and Wigtown.[71]
In England's four border counties there were five towns with either
a Dominican or Franciscan friary: Bamburgh, Carlisle, Durham,
Hartlepool and Newcastle-upon-Tyne.

The evidence of the pele towers is more qualitative than quantitative.
Fortified dwellings were built on both sides of the border in the
fourteenth and fifteenth centuries to a depth of about forty miles. There
were eventually about 180 on the Scottish side of the border and also 180
on the English side. They have been variously classified according to their
style and elaboration: from simple bastles, to more elaborate peles and
tower-houses. Tall tower-houses with battlements were typical on the
Scottish side and account for as many as 170 out of the 180 fortified
dwellings; on the English side crude, very simple bastles were the rule
except on the richer coastal plain. Only about half of the fortified houses
on the English side could compare in splendour and sophistication with
the tower-houses that had proliferated in Scotland. This reflects the
different levels of wealth: by the fifteenth century this was evident in a
social structure that included great lairds like the Pringles of Galashiels
on the Scottish side and very poor squires, like the Halls of Otterburn, in
the North Tyne, Redesdale and upper Coquetdale: 'Their social standing
was high, their resources greater than their neighbours, but even though
they formed the top stratum of society in much of the English uplands
they stand no comparison with the Scottish lairds.'[72]

The outer perimeter of England's frontier province was never any
match for the rich and powerful neighbouring society across the Tweed.
This was the stark and simple lesson of the twelfth century. A more
integrated province of outer perimeter and more richly endowed inner
core was a necessary subsequent development. By the sixteenth century the
mobilization of the six northern counties under the lieutenant of the
North was militarily insuperable: as evident at Flodden in 1513 and in
the heavy-handed 'diplomacy' conducted by Edward Seymour, earl of
Hertford, between 1544 and 1547. This attempt to put pressure on
Scotland to agree to the betrothal of Mary to the prince of Wales was
militarily successful (in spite of French help and a set-back at Ancrum
near Jedburgh in February 1545) although politically disastrous. The
lieutenant of the North (who had been given Wolsey's Yorkshire estates)
waged merciless war not only on Edinburgh and Leith (in May 1544) but

on the border abbeys which were systematically destroyed in September 1545.

Sir George Bowes and Sir Brian Layton had led their raiding parties into the borders in the previous November, however, and reiving parties from Tynedale and Redesdale had entered Pringle lands at the same time. These subsidiary actions occurred within the general context of a national offensive against Scotland and illustrate the different levels at which the military frontier operated. Sir George and Sir Brian with 700 men rode on to the lands of Dryburgh abbey on 4 November 1544 and carried off 100 head of cattle, 60 horses and 100 sheep; the reiving party from Tynedale and Redesdale carried off 600 head of cattle, 100 horses and household furniture from the Pringle estates.[73] Whatever the wider objectives of English national policy, Scotland's rich border abbeys and lay estates were an integral part of perimeter England's bandit economy.

5

From Power to Rebellion

For four hundred years, from the tenth to the thirteenth centuries, the North grew markedly in wealth and power, especially on the east of the Pennines. The most favoured region was eastern Yorkshire, between the Humber and the Tees or, in monastic terms, between Meaux abbey in the south and Guisborough priory in the north, Bridlington priory in the east and Fountains abbey in the west. The new wealth underpinned the power of the northern barons who led the revolt against King John culminating in the Magna Carta of 1215.

Thereafter, from the fourteenth to the sixteenth centuries, the North experienced relative decline in wealth. This helps to explain why the North proved in the end an inadequate power base for Richard of Gloucester of Middleham castle: why he had such difficulties as king after 1483, why his plantation of northerners in the South proved to be so ineffective, and why his brief reign culminated in 1485 in failure at Bosworth Field.[1]

The economic upsurge from the tenth to the thirteenth centuries was part of a wider European movement which arose out of more efficient cultivation of marginal land and steady population growth.[2] But there were also strong local factors: the Danish settlers' stimulus to trade and urban growth; wool production (and high-quality cloth manufacture for a time); and an energetic exploitation of the North Sea trading community. This upsurge in the North was marked by urban expansion which was only exceeded elsewhere in England in Devon and Southampton's hinterland. It was fuelled by migration to new northern towns and development areas (ecclesiastical and lay) and a generally disproportionate population growth: while England's population probably doubled between 1086 (Domesday survey) and 1377 (the poll tax year), the population of the seven northern counties probably increased by a factor of five.[3]

The changing value of the lands held in-chief in Yorkshire by the archbishop of York illustrates the steep economic growth curve in the twelfth century. In 1065 these lands were worth £320; in 1086 in the wake of William's harrying of the North their value had been depressed to £166; but by 1180 they had risen to £1,100.[4] Thus their value had almost quadrupled in a little more than a hundred years.

After, the later fourteenth century the North experienced relative economic decline. Cloth displaced wool as England's principal export and its manufacture flourished in East Anglia (especially around Lavenham) and in the South-west (especially around Totnes), far from the restrictions of the North's over-regulated corporate towns. The wealth of Lavenham, Tiverton and Totnes, as assessed for tax, increased no less than twenty fold between 1334 and 1524, Bury St Edmund's, Norwich and Exeter eight fold, but York and Lincoln remained static and the wealth of Boston declined.[5]

Lancashire actually experienced an absolute decline in wealth, the only county in England to do so. While Middlesex, for example, increased eight fold in wealth and Surrey by a factor of five, Lancashire's wealth diminished by roughly one-sixth. Northern wealth was also increasingly in ecclesiastical hands: while the proportion of clerical wealth declined from 40 to 30 per cent in England as a whole between 1334 and 1515, in the West Riding of Yorkshire it increased significantly, from around 40 to over 60 per cent. In Lancashire it rose from 72 to 76 per cent.[6] This shift had implications for lay power, tending to depress gentry wealth and importance, especially in south and west Yorkshire until after the dissolution.

In 1086 England was worth £71,000 a year; Lincolnshire was worth around £3,500, roughly 5 per cent.[7] But Lincolnshire was 5 per cent of the area of England and so its share of England's wealth was appropriate. By 1352 it had more than its fair share, however, with 8 per cent of the country's wealth.[8] Eastern Yorkshire was probably comparable, but the devastation of 1070 resulted in a dramatic reduction in its value for a time. Only Beverley was spared.[9] Domesday estimates for east Yorkshire manors at the beginning of 1066, in the reign of King Edward, indicate prosperity at least in line with Lincolnshire. Whitby, valued at £112, and Pickering at £88, compared well with Grantham at £52, Caistor at £30 and Louth at £12.[10] In the tax returns of 1352 eastern Yorkshire, some 2 per cent of England's area, had roughly 3 per cent of England's wealth.[11]

England generally was a very rich and highly urbanized country in the tenth and eleventh centuries. That is precisely why it was attacked by Vikings who targeted their raids with precision on the wealthiest zones. The payments (in gold and silver) which were made to Viking invaders between AD 991 and 1012, especially to Cnut in 1016, were huge. The northern areas to which the Humber gave access were a rich prize – comparable to Dorset, which had been the Vikings' first target in AD 789.[12]

The estimates of the wealth of eastern Yorkshire at different times from the eleventh to early fourteenth century suggest steady and significant but not dramatic growth. The truly dramatic increase was in the Holland district of Lincolnshire: from its median position among England's thirty-three counties in 1086, it was actually the richest area in England in 1334. Derbyshire and Lancashire were abysmally poor in 1086 and would remain so (see table 5.1 for a comparison of the wealth of various county areas in later centuries). It was in Stenton's 'essential Danelaw' between the Welland and the Tees that northern wealth was concentrated at the time of the Domesday survey and beyond – as eleventh-century invaders up the Humber were fully aware. This difference between the north of England on the east of the Pennines and the west would persist throughout the Middle Ages.

Chester, it is true, was an important medieval port. It was involved in trade with Ireland and Gascony, and in the transport of troops to Ireland and Scotland. It had three friaries within its walls – important indicators of urban wealth (see below) – a nunnery, and the rich, powerful (and oppressive) abbey of St Werburgh. Unlike Lincoln, York and Newcastle, however, Chester had no Jewish community and it had only slight connections with Italian merchants. (Also unlike York, Newcastle and Lincoln it would never, in the fourteenth century, be a staple town.) After the Welsh wars of Edward I its importance was undermined by peace, and while Newcastle in an analogous position prospered, Chester declined. 'The permanence of the settlement (with Wales) ultimately deprived Chester of its military and political importance.'[13] It weakened its economic importance too.

TABLE 5.1 Lay wealth of countries in England, 1334 and 1515 (value of personal property in Pounds per 1,000 acres)

1334	(£/1,000 acres)	1515	(£/1,000 acres)
Holland (Lincs)	46.4	Essex	102.0
Kesteven (Lincs)	27.8	Surrey	94.1
Lindsey (Lincs)	22.6	Holland (Lincs)	67.3
East Riding (Yorks)	22.2	England (average)	66.0
England (average)	21.5	Lindsey (Lincs)	45.6
Notts	18.7	Kesteven (Lincs)	42.6
Essex	18.5	Notts	32.2
Surrey	17.3	East Riding (Yorks)	25.0
Derby	10.2	Derby	18.7
North Riding (Yorks)	7.0	West Riding (Yorks)	11.3
West Riding (Yorks)	6.5	North Riding (Yorks)	8.1
Lancs	4.6	Lancs	3.8

Source: R. S. Schofield, 'The geographical distribution of wealth in England 1334–1649' Economic History Review, 18 (1965), pp. 483–510.

INDICES OF WEALTH: TOWNS, MONASTERIES, FRIARIES
AND LOST VILLAGES

There are three main indicators of regional wealth apart from potentially treacherous medieval taxation data: the growth of towns, the foundation of monasteries, and the number of friaries. Urban development is an index of general economic advance including population growth, at least until the later fourteenth century when economic development occurred more commonly outside towns. The foundation of monasteries is an index of landed wealth, especially when it is concentrated in relatively few hands. The distribution of friaries is an accurate reflection of urban wealth. On all three counts the North on the east of the Pennines was an area of rapid economic advance between the tenth and the thirteenth centuries.

Castle building, which was also a feature of this period in the North, is less an expression of wealth than a contribution to it – capital investment providing employment and stimulating economic development around it. Newcastle-upon-Tyne is the most obvious illustration. Castle building in the years immediately after 1066 had often been a highly destructive enterprise involving the demolition of houses to provide suitable urban sites. Both York and Lincoln suffered severe impairment in this way. But by the later twelfth century, however, royal as well as baronial castle building was big business, contributing to regional development, and it was often disproportionately heavy in northern England: a quarter of the kingdom often accounted for half of the royal expenditure on castles, as in the two years 1210–1212, for example, when £2,696 was spent in the North out of a total of £5,092.[14]

The twelfth century was the heyday of 'development' in northern England, especially in the later years (the last three decades have been pin-pointed as the peak period for this essentially demographically based development in England as a whole).[15] The great wave of monastic development was over by then (the friaries came later, in the early thirteenth century, underscoring and pin-pointing what was already achieved). The second Norman invasion promoted by Henry I (reigned 1100–1135) had also been accomplished. Henry brought in western Normans and Bretons to settle and develop the northern frontier regions – men possibly less fastidious than William the Conqueror's followers and more willing to eat the oaten bread of these northern lands.[16]

One hundred and seventy new towns were 'planted' by bishops, abbots, lay lords and kings. Northern England on the east of the Pennines played a full part in this prodigious urban development. Nine of these new towns were planted in Northumberland between 1180 and 1250, with a tenth early in the fourteenth century. Another ten 'organic' towns, which had grown out of small village settlements, made Northumberland one of the most urbanized counties in England, similar to highly developed Hampshire which had twenty-two towns, eleven planted and eleven organic.

Devonshire, with almost seventy towns (but only seventeen of them deliberately planted), was the most heavily urbanized county of all, but Beresford brackets it with Northumberland: 'Northumberland is revealed as a little Devon in the degree and timing of its urbanization.'[17] The great success story was the planted town of Newcastle-upon-Tyne, the boom town of twelfth- and thirteenth-century England. The customs and franchises on which it was founded were a model for urban development throughout the North and beyond.[18]

There were some 530 towns in total in late thirteenth-century England, defined as taxation boroughs, parliamentary boroughs, or towns with borough charters (some of course were all three). Northumberland and Durham together had thirty-one – 6 per cent – and the two counties together are 6 per cent of England's area. The North-west, by contrast, was an urban desert (except for Carlisle): there were no urban areas there worth taxing during the reign (1154–1189) of Henry II.[19] Nottinghamshire and Derbyshire were not much better: together the size of Northumberland, they had a total of only eight towns.

The 170 planted towns are the best guide to planned development. The three northern counties which flank the eastern Pennines – Northumberland, Durham and Yorkshire – are one-sixth of England. A significant proportion of their terrain is high moorland and mountain and their population was still relatively sparse; but thirty of the new towns, a little more than one-sixth of the total, were planted in these counties. They constituted a genuine 'development area' in twelfth-century England.

Twelfth-century monastic development tells a similar story. Monasteries reflect great concentrations of landed wealth and in the twelfth and thirteenth centuries they were established throughout northern England, but especially on the east of the Pennines: twenty-five on the west, eighty-two on the east. At the time of the Domesday survey of 1086 a great swath of three dozen rich Benedictine monasteries extended across middle England from East Anglia to Gloucestershire, Worcestershire and Somerset. Their aggregate revenue was roughly one-sixth of the revenue of England. There were no monasteries at all north of a line from

Worcester to Burton-on-Trent and thence to the Wash. Starting from a
zero base in 1086, the northern counties of England redressed the balance
by the thirteenth century. At the dissolution in 1536 107 monasteries (20
per cent of the total) were in these northern counties (which made up a
quarter of England).

The Cistercians were particularly associated with northern England.
Between 1128 and 1153 they established fifty-six separate houses for
monks throughout England, of which eighteen (32 per cent) were in
the northern counties. Again, they were preponderantly on the east of the
Pennines: eleven compared with seven on the west. Only 6 per cent of the
far more numerous Benedictine houses were in the North but the total was
again eighteen: thirteen on the east and five on the west. Cistercian houses,
contrary to common belief, were mostly in rich, if remote, valleys.
Upland Fors near Askrigg in Wensleydale, whose lands were poor, soon
perished.

In the space of twenty years (between 1220 and 1240) the establishment
of friaries broadly confirmed this geographical pattern of wealth. These
mendicant orders – especially the Franciscans and Dominicans – went
with an unerring instinct to the urban centres of wealth and power. The
first Franciscan friaries were in London, at Oxford and at Northampton,
the latter being a pivotal town, occupying a strategic position between the
North and the South. Within five years the Franciscans had advanced as
far north as Lincoln, Stamford and Nottingham. In the next ten years
(1230 to 1240) they established friaries at York, Scarborough, Beverley,
Hull, Scalby (near Scarborough) and Richmond in Yorkshire; at
Durham; at Hartlepool and Newcastle-upon-Tyne in Northumberland;
Carlisle in Cumberland; at Preston in Lancashire; and at Chester in
Cheshire. They established, in total, forty-eight friaries in England,
twelve (25 per cent) in the North. The Dominicans followed an almost
identical geographical spread, establishing ten friaries in five of the seven
northern counties, 19 per cent of the fifty-three friaries throughout
England: in Yorkshire at Beverley, Pontefract, Scarborough, Yarm and
York; in Northumberland at Bamburgh and Newcastle-upon-Tyne; in
Cumberland at Carlisle; in Lancashire at Lancaster; and in Cheshire at
Chester. A number of northern towns supported friaries of both
Franciscans and Dominicans, a sure sign of great urban wealth: York,
Beverley, Scarborough, Chester, Carlisle, and Newcastle-upon-Tyne.
These two fold foundations pin-point the key concentrations of urban
wealth in the North.

Three of these six key points – York, Beverley and Scarborough – are

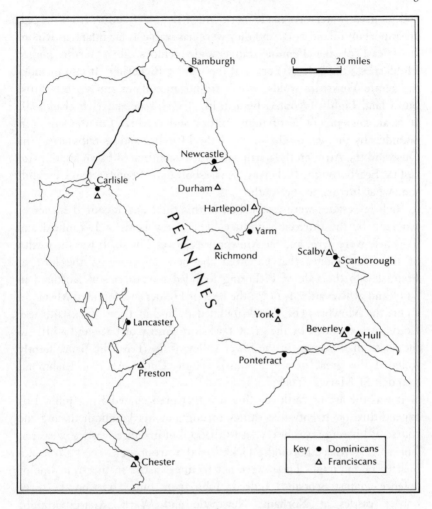

Bamburgh

0   20 miles

Newcastle

Carlisle

Durham △

Hartlepool △

P E N N I N E S

Yarm

Richmond

Scalby △
Scarborough

York

Lancaster

Beverley
Hull

Pontefract

Preston

Key ● Dominicans
     △ Franciscans

Chester

MAP 5.1   Dominican and Franciscan friaries in northern England
Source: author

in eastern Yorkshire, the heart and centre of wealth and power in the
medieval North. It was pre-eminently the land of castles, new towns,
parliamentary boroughs, lost villages, friaries and monasteries – all
strong indicators of power and wealth. Eastern Yorkshire is larger than
the historic East Riding: it extends east from a line which runs north from
Pontefract through Knaresborough to Ripon and Thirsk to the coast
between Scarborough and Spurn Head. It is roughly fifty miles from
north to south and sixty miles from east to west. It is not a highland zone

and its great waterways made York, more than sixty miles from the sea, an important inland port, and they were navigable as far inland as Ripon. It is east of the Pennine range and includes great fertile plains: Holderness, the vale of York and the vale of Pickering. It also includes the gentle Yorkshire wolds, which are not mountains and scarcely hills, but a land highly favoured by a mild, dry climate and rich chalk soil. It is an ancient cradle of high culture and civility. On the east it is bounded by the sea; on the south by the Humber and its tributaries, the Ouse and the Aire; on the north and east it is embraced by an arc of great castles: Scarborough, Pickering, Knaresborough, Pontefract and Tickhill somewhat further to the south.

Rich lay estates were established in this tight and favoured corner of England by the thirteenth century. The Percy lands at Leconfield and Topcliffe were here, and the Mowbray estates at Thirsk. It was the wealth of these lay estates that endowed the new monasteries: the lord of Helmsley in the vale of Pickering founded monasteries at Kirkham in 1130 and at Rievaulx in 1132; the lord of Holderness founded Meaux in 1151; the Mowbrays of Thirsk founded Byland in 1177. Kirkstall, near Leeds, was founded by the great Yorkshire family of Lacy and a little to the north of this area, in the lower valley of the Tees, the Bruce family founded the great priory at Guisborough. Count Alan of Richmond founded St Mary's, York.

It was the arc of castles in this area that preoccupied King John. His expenditure on twenty-five castles throughout his kingdom during the course of his reign was heavy, at £15,000, but just three castles in eastern Yorkshire – Knaresborough, Tickhill and Scarborough – cost £3,800, a quarter of the total. These were not frontier castles in the front line of defence against Scotland. Indeed, John spent only £670 on the three border castles at Norham, Newcastle and Wark. Knaresborough, however, accounted for £1,300, and Scarborough for £2,300.[20] This was a massive investment in royal castles, not to stand against the might of Scotland but against the might of eastern Yorkshire.

By the late thirteenth century eastern Yorkshire was not only encrusted with great abbeys and royal and baronial castles: it had a quite disproportionate number of boroughs sending members to Parliament. When the sheriffs were asked in 1295 for the boroughs of sufficient standing to send two discreet and capable burgesses to Parliament, Buckinghamshire, Hertfordshire and Middlesex made nil returns. Eastern Yorkshire on the other hand was able to send burgesses from eleven boroughs: Beverley, Hedon, Malton, Pickering, Pontefract,

Ripon, Scarborough, Thirsk, Tickhill, Yarm and York. Only two counties in Southampton's hinterland could match this: ten boroughs in Hampshire (including two on the Isle of Wight) sent burgesses to Parliament, and thirteen in Wiltshire.[21] This small corner of Yorkshire was sending representatives from eleven of its boroughs at a time when the average number of boroughs represented in Parliament was seventy-five. (In 1295, 114 boroughs made returns.)[22]

By the end of the Middle Ages eastern Yorkshire also had few serious rivals in the scale of its lost villages. Between the tax year 1334 and a population inquiry in 1517, the East Riding of Yorkshire had lost 13 per cent of its villages (the rather more extensive eastern Yorkshire as defined above had lost a somewhat higher proportion). The poverty-stricken areas of England – Lancashire, Cumberland, Westmorland, Shropshire and Herefordshire – had lost none. But rich Oxfordshire had lost 11 per cent, Warwickshire 13 per cent, and the Isle of Wight eclipsed them all with 22 per cent. Lost villages were the victims not of poverty and decay but of progress and wealth. This was especially so in good arable areas (like the Yorkshire wolds) which could easily convert to pasture for sheep, where villages disappeared as a consequence of 'development'.[23] Lost villages, like monasteries, are an index of landed wealth: 'Many a lost village stands in the shadow of the Great House.'[24]

This small, tight corner of Yorkshire was the only part of the North that would experience the Peasants' Revolt in 1381 – apart from the Wirral estates of the rich Benedictine abbey of St Weburgh at Chester. The three towns whose Dominican and Franciscan friaries signalled their wealth were precisely the towns where disturbances occurred: Scarborough, Beverley and York. There was a strong element of regional separatism in the Peasants' Revolt, resentment against the intrusive apparatus of central government (which failed to secure Scarborough no less than south-east ports from enemy attack) and demand for local autonomy: this was so in the South-east, where the revolt principally occurred, and it was also in eastern Yorkshire.[25] It was a protest of local communities demonstrating their power. The revolt of 1381 both in the South-east and in the North was the revolt of economically highly developed urban–industrial and commercial areas.[26] Lost villages and the Peasants' Revolt were not symptoms of poverty and decline: they were the pathology of development and success.

It was a very active North Sea trading community into which northern England on its eastern side was locked through its great ports from Boston to Newcastle-upon-Tyne. Its main export was wool, although in the twelfth century high-quality cloth was important, too, manufactured in Lincoln, Hedon, Selby, Beverley, Whitby and York. The cloth industry was in decline by the late thirteenth century and the weavers' guilds in eastern Yorkshire were unable to pay their exchequer dues.[27] Wool production and exports were buoyant, however, and principally for this reason Boston was the richest port after London in 1204 and Newcastle-upon-Tyne ranked third among the wealthiest English towns (after Bristol and York) in 1334.[28]

Hull rose in a spectacular way from the late thirteenth century. The great Cistercian abbey at Meaux in the lowlands of Holderness had developed Hull to export its high-quality wool and in the thirteenth century a dynamic group of Yorkshire merchants made use of its facilities. In terms of wool exports it was now outclassed only by Boston and London. A network of a dozen east Yorkshire towns and villages supported Hull's export trade: in Beverley alone there were at least seventy capitalists involved in the trade.[29]

Northern merchants from the old Danelaw counties between the Welland and the Tyne were heavily involved in this North Sea trade in which Hansa merchants were a dominant force. It was a community defined not only by reciprocal trade (indeed true reciprocity was powerfully resisted by the Hansa towns), but by a legal framework of licences, treaties, privileges and exclusions. Oversea staple towns and communities of expatriate English merchants involved northern England in an intricate network of legal and diplomatic relationships. In the twelfth and thirteenth centuries northern merchants sold wool to the Low Countries. It was not until the late fourteenth century that they effectively gained a foothold in the Baltic, principally for the sale of cloth from the colony they established at Danzig.[30]

Merchants were involved in 'diplomatic incidents' and legal contests throughout the Middle Ages. A Beverley merchant negotiated for five years (1305–1309) in the courts of the bishop of Utrecht in an attempt to force Groningen merchants to pay their debts. This raised abstruse questions of German constitutional law.[31] Respected traders were commonly pirates on the side, like Robert Acclom, MP for Scarborough between 1401 and 1404.[32] Merchants of Beverley, York, Scarborough, Hartlepool and Newcastle-upon-Tyne were necessarily skilled in the niceties of European mercantile law and the legal–political structures which in some measure constrained their quasi-piratical trade.

It was thus a rich, sophisticated, cosmopolitan and worldly-wise corner of northern England that was the base for the baronial rebellion against

King John. (When the barons of England needed emissaries to send to Rome to present the case against John they chose two east Yorkshire clerics, John de Ferriby, Vesci's protegé, and John FitzOsbert, Richard de Percy's chaplain.) It was this same rich, international corner of England that would provide a springboard for Bolingbroke when he landed at Ravenspur in 1399. From this base he not only claimed his duchy but obtained a kingdom. There was a strong economic and cultural background to the political rise of the medieval North.

NORTHERN POWER AGAINST KING JOHN

It was in the early thirteenth century, and especially between 1212 and 1216, that the power of the North became manifest, as the northern barons moved politically centre-stage and led the opposition to King John. They were formidable men, but of comfortable independence rather than great wealth: their families were important in their shires as administrators and officials rather than great feudal lords. The chroniclers were unanimous that the opposition to John came principally from the 'Norenses', and although this term gradually lost its geographical specificity and embraced all of John's opponents, its heart and centre was the north Yorkshire moors. All northern counties contributed rebel barons (and eventually an impressive number of rebel knights), but important estates of the key figures encircled the north Yorkshire moors: Ros at Helmsley; Stuteville at Kirkby Moorside; Percy at Whitby; Bruce at Skelton; Vesci at Malton; and Mowbray at Thirsk.[33]

There are four points at which the northern opposition to John is obvious, measurable and disproportionate: the refusal of military service and scutage for the campaign in Poitou 1213–14; the gathering of rebel barons at Stamford in the spring of 1215; the composition of the committee of twenty-five 'charter barons' in June 1215; the writs restoring the lands of rebel tenants who had opposed John in the civil war between 1215 and 1216. There are of course problems with the statistics: in part the unreliability of chroniclers' lists, and the difficulty of assigning men with widely scattered lands to any particular geographical location or sheriff's jurisdiction. Nevertheless, some tentative conclusions are possible and when put together the overall picture is strong.

It was northern barons who disproportionately resisted serving in or paying for the Poitou campaign. The chroniclers said so and surviving records support them. Eastern and home counties' barons (who would later be foremost rebels) served or paid; six prominent Northerners did neither. They were Bruce, Grelley, Montbegon, Percy, Vesci and Mowbray. The last four would later serve on the committee of twenty-five barons appointed to guarantee the 'great charter'. Only Mowbray came anywhere near the landed wealth of the great eastern lords.

The rebel barons who mustered at Stamford early in 1215 were rather unreliably enumerated by chroniclers; but principally on a cautious reading and cross-checking of Wendover's list, the names of forty-five rebel barons have been reasonably established.[34] Twelve of them had most of their lands in Yorkshire, Northumberland, Lancashire and Cumberland; but if Lincolnshire is counted a northern county, then eighteen of the forty-five were northerners. Thus 40 per cent of the rebel barons at this stage came from the still most thinly populated third of England.

Barons from the sparsely populated quarter of England north of a line from the Humber to the Dee (which had perhaps around 12 per cent of England's population in 1215) were one-third of the committee of twenty-five appointed to oversee the implementation of Magna Carta. They were eight in number: John FitzRobert (lands mainly in Northumberland),[35] Roger de Montbegon (Lancashire), Richard de Percy (Yorkshire), Robert de Ros (Yorkshire), William de Fors (Yorkshire), Eustace de Vesci (Northumberland and Yorkshire), William de Mowbray (Yorkshire), John de Lacy (Lancashire and Yorkshire). All held land elsewhere, principally in Lincolnshire.

Nothing is known of the way in which the committee of twenty-five was established or on what basis. The chroniclers who listed their names did so some years after the event. It was clearly a remarkable body, however, with remarkable powers: the authority to command a kingdom and control a king – if necessary by legalized revolt. More than a thousand knights were to be on stand-by to support its authority.[36] The sheriffs of all counties were to obtain oaths of loyalty to the 'charter twenty-five' from the men of their shires. If the king contravened the charter and refused to make amends the twenty-five could seize his possessions, castles and lands. Eight northern barons, all of modest rank, and most of modest wealth, shared in these remarkable powers.

None of the eight was an earl. There were fifteen earls in 1215 and only one in the North – Ranulf of Chester. With his palatine county and extensive lands in Yorkshire and Lincolnshire he was a man of immense resources, power, and prestige. He remained loyal to King John. Six earls (and the son and heir of a seventh) were among the charter twenty-

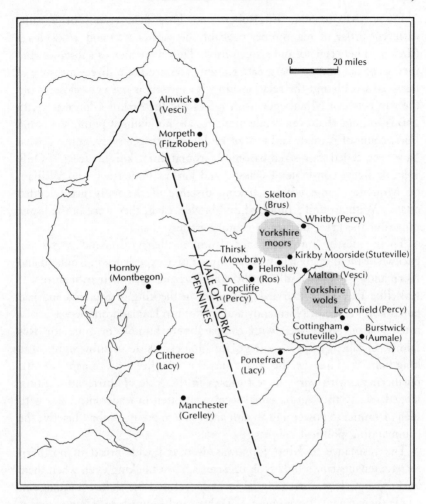

MAP 5.2 Northern barons against King John
Source: author

five. They were not all equally rich and powerful: Robert de Vere, earl of Oxford, held relatively modest estates. But Roger Bigod, earl of Norfolk, and Geoffrey de Mandeville, earl of Gloucester, held extensive lands. Expressed in terms of knights fees, they had some 200 each. These were probably over 30,000-acre estates.[37] William Marshal junior, another charter baron, heir of the earl of Pembroke, would inherit estates of similar size.

Percy, Montbegon, FitzRobert and Fors held estates of a quite different order of magnitude: probably between 1,000 and 3,000 acres (they held between six and sixteen fees). They were men of substance, but they were not among the great. Knights fees are not a direct measure of personal wealth and the relationship with income is not very close,[38] but the gap between Montbegon with 8 fees and the earl of Gloucester with 270 is so huge that even crude measures are not without point. Vesci and Fors, count of Aumale and lord of Holderness respectively, enjoyed what have been called 'fair-sized baronies' (around thirty knights fees).[39] Only John de Lacy, constable of Chester and lord of Pontefract, and William de Mowbray came within striking distance of the truly great landed estates. With around a hundred knights fees each, they were in the lower ranges of the great thirteenth-century estates.

These mostly minor barons from northern England were not backwoodsmen: many had wide administrative experience in England and Normandy: 'They had all seen broader horizons than their own shires.'[40] Ros (like Vesci) had married a daughter of the king of Scotland and had half a knights fee in Normandy and thirteen in England but he was still a minor baron. And yet, 'with comparatively humble origins, the Ros family climbed from a village in Holderness to within sight of a kingdom.'[41] This is the real measure of the achievement of the northerners: with very modest estates in the scale of thirteenth-century landed society they sat on equal terms and often in leadership roles with men of immense power and wealth and came to occupy, albeit briefly, the commanding political heights.

The resistance to King John was deep and widespread in northern society: tenants commonly took up arms against the king even when their lord did not. It was not only barons who refused the Poitevin scutage in 1214: their tenants throughout Yorkshire and Lancashire, from whom it would be raised, refused as well. These men held their land by military tenure: they were mostly of the class of knights. They usually held land from more than one lord and often in more than one county. This was perhaps the basis of the remarkable independence which feudal tenants commonly showed towards their lords.[42]

This independence was shown especially in northern counties in the civil war of 1215–16. In the honour of Richmond they rebelled early, before Runnymede, in June 1215 – they were not 'September rebels', waiting on events, as they commonly were in the South – and although their lord for the past ten years had been the mighty Ranulf, earl of Chester, who remained loyal to the king, they rebelled almost to a man.

They were in a geographically compact area and on the face of it easily subject to the political domination of their lord, but the score or so knightly tenants rebelled in the weeks before Runnymede and they rebelled again in the autumn when the barons' agreement with John broke down.

The writs addressed to sheriffs to restore the lands of rebel tenants at the end of the civil war present their own problems of interpretation. These writs of seisin provide the main evidence of tenants' revolt. They may understate its extent, because many rebel tenants were probably subsumed under the legal action taken against their lord when he was a rebel too. But what is striking is the extent of rebellion by tenants when their lord remained loyal. The great majority (twenty out of twenty-four) of the Holderness tenants of William de Fors rebelled. It is true that de Fors was himself a rebel at first and even one of the twenty-five charter barons, but in August he changed sides. His tenants did not.[43] They had agreed in the previous year to meet the expenses of four knights for the Poitevin campaign (at three shillings a day); but by the time the knights returned their attitude had hardened and they refused to pay at least one of them, Andrew de Faucenberg. (Andrew probably remained loyal to John; his name does not appear in the list of *reversi* when the rebellion was over, although the name of his brother, Peter de Faucenberg, does.)[44]

Hostility to John ran deep and wide in the North. It was widespread among tenants no less than their lords and they took independent action. All five tenants of the Yorkshire loyalist Peter de Maulay rebelled. Even in Westmorland, where the loyalist Robert de Vieuxpont held a tight, compact lordship, sixteen tenants rebelled against the crown.[45]

EXPLANATIONS: ANGEVIN INTERVENTIONISM, NORTHERN SEPARATISM AND NORTHERN WEALTH

The special part played by the North in the opposition to King John calls for an explanation in northern terms: what particular factors were operating in the North but not operating, or not operating so strongly, elsewhere?

The crisis came over military service overseas, especially for the Poitevin campaign planned for 1213; more generally, John's fevered attempts to recover Normandy since its loss in 1204 were a source of increasing baronial unrest. A special northern factor might simply be the remoteness of northern barons from this theatre of action: their interests and involvements (often their wives and estates) were across the border in Scotland rather than across the channel in France. Moreover, some border tenures limited military action to local defence.

There is no evidence, however, that cross-border and cross-channel interests were mutually exclusive. Northern barons with estates in Scotland often had them in Normandy too, and had fought hard to defend them in 1204. Some retained them, like the Balliols of Teesdale. (And a century later, when John Balliol ended his five-year tenure of the Scottish throne, he retired to his Normandy estates and died at Castle Galliard twelve years later.) Service in Poitou might be seen as having less legitimacy than service in Normandy, but there was no reason for this view to be especially strong in the North. The problem of overseas service in general and of the Poitevin campaign in particular look more like a pretext for rebellion than a cause.[46]

It has been said of the revolt against King John that 'It was a rebellion of the King's debtors.'[47] It is true that a number of northern barons were heavily in debt to the crown, but this was far from being a uniquely northern problem. Indeed, a majority of the English baronage, wherever their estates were located, were in debt to the crown; among the northern barons de Vesci, a cautious and parsimonious man, had no debts at all;[48] and when Percy's debt to the exchequer was consolidated in 1211 the total came to £31 6s. 8d., a wholly insignificant sum[49] (some debts were in excess of £10,000). The debts arose principally from feudal 'reliefs' (inheritance tax), and the problem was the accumulation of arrears. But what mattered was the size of the instalments, which could be quite modest (and might take 700 years to pay off).[50] This was a problem for the entire feudal baronage and there is no evidence that it was especially acute in the North.

The root problem in the North was the ancient one: northern separatism. It was a separatism made more self-confident by centuries of steady if not spectacular economic development which produced men of good circumstances to express and defend it. This ancient tradition was now confronted by restlessly interventionist Angevin kings bent on northern integration. The real significance of the loss of Normandy in 1204 was that John had more time and more need to intervene in the North.

Magna Carta was in reality a defeat for the northerners. It was a compromise engineered by moderate southerners, notably Stephen Langton, archbishop of Canterbury, and William Marshall, earl of Pembroke. The northerners did not want a peace treaty with the king;

they wanted to be rid of him. They were outmanoeuvred between February 1215, when they were in the ascendant, and June when they met John at Runnymede; they had renounced their allegiance to John at Brackley in April but were now diverted from civil war and brought to negotiation. But the northerners were leaving the hard bargaining at Runnymede before it was completed, and were taking up arms. 'They intended war; they talked of electing a new king.'[51]

They had first begun looking for a new king as early as 1209. John de Lacy, the eldest son of the constable of Chester, was in league with northern allies and in correspondence with the king of France. John's highly effective military action against the North and King William of Scotland in 1209 was probably in response to this conspiracy.[52] In September 1215 the barons sent a delegation to the king of France offering the English throne to his eldest son.

Stubbs said that the northerners who rebelled against John were drawn from the old 'administrative families'.[53] They had the northern counties in their grip not as great feudal lords but as governors of castles and as sheriffs, offices which they tended to treat as hereditary. Smaller landholders of the status of knight were also getting a grip on their localities as assessors and collectors of taxes, as the revolutionary tax on movables, first successfully levied in 1188, became established. These were the men who felt threatened by John – as indeed they had been threatened by his father, Henry II, who removed sheriffs wholesale.

The small landholders who might expect such fee-paid appointments as tax assessors (the fee was 40s. in the early thirteenth century, £5 by the end) are more elusive to historians than the greater lords who became sheriffs or castellans. But Thomas de Muleton of Cumberland, who held one knights fee in Lincolnshire, was an itinerant justice who served on various commissions of inquiry, was a tallager and tax-assessor, and for a time, somewhat disastrously, even sheriff of Lincolnshire. He rebelled against John in 1215. Roger de Merlay was a similar small landholder in Northumberland who held similar relatively minor administrative posts. He too rebelled against John in 1215.[54]

Sheriffs were still men of great power in the twelfth and early thirteenth centuries and likely to make high profit from their office. Vescis, Stutevilles and Bolbecs treated the northern shrievalties as family concerns. Henry II began to check their pretensions towards the end of his reign; John did so even more vigorously from early in his.

John asserted his authority in the North for two reasons: first to find jobs for his followers who were being displaced from positions in

Normandy; second to bring the northern counties under more effective central control. From service in Normandy Robert de Vieuxpont became custodian of Appleby, Brough and Bowes castles and sheriff of Westmorland; from a similar Normandy background Brian de Lisle became custodian of Bolsover and Knaresborough castles. Under Brian's administration Knaresborough castle became one of the main military and financial centres of the North.

John disciplined the North. His itineraries in the North, often in midwinter were marked by exactions and fines, the confirmation of ancient privileges for huge sums, the weight of royal authority on towns, abbeys and shires. His journeys were punitive: York was fined £100 in 1201 for failing to provide lodgings for his crossbowmen. The expedition to Scotland in 1209 was in fact another 'harrying' of the northern shires. These endlessly restless journeys and heavy and merciless exactions marked, it has been claimed, 'the final integration of the north in the English realm'.[55]

The main impetus to revolt against John came from the North with strong support from eastern counties; but in the year-long civil war that followed the failure of the Runnymede accord, rebellion was much more widespread. It was never strong in western and south-western counties, however: the geographical concentration remained in the North and the East.

Some 1,400 freeholders rebelled, according to the writs by which they were reinstated in their lands when they finally made their peace.[56] 350 of these freeholders were in Yorkshire and Lincolnshire.[57] Yorkshire and Lincolnshire, roughly 15 per cent of England's area (and at this date perhaps 10 per cent of England's population) contributed 25 per cent of the rebels. Norfolk, Suffolk, Essex, Hertfordshire and Cambridgeshire also made a disproportionate contribution, but Staffordshire, Hereford-shire, Shropshire, Gloucestershire, Somerset, Devon and Cornwall contributed a negligible number of small freeholder rebels against John.[58]

There is a broad correspondence between the distribution of landed wealth and of small freeholder rebels. It was the mostly poor western counties that were massively under-represented in the rebellion against King John. The richest counties in 1086 were Oxfordshire and Berkshire – they were still the richest in 1334; the poorest in 1086 were Herefordshire, Devonshire, Shropshire, Cornwall, Staffordshire and Lancashire – these were also the poorest counties in 1334. Some counties changed markedly: those that significantly advanced were Lincolnshire,

TABLE 5.2   The richest and poorest counties in 1086 and 1334

1086 (s./mile²)		1334 (£/1,000 acres)	
Oxon	78	Oxon	42
Berks	70	Berks	31
England (average)	32	England (average)	21.5
Hereford	26	Hereford	14
Devon	24	Shropshire	12
Shropshire	13	Staffs	11
Cornwall	10	Devon	8
Staffs	8	Cornwall	8
Lancs	4	Lancs	5
(with Cheshire)			

Source: H. C. Darby, Domesday England (Cambridge University Press, 1977), p. 359.
R. S. Schofield, 'The geographical distribution of wealth in England 1334–1649', Economic History Review, 18 (1965), pp. 483–510.

Norfolk and the East Riding of Yorkshire. It was where small landholders had grown in wealth, power and self-confidence that the civil war received its strongest support. The rebellion against King John occurred at the point of intersection between Angevin attempts to integrate the North and the steady growth of northern and eastern wealth.

One further circumstance is of great significance in explaining the geographical pattern of opposition to King John: the historically close political and social connection between the Angevins and the West. There was, indeed, a long-standing tension between the Angevin West and the proudly self-conscious Norman nobility of the North, dating back to the reign of Stephen. The west country was the power base of the Angevin party from the time when Empress Matilda (mother of Henry II) contested Stephen's throne: her half-brother Robert, earl of Gloucester, was her principal support. Matilda had married woefully beneath herself both as a Norman (daughter of Henry I) and as the widow of Emperor Henry V; but her son by her new husband, Geoffrey Plantagenet, count of Anjou, would become England's first Angevin king. In the west country the Angevin connection was strong and became stronger. Henry II's son King John was buried at Worcester and his grandson King Henry III was crowned at Gloucester.

The proud and highly cultivated Norman barons of the North had supported Stephen; a number of them, including Balliol, Lacy and Mowbray, were captured with him by west country armies at Lincoln on 2 February 1141. These northern barons were keenly conscious of their Norman heritage: a litany of Norman battle honours was recited by Walter l'Espec before they fought the Scottish allies of the Angevins at Northallerton in 1138. They remained deeply contemptuous of the brash, barbaric, upstart Angevins and their west country friends. But the west country was by no means impotent. It did not save John from political defeat in 1215, but it made a significant contribution to his military success in 1216.

What troubled the northern Norman nobility most under Angevin rule, however, was the increasing weight and pervasiveness of centralized power. The rebellion against John originated in perimeter England around the north Yorkshire moors. It was precisely the families that resisted the take-over by King David of Scotland in 1138 who resisted the take-over by John in 1204–15. It was Mowbray, Percy, Lacy, Stuteville, Brus and Aumale who were to the fore in 1215 as in 1138. There was a major difference, however: in 1138 the northerners had received virtually no help from the South; they achieved victory by themselves. In

1215 only London saved the revolution against King John. The most significant name among the twenty-five charter barons was not Percy, Mowbray or Lacy, but the mayor of London. It was their grip on London – which had supported them and had been their base since May 1215 – that the barons refused to surrender in the Runnymede accord. And indeed, the North everywhere capitulated to John in the civil war: only the castle at Helmsley held out. While the North submitted to John, the citizens of London welcomed Prince Louis of France as their king.

6

War on Two Fronts 1296–1453

FOURTEENTH-CENTURY PERSPECTIVES

The century 1296 to 1399 saw northern England rise spectacularly in military strength and political power. This rise involved northern England more comprehensively than that which culminated in the reign of King John; its basis was essentially strategic rather than economic. Northern society was convulsed, transformed, and pulled out of three centuries of relative isolation by a renewed war with the Scots.

Isolation was decisively ended and power reinforced through the contribution that northern England was making by the 1340s to the Hundred Years War that was now beginning in France. Northerners did not remain locked and isolated in a remote perimeter war. They used their enhanced importance to gain access to the central concerns and preoccupations of England as a channel state. They had not been called to meet any feudal obligation, but were volunteers with agreed contracts on generous terms. A rising reputation and fortune on the northern front were confirmed and consolidated by serving in a good regiment – perhaps with John of Gaunt or the Black Prince – in France. Northern captains and northern families often contrived a remarkable symmetry in their involvement in two wars. While Henry Percy, second baron of Alnwick, at the age of forty-seven commanded at the battle of Neville's Cross near Durham in 1346, his eldest son Henry, at the age of twenty-four, was winning distinction at Crécy in France. It was this dual or symmetrical involvement that gave northern England its power, which was most visibly signalled in 1399 when northern backing, formidably displayed at Doncaster and Pontefract, put the usurper Bolingbroke on the throne.

This was only the prelude to the ascendancy of the North. This ascendancy began with the highly organized war effort against Scotland in the last decade of the reign of Edward I (1296 to 1307). It was confirmed in the reign of Richard II when northern leaders first moved to the front rank of national affairs (1377 to 1399). Culmination came with Richard of Gloucester's lordship of Middleham and finally his brief period as king (between 1483 and 1485). 'In 1399 the northern magnates played a decisive part in national politics for the first time: in the fifteenth century they were to occupy the centre of the stage.'[1]

The key to the rise of northern power in the fourteenth and fifteenth centuries was the erosion of northern isolation. Isolation was almost a mathematical consequence of a unified kingdom in the tenth century; this was confirmed and heavily reinforced by the Norman conquest in the eleventh. To some extent this isolation was mitigated by north-eastern involvement in the North Sea economic community, but for two centuries after 1066 the interests of England's Norman and Angevin kings took them far more often across the channel than across the Humber. The first Angevin king, Henry II, ruled for thirty-five years and spent twenty of those years south of the channel. England was governed by itinerant duke-kings whose interest in their cross-channel duchies remained strong if not paramount.[2] The result was to accentuate the North's isolation and make northern England 'more of an outlying province' than it might have been.[3] Indeed, it often seemed expendable. King Richard I, it is true, baulked at granting the king of Scotland's demand for the four border counties, but would have ceded Northumberland for £10,000. King John was much more attentive to the North, but the importance of the northern province only increased significantly in the second half of the thirteenth century with the growing interest of England's kings in Scottish affairs. Northern England now acquired 'at least a strategic importance'.[4] Politically, the importance of northerners arose from involvement in both centre and circumference. The centre was not only London and the court: it was Normandy, Poitou and Aquitaine.

The north of England's military captains were in France, often in disproportionate numbers, for the profits of war. They had not been summoned across the channel to meet feudal obligations, as in the reign of King John; they were volunteers who raised or served in indentured retinues and received the 'accustomed wages of war' (four shillings a day for a banneret).[5] 'The feudal army had proved unsuitable for war';[6] in fact it had been privatized. County levies, which were not feudal either, were indeed conscript troops, called to service on a selective basis and quite handsomely paid. They were never raised in the four border counties for service in France and very seldom, on a very limited scale, in Yorkshire; and from about 1370 they were not raised at all. The gentlemen-volunteers of northern England served for the profits of war in their various forms: ransom money and pay, offices, land, pensions, influential connections, distinctions and honours (the 'garter' was a coveted honour after the order was instituted in 1348). The profits of war flowed abundantly into the North.

The power of the north of England in the fourteenth and fifteenth centuries is closely connected with the rise of two northern families: the Percies and the Nevilles. The extent of their power and importance both regionally and nationally has often been exaggerated. Their absolutist rule over northerners and the unquestioning loyalty they could allegedly command have been absurdly overstated. The 'rise of the North' meant also the rise of knights, gentry, yeomen, financiers and administrators on whom Percies and Nevilles depended and who defined the limits of their power. Percies and Nevilles mirrored northern society. They were like other military captains who were deeply involved in both the northern frontier and the wars in France. Perimeter importance was constantly reinforced through participation in the centre. This was not achieved only by Nevilles and Percies: even Umfravilles, Feltons, Skeltons and Bertrams emerged from their far-northern lordships to find involvement at both centre and circumference.

Regional power was not self-sustaining. It was reinforced and translated into national power when it gave access to the centre, which was both the court in London and the overseas imperium in France. Henry Percy had 'arrived' in 1377 when in addition to his northern responsibilities he became general of all the forces fighting in France and marshall of England in charge not only of the new king's coronation but of the highly charged situation in which John Wycliffe's London trial was taking place. In 1377 he also became the first earl of Northumberland.

And yet Henry Percy was little involved in the high politics of Richard II's turbulent reign. In 1381 he felt strong enough to challenge John of Gaunt's authority in the North and refuse him entry to Bamburgh's royal castle, and he stationed a body of northern troops in London while he withstood the king's demand that he apologize. In the end his apology was suitably abject. But the dispute was connected with the northern command. When he moved to the very centre of political action at Pontefract and Doncaster in 1399, this was a little surprising.[7] The power of the Percies and the Nevilles rested less on a continuing involvement in the hard graft of high politics than in their audacity as crisis-makers and managers: they were kingmakers for 170 years, from 1399 to 1569. Their power has doubtless been exaggerated by historians, but their story and their fortunes are very closely bound up with the late medieval history of the North. And for northern society especially beyond the Tees their failure as crisis-makers and managers in 1569 was an enormous catastrophe.

Whatever their importance and power in the North, the Percies and the Nevilles did not inaugurate a new phase of northern separatism; indeed they presided over its decline. The fourteenth century saw the beginning of the 'royalist North'. Never since the days of Athelstan had northern England been so courted by kings. From William the Conqueror to John, when England's kings had paid attention to the North, it was usually to harry and punish it. In the fourteenth and fifteenth centuries kings' sons, uncles and brothers held extensive northern estates and gave them their 'good lordship'. But the root of royal favour was the need for northern troops to fight not only in Scotland but France. These military needs were the basis of the 'special relationship' between Cheshire and the Black Prince and his son Richard II, and between Lancashire and Richard's uncle, John of Gaunt.

Cheshire, Lancashire and south and east Yorkshire had particularly strong royal connections in the fourteenth century. So had north Yorkshire (Richmondshire), first through John of Gaunt and again in the later fifteenth century through Richard duke of Gloucester, brother of King Edward IV and the future King Richard III who was lord of Middleham. The land of ancient regalities beyond the Tees, however, was almost a royal exclusion zone: apart from the minuscule Lancastrian barony of Embleton and Dunstanburgh there was no royal toe-hold across the Tees (apart from three royal castles) until the later fifteenth century when Richard of Gloucester gained the lordship of Barnard castle. Nevertheless, kings' sons were appointed to important border commands as overlords of the marches: John of Gaunt in the later fourteenth century and, in the early fifteenth century, John of Lancaster, son of Henry IV, later duke of Bedford and regent of France. And when rebellions occurred in Durham in the fourteenth century, unlike the eleventh, they were not to resist the king's authority but to invite it in to counteract and indeed displace the quasi-regal powers of prince-bishops.

'Good lordship' was not simply a quid pro quo for military support. John of Gaunt, sometime earl of Richmond, was at some personal risk in defending John Wycliffe, the heretical reforming priest from Richmondshire. The meteoric rise of Thomas Langley from obscure origins in

Middleton near Manchester is explicable principally in terms of where he
was born and his service in the local administration of the duke of
Lancaster.[8] He missed becoming archbishop of York only because this
was disallowed by the pope (in the wake of the execution of the
treacherous Scrope), but he became bishop of Durham in 1406. He had
already been keeper of the Privy Seal, chancellor, and ambassador to
France. He would lead Henry V's great embassy to the French court in
1415.

England's kings no longer harried the North. King John had burnt
Alnwick, Morpeth, Mitford and Wark in 1216 (the northern barons had
paid homage to Scotland's king, Alexander II, and agreed to hand over
Cumberland, Westmorland and Northumberland). A qualitative change
in the relationship between England's kings and the north of England was
heralded in the later thirteenth century; it gathered rapid momentum after
1296. England's kings and their sons were now frequently beyond the
rivers Don, Tees and Tyne, leading armies against Scotland and enlisting
military support. This could not be gained on the scale and with the
frequency required simply through coercion or even payment of good
wages and bonuses. Calls for service explained at great length why the
campaign was necessary. In flowery rhetoric the king of England
explained to his northern subjects why the Scots must be punished for
their atrocities and pagan disregard of religion. The king had to negotiate
and overcome opposition in raising county levies. The same men were
often called upon over and over again. Royal representatives –
commissioners of array, captains and custodians – negotiated with local
communities for grants of service.[9] The men who served in the shire
levies were free men, they were paid the king's wages, and when they
were aggrieved their representatives sought out the king at Hartlepool,
Tynemouth or Berwick and settled the terms on which they would serve.
The north of England was becoming royalist in sentiment as well as out of
cold calculation.[10]

A NEW WAR IN THE NORTH

The northern war which began in 1296 and lasted for 300 years was not
simply a renewal of old conflicts: it was a new war with new purposes.
The 300-year war from 1296 to the treaty of Berwick in 1586 was
Scotland's war of independence; the 200-year war which preceded it from
1018 to 1216 was Scotland's war of imperialist expansion. Scotland had

done remarkably well out of the dismemberment of the historic kingdom of Northumbria, especially in acquiring Lothian in AD 973. It intended to do even better. From the battle of Carham on the Tweed in 1018 to the support given to King John's baronial rebels in 1216, Scotland fought expansionist wars to push the border to the Ribble, the Tyne or the Tees, or even to the Ouse. William the Conqueror's military expedition to the Tay achieved no lasting settlement in the treaty of Abernethy of 1073; neither did William Rufus's abortive expedition to the Forth in 1091 or his more effective expedition to Carlisle in 1092. In the middle of the twelfth century Scotland's King David had his capital at Carlisle, kept court at Newcastle-upon-Tyne, and ruled as far south as the Ribble and the Tees.

The new war came after an eighty-year interlude of relative peace between 1216 and 1296. The border had been finally settled by the treaty of York in 1237; in effect it had been settled by Henry II in 1157 when Malcolm IV had surrendered Cumberland, Westmorland and Carlisle. Even this 'retreat' represented an enormous addition of material resources to the kingdom of the Scots, and the border along the line of the Solway–Tweed 'incorporated [into Scotland] territory which well into the twelfth century was still regarded, racially or geographically, as *Anglia*, England'.[11] But this border was constantly challenged after 1157, notably by William the Lion in the reign of King John, and although actual organized warfare between England and Scotland ceased in 1216 (when Alexander II captured Carlisle and John burnt Haddington, Roxburgh and Dunbar), it was only in 1237 that Alexander finally renounced Scotland's claim to England's northern counties. Alexander III married Margaret, daughter of England's King Henry III, at York in December 1251.

The interlude of relative peace between 1216 and 1296 has been romanticized as a time when 'the civilizing arts of peace' prevailed, only to be rudely interrupted by the aggression of Edward I.[12] This is not entirely accurate. The subterranean border warfare of raid and counter-raid continued much as before and there were times of acute crisis, as in 1244 when England's feudal army marched north and faced Scotland's army across the Tyne. A crisis in 1255 led to a distrainment of knights;[13] and at a distraint in 1278 there were more Northumberland knights (forty) than there had ever been before or would ever be again. In this period of peace Northumberland bristled with knights.

The crisis which led to the renewal of war in 1296 arose out of the problem of succession to the Scottish throne and Edward I's claim to 'superior lordship' and feudal service. What made continuing war inevitable, however, was the provocative colonial policy that Edward pursued in Scotland between 1298 and 1305. For Edward Scotland was no longer a 'realm' but a 'land'. By 1302 fifty-one of Edward's English followers had received grants of land in Scotland. Even without the seizure of the Scottish throne by Bruce in 1306, Edward I's 'colonialism' had set his country on a course that could lead only to continuous war.[14]

The new war with Scotland had three distinguishing features: a new leadership in northern England; a very pronounced international dimension; and a high-profile frontier sharply defined not only in military but increasingly in cultural terms. This period finally saw the end of the latent 'kingdom of the North' between the Tees and the Forth, and St Cuthbert, for all his Teviotdale origins and centuries-old connection with Scotland's religious institutions, now became the exclusive property of county Durham. In Scotland men of property now seldom made bequests to honour and commemorate St Cuthbert's name. 'The warfare of the fourteenth century had stimulated the militarization of the supernatural and the mobilization of the saints.'[15] It was this sharpness of cultural definition that would delay by a century the union of the two kingdoms after the union of the crowns in 1603.

The new war was a great turning point in the history of northern England. 'The wars of Edward I with Scotland, unprecedented in their character, were unprecedented in their results.'[16] One of the first results of major importance was to produce new leaders in the North who, under pressure from the Scots, achieved a striking and formidable coherence. They displaced the Balliols, Comyns and Bruces whose cross-border ties were extensive and close. But the new leaders looked very much like those of an earlier day, especially the Percies and Mowbrays, being biased towards east Yorkshire in their origins, as in 1138 and 1215. The Nevilles of Teesdale had estates in the same region. One apparent leader-in-waiting was Thomas earl of Lancaster, but for all his south Yorkshire estates and grandiose castle at Dunstanburgh (which he began building in 1313) he lacked convincing northern credentials (and by 1320 was in treasonable relationship with the Scots anyway). No northern leader of any stature emerged on the west of the Pennines – it would be more than a century before the Stanleys rose to regional power and national significance from their Lancashire–Cheshire base. The Percies had no land in England beyond the Tees before 1309, when they obtained their Alnwick estates.

The east-of-Pennines bias in northern leadership and political importance calls for an explanation. There were two principal reasons: the first was quite simply the use of York as royal headquarters for long periods between 1298 and 1336. If Edward I and Edward III had decided to have a forward base for operations against Scotland at Chester, Preston or Lancaster, northern leadership would have had a different complexion. The de la Poles would never have risen to an earldom; they would have remained modest merchants in Hull. The importance of York was an enormous advantage to ambitious families in east Yorkshire and the vale of York.

The second reason was the disproportionate involvement of the military aristocracy of Lancashire and Cheshire in cross-channel affairs between the battle of Poitiers in 1356 and Verneuil in 1424, almost to the exclusion of service elsewhere. The knights and gentry of Cheshire and Lancashire had contracts of service with the Black Prince who was not only earl of Chester but prince of Aquitaine. The Lancashire gentry also had contracts with John of Gaunt, who was not only the duke of Lancaster but 'My lord of Spain', king of Castille, and with his son Bolingbroke, the future King Henry IV who – like his uncle the Black Prince, but unlike his father – had little interest in and no experience on the northern frontier. Bolingbroke was more interested in Lithuania: on his expedition there in 1390 he was surrounded by the gentry of Lancashire including, for instance, Sir Ralph Staveley, who would be a shire knight for Lancashire in 1404 and 1407 and would fight at Agincourt in 1415 (he never saw service in Scotland), and John Morley, esquire, whose lands were in Lonsdale and near Clitheroe, who was also at Agincourt (and never saw service in Scotland either). Sir William Haryngton, who was the bearer of the royal standard at Agincourt and who, like his brother-in-law John Stanley, esquire, also at Agincourt, had some limited experience in Scotland: he had briefly been deputy warden of the east march, and Stanley had been warden of Roxburgh castle.[17] The close involvement of kings and their sons with Cheshire between 1350 and 1399, and with Lancashire between 1350 and 1435, meant that they called heavily on the military aristocracy of those counties. It remained only a minor aristocracy, however, in spite of its close royal connections, principally because its importance in Normandy or Aquitane found no resonance on the Scottish front.

On the east of the Pennines the military aristocracy exploited their importance to the full on two fronts. Both the Percies and the Nevilles were remarkably self-propelled. Virtually alone among England's fourteenth-century higher nobility they were able, through the geopolitical context in which they found themselves and which they were able to exploit, to advance to the foremost positions of power and wealth without being creatures of the court or close friends or relatives of kings.[18] They were very capable and ambitious military captains already of regional standing who were in the right place at the right time.

The Anglo-Scottish wars after 1296 were not remote, easily isolated frontier wars: they were fought in an international framework. Indeed, they were sustained for nearly 300 years by their international connections, and they finally ended only when the international context radically changed. This happened after the Reformation when Protestant England and Scotland found themselves surrounded by European Catholic powers. Thirty years of Protestantism on the edge of a largely Catholic Europe led to a solution which nearly 300 years of warfare had failed to produce.

The international dimension of the conflict was based on the 'auld alliance' formed between Scotland and France in 1295. It was given enhanced significance when England began the Hundred Years War in 1337. Henceforth border warfare constituted a 'second front' and England's major military initiatives in France were followed automatically by Scottish cross-border raids. The battle of Neville's Cross in 1346 was an integral part of the Crécy campaign; the 'foul raid' of 1416 came in the wake of Agincourt. (The youthful King James I of Scotland, accidentally in English hands, was being held as a hostage with Henry V in France to prevent precisely such raids, but in the event this was of no avail.) The battle of Flodden in 1513 arose out of Scotland's support for France after Henry VIII's victory at the 'battle of the spurs'.

There were other intricately interlocking 'levels' of the northern wars: national, regional and local. At the local level smallholders supported warfare for loot: by the fourteenth century cross-border theft was an essential support for a precarious border economy. At the regional level the Percies and the Douglases confronted each other across the border as lords of estates and wardens of the march. Their rivalry was acute. The two families had risen in step in the fourteenth century as leaders in their respective border zones. They even held adjacent and interlocking estates at Jedburgh: Percy had been granted forests and the castle worth about £270 a year – enough to support a dozen knights – after a successful campaign by Edward III in 1334. The Percies were never dislodged from Jedburgh by military might but forfeited their holding to Henry IV for treason in 1404.[19] The Jedburgh estates kept the conflict between the Percies and the Douglases finely tuned.

These different levels of involvement are well illustrated in the four-year sequence of events which culminated in England's disastrous defeat at Otterburn in 1388. The sequence began at the international level in 1384 when a French army under the famous admiral Jean de Vienne landed in Scotland to maintain the momentum of war at a time when John of Gaunt was establishing good relationships with the Scots. The French had some limited success in border raids and in August 1385 Richard II brought a great army to Newcastle-upon-Tyne (the last 'feudal host') and proceeded to destroy the rich abbeys in the Scottish borders. The campaign which culminated at Otterburn was planned in retaliation against the English invasion of 1385. It was three years coming to fruition, the issue kept alive and finally brought to a head by the tension in the region that centred on the rivalry between Percy and Douglas and the pressure of their followers who were eager for the profits of war. King Richard's well-known political difficulties, and friction between the Percies and the Nevilles, suggested to the Scots that the time was ripe.

The international conflict of 1384–5 had been transposed into purely regional and local terms by 1388. In August 1388 it was two regions rather than two nations at war. The English troops were northern knights and the levies of the border counties. The bishop of Durham led the Durham county levies but failed to arrive at Otterburn on time. The earl of Douglas was killed and Sir Henry Percy (Hotspur) was captured. Froissart was delighted to enumerate the English knights taken and the enormous ransoms they paid: 'I believe the Scots were richer by two hundred thousand francs.' The crown (unusually) contributed £3,000 to the huge ransom demanded for Hotspur. The followers of Douglas who had pressed for this campaign were hugely rewarded and had every reason to encourage such adventures again.

The high definition of the Anglo-Scottish border after 1306 was in sociocultural as well as military terms. (No additions were made to the four twelfth-century castles which stood on the border: the tight eastern cluster of Berwick, Norham and Wark nearly seventy miles from William Rufus's castle at Carlisle.) Edward I had no intention of reviving the Scottish kingship after Balliol's abdication in 1296 and his colonial policy was predicated on an open frontier of minor administrative importance; in the event Edward's implementation of his policies and the emergence of Bruce as king led to a frontier impenetrable to a degree that was without historical precedent even in Hadrian's Wall.

This impermeability was not quite absolute. Landowners on both sides of the border were supervised by their governments with relative ease, but the cross-border migrations of common folk were more difficult to control and certainly occurred. Trade also continued on a limited scale and local shortages as well as English customs duties encouraged commercial arrangements between English and Scots. Even new grants of land were made when the fortunes of war turned, notably after England's victory in 1346 and the capture of the Scottish king: this new colonial phase was not finally ended until Jedburgh was lost to the Scots in 1408. (A new phase of colonial expansion was envisaged for the north-west palatinate that was approved by Parliament for Richard of Gloucester in 1483.) But the monolithic frontier society embracing both English and Scottish marches that appeared to be emerging in the thirteenth century was divided cleanly and decisively down the middle along the course of the Tweed during the years of conflict after 1306.

The militarization of the border that now occurred was principally in the form of a new institution: the wardenship of the march (see below). It was also expressed in new fortifications, however. The militarization of the border had one major consequence for the frontier province: it sharpened the distinction between the forward zone and the support regions in the rear. Pele towers were built all over the outer perimeter; new castles were built (in the later fourteenth century) in the inner core.

Northern England south of the Tees was a major source of victuals and soldiers but was only briefly and exceptionally under direct military attack. Scottish incursions reached the West Riding of Yorkshire in 1318 and 1319 and the East Riding in 1322; the North Riding was raided in 1314, 1318, 1319 and 1322.[20] Thereafter it was the border counties that took the weight of Scottish assaults.

Yorkshire provided soldiers most consistently on a disproportionate scale (though Cheshire occasionally made a huge contribution). The county levies of Yorkshire were very seldom and the four border counties were never raised for service in France (but demands were made on Lancashire and Cheshire for service in both France and Scotland). Yorkshire made the largest contribution to both national and regional armies raised for Scottish campaigns, usually between 1,000 and 4,000 men, exceptionally in excess of 6,000 (6,360 footmen and archers were demanded from Yorkshire for the Roxburgh campaign of 1334–5).[21] This was a high proportion of armies which usually numbered about 10,000 men. On one occasion in 1297, Cheshire made an even more disproportionate contribution in relation to its population, when 4,000 footmen were arrayed for war against the Scots.[22] Yorkshire was asked for 4,000 men for the Bannockburn campaign, a quarter of the infantry raised in all the English shires. Warwickshire and Leicestershire, the most southerly counties, contributed 500, Nottinghamshire and Derbyshire 2,000, Durham 1,500 and Northumberland 2,500.[23] For the battle at Neville's Cross near Durham in 1346, a wholly northern affair, Yorkshire raised 3,064 men, Lancashire 1,204.[24]

Yorkshire was a major and integral part of the northern military complex but was outside the fortress system of the frontier zone. By the later fourteenth century so was the eastern plain of Durham south of the river Wear. The later fourteenth and early fifteenth centuries saw a remarkable spate of castle building across Yorkshire and even beyond the Tees. This has been interpreted as a response to military pressure, marking the southern limit of the militarized zone.[25] In fact these castles were built precisely because they were outside the militarized zone: they were suburban and domestic, not fighting castles. Even in militarily active areas castles had become 'concentration camps' for protecting refugees, along with their livestock, at the height of Scottish attacks. Bamburgh castle and Richmond castle took in better-class local residents who could pay the custodian's entrance fee, and provided a safe base from which to negotiate with the Scots the payment necessary to buy them off.[26] But even this need was of brief duration south of the Tees, although Bywell castle on the Tyne was built by Ralph Neville, the second earl of Westmorland, in the early fifteenth century precisely as such a 'concentration camp' – in which the local population and their livestock could be concentrated during a Scottish attack.

The late fourteenth- and early fifteenth-century castles extended north to south from Chester-le-Street on the river Wear (Lumley castle) to Wressle castle near the confluence of the Yorkshire Derwent and the river Ouse. The six principal castles, all built after 1380, were Lumley, Streatlam and Raby in Durham, Bolton, Sheriff Hutton and Wressle in Yorkshire. Lumley castle was built by the Lumley family, military tenants of the bishop of Durham (would-be kingmakers in 1688, and soon thereafter earls of Scarborough); Streatlam was built by Sir William Bowes in the 1430s when he returned from the French wars; Bolton castle was built in Wensleydale by Richard Scrope when he returned from the French wars half a century earlier; Raby and Sheriff Hutton were built by John Neville, lord of Middleham, and Wressle by Sir Thomas Percy, the future earl of Worcester. Two of these castle builders were 'magnates', but three were not.

The ninety miles from Lumley castle to Wressle measures not the depth of the militarized frontier but the rich backdrop to the forward zone beyond the rivers Tyne and Wear. These late medieval castles were not military fortifications but displays of wealth, opulent, graceful, theatrical, each one a 'princely lodging' (as Leland would later describe Raby). Lumley castle was safely in the suburban lee of Newcastle-upon-Tyne, eight miles from the city centre; Sheriff Hutton is a dozen miles north-east, and Wressle a similar distance south-east, of York. All of them were militarily superfluous in a region already thick with castles from an earlier age (none was ever beseiged). The permission to crenellate was sheer redundancy. The serious business of defence was to the north and west of the river Wear, and its gravity is marked not by castles but pele towers.

Beyond the rivers Wear and Tyne the fourteenth, fifteenth and even sixteenth centuries, were not times for building castles but abandoning them. Safety was in pele towers: cramped, strictly and starkly utilitarian structures with stone walls seven to ten feet thick. The keeper of Prudhoe built a pele tower outside the castle gates in 1326. Preston tower, one of the more elaborate of the English peles, was built at the end of the fourteenth century by the custodian of Dunstanburgh castle, Robert Harbottle, although Dunstan tower (Proctor Steads) was a pele tower already incorporated into the castle complex at an earlier date. Dunstanburgh was a strong castle, but six pele towers were built within a radius of five miles: Craster, Embleton, Dunstan, Preston, Howick and Rock Hall. At Featherstone on the south Tyne a pele tower was built in to the structure of the existing castle in 1330.

The new castles built south of Chester-le-Street in the late fourteenth century betoken the great wealth of northern England arising principally from the French and Scottish wars. They also provide a pointer to the diffusion of wealth. The Nevilles and Percies who built Raby, Wressle and Sheriff Hutton were magnates, but Bowes was upper gentry and even Scrope and Lumley fell well below the magnate class. The Lumley estates were worth £250 a year,[27] ten times the income of a basic knight, but the Percy income was ten times greater than that at around £2,800 (gross).[28] Scrope's Bolton castle cost £12,000;[29] and Lumley castle and Streatlam were of comparable grandeur. One aspect of the rise of the North in the fourteenth and fifteenth centuries is the wealth which undoubtedly came pouring in and was quite widely diffused from the profits of war.

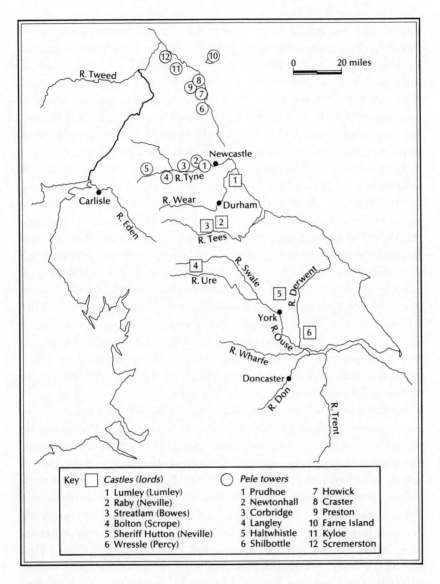

MAP 6.1   Late fourteenth- and early fifteenth-century castles and pele towers
Source: author

NORTHERNERS AT CENTRE AND CIRCUMFERENCE

The Scottish war pulled the political centre of gravity from London to the North for forty years after 1296, time enough for northerners to become disproportionately involved and deeply entrenched in the direction of national affairs. The exchequer was based in York for a total of fourteen years between 1298 and 1338. Not even a branch office was left behind in London and sheriffs throughout England had to travel to York to transact their exchequer business.[30] The chancery was in York continuously from 1332 to 1336, and the common bench was based in York castle from 1333 to 1339.[31] Parliament, which usually met in the palace of Westminster, was called to York on eight occasions between 1298 and 1335. After this, the French wars pulled the political centre of gravity back to the South and between 1338 and 1377 Parliament met nowhere but Westminster. Although eight of the fifty Parliaments that were called between 1377 and 1422 met at provincial centres, none was further north than Shrewsbury, Leicester and Northampton.[32] Parliament met in Lincoln in 1301, 1316 and 1327 to discuss Scottish affairs, but Lincoln was too far in the rear to have any direct bearing on the Scottish conflict (although in 1316 York was vulnerable to attack). Parliament even met at Carlisle in 1307. Despite the location of Parliament however, for a large part of the period 1296 to 1338 (especially 1298 to 1305 in the reign of Edward I and 1333 to 1338 in the reign of Edward III) the virtual capital of England was not London but York.[33]

Northern landowners might, in accordance with their numbers, have been perhaps a fifth or a quarter of the lords summoned to Parliament by individual writ. In fact they were more than a half, even when Parliament was not meeting at York. They made up half the number (twenty-seven out of fifty-three) in August 1295 in the Parliament at Westminster; indeed, 'perimeter barons' from the border regions of Wales and Scotland were 70 per cent of the House of Lords.[34] This was before war with Scotland had actually begun, but Scottish affairs were already a serious issue and those northern barons who had been summoned, 'like Brian Fitzalan of Bedale, Robert de Ros of Wark, John of Greystock, William de Vescy of Alnwick and Robert of Hilton his tenant, were bound to feel the first effect of any assertion of Scottish independence'.[35]

The immediate issue in the autumn of 1295 was France, but a Franco-Scottish alliance was in the making and French and Scottish problems were already intertwined. In any event, 'The magnates whose power was centred in the midlands, south or east hardly enter into the list.'[36] When the war with Scotland had actually begun the northern bias in the embryo peerage was still more pronounced; indeed, a list of landowners who were to be individually summoned for military service in Scotland in 1299 (issued in September 1298) now became the basis of parliamentary writs: 'It provided an authoritative record of the hundred or so most important and reliable military leaders, whose status also entitled them to a leading part in the deliberations of the nation, and it was accordingly the basis of all the military and parliamentary summonses of the rest of the reign of Edward I.'[37] It was Edward's method of summoning magnates for service in war and attendance at Parliament that 'contributed substantially to the development of a real peerage in the fourteenth century'.[38]

The northerners who were summoned to Parliament by individual writ were by no means invariably the king's tenants-in-chief. Brian Fitzalan of Bedale held his land from the honour of Richmond, but he had substantial military service in Scotland, had been castellan of Roxburgh and Jedburgh, and one of the guardians of Scotland during the vacancy of the throne. Sir Robert Holland was a powerful official and tenant of the honour of Lancaster: he received an individual writ to attend the parliament at York in 1314. Thomas Grelley, another 'honourial baron' of the Lancaster estates was on military service in Scotland in 1300, 1301, 1303, 1306, and 1308–11; he was summoned to Parliament by individual writ six times between 1308 and 1311.[39]

Clerks from Howdenshire dominated the great departments of state. They held the key posts in the chancery and effectively monopolized the small but powerful wardrobe (which handled the finances of the Scottish campaigns). They dominated the exchequer, too. Twenty east Yorkshire clerks entered royal service at York between 1298 and 1304, a further twelve between 1304 and 1307. Their names are redolent of east Yorkshire: John Cave, Nicolas Huggate, Richard Ferriby, Robert Cottingham, John Swanland, Walter Wetwang. Most important of all were William Hambleton from Selby, a chancery clerk, and William Melton from Howden who first became a wardrobe clerk in 1294. They were established officials before the royal administration moved to York in 1298. These senior civil servants were recruited through kinsmen already in post and the diocesan administration of York, not through the influence of northern magnates. They did not need or seek magnate patronage. They were the king's constant advisers; it was not they who sought magnate patronage, but magnates who sought theirs.[40]

These were wealthy men. Operating on the frontiers of the exchequer and army they had every opportunity to enrich themselves.[41] But in any event the incomes they received from the benefices they held were often huge. William Melton had an income of £800 a year long before he became archbishop of York – a good income at this date for an earl. And from their wardrobe clerkships they went on to be canons, deans and bishops. John Sandal from Doncaster was an exchequer clerk in 1294; in 1297 he was in Gascony as controller of the duchy receipts; in 1305 he was appointed chamberlain of Scotland; in 1307 chancellor of the exchequer. He became bishop of Winchester in 1316 and refused to ordain anyone who was not a Yorkshireman.

In the forty years 1296 to 1338 the Scottish wars brought a disproportionate number of northern landowners to the House of Lords and east Yorkshire clerks to a position of dominance in the exchequer and especially the wardrobe. The wars also brought northern merchants and prelates to great power and importance in army purveyance and royal finance. Especially notable as financiers were Archbishop Melton and William de la Pole.

The abbot of Fountains abbey and more especially the abbot of St Mary's, York, were also involved in the financial administration of the Scottish wars,[42] but Melton was a war financier on a grand scale. During his twenty-two years as archbishop of York (1317–40) he made some 400 loans totalling £23,551. This was not on the scale of the Italian bankers, the Bardi and the Peruzzi, or of the brothers Richard and William de la Pole, but it was substantial. Between 1332 and 1337 he made loans totalling £6,351 to Yorkshire knights to finance their military operations in Scotland with a reasonable expectation that his investment would make an adequate return.[43] The de la Pole brothers made their first loan to Edward III for a Scottish campaign in 1327: it was £4,000. In 1338–9 the two Italian banking houses raised £125,880 (this was for war in France); William de la Pole almost matched this joint Bardi–Peruzzi contribution with loans amounting to £111,000.[44]

It would be difficult to overstate the importance of royal connections and appointments generally in the rise of individuals to power. The de la Poles did not rise from their obscure origins in Hull because they were merchants supplying the king's armies in the North or even as financiers to the king on a formidable scale; they rose because they became royal servants, incorporated into the royal bureaucracy. Their rise was spectacular. It was seventy years from the appointment of William de la Pole as deputy to the king's butler in Hull in 1317 with the principal duty of importing wine for the king's use, to the elevation of his son Michael to the earldom of Suffolk in 1385 (only eight years after Henry Percy became earl of Northumberland). William's rise was through service in the Scottish wars: he became a knight banneret for financial services to the crown with an income from land of £333 6s. 8d. a year to support the dignity of his office. His son made the necessary strategic move to the centre and saw military service in France first with the Black Prince and then with John of Gaunt. Only one thing more was necessary: the hand of a rich heiress. And even the East Anglian heiress whom he married was a daughter of another of the Black Prince's men. Success in the North in one generation had been consolidated in the next through appropriate connections at the centre.

The major and disproportionate involvement of northern gentry in the French wars did not vary significantly overall between the heroic period of Crécy to Poitiers (1346–1356) and the no less heroic period of Agincourt to Verneuil (1315–1324). At the parliamentary elections of 1414, the gentry of Lancashire showed great impatience for a new phase of active warfare to start.[45] The Derbyshire gentry, through their duchy of Lancaster connections, were much more prominent in the second phase, especially in the conquest and administration of Normandy, and the Cheshire gentry much less – although William Troutbeck, esquire, chamberlain of Chester, was at Agincourt with by far the largest contingent of archers: 650 men.[46] The gentry of Lancashire continued to make the high level of contribution that was evident at Poitiers in 1356 and even more evident at Najera in 1367; the contribution of the northern border counties remained at least constant and from Richmondshire up to the Tweed probably increased, but their contribution to the northern front was in no way impaired.

The Cheshire contribution was at its height when the earl of Chester, Edward of Woodstock (the Black Prince), was not only a leading military commander but for eight years (1362–71) ruler of Aquitaine. Cheshire knights rose to prominence and wealth, notably Sir John Chandos, who fought at Crécy and Poitiers, Sir Hugh Calverley who fought with Chandos in later campaigns and was governor of Brest, and Sir Robert Knollys who first saw military service in Brittany in 1346 and amassed great wealth (and in 1381 guarded his fortune in his London house and led Londoners against Wat Tyler's rebels). The Black Prince never saw service on the Anglo-Scottish front (neither did his son, Richard of Bordeaux, who became King Richard II) and his principal Cheshire knights fought only in France and Spain. This in the long run was a weakness for Cheshire, quite apart from being a favoured province of a king who was deposed in 1399. The eminence of Cheshire knights abroad was never translated into pre-eminence at home.

What is striking about the northern border counties is their large and sustained contribution to war on two fronts. Northumberland knights fought in Scotland and served with distinction with Edward of Woodstock, too. Sir Thomas Felton, a younger son of the governor of Alnwick, fought at Crécy and Poitiers and served the Black Prince as seneschal of Aquitaine. He was taken prisoner by the French near Bordeaux in 1377 and the king granted him 30,000 francs from the ransom money of two French prisoners to secure his release. He was appointed a garter knight in 1381.

Sir William Felton of Northumberland had a longer and more distinguished career in border warfare before proceeding to France. He had fought at the battle of Halidon Hill in 1333, had been governor of Bamburgh castle in 1334 and in 1338 was in command of Roxburgh castle which he defended against the Scots. In 1342 he was sheriff of Northumberland and governor of Newcastle-upon-Tyne, but in 1343 he was in France at the seige of Nantes, subsequently at Crécy and Poitiers and was eventually seneschal of Poitou. He was killed in 1367 in a skirmish before the battle of Naverette.

The closely interconnected military families of north Yorkshire and Northumberland and Durham – Scropes, Fitz Hughs, Nevilles, Umfravilles, Elmedens, Percies and Eures – contrived remarkably symmetrical careers as soldiers and military administrators (and often as ambassadors) on the Anglo-Scottish borders and in France. Thus Richard, first Baron Scrope of Bolton in Wensleydale had already served in Brittany before he fought at Neville's Cross at the age of nineteen and was knighted in the field for valour. Thereafter he went to join Edward III at Calais, served with John of Gaunt and fought at Najera in 1367. At the age of fifty-five he was home building his great castle in Wensleydale; he now became warden of the march. At the age of fifty-eight he fought in Richard II's Scottish campaign of 1385 and thereafter, until his death in 1402 served on various embassies to Scotland and France. This 'symmetrical' career contrasts with that of many Lancashire and Cheshire knights who retired on very handsome pensions but often to relatively minor and even pseudo-jobs in, for instance, forest administration. An example is Sir Thomas Banastre KG who was also at Najera (but never on the Scottish front) and retired to a post of considerable local but scarcely national significance as forester of Rossyndale chase. Chandos retired as surveyor of Cheshire forests on £53 13*s*. 4*d*. a year – a newly invented and wholly superfluous post.[47]

John, third Lord Neville of Raby was too young to fight at Neville's Cross. He was only five years old in 1346, but his father carried him to see the battle. One of his earliest appointments was as one of the commissioners of the east marches towards Northumberland, but he was soon in France. His Teesdale archers regarded southern England as hostile territory, did great damage around Southampton in 1373, and he was impeached in Parliament on the charge that his troops treated the inhabitants of Hampshire as the king's enemies. He was governor of Bamburgh castle in 1377 and repelled a Scottish attack on Berwick, but in the following year was invested as lieutenant of Aquitaine. He conducted war in Gascony for seven years and secured huge ransoms. His frequent and onerous involvements in Scotland never precluded frequent and lucrative involvements in France.

Thomas, Lord Ughtred of Scarborough and Henry, Lord Percy, first earl of Northumberland, enjoyed long and finely balanced careers in the North and in France. Ughtred spent a quarter of a century fighting in Scotland before 1340 and a quarter of a century afterwards fighting in France. He was at Bannockburn, subsequently admiral of the fleet from the Thames northward, and in 1339 he was driven from Perth, which he was defending, and was the subject of a parliamentary inquiry (he was exonerated). He recovered his reputation and fortunes fighting in France until his death in 1365. He was appointed a garter knight in 1358.

Henry, Lord Percy's career was less tidily balanced but reached far greater peaks. He spent ten years fighting in France and Spain (he was at the battle of Najera in Castile in 1367 with John of Gaunt and the Black Prince) before he was appointed warden of the marches towards Scotland in 1369. In 1373 he was in France again with a large contingent of 24 knights, 175 esquires and 300 archers. In 1376 he was marshall of England inspecting the forts and castles of the Calais march; in 1377 he led a punitive expedition against Scotland and took Berwick in 1378. He had been made earl of Northumberland at Richard II's coronation in 1377.

North-eastern knights still had the same career patterns forty years after Henry Percy became an earl: at the time of Agincourt and Verneuil they still served on the Scottish frontier, and they also served in France. Even Robert Umfraville of Redesdale appears in the roll of arms of those who fought at Agincourt: he is listed as an esquire commanding twenty men-at-arms and forty archers.[48] But he had always maintained that it should be unnecessary to go to France to gain military honour and for two years he 'made warre on the Scottes to have name'.[49] (The name that he got was 'Robin Mendmarket' for burning the town of Peebles on market day.) Robert was a younger son whose estate was worth only 100 marks a year; but he became vice-admiral of the North and chamberlain of Berwick, and in the income tax return of 1436 he was one of only ten knights in England with an income of over £400 a year. His brother, Sir Gilbert, was less fortunate. His military career in France was very distinguished and he received liberal gifts of forfeited Norman estates, but he was killed in 1421, ironically by a contingent of Scots fighting in France.

The Bowes family of Teesdale established their fortune and reputation at this time through service on both fronts. Their position over the next century and a half illustrates the importance of the substantial northern gentry who prospered through military service but remained in the ranks of knights and esquires. William Bowes was of sufficient standing to marry a daughter of Ralph, Lord Greystoke, but when she died within a year William went to France, fought at Verneuil in 1424, was knighted in the field, and later served John, duke of Bedford, as his chamberlain. When he returned to England he consolidated his position not only by building Streatlam castle between Raby and Brancepeth but by serving as warden of the middle march and governor of Berwick.

Bowes was one of the first generation of royalist northern gentry. He had prospered in the service of a king's son, John, duke of Bedford. The Bowes family continued to give devoted service to the crown especially on the borders. They were typical of a great race of northern gentry who would not bow to Neville, or Percy. George Bowes would be knighted at Berwick in 1560 and entrusted to escort Mary Queen of Scots from Carlisle to Bolton castle in Wensleydale in 1568. The following year he stood out gallantly at Barnard castle against the rebellion of the northern earls.

Northern gentry were significantly over-represented among those who served in France. The knights of the shire who were returned to Parliament in 1422 provide a representative national sample, although the two northern palatine counties, Cheshire and Durham, did not return shire knights. The remaining thirty-nine counties returned seventy-eight. Sixteen had served in the Agincourt campaign, a further fifteen had seen service in France in the following six years: a total of thirty-one (40 per cent). If 'northerly counties' are taken as comprising Cumberland,

Westmorland, Northumberland, Lancashire, Yorkshire, Derbyshire, Staffordshire and Lincolnshire, then northern England furnished sixteen shire knights and nine of these (56 per cent) had served in France. The remaining counties had returned sixty-two knights and of these twenty-two (35 per cent) had served in France.[50]

No shire knight from the south-eastern counties of Norfolk, Suffolk, Hertfordshire or Surrey, or from the southern counties of Hampshire and Wiltshire (or from Gloucestershire) had served in France. But shire knights from Northumberland (Elmedon and Bertram), Derbyshire (Cockayne and Vernon) and Lincolnshire (Graa and Roos) had done so, as had Eure of Yorkshire, Skelton of Cumberland and Gresley of Staffordshire. Sir William Elmedon (Northumberland), the son-in-law of Sir Thomas Umfraville, fought at Agincourt and was later appointed custodian for life of the royal castle at Bamburgh. Sir John Bertram, a frequent commissioner for settling border disputes, had been keeper of the castle of Fronsac in the Bordelais. Sir William Eure had in effect been 'borrowed' by Yorkshire from Durham: his main estates were at Witton-le-Wear and he was much involved in the affairs of the palatinate and in military service on the border, but he had some Yorkshire land and had married a daughter of Henry, Lord Fitz Hugh of Ravensworth in Richmondshire (Henry V's chamberlain and sometime treasurer of England). He was in the retinue of Fitz Hugh – then sixty-three years of age – at Agincourt.

Northern England was now strongly represented at the centre, whether defined as the king and his court, the colonial enterprise in France, or England's still very small and very exclusive higher nobility. In 1307 there were only nine earls (and no dukes apart from the king who was duke of Aquitaine); none of them was a northerner. Ninety years later there were eighteen earls (and six dukes and one marquis, all connected with the king by blood or marriage). Four of the earls in 1397 were northerners. (Michael de la Pole, son of the Hull merchant-financier, had been made earl of Suffolk on the Scottish campaign of 1385 but had died in exile in 1389.) The northern earls were two Percies, a Neville, and a Scrope. All four were ennobled by Richard II. Henry Percy became earl of Northumberland, a 'coronation earl', in 1377, his brother Thomas became earl of Worcester in 1397 and at the same time William Scrope became earl of Wiltshire and Ralph Neville earl of Westmorland. All were sons of northern families which began their rise to eminence through military command in the northern wars and had built up great northern estates, but none of them was ennobled simply or even

principally because he was a potentate in the North. They were all deeply
involved in the centre and were rewarded for this involvement, and three
would die because of it: the earl of Wiltshire, executed as a traitor in
1399; the earl of Worcester, executed as a traitor in 1403; and the earl of
Northumberland, killed as a traitor in battle on Bramham moor in 1408.

Thomas Percy, earl of Worcester, who built a castle at Wressle near
Howden, less than 200 miles from London up the great north road, had a
long career of military involvement in France and Spain with Sir John
Chandos and John of Gaunt. He was for a time joint warden of the eastern
marches and constable of Roxburgh castle, but his service was principally
in the royal household and with Richard II in Ireland. William Scrope,
earl of Wiltshire, was likewise essentially a man of the centre, serving
in Gascony and as captain of Cherbourg and Brest, and later as
chamberlain in Ireland. Like Thomas Percy he gave loyal service to
Richard II against his enemies. Ralph Neville, earl of Westmorland, was
more circumscribed by the North: he saw military service in France in his
youth and was knighted there, but his important public service was in the
west march towards Scotland. But the Neville position in the North was
now of sufficient importance to give access to the centre in a different way:
Ralph Neville's second wife, whom he married in 1396, was Joan
Beaufort, cousin of Richard II and half-sister of the future King Henry
IV. This brilliant second marriage was a source of great power and
wealth, and the fourteen children in turn made in many cases brilliant
marriages, not, like the nine children of the first marriage into the northern
aristocracy, but into the higher nobility of England. In the course of a
century the Nevilles had risen from northern obscurity; the first Neville
earl was brother-in-law of the first Lancastrian king.

POWER, WEALTH AND MODERNITY IN THE
NORTHERN MARCH

The military emergency on the northern frontier after 1296 was a forcing
house of modernity: it promoted military organization based not on
tenure and homage but contracts and cash. Modernity was not entirely
unheralded in 1296, but it found a powerful expression in the entirely
voluntary indentured retinue which developed over the next fifty years,
first in the wars against Scotland, and reaching fruition in the wars against
France. 'The king required the services of the best fighting men,
irrespective of the amount or type of tenure of land they might possess.'[51]

Contract service brought rationality, flexibility and efficiency, avoiding the rigidities, dubieties and potential conflicts of the tenurial bond.[52] And the purely voluntary, contract captain of the new order *par excellence* was the warden of the march.

'Modernity' in fourteenth-century England was contracts, the 'use' and the last will: instruments of flexibility and choice, extending options far beyond and outside what was prescribed by tenurial obligation or the common law. Service contracts were certainly not new in 1296. They had developed over the previous century as estate management was professionalized and an army of lawyers and accountants was engaged as receivers, auditors, treasurers and bailiffs. They received contracts of service, and thus the needs of estate management produced 'a versatile instrument of social organization which could be used in many different circumstances'.[53] One circumstance in which it was particularly relevant was the new post-feudal structure of northern defence.

It is possible to exaggerate the modernity of Edward I: his military structures retained strong traditional features.[54] Nevertheless, his Scottish wars were powerful agents of change. Contracts and a system of ensuring the regular payment of troops engaged at the king's wages called for an efficient bureaucracy and an organization of mobile paymasters in the field.[55] The key institutions of warfare by 1307 were the exchequer, which handled the contracts and the wardrobe, which paid the king's wages. Both exchequer and wardrobe were based for long periods at York. Contractor-captains negotiated short-term contracts with the exchequer, but individuals serving in retinues might have life-contracts with captains for service in peace and in war. Contracts were not exclusive, however, although a man might bind himself to serve one lord 'above all others' within the terms of the agreement. Modernity was being forged in the crucible of war in the North.

The institution which represented modernity in northern frontier defence was the wardenship of the marches towards Scotland. It began in a simple, provisional and *ad hoc* manner in 1297 to meet the emergencies of border defence. Wardens were being appointed regularly after 1309, indentures were well established by 1319 and developed apace in the new phase of warfare which opened in 1327. In that year Sir Henry Percy obtained a contract for the general defence of the North for a period of three months at an inclusive fee of 1,000 marks (around £660). For this he was to recruit and pay 100 men-at-arms and 100 hobelars.[56] Sixty years later (1388) the contract of Sir Henry Percy (Hotspur) for the east march and Berwick castle alone, was to serve for three years for a fee of

£12,000 in war and £3,000 a year in peace. The warden could now decide how many troops he need employ. The size of the fee, the duration of the contract and the discretion allowed to the warden in the recruitment of troops are a measure of the extent to which the wardenship had increased in importance and power over a period of sixty years. It was now the most highly paid royal appointment in the land.[57]

The wardenships were created because of the manifest deficiencies of feudal border defence.[58] Their growing importance in the first half of the fourteenth century is easily explained in terms of the military needs of the North, but this is not a sufficient explanation of their end-of-century importance. Their growing power had given them relevance to the high politics of the centre, and they were further developed (and enriched) as a form of patronage and means of political manipulation with consequences far beyond the frontier province of the North. They are at the heart of revolution and counter-revolution in the crisis years 1388 to 1408: sources of wealth and power, they were centres of political intrigue and conflict at national as well as regional level. It was at the time of acute political crisis at the centre in 1388 that the wardenships became so highly paid. It was the gross mismanagement of wardenship appointments that helped to unite Percy and Neville against Richard II in 1399. Bolingbroke had promised the earl of Northumberland the wardenship of the west march two months before he became king, and once on the throne he lavishly rewarded Hotspur and his father for their treason by giving the former the east march and Berwick, and the latter the west march and Carlisle, all at the high rates of remuneration established in 1388: a combined annual fee for both marches of £18,000 in time of war and £4,500 in time of peace.[59]

In the early fourteenth century the warden of the march was in effect a 'super-sheriff' with enlarged powers of military command and array extending at times over three, four, five or even six counties, to cope with the exigencies of border defence. The institution developed into an elaborate military bureaucracy restricted to the border counties with wide-ranging judicial, administrative, military and diplomatic powers and responsibilities. One of the early fourteenth-century wardens was in fact a sheriff: Sir Andrew Harclay, sheriff of Cumberland and custodian of the castle at Carlisle. Ten days after his spectacular military victory at Boroughbridge on 16 March 1322 he was made captain and warden of the six northern counties 'for the purpose of repelling the Scots'. He was also created earl of Carlisle. Lancashire was included in his command and he made heavy demands on Lancashire knights to support his endeavours which unfortunately degenerated into treasonable dealings with the Scots. The earl-warden of exactly one year's standing was executed for treason on 3 March 1323.[60]

The wardenship became a complex structure of border administration and military command which was divided into east and west march wardenships in 1345 and a middle march wardenship in 1381. Before this date there were commonly three joint wardens, and sometimes, as in 1379, as many as six. Each warden appointed at least two deputy wardens, two warden-serjeants and lesser officials. The command of the castles at Berwick and Carlisle was closely linked with the wardenships, although the town of Berwick had its own separate warden with full powers of a warden of the march. He was usually of the same status as deputy wardens in the east and west marches: very substantial northern knights like Sir Arthur Lacy (1334–8), Sir Richard Talbot (1338–9) and Sir John Mowbray (1340–1), who would be one of the military commanders at Neville's Cross in 1346. The warden of Berwick town in the mid-century commanded 10 knights, 3 bannerets, 120 men-at-arms, 100 hobelars and 200 archers.[61] The militarized border of the fourteenth century provided well-paid and prestigious appointments for scores of knights and gentry of northern England, financed from central government funds.

The wardens had great power – in diplomacy, peacemaking and peacekeeping, as well as in raising troops and conducting war – and they exercised it in a region of extensive franchises, liberties and palatinates. Some historians have emphasized these regalities as restrictions on their power. The only way to control the regalities, it has been said, and raise their inhabitants for defence and war, was to make their lords wardens of the march.[62] And it is true that the Umfraville lords of Redesdale were frequently joint wardens down to 1381. But Percies and Nevilles were not lords of regalities, and in fact the wardens effectively exercised an overriding authority in military matters in all the franchises including the palatinate of Durham itself.[63]

The heyday of the wardenships of the marches towards Scotland lasted for a century, from 1388 when very favourable contracts were introduced (fees were significantly reduced in 1411), to 1489 when the earl of Northumberland was killed and Henry VII's son Arthur at the age of three was installed as warden-general of the march. There was now a deliberate downgrading and under-funding which reflected not only a change of dynasty but the underlying long-term decline of northern England. The border would remain a problem down to the 1560s and the years 1558 to 1566 saw heavy investment in Berwick's defences; but 'by the reign of Henry VIII the fees (of wardens) had sunk to a derisory level'[64] and no-one of consequence would take the job on.[65] It was now done by deputies like Robert Carey: impecunious courtiers on the make.[66]

For Percies and Nevilles in the fourteenth and fifteenth centuries, however, the wardenship of the march was the vehicle on which they rode to power and wealth. Percies and Nevilles were not the exclusive wardens of the march; but in the century after 1388 there were Percy wardens of the east march for eighty-one years, and Nevilles held the west march for a total of fifty-nine. But non-northerners of eminence, including royal dukes, now held appointments in the northern march. John of Gaunt was given overriding command of the marches in 1379, again for three years in 1381, and finally in 1398. Thomas Mowbray, earl of Nottingham, became warden of the east march in 1388; Edward duke of Albermarle warden of the west march in 1398. Henry IV's son, John of Lancaster, the future duke of Bedford and regent of France was appointed custodian of Berwick and warden of the east march in 1403 and held this difficult post (at a very difficult time) conscientiously for the next twelve years. The appointment of such men was partly to bring some central control to the northern marches, but on any count it was a tribute to their remarkable importance and power.

They were a source of great wealth, not only for magnates who were full wardens, but for the northern gentry and the northern county communities. The crown was chronically dilatory in the payment of fees; even the king's son, John of Lancaster, spent an inordinate amount of time and effort trying to get the money from London which was his due.[67] The arrears, perhaps as much as £20,000, owing to the earl of Northumberland in 1403 were part of the reason for his rebellion.[68] Nevertheless, the profitability of the militarized frontier to the nobility, the gentry and the general population of the border counties over a period of time was huge. Even non-payment by the crown had its advantages: the Percies built up their great northern estates in the early fourteenth century by taking land from the king from time to time in lieu of fees; they also received grants from the customs of Berwick-on-Tweed; and although receipts from the crown in respect of the east march over the period 1440 to 1457 were only £36,000 and should have been £53,000, a licence granted to the third earl of Northumberland to ship wool abroad would be more than ample recompense.[69] The profitability of the wardenship probably declined after 1453 but up to that time it was substantial.

When the fees were at their maximum, between 1388 and 1411, they amounted to a total for the east and west marches of £18,000 in time of war and £4,500 in time of truce. They would be spent very largely on the knights, esquires and archers serving in the wardens' contract retinues. This was an enormous financial underpinning of northern England's military aristocracy. Even as early as 1319, when the fees were relatively quite small, the 'keepers of the march of Northumberland' had 35 knights and 250 esquires in their pay.[70] This was at a time when the total number of knights in the whole of Lancashire was only thirteen, and the number of esquires fifty-one.

The disbursement of £18,000 (or even £4,500) in one year among the military families of the border counties should be seen against the poverty of the area. This was wealth flowing into counties which at the tax assessment of 1307 contained personal wealth amounting to £1,407 (£470 in Cumberland, £252 in Westmorland and £685 in Northumberland).[71] At the assessment of 1352, after years of Scottish devastation, the total for these three counties was only £772.[72] In Hampshire, by contrast, the value of personal property in 1307 was £750 and by 1352 had doubled to £1,340. In relation to the border counties' level of wealth, the end-of-century fees of wardens of the march — even when only partly paid and seriously in arrears — were remarkable.

The fees paid to the wardens of the march are a major though perhaps not a sufficient explanation of the wardens' power. Extensive landed estates and numerous tenants might help but were not crucial. It was certainly not the case, as some historians have suggested, that the great lords of northern England subsidized the wardenships by providing their own retinues at their own expense.[73] Sometimes, indeed, contracts were framed to preclude any such use of a warden's local resources: in 1386 new joint wardens of Berwick were appointed and required to recruit 160 men-at-arms and 320 archers of whom all but forty had to come from south of Richmond and Craven.[74] Thus the wardens would have as much difficulty in subsidizing the defences of Berwick as they would in using the funding of the crown to subsidize their own private retinues (although this undoubtedly occurred on a very considerable scale).

Richard Neville, earl of Salisbury, had neither estates nor tenants on any significant scale in Cumberland and Westmorland, where he exercised enormous power as warden of the west march for a total of thirty-five years between 1420 and 1460. His title and most of his lands came from his wife; his mother made him a grant for life of the lordships of Middleham and Penrith. The lands he held from his wife's inheritance provided an income of £1,240 a year; his income from the wardenship of the march was £1,250 a year. He retained twenty knights and esquires in northern England widely scattered between north Yorkshire and Northumberland. There was no particular geographical concentration and some of the men he retained were important, even formidable, in their own right. The fees they received were a small proportion of their income, their contracts were not exclusively with the earl, and mostly they were not for life. In short, their importance as a power base for the earl of Salisbury was not great. The point has been made that they were scattered throughout mainly Percy territory, but this was a source of weakness rather than strength. Sir Robert Ogle of Northumberland, a man of considerable stature, was retained for £20 a year, as was Sir Thomas Lumley of Durham. Sir John Middleton of Northumberland was retained for £6 13s. 4d., Ralph Rokeby of Rokeby for £4, Ralph Pollard of Durham for £1 6s. 8d. The only geographical cluster was seven gentry around Middleham.[75]

In Cumberland and Westmorland the earl of Salisbury in his castle at Penrith was an outsider among Cliffords and Dacres who had the land and the tenants. This was an irrelevance. The earl of Salisbury was one of the most powerful men in the north of England.[76] There were three reasons for this: he was a trusted and valued senior officer of the crown; his fee as warden (£1,250 a year) was equivalent to an income from a great landed estate, and he kept in close touch with the centre. He attended the king in France in 1431; he was on military service in France in 1436; in 1437 he became a member of the King's Council and was granted a salary of £100 a year.[77] Wealth was certainly not enough: the key to power in the North was wealth plus the right connections in the South.

The wardens of the march were fee-paid professionals who engaged other fee-paid professionals; their power was not based on tenurial but contractual obligations. They did not become wardens because they had great landed estates in the North; they gained great landed estates because they were wardens. They had risen as military captains of proven competence and established loyalty. They were highly paid office-holders of the crown presiding over one of the most complex military bureaucracies of the age (which never quite achieved effective overall co-ordination). They were the representatives of the post-feudal society: northern England at the leading edge of modernity.

BALANCE SHEET: PROFIT AND LOSS IN THE NORTH

Any balance sheet for northern England for the years of warfare on two fronts between 1296 and 1453 must show huge net gains. There was much material loss, but material profits, which were quite well distributed, were immense. But above all there was the heightened political importance of the northern province and a wide diffusion of power and wealth through the ranks of gentry and knights. These were the 'overmighty subjects' of northern England which in fact, for all the pervasive power of the Percies and the Nevilles and especially after 1399, was characterized by huge magnate-free zones.

The damage done by the Scots especially in the two decades after 1310 was extensive and grievous. Any resident in the border counties needed to be not only well-armed and courageous but sufficiently well off to pay repeatedly for the Scots to leave and for refuge inside some castle's walls. Those unable to meet these costs simply migrated either to Scotland or to England south of the Tees. There was also ransom money which the Scots probably received more often than they paid. Against these losses must be set the huge payments made to troops from central funds and the booming war economy of north-eastern coastal towns, especially Newcastle-upon-Tyne which ranked third in wealth among England's towns in 1334, inferior only to Bristol and York.[78] This was a remarkable improvement in its relative position: a century or so earlier it ranked thirteenth.[79] In 1326 it was made one of England's eight staple towns for managing the export of, and collecting the customs on, wool.

Over wide areas of northern England land values, rents, and the value of personal property (including livestock) were often halved between 1311 and 1329. Church lands at Northallerton, which in 1292 were valued at 1,467 shillings, were valued at 533 shillings in 1318. At Filey and Scarborough, however, values were unchanged: the east coast region had made a deal with the Scots.[80] In October 1320 the archbishop of York wrote to eight Augustinian houses asking them to take in the canons of Bolton priory because Scottish raids and a 'calamitous murrain of beasts' had made their own resources insufficient to support them.[81] In 1322 the monks of Bridlington shipped their valuables south of the Humber; in Knaresborough 140 out of 160 houses had been destroyed.[82] The county of Durham escaped serious damage because between 1311 and 1327 it made eight payments totalling £5,337 to the Scots. Northern England probably paid out a total of £20,000, and during these two decades 'the king of Scotland wielded more power in, and drew more revenue from, the north of England than did the English king.'[83]

It would be difficult to overstate the severity of the Scottish raids, although in the worst years between 1316 and 1319 bad weather, poor harvests and cattle disease deepened economic decline and distress, especially in Yorkshire. But the northern economy showed striking resilience, even in areas north of the Tyne where the sowing of corn might be prevented in four consecutive years.[84] The devastation probably made no significant contribution to the long-term economic decline of northern England which had undoubtedly begun by this time; the long-term decline in income from lay and monastic estates was due to reasons other than Scottish attacks.[85] The income from some of the archbishop of York's estates was halved between 1317 and 1318, but by the 1330s the archbishop was financing Edward III's Scottish wars on a significant scale.[86] The stimulus that war gave to the economy almost certainly outweighed the damage done by the Scots. Thus the northern counties were the principal market-place for providing replacements for horses lost in Scottish campaigns. In 1300 central government paid £2,000 for replacement horses; in 1327 it paid no less than £28,076.[87]

In fact enormous resources were poured into northern England in the century after 1296. The Neville's Cross campaign. which was only five days at the king's wages, cost only £307, all of which went to northern counties,[88] but the wages bill for the Scottish campaign of 1300 was £8,561 (£5,500 for archers and infantry), for the campaign of 1301 it was £15,746 (for infantry alone); and in 1327 it was £39,655.[89] Northern counties contributed between a quarter and a half of the national armies that fought in Scotland: in 1327 at least £10,000 would be received by soldiers from counties in which the total value of all personal property including cattle, horses, sheep, other livestock, tools, implements, stores of grain and the like was under £4,000.[90] In the enormous ninety-day summer campaign of 1335 – one of the most gigantic if unspectacular failures in England's war with Scotland – a vast army of possibly 15,000 was deployed, as big as the army in the Calais–Crécy campaign.[91] The five northern counties contributed half of the 5,000 mounted archers and foot-archers who were paid 6d. and 3d. a day respectively. Lancashire contributed 232 mounted archers and 618 foot-archers; their pay for ninety days would be £1,215. The total value of personal property in Lancashire at this time was some £377.

One historian has said that for the medieval peasant, serving in the king's army might be an alternative to starving in the village.[92] He has been sternly rebuked for saying so. These may not, indeed, have been alternatives: the attractions of war service were considerable for peasants who were far from starvation. But to claim that the expenses incurred by villages in sending men to war far outweighed any advantages[93] is to misconceive the sheer scale of these repeated military, operations and their aggregate returns. Even if wages were in arrears, only partly paid, or paid in some measure in kind, the repeated inflow of army wages amounting in total to over £1,000 into counties with personal property (including all livestock) worth altogether only two or three hundred, was on any reckoning an enormous net gain.

The wages that archers earned in either Scotland or France were not a negligible element in northern England's economy, but the really significant financial gains were made by gentry and knights. The pay agreed in their indentures was the least of it, 'but it must not therefore be regarded as trivial'.[94] The bonuses they received were generous, ransom money and loot even in Scotland could be very worthwhile even when superior officers had taken their share (usually a third), and the proceeds from colonial offices in Normandy or Gascony which military captains like Richard Scrope and William Bowes remitted home were 'sheer profit'.[95] This was an addition to the wealth not only of English knights but to the wealth of England.

The men who fought in France in the mercenary armies of Edward III and Henry V 'saw war as a speculative, but at best hugely profitable trade'.[96] Those who fought in Scotland had more pressing and down-to-earth problems of defence and survival in mind, but war in Scotland was a speculative enterprise, too, and from 1296 had strong colonialist objectives and overtones. The sheer magnitude of the ransoms after Homildon Hill in 1402 and the problem of sharing them were the cause of serious conflict between the earl of Northumberland and Henry IV.

The prospect of plunder and ransom money was written in to the call to arms for Scottish campaigns, and it was in the invasion of 1385 that the 'ordinance of Durham' laid down the 'rule of one third' for the distribution of spoils.[97] Some northern families were ruined, but for some the gains were enormous. The ransom of £66,000 for the Scottish king taken at Neville's Cross in 1346 did not go to Sir John Copeland, the northern knight who captured him, but to the king. Large ransoms for important prisoners of war went in the main to the crown, but Sir John received a pension of £500 a year, which compares well with upper gentry incomes from land at this time, and very well with the income that a knight would get for one year's service at the standard rate of 2*s*. a day: some £35.

War in Scotland and France was not *la carrière ouverte aux talents*: pikemen did not rise to become knights with landed estates. The rule of a third itself meant that a military captain did very well out of enterprising subordinates; rewards went disproportionately to those already well placed. Lesser gentry became greater gentry and esquires became knights.[98] But at this level rewards were widely spread.[99]

Lucrative posts in the colonial administration of Gascony went disproportionately to the Black Prince's Cheshire knights in the decades after the battle of Poitiers in 1356; posts in the colonial administration of Normandy went disproportionately to Derbyshire knights after Agincourt, in the years 1417 to 1450. Derbyshire knights were prominent at Agincourt: both father and son from the Cockayne, Longford, Gresley, Shirley and Vernon families were there, and Vernons, Gresleys and Blounts held important imperial posts in Normandy down to the 1440s. Richard Vernon became treasurer of Calais, Thomas Blount treasurer of Normandy and John Gresley lieutenant-general of Rouen.[100] And apart from the profits of war and proconsular office there were now handsome profits to be made in Normandy from dealing in land.[101]

Historians have fiercely debated the problem of overall profit and loss in fourteenth- and fifteenth-century wars. It is probably true that the enormous ransoms of the 1360s (three amounted to £268,000) 'like so many other war-time windfalls, washed over the economy of Britain without even wetting it'.[102] But what is at issue here is the gain by a region, the North, and by some individuals living in the North (even they are not necessarily precisely the same thing). Some northern gains arose through the redistribution of wealth within England: the payment of northern troops by the national exchequer is an obvious case. Sometimes individuals became rich through the redistribution of wealth in a region, as happened in Cheshire. In 1370 twenty-seven Cheshire gentlemen who had served in the Black Prince's retinues in France were in receipt of annuities totalling £1,500, an average of £55 each; good gentry incomes. But the £1,500 came from the revenues of Cheshire and Flintshire which in total amounted to £2,500.[103] The cost of the annuities was only a third of the revenues by 1374, but still an enormous burden on the palatinate's resources. The minor military aristocracy of Cheshire was prospering at Cheshire's expense.

But the broad picture in northern England is one of substantial net gain. The frontier province was awash with wealth and power. It was a land of highly independent gentry and knights whose military importance, responsible proconsular experience and increasing wealth bred a supreme and formidable self-confidence. They did not live in cosy county communities even when they had served in the same regiment in Scotland and France. They fought each other, and they challenged the power and pretensions of prince-bishops and palatine-earls. Their feuds were civil wars, fought principally over local administrative appointments, they were not class-based peasant risings against oppressive landlords but conflicts within the ruling class.

The military importance of Cheshire knights to the Black Prince – as well as their importance in consenting to extraordinary taxation – made it impossible for him to circumscribe their growing local power and outrageous abuse of local offices, although on two occasions, in 1353 and 1358, he visited Chester expressly to do so. It was precisely men like Adam Mottram and Sir James Andley, who had fought at Poitiers, who were leaders in extortion and corruption in the palatinate.[104] Richard II's favoured treatment of Cheshire and reliance on his indentured retinue of Cheshire archers put even more power into the ranks of the gentry. It was Cheshire knights with vast military and administrative experience in Scotland and France – Sir Thomas Talbot and Sir Nicholas Clifton – who took up arms in 1393 to resist the peace policy of great magnates, the dukes of Lancaster and Gloucester and the earl of Derby.[105] Talbot had been joint keeper of Berwick and keeper of the castle of Guisnes in the Calais march. War had given such men power and they were prepared to use it to safeguard the prospect of further lucrative service abroad.

The fourteenth-century wars consolidated the palatinate of Durham in its regalian powers, but as the liberties and franchises of the bishop increased, the power of knights in the palatinate advanced *pari passu*.[106] The balance was tipped somewhat in the favour of the latter in the course of the fourteenth century:

The balance between the bishop and his subjects was . . . disturbed after the 1290s by the flood of wealth which the Scots campaigns brought into the region: wealth expressed in terms of armed men. Thereafter the bishop was trying to control an area where nearly every landholder was a mercenary captain, allied to a national faction, and commanding a force trained and paid for by national wars. By 1300 it was hardly possible for the bishop to overawe his 'subjects' collectively; by 1400 he could not overawe many of them individually. Whereas Puiset in the twelfth century had dominated his bishopric in solitary splendour, Langley in the fifteenth was hardly *primus inter pares*.[107]

Antony Bek, the great bishop of Durham and close friend of the king, was obliged to concede a charter of liberties to the freemen of Durham in 1303. The pressure had been put on him by Sir John Marmaduke, a notable soldier, who organized resistance in Durham to repeated demands for fighting the Scots. But the men of Durham had been fighting with distinction, notably at Falkirk in 1298, for nearly four years when they refused their service and made their demands after the winter campaign of 1299–1300. The charge against Bek was that he was usurping the king's powers. Although a *magna carta* confirming civil liberties was agreed in July 1303, it represented a climb-down from the original demands which would have severely restricted the range of military service. This would not have been in the king's interest, and although Edward I listened sympathetically to Marmaduke's case and brought the bishop to account at Tynemouth in June 1303, the final result was a compromise which satisfied Marmaduke's honour but left the bishop's powers essentially intact.[108]

Sir Gilbert Middleton's Northumberland rising in 1317 was marked by even greater audacity. The central action was the abduction of the bishop-elect and two French cardinals as they travelled north for the new bishop's consecration. Sir Gilbert and a group of northern gentry abducted the episcopal party and imprisoned them in Mitford castle. This was at least in part a political protest against royal administration and policy in the North: there was widespread resentment against the keepers of Barnard castle and Bamburgh, against the king's inadequate response to the Scottish attacks, and against the king's appointing Lewis Beaumont, relative of the queen and brother of the constable of Norham, as bishop despite the fact that the monks of Durham had voted for a different candidate. Sir Gilbert was challenging the king and the charge against him was treason, for which he was in due course shipped to London and executed.[109]

Sir William Eure, like Sir John Marmaduke a century before him, pursued a more legalistic course in opposition to power in the North: for more than four years (1433–7) he pursued Bishop Langley relentlessly through the courts, challenging his exercise of regalian authority. An unscrupulous, resourceful and well connected man of considerable legal ability, he had seen military service in France and in the east march. Eure challenged the bishop's palatine rights before a royal commission at

Hartlepool in 1433 and before the king's bench. Like Marmaduke before him, however, he failed to make any serious impact on the bishop's powers.[110] It was still not in the king's interests that the power of the great northern bishopric should be significantly reduced.

The gentry of northern England in the fourteenth and fifteenth centuries was concerned about power in their regions and the appointments by which it was conferred. It was just such an issue – prestigious appointments – that lay behind Beckwith's protracted warfare between 1388 and 1393 against Sir Robert Rokeley, steward and constable of the Lancastrian castle at Knaresborough, and Henry Bellingham's sustained assault on Sir Henry Parr, Lord Clifford's sheriff in Westmorland, in the 1440s. The shrievalty of Westmorland was one of five throughout England that were not crown appointments but held in fee, and as such a focus of gentry hostility to magnate power. Bellingham appealed to chancery to have Parr removed from office (although this was not in fact in the chancellor's power), and, when this failed, plotted his murder in London when he was there attending Parliament as a shire knight for Westmorland. In Northumberland the Heron faction backed by Sir Robert Umfraville was in bitter conflict with the Manners faction backed by Sir Robert Ogle;[111] in Derbyshire the Longfords attacked Blount's manor house at Elvaston with a thousand men on 28 May 1454. Longfords and Blounts had served together in France with John of Gaunt and both families provided military administrators for Normandy after 1417. Longford now refused to accept letters from the King's Council and threatened to kill the king's messenger. Foljambes and Bradshaws had also been Gaunts' retainers; their factions were at prayer in Chesterfield church on New Year's Day 1434 when the Foljambes murdered William Bradshaw and Sir Henry Pierpoint. These were the families that provided the county's sheriffs, justices of the peace and members of Parliament; that is precisely why they murdered one another.

These were the men who were waiting for Bolingbroke at Ravenspur in July 1399. They were Watertons and Leventhorpes, estate officials of the duchy of Lancaster without even the dignity of knighthood, along with the foresters of Knaresborough chase. Robert Waterton was the constable of Pontefract castle, later chamberlain of the duchy; John Leventhorpe was the receiver-general. Their first move was to take Bolingbroke to Pickering castle, thence to Knaresborough, and finally to Pontefract. At Pontefract, according to the chronicler, 'a great force of well-born knights and esquires' had come quite independently out of Lancashire and Yorkshire to support him. The subsequent meeting at Doncaster with Henry Percy, earl of Northumberland, and above all Richard Neville, earl of Westmorland, was certainly important in confirming Bolingbroke's bid for the throne. But the lesser men assembled earlier at Ravenspur, waiting in the castles at Pickering and Knaresborough, congregating at Pontefract, were the true reflection of the rise of the North over the previous century. War in both Scotland and France had produced widely diffused wealth and power, sufficient to provide a successful launch for a usurper-king who was not himself very strongly identified with the North – he was better known in Danzig than in Northumberland.

The revolution of 1399 somewhat distanced the crown from the North: henceforth the dukes of Lancaster were duke-kings.[112] The link was not broken, however, and was by no means unimportant in securing advancement. It was after 1399 that Langley was plucked from obscurity in Lancashire to national and even international eminence and power. Preston, it is true, was now subordinated to a London-based bureaucracy, but the duchy was not simply incorporated into the kingdom. It retained its separate identity, administrative and financial arrangements. But 1399 was a defeat for Cheshire, which had been the pampered power base of the now deposed King Richard II, and both the 'Cheshire rising' of 1400 and Cheshire's involvement in Hotspur's insurrection in 1403 at the battle of Shrewsbury were a dethroned principality's protest against demotion.[113] Nevertheless, 1399 was a high point for northern England: not only for its earls, but for its self-confident, self-assertive and formidable gentry class. The seventeenth century would be London's century, but the fifteenth would be the century of the North.

7

To a Golden Age 1351–1485

England in the later Middle Ages was a country with a weak, disturbed, over-extended (and chronically underfunded) centre and powerful perimeters. The rise of the North was one aspect of this more general circumstance. Those sectors of the perimeter that had at various times experienced long exposure to outside attack had deep accumulations of power: the Welsh march, the northern march, and the 'barbican' constituting Normandy and Aquitaine. But the prepotent sector of England's perimeter by the early fifteenth century was the Calais march.

The fifteenth century was the century of the North, but it began disastrously with an over-ambitious assertion of northern power by the Percies (the earl and his son Hotspur) between 1403 and 1408, and it ended abruptly and catastrophically in 1485 on Bosworth field. The high points were the three and a half years between 1461 and 1464, when a young and inexperienced King Edward IV ruled nominally in the Midlands and the South while Richard Neville, earl of Warwick, at his established Yorkshire base, 'governed in the saddle from the periphery of the realm';[1] and the twelve years from 1471 to 1483, Edward's highly effective 'second reign', when his brother, Richard duke of Gloucester, based in north Yorkshire at Middleham and Sheriff Hutton, was not only the viceroy but the darling of the North.

Northern families that had risen in wealth and importance in the fourteenth century were deeply involved in the great affairs of fifteenth-century England. The position they had achieved secured for them offices, alliances, and above all advantageous marriages which consolidated their power. But after Archbishop Scrope's remarkable rebellion and still more remarkable execution in 1405, the great political initiatives did not come out of the North: they came out of the Welsh march. The key to power in fifteenth-century England was Ludlow rather than Alnwick, Middleham, or Berwick-upon-Tweed.

This is particularly true of the thirty-year civil war (1455–87) commonly known as the Wars of the Roses. They have often been interpreted as the outcome of Percy–Neville feuds which escalated until they involved virtually the entire ruling class: 'The Neville–Percy feud was the chief single factor which turned political rivalry into civil war.'[2] This is grossly to overstate the importance of northern England in general and of the Percies and the Nevilles in particular. The Wars of the Roses arose out of concern for effective kingship and central government; this concern was properly expressed by those whose pedigree and power gave them some authority to challenge and possibly replace inadequate kings and their advisers.[3] In northern England there were kingmakers; there were no kings-in-waiting. These also were to be found in the Welsh march. Northerners were important not as initiators but as allies. This was more than a minor importance: without their contribution and above all their private armies the wars which they did not initiate could not have been fought.

Kingmaking by Percies and Nevilles over a period of 170 years was certainly a manifestation of northern power. It occurred on eight occasions: in 1399, when Henry IV became king; in 1403 with an unsuccessful Percy rebellion in favour of the Mortimer earl of March; in 1461 for Edward IV; in 1470 and 1471 with Edward IV in exile, Henry VI briefly restored then Edward IV returned; in 1483 for Richard III with Percy support; 1485 for Henry VII; and 1569 with an unsuccessful rebellion in favour of Mary Stuart. But the initiative came from Percies or Nevilles only in the case of the two failures and the re-adeption of Henry VI in 1470; in the other instances Percies or Nevilles were involved only at a relatively late stage, when they gave or strategically withheld their support. Their calculated inaction could be of crucial importance, as in 1471 when Edward IV returned to his kingdom via Ravenspur in effect by courtesy of the earl of Northumberland; and in 1485 when the earl of Northumberland withheld support from Richard III at the battle of Bosworth. Even in the critical year 1461, however, when the Lancastrian dynasty fell and a Yorkist became king, it was not Neville initiative that put a new king on the throne: 'The consent and support of the Neville clan was necessary for Edward to assume the throne, but we have no good reason to assume that the initiative came rather from Warwick than from the confident young Edward himself.'[4]

There is an air of contrivance about the culmination of northern power in the years 1471 to 1485: it rested too heavily on the 'tidy-minded regional policy' of the Yorkist kings.[5] The perimeters had accumulated power; the Yorkist kings quite deliberately gave them more. The power of northern England in the early thirteenth century had been firmly rooted in a long period of economic growth (see chapter 5); in the fourteenth century in the crucial military function of a strategic frontier zone (see chapter 6); in the fifteenth century its importance was more contrived. The North was in relative economic decline; its magnates were still rich, but their opponents – especially those with a significant part of their income from the Welsh march – were richer still. But it was given enhanced significance through the devolutionary policies of the late medieval state. Richard duke of Gloucester was in the end the victim of this regional policy which as king he was unable to transcend. The North was victim, too, unable to survive the death of Richard, a change of dynasty, and the policy changes that ensued.

PERIMETERS AND POWER

There is nothing surprising about the tendency of perimeters to collect power. If they are highly vulnerable to outside attack and exposed to incursion for long periods of time, it would be remarkable if it were otherwise. Their importance in the defence of the realm guarantees them privileges, exemptions and subventions; they offer lands and careers to men of initiative and enterprise. Even when their own resources are meagre and their lands poor, they draw in the wealth needed for their task of defence, as in the northern march. If their lands are rich and they have a breathing space to develop them, their own wealth may be immense, as in the marches of Wales. By the fifteenth century England's perimeter was the home of very wealthy, well-connected, and interrelated families which could provide an entirely credible and even constitutionally legitimate alternative to the men at the centre, including the king. When the centre was manifestly inadequate – and it was demonstrably so by the 1450s, especially after the loss of England's empire in France – the perimeter moved in. This movement was the Wars of the Roses.

The personnel of the different sectors of the perimeter were now virtually interchangeable. And so we have the remarkable spectacle of a man with his family roots deep in the Welsh march, Richard of Gloucester, brother of the earl of March, chief steward and chamberlain of south Wales, as the embodiment of northern interests and power after

1471: an ersatz northerner, a substitute Neville, and from 1483 to 1485 England's first and only 'northerner' king.

England's exposed perimeters, including the south-east coast and the Cinque Ports (which now numbered eight), had gathered great power in the three centuries after the Norman conquest; in the following century (specifically between 1351 and 1483) they gathered even more. Defence was still highly important and justified an extension of the outer perimeter to include Calais (1347) and Normandy (1417), but there were three further reasons. First and most general was the growth of strong centrifugal influences in English society as feudalism declined and 'bastard feudalism' rose; second there was deliberate government policy of decentralization and devolution, taking pressure off central administration and resources, which culminated under Yorkist rule between 1461 and 1483, but had led to the creation of 'anachronistic' palatinates, and other decentralizing measures, in the previous century; and third there was tension and conflict in the centre itself (composed of London and the court) which promoted flight to the perimeter. The flight of Richard II took him principally to Chester, but also to Ireland and York.

Feudalism was centripetal, bastard feudalism was centrifugal. Feudalism placed the king in direct relationship with some 3,000 landholders throughout the kingdom, his tenants-in-chief. As England's sole landowner he had a claim on their services and estates which his officials, notably escheators and sheriffs, enforced. It was a fiscal at least as much as a military system;[6] but in any event it was a pervasive, centralizing device. The Tudors understood this perfectly well, which is why they revived it in the early sixteenth century.

Feudalism was in large measure (though never entirely) superseded by so-called bastard feudalism in the course of the fourteenth and fifteenth centuries. This is a pretentious and misleading term: feudalism was about fees, heritable parcels of land with fiscal and military obligations attached, but bastard feudalism had nothing whatsoever to do with holding land. It was simply paid employment, usually part-time, often but not necessarily in the form of service in private armies.

Tenurial obligations were replaced by contracts and cash. This weakened the power of the centre to an enormous extent. The tenurial relationship between the king and his landowners did not simply 'decay'; but was circumvented by legal inventions such as the 'use' and the 'entail' which in effect set up trusts, defined owners as life tenants and so relieved them of many of an owner's fiscal and other obligations. (Their estates escaped confiscation when they committed treason because they were not 'really' theirs.) This is what Sir John Fortescue (a former chief justice) principally complained about in the treatise he wrote in 1470 on *The Governance of England*: these legal stratagems weakened and impoverished the king *vis-à-vis* his great landowners.

Landowners no longer raised armies because their tenurial obligations to the crown required them to do so; they raised them because they wanted to and could pay for them. (For overseas and Scottish expeditions they raised them at the king's expense.) Magnates kept gentry on standby for military and menial estate duties for an annual fee, typically quite small, seldom more than £6 13s. 4d. These 'affinities' were in fact quite small, ramshackle retinues; the fee was usually only a small proportion of a gentleman's total income. Sir William Mountford, a member of the Beauchamp affinity in the early fifteenth century, received an unusually large fee of £26 13s. 4d. but his total income from all sources was £258.[7] Magnates were not tied tightly to the king; gentry were not tied tightly to magnates. The gentry who fought in the Wars of the Roses did not do so because they were constrained by the ties of bastard feudalism; 'they freely chose their part'.[8]

These weak, non-exclusive, flexible links suited a restlessly aspiring gentry class.[9] This was a 'loosely knit and shamelessly competitive society', marked by shifting loyalties, in which 'politics was a joint-stock enterprise'.[10] Bastard feudalism was the perfect recipe for a very loose confederation of regional magnates unconstrained by a powerful centre. To a far greater degree than the far-northern regalities, bastard feudalism stood outside and endangered royal authority.[11] It was entirely congruent with, and indeed promoted, a weak centre and powerful perimeters.

To deliberately create new palatinates at this time and in these circumstances looks like perversity. Yet that is precisely what happened. In addition to the ancient palatinates of Chester and Durham, the year 1351 saw the creation of the palatine county of Lancaster. The county palatine of Chester was elevated into a principality in 1397. Perhaps most remarkable of all, 1468 saw the creation of the Norfolk liberty with the full panoply of franchisal exclusions and privileges.[12] In 1483 Parliament approved a new palatine county of Cumberland–Westmorland and the derogation of the wardenship of the west march from royal into private hands in perpetuity. This, like the principality of Chester, was overtaken by events, but it was part of a continuing policy of decentralization and delegation which created a late medieval perimeter awash with privilege and power.

Historians have been united in regarding the Lancaster palatinate as an anachronism. Lancashire men at the time were united in regarding it as a grievous exclusion from royal justice. They frequently petitioned Parliament to change a system which placed them at the mercy of palatine courts.[13] The palatinate could certainly not be justified, like Durham, in terms of frontier defence. Edward III created the palatinate and duchy to honour his cousin, the distinguished soldier, Henry of Grosmont; it was a grant for life. But the king revived the full *jura regalia* for his son, John of Gaunt, in 1377. 'The concession made in 1351, equally with that made in 1377, was politically indefensible.'[14]

The palatinate, it has been said, was 'useless', and historians have been quite clear about 'the unwisdom of creating this subordinate regality'.[15] 'The charter of 1377 was an act of retrogression.'[16] Late-Victorian English historians always regarded as retrograde any measure that did not lead to the triumph of the highly centralized late-Victorian state. In the long run it is true its special status isolated Lancashire (and Derbyshire) from the mainstream of English life, but for a century its royal connections, even after 1399, involved this poor, remote region in the great affairs of the day and secured for men of the palatinate distinguished careers on an international stage. And it relieved central government of some of its financial burden and exploding administrative responsibilities as the empire expanded apace overseas.

The devolved principality of Aquitaine between 1363 and 1371 is part of this picture. It was in just these terms of an over-extended centre that Edward III devolved Aquitaine on to another son, the Black Prince, in July 1363. This ancient Angevin inheritance had been held since 1154 by king-dukes. The charter of 1363 said in its preamble that the king was unable to be directly involved in the affairs of all his lands and his eldest son should help.[17] The reasons were certainly more complicated than that: this elevation of the duchy to a principality in the hands of the Black Prince enlarged its independence, a necessary price for Gascon military service (which in any event was never to be used against the king of France).

But Aquitaine was being off-loaded from the centre not only as the administrative responsibility but as the source of income of the Black Prince. The principality was to be financially self-sufficient. This was a serious and rather puzzling, miscalculation. The net cost of Aquitaine in the middle of the fourteenth century was usually about £3,000 a year. The revenues raised in Gascony, principally the duties on wine at Bordeaux, never covered the pay of the three chief (English) officials: the seneschal, the controller, and the constable of Bordeaux, who cost about £750 a year.

The annual net cost would rise to around £6,000 a year in the early fifteenth century. Gascony was referred to in Parliament as the 'barbican and defence of England' when this expense had to be justified.[18]

The new prince was appointed for life; in the event he ruled Gascony for eight years (but lived for five years after that). When he took up his appointment he was granted £15,004 19s. 4d. 'for going towards the parts of Gascony'. The constable of Bordeaux received £9,350 for the prince's retinue. This total sum of £24,000 would run out in eight years if net costs remained at about £3,000 a year, and no money was sent from England to Bordeaux, and that is exactly what happened (no money was sent). In 1371 Edward of Woodstock came home. He handed back his principality to the crown explicitly because he could not afford it.

The problems of the centre contributed to the extensive build up of power on the perimeter. The centre was London plus the king and his court. London was immensely powerful in its constituent parts: the mob had great political power; the small elite of freemen even more; the twenty-five aldermen were almost omnipotent. London's political and above all financial power would be used in the interest of the first Yorkist king, Edward IV, who benefited hugely from popular backing and especially the financial support which was 'vital to the regime'.[19] But London was a serious problem for Edward III, his son John of Gaunt, and above all his grandson, Richard II. This largely accounts for the massive injection of power into the perimeter at Chester in the closing years of the fourteenth century.

The crisis year for Richard II in his dealings with London was 1392. In May he removed the Court of Common Pleas, the chancery, the exchequer and the inmates of the Fleet prison to York so that London would suffer from this absence of the machinery of government. In June he summoned the mayor, sheriffs, aldermen and twenty-four leading London citizens to Nottingham to account for their administration, removed the mayor and the sheriffs from office and sent them to prison.[20] There were rumours that Richard might make his capital at Chester or York. By 1397 he had elevated the Chester palatinate to a principality and by 1398 had established his exclusive, highly paid corps of Cheshire archers. It had a permanent establishment of ten knights, ninety-seven esquires and 300 archers; it cost £5,140 a year.[21] This was even more than the fees paid for the maintenance of the northern march at this time in periods of truce. In fact it was a comparable power complex, but with the king as warden of the march.

There was only one sector of England's perimeter that was more remarkable in its resources, power (and cost): Calais and the Calais march. Conquered in 1347 it had become a formidable complex of military and financial power: a small portion of England overseas. Incorporated into the English crown with absolute sovereignty, ecclesiastically part of the diocese of Canterbury, it was the home of the immensely rich company of the staple and a thousand-strong garrison based on five castles in the English march: the largest body of professional soldiers in the pay of the English crown.[22] The captain of Calais was a man with enormous responsibility and power. (Henry of Monmouth, the future Henry V, held the captaincy for three years between 1410 and 1413.) It cost at least £19,000 a year in time of war, £12,000 in time of peace. The town contributed around £3,500 but the balance came from the English exchequer – or when this failed, from loans made by the company of the staple.[23] Men, money and victuals were poured into English garrisons from Calais to Cherbourg, Brest and Bordeaux and as far south as Bayonne, but into none on a greater scale than Calais.

Two sectors of the strategic perimeter placed little or no financial burden on the centre: Normandy (at least before 1424) and the Welsh march. Normandy after its conquest in 1417 had an army of occupation of some 12,000 men and so was at least ten times as expensive as Aquitaine, but a remarkably successful effort was made to make Normandy pay for itself. Norman and French administrative machinery and methods of taxation were taken over and operated very effectively at least during the lifetime of Henry V; and when the duke of Bedford was ruler of Normandy thereafter his financial problems were infinitely less than during his twelve harrowing years as captain of Berwick and warden of the east march.[24] Taxes raised in Normandy amounted to £24,000 in 1420, but although they rose to £84,000 by 1424, they were now being outstripped by rising expenses. Verneuil was a military high point, but it marked the beginning of financial collapse.[25]

Only the Welsh march remained outrageously rich and placed no financial burden on the English crown; on the other hand it provided no alleviation either because the lands of the lords marcher were untaxed. They had grown enormously in wealth as they developed their estates in the relative peace (for Wales) of the fourteenth century. Their numbers had diminished from twenty-five at the beginning of the century to fifteen by the end and individual estates had grown correspondingly. Estate development had been ruthless and highly successful. Mortimers, Fitzalans and Bohuns as well as the house of Lancaster drew large profits which were generally transferred to their English accounts. In December

1387 eleven archers accompanied the treasure-carts which carried bullion worth £1,400 to London from the Mortimers' Wigmore estates. Some 70 per cent of the Mortimer income of £3,400 in 1398 came from their marcher lands.[26] This was the land of the major players in English politics: in 1307 seven of England's ten earls were Welsh marcher lords.[27] The first duke of Lancaster drew the largest slice of his income (about 15 per cent) from his Welsh estates;[28] ten of the duchy of Lancaster's thirty castles were in the Welsh march (four were in Lancashire).[29]

By the early fifteenth century England's outer perimeter was a threat to the centre because of both its cost and its array of rich and powerful men. The centre derived power from the perimeter principally through the patronage involved in making appointments to a vast range of imperial posts. But the perimeter's estimated cost in 1411 was £41,000 out of a national budget of £64,000: 75 per cent. The estimated cost of Calais was £22,500, of the Scottish march £8,700, of Aquitaine (including the castle at Frounsak) £8,200, and Ireland, now a rising cost, £2,666. In the 1421 budget perimeter costs were 60 per cent of the total budget, in 1433 only 40 per cent, but this was because the expenditure on the Scottish and Calais marches had been estimated as for times of peace.[30] It was in this sheer financial weight that the perimeter finally placed a burden on the centre that it could not possibly bear, and the overseas empire collapsed.

Calais remained, however, and in the nine months between June 1460 to March 1461 the crowded events and high drama which changed the dynasty were played out between three key points on the perimeter: Calais, Ludlow and Pontefract. In June a Neville moved in to secure London, not from the wardenship of the west march with northern backing, but from the captaincy of Calais with the backing and gratitude of the men of Kent. In October the duke of York moved in from Ireland to claim the throne but was accepted only as 'protector'. In December he was in south Yorkshire to repel Pontefract-based attacks on his estates and was killed at the battle of Wakefield. In March his son the earl of March moved in from Ludlow, was acclaimed king in London, went north to reverse the Yorkist defeat at Wakefield and did so convincingly at Towton near Tadcaster. These movements and events on England's strategic perimeter saw the end of the Lancastrian dynasty and the establishment of a Yorkist king.

NORTHERN ASPECTS OF THE CIVIL WAR 1455–87

In the seventeenth-century civil war England's inner core, London and East Anglia, challenged and deposed the king and his ministers; in the fifteenth-century civil war England's perimeter challenged and deposed kings and their ministers. In the seventeenth century wealth, power, and cosmopolitan experience and ideas were concentrated in London and East Anglia; in the fifteenth century they were much more heavily concentrated in strategic sectors of the perimeter. Both civil wars were conflicts within England's ruling class, both arose out of deepening disquiet with the quality and adequacy of kings, but the geography was different. Cromwell came in from Huntingdon; Richard duke of York and his son Edward came in from the Welsh march.

The fifteenth-century civil war was not a centre–perimeter conflict because a strong centre was trying to rein in an independent perimeter – like the civil war in the reign of King John and some of the provincial risings under the Tudors. On the contrary, it was because the centre was exceptionally weak. Kings, especially Henry VI, were weak; but so was kingship. This weakness was a cause for concern among men who had some weight and responsibility in the conduct of the nation's affairs. Such men were disproportionately those with lands or offices in the Welsh, northern or Calais march. These reasons are simple but perfectly adequate (we have been properly warned against temptations to profundity in explaining the Wars of the Roses).[31]

The problem was not settled when Henry VI was finally deposed. Three kings were crowned and ruled in the fifteenth century after him: Edward IV (1461–83); Richard III (1483–5); and Henry VII after 1485. Their adequacy too was initially suspect and challenged. This was the basis of recurrent war. The final challenge came at Stoke in Nottinghamshire in June 1487: the alternative (Yorkist) government presenting itself was effectively defeated in battle. This was the end of the Wars of the Roses. It was also the end of northern pre-eminence. Henry VII spent the summer on a royal progress in the North from Pontefract to York, Durham and Newcastle. It was not really necessary: the North, and notably York, had given no support to this Yorkist challenge to Henry Tudor. But Henry still felt it worthwhile to make his point.

There has been little agreement among historians about the geographical basis, if any, of the Wars of the Roses. McFarlane said geography was irrelevant: 'These were neither wars between north and south nor between lowland south-east and the dark corners of the north and west. The sides had no frontiers to defend.'[32] Trevelyan located the sources of the troubles on the northern and Welsh frontiers where 'Mortimer in Wigmore and Percy in Alnwick lived constantly under arms' but gave particular importance to the Welsh march: 'the Wars of the Roses were to a large extent a quarrel between Welsh Marcher lords, who were also great English nobles, closely related to the English throne.'[33] Others have seen northern feuds as the key issue, especially conflicts between the Percies and the Nevilles, escalating into national conflict. Although they were not the sole cause of the civil wars, it is said, they had far-reaching consequences.[34]

Certainly the nobility quarrelled over land and appointments in the North but not, at least on anything like the same scale, in the Welsh march. Four great men had interests which converged in south Yorkshire and might well lead to conflict under a weak king: the earl of Northumberland; Richard Neville, earl of Warwick; Richard, duke of York, and the king himself as duke of Lancaster. There were indeed bitter conflicts in south Yorkshire like the 'battle of Heworth moor' on 24 August 1453, when a contingent of Percy supporters (including numerous merchants from an economically depressed York) led by Lord Egremont, ambushed a Neville wedding party returning from Lincolnshire to Sheriff Hutton a few miles outside York. This has been seen as a prelude to the Wars of the Roses.[35] But these rivalries and conflicts in the North were scarcely a cause of these wars: they really decided which side northern families would take. Whatever side the Nevilles were on, Percies would be on the other.

In the early years of the fifteenth century it would have seemed likely that any challenge to the house of Lancaster would have Percy support. The rebellion of 1403 (which led to Hotspur's death at Shrewsbury and, five miserably fugitive years later, to the earl of Northumberland's death in battle as Bramham moor, near Tadcaster) arose out of Percy disenchantment with the Lancastrian king they had helped to put on the throne in 1399. The penalties the Percies suffered because of their rebellion significantly weakened their power. 'The Percies never again dominated national politics as they had done between 1399 and 1403.'[36]

The Percies would still be a family of consequence, especially after the downfall of the Neville earl of Warwick (the 'Kingmaker') and his death in battle at Barnet in 1471, but the Nevilles had, overall, greater fifteenth-century importance, wealth and power. Two kings were Nevilles on their mother's side: Edward IV and Richard III (their father,

Richard duke of York, had married Cecily, daughter of Ralph Neville, earl of Westmorland). Edward became king in 1461 with active Neville support; Richard, who had himself married a Neville, became king in 1483 from his Neville power base in the North.

The Nevilles had become much richer than the Percies. They were no longer simply landowners and military leaders in the North. Two brilliant marriages had greatly advanced their fortunes: Richard Neville's marriage to the Salisbury heiress, and his son Richard's to the Beauchamp heiress. But for the wealth from these two highly advantageous marriages (and the first made possible the second), the Kingmaker would have been merely Sir Richard Neville, a substantial north country knight. His income was twice as big as the Percy earl of Northumberland's, however, and rivalled the duke of York's. The richest man in England around the middle of the fifteenth century was the duke of York with over £6,000 a year; the Beauchamp estates which came to Richard Neville through his wife in 1449 produced a landed income of around £5,500; but the earl of Northumberland's income – given as only £1,210 in the income tax assessment of 1436 – was in total probably only around £2,800.[37]

It was not as a northern landowner or warden of the northern march that Richard Neville supported the successful Yorkist bid for the throne (1460–1), but as captain of Calais. He had behind him the immense resources of the Calais military establishment as well as the support of south-east England whose interests his naval forces had protected. Indeed, he had become strongly identified with southern interests. The Percies remained much more completely a family of the North.

There were, in fact, two periods when the Wars of the Roses took on a strong north versus south complexion, although this was not their essential nature: the first was in the events surrounding the usurpation of 1461; the second the usurpation of 1483. The first took on the character of a London-based attack on the North; the second a Yorkshire-based attack on the South.

The castle at Sandal near Wakefield was the administrative centre of the duke of York's Yorkshire estates (they contributed roughly 10 per cent of his total income which came preponderantly from the Welsh march). His estate officials were being harrassed in the summer of 1460 by Lancastrians in nearby Pontefract. On 9 December the duke went north; on 30 December he was killed in a battle with Lancastrians at Wakefield. The duke was now 'protector' and on 8 November had been proclaimed heir-apparent. His arrival in south Yorkshire was not simply that of a landowner dealing with the problems of his estates: he represented royal authority and the South. When his severed head was placed on the walls of York it was adorned with a paper crown. Like Archbishop Scrope's rising in 1405, the attack on the duke of York at Wakefield was resistance to over-intrusive royal authority in the North.

The duke's son Edward now seized the throne in some measure at least as saviour of the South, and for the next decade, for all his Neville connections, was strongly identified with London (where he found powerful popular and financial support) and the South. After Wakefield northerners marched south and pillaged as they went, Edward earl of March came in to stop their advance and take the throne. It was as the 'Rose of Rouen' defending the South against barbarous northerners that he was celebrated in ballads of the time. The lords of the North would have destroyed the south country and 'Had not the Rose of Rouen been, all England had been shent.' He stopped them at St Albans, was acclaimed king by Londoners and decided he must deal with continuing Lancastrian opposition in the North. Before setting out on his northern expedition in March he addressed thirty-three loyalist counties through their sheriffs as their new king: all were south of the Trent with the curious exception of Northumberland.

Edward's army was drawn from London, Kent, East Anglia, the Midlands and the Welsh march. He met the Lancastrian forces at Towton near Tadcaster, an important Percy estate, on 29 March 1461. His overwhelming victory was a major military disaster for the north of England: the slaughter was immense and the earl of Northumberland and Lord Dacre of Gilsland were killed. It was also politically decisive;[38] but northern resistance continued for three years and three castles, Alnwick, Bamburgh and Dunstanburgh had to be overcome not once but on three occasions: in September 1461, July 1462 and January 1463.[39] This was quite remarkable persistence in circumstances which were now clearly without hope.

Edward was generous in his treatment of the Lancastrians in the North, but they had not forgiven him ten years after Towton. In March 1471 he was returning from exile by way of Ravenspur (his preferred point of entry had been Cromer) when he met with a reception in east Yorkshire very different from Bolingbroke's in 1399. The contemporary narrative, the *Arrivall of Edward IV* said that 'the people were sore induced to be contrary to him, and not to receive, ne accept him, as for their king.' They would take their cue from the earl of Northumberland; but Edward had come to terms with the earl a year before and now the earl 'sat still'. This was the most that Edward could expect, but the earl's inaction 'did the king right good and notable service'. He came through this hostile territory unscathed, reached London and defeated and killed Richard Neville, earl of Warwick, at the battle of Barnet. This was a triumph for the Percies and for the north of England, which now entered into its golden age.

The next usurpation, in 1483, was again played out as a conflict between the North and the South. In 1461 Edward earl of March had come in from Ludlow to claim the throne; his heir, the twelve-year-old Prince Edward, was at Ludlow when he died on 9 April 1483; his brother Richard was at his base at Middleham in Richmondshire. By 29 April Richard had moved south to Northampton to intercept Prince Edward on his way to London and did so at Stony Stratford in Buckinghamshire. These movements from the perimeter, converging on London, were again the prelude to a seizure of the throne, and as in 1460–1 they took on a strong north versus south complexion. Whereas Edward IV in 1461 established himself as king through a southern, London-based assault on the North, however, Richard in 1483 established himself through a northern, Yorkshire-based assault on the South.

Richard obtained the throne with the backing of northern arms. He arrested the boy-king Edward V, his uncle Earl Rivers and half-brother Richard Grey on 30 April. Rivers and Grey were dispatched to Sheriff Hutton and Middleham respectively; both were beheaded at Pontefract on 25 June. Meanwhile Richard had summoned troops from York, and it was the threat of this northern army that made possible his peaceful usurpation of the throne on 26 June and his coronation on 6 July. In the background was the earl of Northumberland whose implicit support was crucial for Richard's success.[40]

His reign was seen in the South as a 'tyranny' by the North. It was indeed a period of aggressive northern colonialism. A 'plantation' of northern gentry occupied key posts, as sheriffs, custodians of castles and on commissions of peace throughout the South but especially in the South-west. After rebellion in the South and the act of attainder by which rebels' lands were forfeited, the invasion of northerners became a flood. A further forty northerners at this point received lands, offices and annuities from confiscated estates. The gains of northerners were comparable to what they might have got sixty years earlier in Normandy. Thus John, Lord Scrope of Castle Bolton in Wensleydale became constable of the castles at Barnstaple and Exeter and received estates in Cornwall, Devon and Somerset worth £200 a year.[41]

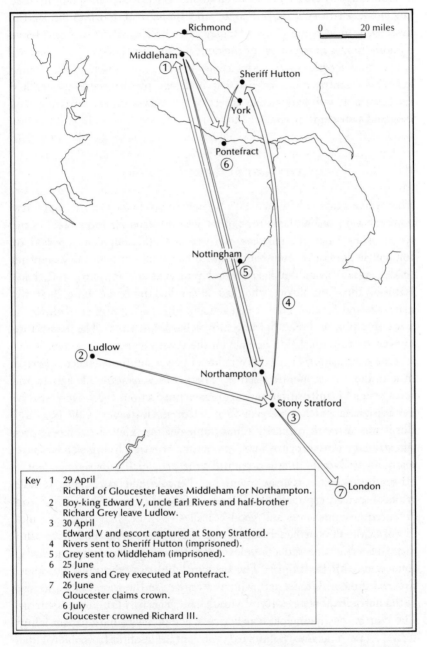

Key 1 29 April
        Richard of Gloucester leaves Middleham for Northampton.
     2 Boy-king Edward V, uncle Earl Rivers and half-brother
        Richard Grey leave Ludlow.
     3 30 April
        Edward V and escort captured at Stony Stratford.
     4 Rivers sent to Sheriff Hutton (imprisoned).
     5 Grey sent to Middleham (imprisoned).
     6 25 June
        Rivers and Grey executed at Pontefract.
     7 26 June
        Gloucester claims crown.
        6 July
        Gloucester crowned Richard III.

MAP 7.1   Centre and perimeter: the usurpation of 1483 (29 April to 6 July)
Source: author

Ironically, Richard III was defeated at Bosworth principally because key northerners – notably Stanley and the earl of Northumberland – deserted him. Thomas, Lord Stanley placed Richard's crown on Henry Tudor's head and received an earldom for his treachery.

But the north–south dimension should not obscure the wider perimeter–centre relationships that underlay the late fifteenth-century civil wars. It was simply one aspect of the late-medieval importance of England's strategic perimeter.

THE GOLDEN AGE 1471–85

The twelve years of Edward IV's 'second reign' from 1471 to 1483 saw northern England near the peak of its political standing and power; in the reign of Richard III its peak was reached as it enjoyed a period of colonialist dominion over the South. The years 1471 to 1485 were its golden age. It was not harried and punished for supporting Richard Neville, the Kingmaker who had quarrelled with the king over his marriage and foreign policy, had actually imprisoned him at Middleham castle in 1469, and died fighting him at Barnet in 1471. The North rose to even more remarkable heights on the great northerner's grave.

This culmination of northern political power and importance occurred in a context of economic decline. There was a nation-wide fall in the acreage under cultivation and aggregate production; there were special circumstances which made economic decline even steeper in the North.[42] But it was an extraordinarily comfortable decline. Deflationary pressures and stable or falling prices made this a time of rising living standards for many in the North. It was a painful time principally for the mercantile classes in ancient corporate towns like Lincoln and York. The middle ranks of society, especially small landowners and peasant farmers, were in favoured circumstances and good heart.

Politically the north of England after 1471 was a loose confederation of magnates which enjoyed a high level of autonomy while remaining closely connected with the centre. The principal link was the king's brother, Richard duke of Gloucester, who was warden of the west march, keeper of the northern forests, lord of Middleham, Sheriff Hutton and Penrith. The North was a principal beneficiary of the policy of regionalism which Edward IV vigorously pursued less out of political necessity than deliberate choice.[43]

For England this was a time of political stability and internal peace; for the North it was a time, especially between 1480 and 1483, of sharply resurgent war with the Scots when Berwick was once again recaptured and Edinburgh occupied. This was also entirely to northern England's advantage: it enabled Richard of Gloucester finally to confirm himself as a true northerner in overall military command as the king's lieutenant in the North, and reaffirmed the importance of northern England in its historic role of frontier defence.

Richard of Gloucester was a power in the North for three main reasons: he was an adoptive Neville; he was the king's representative in military affairs; and he held a vast array of key offices throughout the North. In typical fifteenth-century fashion he was not powerful principally through land and tenants but offices and men. Above all he was a royal creation and had access to the king.

His mother was the 'Rose of Raby' who had in fact left Raby at a tender age. Richard spent his boyhood with her at Ludlow, but at the age of thirteen, in 1465, was in the care of his cousin, Richard Neville, earl of Warwick, at Middleham castle in north Yorkshire. In 1472 he revived and reinforced his Neville connection by marrying the Kingmaker's daughter, Anne. As a substitute-Neville he had a ready-made following in the North.[44]

He was indeed lord of the North, but he was not the principal landowner in any of the six northern shires. He had no land at all in Northumberland and Westmorland, very little in Durham, and even in Yorkshire and Cumberland he had only a relatively small part of the land. In Cumberland he took second place as landowner to the earl of Northumberland; in Durham he was wholly overshadowed by the bishop, the prior and the earl of Westmorland; in Yorkshire he had significantly less land than the duke of Lancaster (the king, his brother) and the archbishop of York.[45] But he held a formidable number of important offices throughout the North.

He had been warden of the west march, and in receipt of its substantial salary, since 1470. He now became keeper of the northern forests, chief steward of the duchy of Lancaster in the northern parts, sheriff of Cumberland for life, justice of peace in all the northern counties, and military commander-in-chief against the Scots. His lordships and castles were Middleham, Sheriff Hutton, Sandal, Penrith, Skipton-in-Craven, Richmond, Helmsley and Barnard. He had scores of jobs to dispose of as custodians, keepers, bailiffs, foresters and their deputies and lieutenants. The ambitious northern gentry, and especially the numerous 'small gentlemen' of Richmondshire, were hungry not for land but for jobs. The myriad of prestigious regional appointments at his disposal was the basis of Richard's power. His control of the historic twin poles of Yorkshire is of particular importance. His power was not only at the north pole in Richmondshire; as chief steward of the duchy of Lancaster north of the Trent he was in control of Pontefract, too.

The commanding heights of power in the six northern counties were shared informally among the duke of Gloucester, the earl of Northumberland and the Stanleys of Lancashire. Regional power in the North was in effect a condominium. It was never an easy relationship between the three principal partners. Richard of Gloucester's alliance with the Stanleys was a particularly difficult one, although the Stanleys were not of the stature of the Percies; in their feud with the powerful Harringtons of Lancashire their ascendancy was by no means automatic and assured. Richard of Gloucester had close connections with the Harringtons and at times supported them in their conflicts over offices and estates, but he was withdrawn from the Lancashire lordships of Halton and Clitheroe by Edward IV who seems to have decided, however reluctantly, that in Lancashire the power of the Stanleys must prevail.[46]

The earl of Northumberland was the third component of this tripartite system; his support was essential to ensure Gloucester's dominance in the North.[47] He was particularly independent in the county of Northumberland, and although they shared power in parts of Yorkshire, Percy had an unchallenged supremacy in the East Riding. But their relationship was formalized in an indenture drawn up in 1474 which gave Gloucester a decisive edge over Percy in the politics of the North. Gloucester promised not to lay claim to any grants that the earl received from the king, but the earl promised to be Gloucester's faithful servant, and in effect the Percy retinue became a component of the ducal affinity, and Northumberland's men became Gloucester's men at one remove.[48] Latent conflicts remained, but for the next decade the relationship worked well and 'Whether singly or in collaboration, the duke and the earl and their private councils had come to wield a quasi-royal authority in the north.'[49]

The regionalism of Edward IV was highly personal – this was its crucial long-term weakness – but it worked and produced a striking stability towards the end of a turbulent century. The continuator of the Croyland chronicle paid tribute to the effectiveness of the king's regional lieutenants in upholding peace and claimed that Edward had close personal relations with them.[50] Wales and the marches, the Midlands and the South-west as well as the North, were regions effectively controlled by magnates, some recently of only gentry status, now advanced to regional prominence. But in East Anglia it was no upstart who had supreme power: in 1468 Edward IV granted a private franchise to John, the third Mowbray duke of Norfolk, whose 'liberty' extending over some 600 square miles admitted no royal officials and 'being outside the normal bounds of royal justice and administration was an *imperium in imperio*'.[51]

The most spectacular of the late-medieval regalities, however, was the north-west palatinate authorized by Parliament for Richard of Gloucester in 1483: an hereditary palatine lordship embracing the counties of Cumberland and Westmorland and any parts of south-west Scotland that might afterwards be conquered. He was to enjoy the same high immunities as the bishop of Durham. More even than the bishop of Durham, the lord of this new palatinate was to be hereditary warden of the west march, and thus a major military command under the crown passed out of direct royal control and became an hereditary possession in private hands.[52] Here was an over-mighty subject on a truly majestic scale, created at the king's command.

This summit of northern political independence and power was reached against a background of economic decline in England in general and in the North in particular. Indeed, there was a deep agricultural recession throughout Europe which arose essentially from population decline. 'That the total national income and wealth (of England) was declining is shown by almost every statistical index available to historians.'[53] Land went out of cultivation, rents and land values fell. The great landowners were particularly hard hit. ·

And yet this was a time of high prosperity for most people in England, including those in the North. The economy was another dimension of the North's 'golden age'. This adds to the sense of unreality and contrivance in the final phase of northern power and importance which reached its peak in Yorkist England. It was highly precarious, both in its political construction and its long term economic base. Its fragility would be cruelly exposed when government policies changed and population began to rise.

Amidst all the signs of economic contraction the standard of living rose as food and commodity prices fell or remained static for long periods, and (with labour shortages) wages tended to rise. The quarter of a century between 1451 and 1475 has been identified as a period of marked price stability; it also turns out 'to have been a time of exceptional prosperity'.[54] The standard of living of a skilled craftsman (mason or carpenter) had doubled in the two centuries since Edward I became king. It would never reach the same level again, after falling to its lowest point in the age of Shakespeare, for another four centuries, until 1880.

The economic predicament of the great landed estates was not in fact cataclysmic. There was considerable cushioning by the deflationary tendencies of the age. Four fifteenth-century estates have been closely studied: Durham priory, Bolton priory, the estates of the earl of Northumberland and those of the duke of York. The evidence of decline on the Durham priory estates is particularly elusive, and although there were problems of undoubted severity in the early fifteenth century the priory showed remarkable resilience and 'the regional economy of this area in the later middle ages remains profoundly mysterious'.[55] At Bolton priory in Wharfedale rents remained fairly static and the evidence is of stagnation rather than catastrophe.[56] On the duke of York's estates, which were extensive in Suffolk, the South-west, the Welsh borders and Yorkshire, there was evidence of declining land values between 1411 and 1460 only in Suffolk, but even here 'a financial crisis does not seem to have been imminent'.[57] The duke of York's economic problems were not apparently of great severity: 'Poverty was not the spur which drove Richard of York to opposition and rebellion.'[58]

The earl of Northumberland's estates showed more serious problems. Between 1416 and 1470 the revenues of the Cumberland estates declined by at least a quarter, and those of the Northumberland estates by as much as a third in the first half of the fifteenth century. Overall the Percy estates probably lost a quarter of their value between 1400 and 1460. But even this significant deterioration was offset in some measure by price fluctuations which overall fell by 11 per cent in the same period.[59]

The middle ranks of landowners and substantial tenants were doing particularly well, not least in Richmondshire. This was the century not of the great lord but of the small- to middle-sized landowner. Parliament in 1429 made the forty-shilling freeholder the basic political unit of English society and he would remain so for the next four and a half centuries. (A forty-shilling freeholder would have about eighty acres.) Freehold property would never be so widely distributed again in England's history. This was the 'distributive state':[60] the 14,000 or so commoners with incomes from land in 1436 ranging from £2 to £400 a year were an effective counterpoise to the fifty or so peers with an average (net) income of £800.[61] It was this England of small, independent property-holders that Sir John Fortescue celebrated in the 1470s towards the end of his long and eventful life.

He had no doubt of their prosperity and general well-being which was the basis of their independence and incorruptibility (when serving on juries, for instance). Fortescue had been chief justice of the king's bench in the reign of Henry VI. He had been deeply involved near the centre in the century's vicissitudes, but when he surveyed the state of his country in old age he was loud in his praise of its laws, social structure, and above all its numerous and prosperous knights, gentry, yeomen and franklins. In his /Latin treatise, *De Laudibus Legum Angliae*, he claimed that England was 'thick-spread and filled with rich and landed men'. There were even many yeomen with £100 a year: 'Wherefore it is not to be imagined that persons in such wealthy circumstances can be suborned or prevailed on to perjure themselves.'[62]

His perceptions are entirely in line with the picture that a modern historian has drawn of Yorkist Richmondshire. There were a dozen or so gentry with substantial incomes of around £200, another fifty with incomes between £20 and £100, perhaps a score with £10 a year. They were the basis of the Neville political strength, of sufficient consequence to be the mainstay of national figures like the earl of Warwick and the duke of Gloucester.[63] Richard Clervaux of Croft was reasonably representative: he had an estate with some two dozen tenants and his rents were about £20 a year; his total income was perhaps £50 after he received a royal licence to trade with two ships to Iceland. In the middle of the century 'he maintained an impressive standard of living'.[64] This picture of Richmondshire is rather overdrawn, but there was certainly little evidence of north-country decline at Croft near Darlington.

And yet the trend towards economic decline was firmly established, and had been since about 1360 when the overseas demand for English wool began a steep decline. Quite apart from the effects of England's falling population, this reduced demand for England's wool had the gravest economic consequences, especially for the North. Continental cloth industries were either contracting or turning elsewhere for supplies. What they wanted from England was a greatly reduced quantity and higher quality. Good quality Cotswold wool was in demand in this declining market; the relatively poor quality northern wool was not. England's own cloth manufacture did not expand sufficiently, even in new centres like Lavenham, or the West Riding, to compensate for this reduction in demand.[65]

The clearest evidence of declining wealth and population was in the large towns of Lincoln and York. In 1440 Lincoln obtained total tax exemption on the grounds of poverty.[66] York's cloth manufacture declined and population fell steeply in the fifteenth century.[67] This may not have been an 'urban crisis' leading to the breakdown of law and order, but there was an undoubted century-long recession in York.[68] Guild restrictions had much to do with it. The weavers of York were undoubtedly over-taxed and over-regulated,[69] but this was not peculiar to York or to the North, and other major provincial centres also declined.[70] And yet London boomed. Whereas it accounted for perhaps 2 per cent of the assessed wealth of the country in 1334, in 1515 it accounted for nearly 9 per cent.

What is quite clear is that the new centres of cloth manufacture were not, in general, in the North. Lavenham, Tiverton, Totnes and Lewes were the rapidly growing textile towns of the fifteenth century. The assessed wealth of Lewes multiplied tenfold between 1334 and 1524, Lavenham, Totnes and Tiverton increased around twentyfold.[71]

The gap between northern and southern England widened enormously between the tax assessments of 1334 and 1515. During this period of almost two centuries the overall wealth of England's counties more than trebled; the wealth of no northern county even doubled. The greatest increase was in the West Riding of Yorkshire (by a factor of 1.74); Lancashire experienced an absolute diminution of wealth (by roughly one-sixth), the only county in England to do so. The wealth of Hertfordshire, Suffolk and Kent quadrupled; that of Essex, Surrey and Somerset increased fivefold, the wealth of Middlesex increased by a factor of eight.[72]

In absolute terms north–south differences are even more striking. The value of assessed wealth in Lancashire in 1515 was £3.8 per 1,000 acres; in Essex it was £102. In the North Riding it was £8.1, in the West Riding £11.3, but in Hertfordshire £90. In Derbyshire the figure was £18.7, in Somerset £104. Nearly two centuries earlier, in 1334, Essex (£18.5) and Somerset (£19.3) were poorer than the East Riding (£22.2) which was exactly the same as Hertfordshire. In 1515 the East Riding's wealth had declined to only a quarter of that of Somerset.

In these circumstances the reign of Richard III and the northern plantation in the South look like northern colonial exploitation of a richer, conquered land. Richard certainly maintained a close involvement in northern affairs and continued to further northern interests throughout his brief reign. The youthful Prince of Wales was left at Middleham as an informal centre of royal authority in the North but died there in April 1484. Northeners continued to receive lands and offices in the South and became particularly strong in Kent as well as in the South-west. Robert Brackenbury from Durham became the new sheriff of Kent in November

1484. Richard remained trapped by his brother's regional policy; both he and the north of England were its victims in the end.

MILITARY NORTH, CIVIL SOUTH

By the fifteenth century England's wealth was concentrated in a broad belt of a dozen counties extending south-west to north-east across the Midlands: from Wiltshire, Somerset and Gloucestershire through Oxfordshire and Berkshire to Hertfordshire, Essex, Bedfordshire, Suffolk, Huntingdonshire, Northamptonshire and Norfolk. Broadly (although not exactly) coincident with this diagonal of wealth (spilling over a little to the north) were Lollards, literature, and organized gentry-bandit gangs. Northern England did not have in any marked degree these three symptoms of the new wealth.

Northern England was now strongly marked by more than a century of disproportionate involvement in northern and continental wars. A region characterized by light feudal obligations after 1066, it was now pre-eminently a post-feudal military society. The lawyers were taking over in the South (appearing increasingly as parliamentary shire knights), even the duchy of Lancaster after 1399 was run increasingly by London lawyers rather than northern knights. Southern England was becoming an urban, civil society but the northern frontier region remained a highly militarized zone.

The 'civilianization' of England occurred in its most brilliant and successful period in arms: between Crécy in 1346 and Agincourt in 1415 the size of English armies halved;[73] the number of knights reduced probably by an astonishing 70 or 80 per cent; and the standard of living of ordinary people doubled.[74] This was an expansive, exuberant and increasingly urban society no longer so disproportionately committed to war.

The number of knights in England reached a peak in the first half of the fourteenth century. Edward I's mass knightings for the Scottish campaigns – he knighted 297 in Westminster abbey on Whitsunday in May 1306 – made a significant contribution. There were 500 knights in the Scottish campaign in the summer of 1335;[75] 950 knights served in France in the Crécy campaign, 1346–7, and at least 680 were serving in France in 1359–60.[76] There was probably a total of around 1,250 knights fit for active service in the first half of the century.[77] This number of knights would never be reached again until the early seventeenth century when, according to Gregory King, there were 600 knights and 800 new-style knights, the baronets.

The decline in the number of knights occurred at the very end of the fourteenth and in the early fifteenth centuries. While 950 knights served in the Crécy campaign, seventy years later there were only ninety-one in the Harfleur–Agincourt war, and two years after that, in 1417, there were eighty-seven in the invasion of Normandy.[78] While the army had been reduced to a half of its former size, the number of knights had been reduced to a tenth.

Of course the 'pool' of knights in England available for active service was very much larger than the ninety or so who actually served by the early fifteenth century. But there were probably no more than 200 compared with around 1,250 a century before.

The evidence for the total number of knights in England comes principally from the income tax returns of 1436 supplemented by information from commissions of 1434 which were concerned with local provision for maintaining law and order. Unfortunately the income tax returns survive for only sixteen counties and many of them are incomplete at relevant points. The returns gave details, by county, of residents' income from land and social status. It is relevant that at this time an official regulation of 1430 required all men with a landed income of £40 or more to become knights. It has been estimated that a little over 1,000 men below the ranks of the peerage had incomes of that order.[79]

There were nine counties for which both the incomes and status of taxpayers were given: 171 men in total had incomes of £40 or more, but only 32, or 18 per cent, were knights.[80] The nine counties were Cambridgeshire, Derbyshire, Essex, Hertfordshire, Huntingdonshire, Lincolnshire, London, Middlesex and Warwickshire. If they were representative of the country as a whole, with 18 per cent of their 'qualified' men being knights, the total number of knights in England was 180. There may have been a few more than this, but probably no more than 200.[81]

The number of knights (but not the incomes of taxpayers) is known for four other counties around this time: Cheshire,[82] Lancashire,[83] Northumberland and Yorkshire.[84] One striking contrast that emerges from this admittedly very fragmentary picture is that there was one knight in Cambridgeshire, one in Hertfordshire, one in Huntingdonshire and none in Buckinghamshire; but in Lancashire there were eighteen, in Yorkshire twelve, in Cheshire twelve, in Northumberland nine, in Lincolnshire eight and in Derbyshire four.

The North–South-east difference is more striking still when the number of knights in relation to incomes, where these are known, is taken into account. Lancashire was a particularly poor county, and its eighteen knights, compared with only one in enormously rich Hertfordshire, is striking. But there are no precise details of incomes in Lancashire to make an exact comparison. For Huntingdonshire, Hertfordshire and Cambridgeshire, however, the details are known: they had thirty male residents with £40 a year or more and three of them, 10 per cent, were knights – the same proportion as in the county of London, where forty-seven men had landed incomes in excess of £40 a year but only four were knights. In Lincolnshire and Derbyshire, however, there were thirty-three men with more than £40 per year and twelve of them, 36 per cent, were knights.

Derbyshire and Lancashire are of particular interest and significance. Both were very poor counties greatly influenced by the duchy of Lancaster's military commitments both in the time of John of Gaunt's ascendancy and for half a century after 1399. Lancashire was probably the only county in which the national trend towards a drastically reduced number of knights was actually reversed. At an enrolment in full county court on 9 May 1324 there were thirteen knights in Lancashire;[85] a century later the number had not diminished but had risen to at least eighteen. Lincolnshire was more representative of the country as a whole: between the enrolment in 1324 and the tax assessment of 1436 the number of Lincolnshire knights fell to less than a tenth, from ninety-five to eight.

There is no information for Derbyshire at the earlier date, but in 1436 it stands in a class by itself with regard to the proportion of men with incomes over £40 a year who were knights. There were twenty-one men in Derbyshire with an income of over £5 a year and so included in the tax return. Seven of these had in excess of £40, and of these seven, four were knights: 57 per cent. The four were Sir Thoms Blount, Sir Joseph Cokayn, Sir John Gresley and Sir Ralph Shirley, and their average income was £204. (The average income of all the other men assessed was £22.) There was only one peer in Derbyshire – this was not a region dominated by resident magnates – Lord Grey of Codnor, whose income as declared to the tax assessors was £403, less than half of the average declared baronial income (£865). The four well-to-do knights in this very poor county all came from families with a long tradition of military service in France and, for the previous twenty years, in Normandy.

The dramatic decline in knights to at most a sixth of their earlier numbers during a century of sustained and successful war is a remarkable phenomenon. Military reasons may be that knights were expensive and esquires could be employed in armies at half the cost to the same effect, and as county levies fell into disuse there was less need for knights as military leaders and administrators in the English shires. These are unlikely to be the sole reasons for the decline in the number of knights, but the contention that men avoided knighthood because of the financial obligations that it entailed is not very convincing in this age of acute sensitivity to finely calibrated social rank and degree.

The undifferentiated thirteenth-century aristocracy (which included a small number of apparently obsolescent earls) was finely tuned between 1348, when garter knights were instituted, and 1611, when baronets were created. The first non-royal duke was made in 1351, the first peer by royal patent in 1387,[86] and a college of heralds was established in 1483. Knights were now celebrated and glamorized in highly popular Arthurian legends, and by the fifteenth century earlier 'congeries of knights and barons' had been 'transformed into a highly self-conscious aristocracy, punctilious in regard to rank and precedence'.[87]

As the late-medieval ruling class ran out of land it ran out of power. The baronage ran out of land to grant to followers as a consequence of the Edwardian statute *Quia Emptores*,[88] while the king ran out of land as a consequence of the collapse of empire in Scotland and France and the tendency to reverse acts of attainder which gave him forfeited estates.[89] Instead of land kings now gave their followers peerages and the barons gave pensions. Richard II and Edward IV were particularly lavish in their creation of peers, but as the peerage expanded the number of knights dramatically fell. And yet all these dignities of rank and degree were eagerly sought after. In 1417, before the invasion of Normandy, Henry V instructed sheriffs publicly to proclaim

> that no one, of what estate, degree, or condition soever he be, do take upon himself such Arms or Coats of Arms, unless he possess, or ought to possess them, by right of ancestry, or by grant of some person having sufficient power thereto . . . except those who bore arms with us at the Battle of Agincourt, under penalty of being refused to proceed in the aforesaid expedition.[90]

There was a clamour for titles of dignity, and a need to bestow them as the new form of patronage, and yet the number of knights declined.

'Knight' was no longer merely a trade description. It was a title of high distinction, but it still retained strong military connotations, and in spite of wars at home and abroad, this was an ever more civilian age, especially in the South. It was northern estates that paid an astonishingly high proportion of their revenues in fees to retainers (although it is difficult to distinguish civilian estate employees from military personnel).

The duchy of Lancaster and the earl of Northumberland's estates paid out between a quarter and a half of their gross revenues on retainers. Elsewhere, in the Midlands and the South, the proportion was generally less than 10 per cent. The northern circuit of the duchy paid an average of £4,500 a year out of a gross income of £7,400 in the early years of the fifteenth century;[91] the earl of Northumberland, around the year 1440, paid between £1,000 and £1,400 out of a gross revenue of £2,800;[92] but Richard Beauchamp, earl of Warwick, in the 1420s paid £250 out of total revenues of £5,500 from his mainly west Midlands estates, and only half of this was spent on military retainers.[93] The payment on fees and annuities made by the duchy of Lancaster's receivers at the end of the fourteenth century – in excess of £3,000 a year – has been described as 'a scale of expenditure to which it would be hard to find a medieval parallel . . . it was payment for menial and military services rendered and to be rendered; it was no part of the ordinary expenses of running an estate.'[94] The duchy's huge military expenditure had reference principally to warfare in France. The £2,400 paid in annuities between 1418 and 1419 (apart from £1,500 paid in fees) went to Lancashire gentry most of whom had served with the king-duke at Harfleur.[95] It was the duchy of Lancaster's heavy commitment to the defence of England's outer perimeter in France, as much as the Percy commitment to defending the perimeter towards Scotland, that accounts for the disproportionately military character of society in the North.

When the earl of Northumberland attended Henry VII in York in 1486 he did so with thirty-three knights (in addition to yeomen and esquires).[96] This was quite a small number by fourteenth-century standards, when John of Gaunt's retinues might contain more than 100 knights drawn mainly from the North.[97] But in 1486 the earl's thirty-three knights were probably one-sixth of all the knights in England.

The Midlands were now much richer and more civilian than England north of the Trent – although Yorkshire 'belongs' in this sense more to the Midlands than to the outer perimeter. The distribution of wealth accounts for the geographical distribution of highly organized gentry-bandits in the fourteenth and fifteenth centuries: Sir Eustace Folville's gang operated in Leicestershire, Malcolm Musard's in Worcestershire, Richard

Stafford's in Surrey, Charles Nowell's in Norfolk. They arose where there was wealth that made upper-class banditry worth while. This wealth included rich heiresses who might be abducted and forced into marriage, like the widowed sister-in-law of Sir John Shardelowe of Cambridge who was abducted and married by the gang-leader John Pelham in 1387. Pelham was the son of a Sussex knight and a retainer of the earl of Derby; he became treasurer of England in 1411.

There was a marked concentration of gentry-bandits in East Anglia in the mid-fifteenth century. Charles Nowell, who tyrannized the region in the 1450s, was one of the duke of Norfolk's squires, Sir Thomas Tuddenham who terrorized Suffolk, was fined £1,396 in 1450. He was in receipt of a crown pension as a keeper of the great wardrobe.[98]

The religious reformers who followed Wycliffe and are known as the Lollards had less aristocratic connections,[99] but they had a similar geographical distribution. The movement depended on a literate following which was found through the rich territory extending from the south Welsh march through Worcestershire and Warwickshire to Leicestershire and Northamptonshire. Lollards were associated with areas of 'development', with literacy and with weavers.

The literary flowering of the late fourteenth and fifteenth centuries had broadly the same geographical distribution with a more northerly overspill in the miracle play cycles originating in Chester, Wakefield and York. It, too, had strong gentry-bandit connections. Chaucer and the poet Thomas Hoccleve were Londoners; Chaucer's friend, the poet Gower, was a man of Kent. William Langland, who wrote *Piers Ploughman*, however, was a Malvern man, the poet John Lydgate was from Suffolk, and Sir Thomas Malory, who wrote *Le Morte D'Arthur* was a midlander and lived at Newbold Revel in Warwickshire and at Winwick in Northamptonshire. He was a fairly typical knight-criminal of his region and probably wrote most of his twenty-two volumes on the virtuous achievements of King Arthur's knights while serving prison sentences for serious crimes, including attempted murder. He was the Member of Parliament for Warwickshire in 1456.

The perimeter had its own sources and varieties of lawlessness: rights of sanctuary in regalian franchises and the protection from royal justice afforded by palatinates made perimeter England a dangerous and lawless place. But poverty was increasingly its hallmark, as well as privilege: it had been camouflaged by falling or stable prices and the regional policies of Yorkist kings. The golden age of the northern perimeter ended abruptly in 1485.

8

The Tudor Challenge

The sixteenth is the first of two centuries of northern decline. The sixteenth and seventeenth centuries are the low point between the twin peaks of medieval power and nineteenth-century industrial might. In 1485 the North lost its northerner king, Richard III; in 1536 it lost its historic franchises, sanctuaries and 'liberties'; in 1569, after the 'northern rebellion', it lost its great earls, who linked this perimeter zone with the centre; in 1603 it lost its historic defensive role against Scotland and its wardens of the march (by now somewhat downgraded in dignity to the point where it was difficult to make appointments).[1] It is true that it gained an additional bishopric, Chester, as some sort of compensation for the dissolution of the monasteries, but central and southern England gained four. In 1641 it lost its King's Council in the North. In the seventeenth century, too, it lost its yeomen, who left or became tenants-at-will – of economic no less than military significance in a frontier society, they had been protected by the Tudors but were victims of the union of the English and Scottish crowns. This catalogue of loss spells the decline and fall of the north of England from its medieval eminence.

Among the losses in the sixteenth century the aftermath of the rebellion of 1569 was probably the most damaging. The retribution exacted against northern England, especially beyond the Tees, was ferocious. The region was stripped of its higher nobility: the Percy earls of Northumberland were confined henceforth to Sussex; the Neville earls of Westmorland were exiled and lost their estates. Only lesser peers of no more than regional significance were left: Darcys, Whartons and Scropes. By the 1580s there was only one resident aristocrat in Northumberland: Cuthbert, seventh Lord Ogle of Bothal.[2]

THE TUDOR SOUTH-EAST

Under the Yorkist kings in the later fifteenth century there was an increasing divergence between the geographical distribution of wealth and the distribution of power: as political power grew in the North, wealth grew more rapidly in the South. The Tudors brought wealth and power back into tidy alignment in the South-east.

By the middle of the sixteenth century the bias in wealth and power towards the South-east was far advanced and formidable. It had been implicit in the capture of Calais in 1347. As Calais rose in military, political and commercial significance, south-eastern England was given not only more adequate protection but pulled into heightened political prominence. After the loss of all England's possessions in France except Calais in 1453 the road from London to Dover acquired even greater significance.

It was the Tudors, however, who confirmed and consolidated the importance of the South-east and made it the heartland of royal power. They recruited such key royal servants as the gentlemen of the Privy Chamber disproportionately from this region and made grants of land to courtiers and planted them there. The roads from London to south-eastern ports were flanked by a remarkable concentration of royal palaces (among the nine in Kent were Dartford, Otford, Charing and Knole). The roads led to Sandwich, Dover, Hastings and Calais (and in 1520 to the Field of Cloth of Gold).

In the early Middle Ages economic advance in northern England had been notable on the east of the Pennines, and the area between the rivers Welland and Tees was one of the richest in England. Indeed, the Holland district of Lincolnshire was the richest of all, ranking first in wealth among thirty-eight counties at the tax assessment of 1334. The East Riding of Yorkshire ranked sixteenth (see chapter 5). In 1515 the Holland district had declined to nineteenth, the East Riding to thirty-second. Lancashire was thirty-eighth in 1334 and thirty-eighth in 1515 (although if the clerical wealth of all counties is taken into account, Lancashire was thirty-third in 1334 but still thirty-eighth in 1515).[3]

In 1334 the East Riding was as rich as Hertfordshire and Suffolk, and significantly richer than Essex and Surrey, but in 1515 the East Riding had declined from sixteenth to thirty-second, Hertfordshire had risen from seventeenth to eighth, Suffolk from eighteenth to seventh, Surrey from twenty-eighth to fifth, and Essex from twenty-fifth to third. The richest county was Middlesex which had risen from seventh.

In 1515 the richest counties in England 'formed two well defined areas, joined together by Berkshire. In the west there was a group comprising Gloucestershire, Somerset and Wiltshire, and in the east a block of counties grouped round London, comprising Kent, Surrey, Middlesex, Hertfordshire, Essex, and Suffolk'. London itself was advancing ahead of everywhere else in a striking fashion: while England's wealth trebled over the two centuries between 1334 and 1515, London's wealth increased fifteenfold. 'In general the south was pulling further ahead of the north.'[4] In 1334 the richest counties were associated with the production of wheat; by 1515 with the production of cloth.[5]

The West Riding of Yorkshire, for precisely this reason, stands out from the general picture of relative northern decline. In terms of lay wealth, the West Riding's rank among England's counties in 1334 was thirty-seventh, and in 1515 thirty-sixth. But clerical wealth was a high and rising proportion of the West Riding's wealth, and when the clerical wealth of all counties is taken into account, the West Riding's rank in 1334 was thirty-sixth, in 1515 it was twenty-fourth, roughly equivalent to Cambridgeshire and Worcestershire.

The proportion of the West Riding's urban wealth doubled between 1334 and 1524, from 11.7 per cent to 22.5 per cent (but in Lincolnshire, for example, it rose only from 5.9 per cent to 10.8 per cent);[6] its proportion of clerical wealth rose between 1334 and 1515 from 42.5 per cent to 62 per cent. The connection between these two facts is wool. As West Riding towns required more wool for a rising textile industry, the great monastic sheep-runs of West Yorkshire supplied it.

The old industrial towns of eastern Yorkshire like Beverley, Malton, Hedon and Scarborough were now poor, strangled by guild restrictions and urban taxation: the textile industry moved westwards.[7] Leeds, and indeed York, prospered especially in the later sixteenth century as the export trade in cloth for the Baltic towns expanded through Hull.[8] When the London-based Eastland Company for trade mainly with Riga and Danzig was established in 1579, Hull merchants drawing supplies of cloth from the West Riding were significantly involved.[9]

A high and rising level of clerical wealth in relation to lay wealth is a distinguishing feature of northern England's economy and society in the later Middle Ages. In Lancashire the proportion was very high in 1334 and it remained so. In the West Riding of Yorkshire it was 42 per cent in 1334, only a little over the national average of 39 per cent, but by 1515 it had risen to 62 per cent, while the average for England had fallen to 31 per cent (see table 8.1). This was of political no less than economic and social significance: any attack on the resources of the church in northern England was an attack on the region's preponderant wealth. The dissolution of the monasteries was an altogether disproportionate assault on northern England compared with the South.

The West Riding stands out as an exception to the relative economic decline of the North; Sussex stands out as an exception in the rise of the South-east. This poverty-stricken county remained poverty-stricken (although the exclusion of privileged Cinque Ports from taxation leads to some understatement of the county's wealth). Sussex stagnated in relative poverty over three centuries, between tax assessments in 1334, 1515 and 1636, at roughly the same level as Cornwall. Both fluctuated around thirtieth among England's counties in rank-order of wealth.[10]

It was across southern England, starting in Cornwall, that economic misery erupted into riot and rebellion in the summer of 1549. This was one of the major crises of Tudor society and northern England was wholly uninvolved. In this pinched and penurious century of rising population and inflation, the living standards of average people everywhere fell relentlessly from about the time that Henry VIII became king until some years into the reign of James I.[11] The tensions that this engendered were particularly acute among the more vulnerable tenantry of large parts of southern and eastern England (see chapter 4). In Sussex in the summer of 1549 Henry Fitzalan, fourteenth earl of Arundel, a man of vast wealth and estates, sat in his castle to deal with rebels' complaints which were mainly about rents and evictions. His rank and authority enabled him to do this with quite remarkable success.[12] He was interceding in a bitter class war between landlords and tenants. There was no class warfare at this time in northern England and there would not be throughout the Tudor century.

The rich block of south-eastern counties immediately adjacent to London – Kent, Surrey, Middlesex, Essex and Hertfordshire – were also unaffected in the summer of 1549, perhaps because they had been saturated with royal influence and favour. The royal presence in these counties was palpable. The Tudors built or acquired eighty-six royal palaces: forty-one of them were in London, Surrey, Middlesex, Kent and Hertfordshire and only two were north of the Trent – former monastic properties in York and Newcastle-upon-Tyne to house the officials of the King's Council in the North. In Surrey, however, there were twelve, including lavishly built houses like Richmond, Oatlands and Nonsuch.[13]

TABLE 8.1 Lay and clerical wealth in the North and Southeast 1334 and 1515

	1334			1515		
	Lay clerical (£/1,000 acres)	Clerical (£/1,000 acres)	Clerical (%)	Lay clerical (£/1,000 acres)	Clerical (£/1,000 acres)	Clerical (%)
Lancashire	16.6	12.0	72.0	16.4	12.6	76.0
West Riding	11.3	4.8	42.5	36.1	22.4	62.0
Kent	44.2	19.7	44.5	129.5	29.0	22.4
Surrey	28.9	11.6	40.0	123.5	29.4	23.7
England	35.4	13.9	39.3	97.6	31.6	31.1

Source: R. S. Schofield, 'The geographical distribution of wealth in England, 1334–1649', Economic History Review, 18 (1965), pp. 483–510.

There was a similar geographical bias in the composition of the royal retinue that proceeded to the great display of wealth and power in 1520 on the Field of Cloth of Gold in the Calais march. A hundred knights and esquires were called to accompany the king, along with ten earls and five bishops. Two of the earls – Ralph Neville, fourth earl of Westmorland, and Henry Algernon Percy, fifth earl of Northumberland – and one of the bishops – Thomas Ruthall, bishop of Durham – were northerners. At this level, with 20 per cent of the higher dignitaries, northern England was adequately represented: earls and bishops were still the crucial links between the centre and the northern perimeter. At the level of knights and esquires, however, northern representation was abysmal. While the six home counties contributed thirty-six, northern England contributed three: all of them from Yorkshire.[14]

This assemblage at the Field of Cloth of Gold in fact reflected the realities of the structure and distribution of power in early Tudor England. The three Yorkshire knights were drawn from families of real political significance and weight: Sir Robert Constable. Sir William Bulmer and Sir Richard Tempest. All three families would be deeply involved in leadership of the Pilgrimage of Grace sixteen years later. Sir Richard's heir, Sir Thomas Tempest, contributed an important and influential policy memorandum to the pilgrims assembled at Pontefract in November 1536.[15] His son Nicolas Tempest would be executed at Tyburn in June 1537 along with Sir John Bulmer, Sir William's heir. Sir Robert Constable, now a very old man but, after Ashe, the most prominent leader in the Pilgrimage of Grace, was executed at Hull. The call to the king's retinue in 1520 had not bought the conformity and compliance of Tempests, Bulmers and Constables; it had picked out the families of initiative in northern society. But the Pilgrimage of Grace was a 'loyal rebellion', and Sir Thomas Tempest's memorandum at Pontefract made it clear that the insurrection was in the king's best interests, designed to rid him of Thomas Cromwell and other evil counsellors. In fact Sir Thomas would survive the rebellion and become one of the most important members of the reconstituted King's Council in the North after 1537.

Also at the Field of Cloth of Gold, one of the eight knights summoned from Kent, was Sir Thomas Boleyn, father of the future queen. Here, in fact, in the Calais march in 1520, was a microcosm of the political nation, a show of national power and unity behind the king in which were concealed the court factions of the 1530s in embryo: the Kentish knights foreshadowed the Boleyn faction, the Yorkshire knights the Aragonese faction which would rebel in 1536 in part at least to ensure the succession of Queen Katherine's daughter, the Princess Mary. Three knights, two earls and a bishop from north of the Trent against ninety-seven knights, eight earls and four bishops from the South picked out in a remarkably accurate fashion the geographical distribution of significant and effective power in the early Tudor state.

By the middle of the sixteenth century the commitment of the home counties to the new order was solid. While the provincial insurrections that plagued Tudor England were in support of the old, the one home counties rebellion was to preserve the new. This was the rebellion led by Sir Thomas Wyatt of Allington castle near Maidstone in 1554. It was a rebellion of home counties' gentry who had served the early Tudors loyally and had prospered under their rule: their rising was against the proposed marriage of Queen Mary to Catholic Prince Philip of Spain. It came nearer than any other rising of the sixteenth century to overthrowing the monarch. Wyatt had been sheriff of the county and after the southern risings of 1549 had taken steps to organize a local militia to preserve the tranquillity of Kent. His rebellion does not show the disloyalty of the home counties to the Tudor regime: on the contrary, its whole purpose was to preserve its achievements. This was the exception that proves the rule.

REGIONAL CONTROL: THE STANLEY EARLS OF DERBY AND THE KING'S COUNCIL

The two centuries between 1485 and 1688 were a period marked by a dominant centre and weakening perimeter: as the north of England declined in wealth, the power of London, the home counties and the organs of central government grew in political significance and pervasive influence. Policies of governments increasingly pulled power to the centre, especially those directed by Thomas Cromwell in the 1530s, by Oliver Cromwell in the 1650s and (now against a strong contrary current) by James II after 1685. The strengthening of the centre and weakening of the perimeter were in part a semi-automatic process of readjustment after two centuries of pronounced perimeter power reflected in often outrageously irrelevant privileges (like the rights of sanctuary in the Cheshire 'avowries'). The policies of governments broadly reflected these underlying rhythms of inter-regional adjustment and change.

The Tudors have been seen as centralizers *par excellence*, the architects of the modern centralized state.[16] This is essentially true (although 'modernity' did not preclude the deliberate and systematic revival of feudalism and centralization seemed actually to require it), but it was not achieved by stripping power out of the provinces, but by increasing it. A strong centre needed strong regional agents. The Tudors developed two in the North: the house of Stanley on the west of the Pennines, and the King's Council of the North on the east. Both were local centres of power based on local men. Neither provoked revolution; both, in quite different ways, prevented it. But success had its price. On the west of the Pennines it was intense isolation and on the east resentments which long term, in the seventeenth century, contributed to the outbreak of the great civil war.

For all the efforts and achievements of Tudor centralization – which was not a single, coherent, self-conscious policy, but an attack on a range of *ad hoc* problems mainly of law and order and government finance – the ancient distinction within the northern province re-emerged in a new way: between a poorer, more isolated outer perimeter – Lancashire and the four border counties – and the much richer, more integrated 'inner core' – Yorkshire (see chapter 4). The border counties, like Lancashire, were never accommodated within the jurisdiction and administrative framework of the Council of the North, although strenuous efforts were made to achieve this, notably after 1525 and again after 1537. The northern marches retained their own separate, essentially military, administration down to 1603; Lancashire was ruled by the Stanleys; and the palatine county of Durham was still set apart. Tudor England saw a great proliferation of new parliamentary boroughs around its perimeters, and even the recently conquered Tournai (in 1514) and Calais (in 1536) sent members to Westminster, but it would be more than another century before Durham would do so. The bishop remained a man of great independent power, which was increased rather than circumscribed when Bishop Cuthbert Tunstal became lord president of the reconstituted King's Council in the North in 1537.

Centralization depended on strong centres of regional power. The problem faced by the Tudors was not the number of mighty subjects throughout the provinces but the lack of them. Sixteenth-century Yorkshire was curiously bereft of great aristocrats. The only resident aristocrat in the West Riding in the earlier sixteenth century was Thomas Lord Darcy, on the lowest rank of the peerage, whose power in any event came from royal appointments as steward and constable of Knaresborough and Pontefract.[17] Two measures were taken to create responsible centres of power, one specific to Yorkshire, the other general throughout the country. The first was the King's Council of the North; the second was the inspired invention of the mid-century, the lords lieutenant of the shires.

The lords lieutenant were not competing centres of power: they reinforced existing centres. The Stanley earls of Derby were invariably the lords lieutenant of Cheshire and Lancashire; the lord president of the Council of the North was always the lord lieutenant of Yorkshire. This reinforcement of regional centres of power was not peculiar to the North. The mighty Howard dukes of Norfolk, confirmed in their East Anglian palatinate in 1559, were invariably lords lieutenant of Norfolk and Suffolk. This enormous accumulation of regional power did not save the duke of Norfolk from execution for treason in 1572.[18]

The lord lieutenancies were rather quirky appointments with mainly military responsibilities, at first commonly short-term, to deal with particular emergencies. Different counties were often combined in a somewhat arbitrary way. But they were powerful posts: justices of the peace and sheriffs were subordinate to them; in the Durham palatinate, while the bishop still appointed his own sheriff, the lord lieutenant was appointed by the king. Appointments were for limited periods. Only in Lancashire was the lord lieutenancy in practice hereditary, held in succession by the third, fourth and fifth earls of Derby between 1553 and 1593 and renewed to the sixth in 1607.[19]

The Tudors were quite prepared, even impatient, to use the Percy earls of Northumberland in top command posts on the northern frontier and the earls were quite willing to serve as their regional agents. (It is true that Thomas Cromwell made opportunist moves against the indebted estates of the rather gullible sixth earl in the 1530s; it is also true that the crown restored the Cumberland Percy estates in 1535 on the grounds that the border area was more naturally led by the earls of Northumberland than anyone else.)[20] Indeed, it was precisely because he was acting as the king's agent that the fourth earl was murdered by commoners at Topcliffe near Thirsk on 28 April 1489. The earl was collecting a highly unpopular tax and had read out peremptory instructions he had received from the king which he entirely endorsed.[21]

He had been restored by Henry VII to a panoply of regional posts. Imprisoned after the battle of Bosworth he was released in 1486 and made warden of the two eastern marches, constable of all royal castles in Northumberland, sheriff of Northumberland for life, steward of Knaresborough, bailiff of Boroughbridge, and chief justice of forests beyond Trent. The temporary disappearance of earls of Northumberland from top command posts in the northern marches occurred because the fourth earl's son and heir was only one year old when the earl was killed.

It was important to be an earl or a duke for top regional posts, or a bishop for the lord presidency of the Council of the North. A baron would not now suffice. The earl of Surrey was now made the supreme commander of the northern marches. There was a general insufficiency of earls.

Peerages still became extinct from natural causes at an average rate of one every two or three years. Henry VIII more than made good this natural wastage and there were fifty-one noblemen when he died in 1547 (compared with forty-two at the time of his accession thirty-eight years earlier) although two-thirds of these were only barons and half of those were Henry's own creations.[22] They were not men of appropriate regional weight.

The choice of the earl of Surrey as commander of the North after the murder of the earl of Northumberland is curious. He was the son of the duke of Norfolk and like his father a Yorkist; both had fought on the losing side at Bosworth where the duke was killed. Surrey was imprisoned, eventually released, and employed to bring order to the North after the rebellion of 1489. His loyalty to the new dynasty was far more suspect than the earl of Northumberland's, but as a Yorkist he was in fact more acceptable to the men of the North. He commanded their loyalty and respect and at the age of seventy led them to spectacular victory at Flodden in 1513. This was a very northern affair and the battle was fought beneath the banner of St Cuthbert that had been carried from Durham cathedral. It was only now that Surrey was granted his father's title, twenty-eight years after his death. Surrey had not been appointed to a northern command because he was an outsider who could mobilize no threat to the centre. He was appointed precisely because, as a supporter of Richard who had kept faith, he could expect the support of the North. The fourth earl of Northumberland was a deserter and could not. The chronicler said that 'the northerne men bare against this erle continuall grudge ever since the death of King Richard.'[23] The fourth earl of Northumberland proved to be something of a liability to Henry VII not because he was too strong in the North, but because he was too weak.[24]

The basic structure of regional control that was developed in northern England under the Tudors was Stanley power on the west of the Pennines and the King's Council of the North on the east. The intention was that the Council should supersede the wardens of the march but attempts to achieve this were short-lived and the wardenships were always restored (see below). The Council was established in theory for all counties north of Trent and at first followed a regular routine of sessions at York. Newcastle, Hull and Durham (but never at Preston or Lancaster). In effect it became the King's Council in Yorkshire, where there was a real power vacuum arising from the maldistribution of northern England's higher nobility.

There was no vacuum in Lancashire. The Stanleys were earls and they were available. Principal beneficiaries of Yorkist regional policy in the fifteenth century, even to the disadvantage of the duke of Gloucester, earls since 1485, ambitious, deeply self-interested, cautious, circumspect, and without serious competitors, they were eminently suitable for viceregal power in the North-west. Thomas Stanley, like the earl of Northumberland, had also deserted Richard III at the battle of Bosworth, but this was no disability on the west of the Pennines. Lancashire had never been so committed to Richard of Gloucester and had never held him in such affection (or enjoyed his good lordship) as Yorkshire, Durham and Cumberland.

Sixteenth-century Lancashire and Cheshire under the rule of the Stanleys are a striking illustration of strong central government exercised through extraordinary regional power. Neither of the two great northern rebellions of the sixteenth century, the Pilgrimage of Grace in 1536 and the rising of the northern earls in 1569, found significant support in Lancashire, and virtually none south of the Ribble. The reason is quite simple: the earls of Derby forbade it. The result was not only internal peace but intense regional isolation.

Other regional institutions – the palatinate of Lancashire and the duchy of Lancaster – reinforced this conjointly with the Stanleys. Together these institutions provided such an effective insulation against the wider world that the King's Council in the North never established its jurisdiction west of the Pennines. The duchy of Lancaster's own administrative machinery, and not the central government's Court of Augmentations, handled the dissolution of the monasteries in Lancashire (and did so with well below average compensation for the monks). The earl of Derby had his own council which was the link between central and local government: it was the earl who decided how instructions from central government were to be implemented and made appropriate arrangements with justices of the peace.[25]

The power of the Stanleys was not an outgrowth and expression of Lancashire's power. It hadn't got any. It was essentially an extension of royal power. The Stanleys never at any time challenged the king and the central government, even after 1530 when they were profoundly unhappy with their religious policies. And there was no one of any real weight to challenge (or indeed to support) the Stanleys in Lancashire: there were as yet no rich and powerful urban centres, the gentry were poor, there was not even a bishop until the Chester diocese was established in 1541, enormous in extent, grotesquely underpowered and over-extended, inadequate even for imposing the Tudor religious settlement. The abbots were weak, none of them were lords spiritual in the House of Lords, and the earls of Derby were stewards of the major abbeys – Whalley, Furness and St Werbergh.

The Stanley tie with the centre was close. It was the Privy Council that ordered the imprisonment of Sir Richard Molyneaux in 1593 because he had been discourteous to the earl in not informing him that he intended to enter Parliament as a knight of the shire. Earlier in the century Sir Thomas Butler, in dispute with the earl of Derby over titles to land, took his case to the central Court of Star Chamber because he could not expect a fair hearing in Lancashire, where Earl Thomas 'is of such kynn alliaunce and strengthe in servants within the said countie palatyn'.[26] Sir Thomas gained no redress but when the earl called on Lancashire for support against the Pilgrimage of Grace joined his forces with 368 men.

Stanley power was reinforced with elaborate ceremonial on set piece occasions like the funerals of earls and the coming-of-age of the eldest son, and the region's isolation was constantly reaffirmed in the ritual crossing of boundaries. The earl returning from London was met by the sheriff and gentry of Cheshire as he crossed the Cheshire–Shropshire border, and then by the sheriff and gentry of Lancashire as he crossed the Mersey. Nearly a thousand horsemen then accompanied him to a great banquet at Knowsley.

The sixteenth-century power of the Stanleys has been called feudal;[27] it was not. When the earl raised nearly 8,000 men in arms in 1536 he had received a commission of muster from the crown and acted as a commissioner of muster as specifically instructed; likewise in 1545 and 1557. The antecedents of this military organization were in the pre-feudal Saxon fyrd and not in the medieval feudal host. Men of Lancashire were mobilized not because they were the earl's tenants but because they were the king's subjects.

The Stanleys were regional agents of the crown albeit of great power. Their position was not analagous to that of twelfth-century lords of great honours like Richmond and Pontefract, but to that of the lord president of the King's Council in the North across the Pennines. They faced no regional opposition and offered none; they created an intensely insular provincial society. The gentlemen of Lancashire had found international significance with the fourteenth-century dukes of Lancaster in high command in France; with Henry of Lancaster in Lithuania; with John of Gaunt in Spain; with Edward of Woodstock in Aquitaine. The sixteenth-century earls of Derby issued them with a badge with three legs and took them to the Isle of Man.

The Council of the North was far less reliable and far less insulating than the earls of Derby. It certainly connived at, if it did not aid and abet, the Pilgrimage of Grace. It was not an aristocratic body and had no direct military functions: essentially a court of law intended to bring speedy justice to the North, especially to tenants, it was composed of lawyers, gentry and clerics. It was certainly an instrument of central policy and had an important role in establishing the Tudor religious settlement in the North and the new Poor Law administration. It also handled cases of debt and breach of contract and so was important to the commercial community in the developing West Riding, but it inevitably offended powerful interests, principally the greater landowners. Its lawyers kept it abreast of progressive legal opinion and practice and were in close touch with Parliament and the Inns of Court.

This contact with Parliament became closer as the Council instigated the creation of new constituencies in the old, decaying and depopulated east Yorkshire boroughs of Hedon, Aldbrough and Boroughbridge and the somewhat less decayed towns of Thirsk, Knaresborough, Ripon, Richmond and Beverley. There was no question of new northern parliamentary boroughs representing rising wealth and population in the West Riding. They were nomination boroughs; they represented the Council of the North.[28] The Council or important members determined who the MPs would be; in the case of Ripon (enfranchised 1555) the archbishop of York and the lord president of the Council shared the two nominations.[29] An even bigger explosion of parliamentary boroughs occurred in Cornwall apparently at the instigation of the duchy of Cornwall. This was a somewhat indirect process of Tudor centralization whereby the centre's regional organs themselves initiated closer ties with the centre. (Two centuries later most of these same nomination boroughs would serve an entirely opposite purpose, promoting not centralization, but Yorkshire particularism. The Council of the North will have long ceased to exist, and the boroughs would be in the hands of private patrons: Whig squires and aristocrats. Aldborough, Knaresborough and Boroughbridge would be in aristocratic hands; Ripon,

Richmond and Thirsk in the hands of Yorkshire squires, all would be used to support separatist Yorkshire interests. They were an important element in the powerful movement towards regional independence that occurred in the eighteenth century. See chapter 10.)

The King's Council of the North had its origins in the magnate council of Richard of Gloucester. When Richard became king in 1483 and his son, the Prince of Wales, died at Middleham in April 1484, new arrangements were needed to represent royal power in the North and the King's Council of the North was established in July 1484. It met regularly at Sheriff Hutton and Sandal to administer justice. It was never the council of the king's lieutenant in the North; it was never merely an offshoot of the central king's council: it was of independent origin. It was the King's Council *in the North*.[30]

The Council lapsed under the early Tudors until it was revived in 1525 by Wolsey, essentially to cope with increased litigation and to take some of the weight from an overburdened Star Chamber, but its days of greatest importance came after reorganization with enhanced power (the president now became lord president) which followed the Pilgrimage of Grace. Common lawyers and bureaucrats were now its predominant element and it became 'an efficient instrument for government in the king's interest, as well as a useful and much employed institution for resolving local litigation and disputes'.[31]

The King's Council in the North in the sixteenth century, especially after 1537, has received the unanimous acclaim of modern historians: while it did not entirely solve the centuries-old 'problem of the North', said Lapsley, it very nearly did. The 'problem' was northern England's separateness, and the Council was a major step towards the assimilation of this outer province, enabling it eventually to take its 'natural place in the kingdom'.[32] This analysis is seriously flawed since it takes no account whatsoever of the special circumstances of Lancashire and the border counties. The King's Council in the North, however, certainly brought Yorkshire into closer relationship with the centre and fostered a progressive, cosmopolitan society throughout the county, especially in the East Riding and the vale of York.

The signal achievement of the Council of the North, which in fact marked off the northern counties from the rest of England, has passed curiously unremarked by historians. This was the high degree of social-class harmony which kept the northern counties from civil war when the southern and eastern counties erupted into class warfare in 1549. The regional contrast and the immunity of the North have not generally been thought worthy of comment except to express surprise that the wild North was quiet. Elton did indeed ask the question: 'The supposedly volatile North remained virtually at peace – why?'[33] But he refrained from offering an answer.

The men who were in revolt in the southern and eastern counties were not starving labourers, as they were in the same areas in the 'swing' riots of 1830 (see chapter 11), they were quite substantial 'customary' tenants. Their counterparts in northern England were likewise customary and 'tenant-right' tenants who had held land by the custom of the manor from 'time out of mind'. They were certainly not richer but they were undoubtedly more secure in their tenancies and less oppressed (in rents, 'entry fines' and the like) by their lords. The reason was partly the ancient, and still continuing, problem of settlement and defence in an exposed frontier zone. The terms on which men were prepared to settle and fight had always necessarily been good. The Council of the North further safeguarded these anciently favoured tenures. It had done so when it was Richard of Gloucester's council at Sheriff Hutton, and it was expressly instructed to do so by the Tudors.[34] The result was a region remarkably free from the class hatreds that afflicted richer, more anciently feudal, areas of the South. Even Tawney could find no element of class antagonism in the Pilgrimage of Grace of 1536 (although he thought it might be 'latent').[35] The Council of the North, which surrendered with astonishing speed to the 'pilgrims', must have some credit for this, too.

PROVOCATION AND PROTEST: 1536

The first great Tudor affront to the north of England was to defeat and replace King Richard III in 1485; but the first half of 1536 saw a succession of highly provocative measures embodied in four acts of Parliament, the most disturbing being the act for dissolving the lesser monasteries, which was passed in March. This raised large questions of the north of England's viability as a stable society capable of performing its historic and still urgent military tasks. Other measures of 1536 would reinforce these fears. This is the relevant background to the northern rising between 13 October and 8 December which was called by its leader and has been known ever since as the Pilgrimage of Grace.

The 'pilgrimage' was ostensibly about defending the church; but the grievances aired were diverse. What was fundamentally at issue was the 500-year military role of northern England *vis-à-vis* the Scots. The loss of monastic lands and the earl of Northumberland's estates to the crown in 1536 undermined northern England's capacity for war on the nation's behalf.

The Scottish danger pervaded the thinking of the leader, east Yorkshire landowner, London lawyer, and legal adviser to the earl of Northumberland, Robert Aske. It was his central concern when he first entered into discussion with the lords at Pontefract on 19 October 1536. The closing of monasteries, the loss of their local community services, and the diversion of their revenues to the king threatened not only the economic viability but the social cohesion of northern society. This was a serious enough matter in itself, but no more so than in many other of the poorer parts of England. What made the impoverishment and destabilization of northern society especially, indeed uniquely, grave was that it undermined its military effectiveness. In these circumstances, said Aske to the lords at Pontefract, northern society would be weak, vulnerable, in conflict within itself, and the north parts would of necessity 'patyssh with the Scots'.[36]

The religious policy of the government after 1530 exacerbated the Scottish threat and the problem of northern defence in other ways. The exclusion of Princess Mary from the succession to the throne opened the way to the crown itself passing to a Scottish heir. This would be seen as a solution fifty years later, but in 1536 it was only a problem, and the clause in the Pontefract articles which referred explicitly to this Scottish danger was probably drafted by Aske himself. There was also the rising discontent of tenant-right tenants, the very backbone of northern defence, who felt increasingly oppressed and particularly insecure if their tenancies were on monastic estates which were now to be 'dissolved'. Another clause in the Pontefract articles referred specifically to the problems of tenant-right tenants on abbey lands in Mashamshire and Niddersdale, as well as in the north-western counties more generally, and demanded that their tenures and conditions should be given statutory guarantees.

The Scottish danger was omnipresent and palpable. This was the principal reason for Aske's insisting on a peaceful demonstration and requiring the pilgrims to take an oath against murder and bloodshed: only the Scots would benefit from civil commotion in the North.

The Pilgrimage was an apparently spontaneous and uncoordinated mass movement throughout the North – although the assembly of 30,000 pilgrims at its focal point, Pontefract, in early October does look a little stage-managed. It was very northern, and although many of the issues it addressed were of national concern – including the flagrant misuse of

Parliament by Henry VIII and his ministers – the pilgrims never went south of the Don. This was the southern frontier, seemingly fixed and impermeable, of the Pilgrimage of Grace. There was conceivably a national plan of campaign originating in court factions which was primarily concerned to secure the succession of the Catholic Lady Mary;[37] indeed, the two northern peers implicated in the Pilgrimage, Lord Hussey and Lord Darcy, had long service at court in the Aragonese interest, and Hussey had been Mary's chamberlain. But if a national insurrection had been centrally planned, what still calls for explanation is active mobilization and support only north of the Don. The pilgrims were very conscious of their northern identity: they carried not only the banner of the five wounds of Christ, but the banner of St Cuthbert, just as their fathers and indeed some of them had carried it to Flodden and heroic victory over Scotland some twenty years before. In 1536 northern England was deeply conscious of half a millennium of northern history.

It was, indeed, an intellectuals' rebellion (rather like the Campaign for Nuclear Disarmament in the mid-twentieth century), managed by lawyers and historians, a campaign bristling with manifestos which brought together the separate labours of various working parties culminating in the Pontefract articles of 4 December. Perhaps most indicative of the intellectual quality and progressive outlook that characterized the movement was the memorandum that Sir Thomas Tempest, MP for Newcastle-upon-Tyne, addressed to the pilgrims at Pontefract: an historical analysis of comparable situations in the reigns of Edward II and Richard II, and a deeply felt and informed view of constitutional practice and the king's abuse of Parliament and the machinery of local government.[38]

The Pilgrimage of Grace was virtually the entire northern community in action: aristocrats, gentry, abbots and yeomen. It was not an example of class conflict but of co-operation, and although there are some signs of class conflict on the earl of Cumberland's estates in West Yorkshire and Westmorland, this was certainly not a principal cause of rebellion in 1536.[39]

It is true that the aristocrats, gentry and abbots said afterwards that they were coerced by the 'commons' (i.e. commoners). In the case of the abbots (who were disinclined to lose their pensions and redundancy pay) this was probably true, and some of the nobility remained aloof and some actively opposed the rising, notably Lord Dacre and the earl of Cumberland as well as the earl of Derby. But overall the solidarity was impressive: 'The rebels of 1536 were not a class, but almost the whole society of northern

England, which suddenly rolls forward with all its members, spirituality and laity, peasants and peers, in fervent motion together.'[40] The only centres to stand out against the rising were Scarborough, Carlisle and Berwick, as well as the castle, but not the township, of Skipton. (Lancashire south of the Ribble was effectively neutralized by the earl of Derby.) The Pilgrimage of Grace, for all its immense geographical scatter and some regional differences of emphasis, looked solid and both morally and practically irresistible.

A one-week rebellion in Lincolnshire, centred on three towns with particularly rich churches (Horncastle, Caistor and Louth), had occurred between 4 October and 11 October. It was directed against suspected government measures to close parish churches and confiscate their jewels and plate, and local priests played an important part in it. Its first act was to place an armed guard on the treasure-house of Louth church. It was certainly not committed to non-violent demonstration and the bishop of Lincoln was killed. This was a rebellion to defend local church property. It was the men of Horncastle who designed a banner representing the five wounds of Christ and hung it in their church.

This brief and violent Lincolnshire rising was over when the Pilgrimage of Grace erupted in Yorkshire in the middle of the month. The northern movement had echoes of the rising in Lincolnshire and Aske had Lincolnshire connections, but its organization was quite independent and it proceeded over the next two months without Lincolnshire support. It was essentially a separate event.

By 16 October the East Riding pilgrims had taken York (where the citizens had declared for them three days before anyway); by 19 October the king's representative at Pontefract, Lord Darcy, had placed himself and the castle in their hands; by 24 October pilgrims were converging on Doncaster from all parts of Yorkshire carrying the banner of St Cuthbert, and on 27 October their representatives negotiated terms with the king's ambassador, the duke of Norfolk, on the bridge over the river Don. By 8 December the pilgrims had drawn up their grievances and remedies at Pontefract, presented them to the king and received his pardon. They were all home for Christmas and had apparently won.

It was not altogether clear what had been won, however. A small-scale east Yorkshire rising in the following spring was an expression of this uncertainty. It was over-ambitious and rapidly failed; it gave the king an excuse to revoke the pardons of 8 December. By the end of June 1537, in addition to 50 rebels executed for their involvement in the Lincolnshire rising, 130 'pilgrims' and their supporters had been executed at Tyburn.

Aske was executed at York and the East Riding gentleman Sir Robert Constable at Hull.

Among those executed were the two elderly peers, Lord Darcy of Yorkshire and Lord Hussey of Lincolnshire, as well as other members of aristocratic houses, notably the earl of Northumberland's brother, Sir Thomas Percy. There were numerous gentry and a handful of knights including Sir Robert Constable whose father at seventy had distinguished himself for valour on Flodden field. Lancashire made only a minor contribution to these executions, losing sixteen, of whom six were monks.[41] Apart from the abbot of Whalley, all the heads of religious houses who were executed were from Yorkshire: the abbots of three Cistercian houses, Jervaulx, Sawley and Fountains (none of the rich Benedictine abbots was implicated), and two Augustinian priors Bridlington and Guisborough. The Pilgrimage of Grace was essentially a demonstration rather than a rebellion;[42] the violence was not in this protest movement itself but in the judicial retribution that followed its defeat.

The four acts of Parliament which were passed in 1536 and were a prelude to the Pilgrimage of Grace were the Statute of Uses; the act dissolving the lesser monastries with revenues less than £200 a year; an act against franchises; and an act transferring the Percy estates to the king after the sixth earl of Northumberland's death. The Statute of Uses, the act dissolving the monasteries and the abolition of franchises were explicitly opposed in the articles drawn up for the king's instruction at Pontefract.

The first two measures were designed by the government to take wealth from England's landed estates. The dissolution of lesser monasteries in fact took wealth disproportionately from northern England; the Statute of Uses, in the longer term, would do so, too. There were far more smaller monasteries in northern England than elsewhere: in the four border counties twenty of the twenty-four monasteries had revenues under £200 a year; even in Yorkshire half of the monasteries were 'lesser' ones; but in Dorset, Somerset, Wiltshire, Gloucestershire and Hampshire, they were less than a third.[43] When nunneries are taken into account these regional differences are even greater. In the border counties priories of great social importance like Hexham, Jarrow, St Bees, Alnwick, and Shap had revenues under £145 a year – the sum that Glastonbury paid out annually on charities. In terms of monastic revenues lost to the crown the regional contrasts are equally striking: by the act of 1536 eastern Yorkshire lost 19 per cent of its monastic revenues, the south-western counties lost 7 per cent.[44]

The Statute of Uses restricted the ability of landowners to dispose of their property by will and restored the common law rule of male primogeniture. Landowners resented the interference in family life, and the restriction on their ability to provide for daughters and younger sons. The 'York articles' which Aske drew up on 15 October gave details of these restrictive consequences; the Pontefract articles of 4 December demanded tersely that 'the statute that no man shall wyll hys lands be repellid'.

The act was essentially a means of taxing land which had avoided feudal incidents (inheritance duties) and the drain on an estate's resources that occurred through wardship when the heir was a minor: the 'use' was a device whereby the land was technically owned by a trust or corporation which did not die and therefore did not inherit and pay inheritance dues. The Statute of Uses was a major element in the Tudors' systematic revival of fiscal feudalism.[45] It would press disproportionately on northern England when monastic lands were sold off as knight-service tenures. No northern monastic lands had ever been held 'in chivalry'. It was by feudalizing hitherto unfeudalized northern estates that Henry VIII would augment his revenues. This was probably foreseen by lawyers in 1536: the first two Tudor kings never sold or made gifts of land except by knight service *in capite*. And indeed another statute of 1536 which established the Court of Augmentations to deal with monastic estates made it quite clear that any permanent alienation of land would be by military tenures-in-chief.[46]

The act against franchises was a law and order measure; it was also an attack on the church and was generally seen as such. Many northern ecclesiastical corporations like Beverley, Ripon and Tynemouth enjoyed ancient immunities and rights of sanctuary; there were only two or three in the south (Westminster, Glastonbury and St Martin le Grand). The privileges of the Welsh marches and the Cheshire avowries would be dealt with separately, but the 'act for the resumption of jurisdiction' of 1536 'opened up all the great liberties of the North, even the county palatine of Durham, to the king's criminal justices'.[47] The 'liberties' had been a defining characteristic of northern England for more than 500 years, and although many of their inconveniences were now manifest, the Pontefract articles demanded that 'the liberties óf the church' be restored.

The Percies had a comparable symbolic significance: they were at the heart of northern England's sense of identity. In 1536, more through the accidents of personality than long-term government design, they were very clearly vulnerable and were outmanoeuvred by Thomas Cromwell and the king. The sixth earl was weak, ill, unstable, childless, separated from his wife, in debt, and apparently trying to buy the king's favour. But there was already talk in the North of a 'second coming': 'The moon shall kindle again and take light of the sun, meaning by the moon the blood of the Percies.' But the handing over of Percy estates to the crown under the terms of the act of 1536 had more than symbolic importance. The revenues of the earl of Northumberland's estates which would now go to the king were over £3,000 a year, more than twice the total revenues of the twenty monasteries in the four border counties now due for dissolution, which amounted to £1,467. There is little doubt that the prospective loss of Percy estates to the crown was deeply resented and a potential cause of serious disturbance throughout much of northern Enland.[48]

The Percies and the military role of northern England are quite central to the Pilgrimage of Grace. The earl of Northumberland refused to be involved in the rising, but a myriad of Percy tenants and officials took part. His mother gave the movement her support; his two brothers, Sir Thomas and Sir Ingram, were important leaders. Sir Ingram constable of Alnwick castle, led the Northumberland pilgrims. Sir Thomas entered York with the pilgrims on 16 October, a powerful, gorgeously attired military figure on horseback, acclaimed by the citizens of York who saw him as 'the lock, key and wards of this matter'. Lawyers organized and co-ordinated the Pilgrimage and drafted memoranda, but men with a grasp of northern military affairs were chosen as its ambassadors.

When two emissaries were needed after the meeting on Doncaster bridge on 24 October to proceed to Windsor and explain northern problems to the king, the men chosen were Robert Bowes of Streatlam castle in Durham, and Sir Ralph Ellerker, an east Yorkshire gentleman. Bowes was a member of a family with long and responsible involvement in border affairs; Sir Ralph had actually fought at Flodden and had been knighted for valour on the field of battle by the earl of Surrey. Both would serve after 1537 on the reformed Council of the North; both would be very active in border surveys and indeed in renewed border wars. These were not men with any special knowledge of monasteries and churches who went to talks with the king at Windsor on 2 November 1536; they were military men with the border problems in their bones.

After the meeting on the bridge at Doncaster, and while Ellerker and Bowes were preparing for their mission south, Aske and Sir Thomas Percy took time off from their revolution to visit Wressle. On 25 October they dined with the abbot of St Mary's at York and then went south to call on the earl. They went for only one purpose, to persuade the earl to make his brothers Sir Thomas and Sir Ingram wardens of the east march and of the middle march respectively. The earl refused. Aske's followers waiting outside the castle were for assassinating the earl: 'it was openlye spoken of the feeld, "strike of the hedde of the Erle and make Sir Thoms Erle".'[49] (Aske was able to get the earl away to a safe house in York.) Support by the commons of northern England for Percy earls was strictly conditional: earls were expected to live up to their name and traditions, to provide effective military services and to stand up for northern interests against central government and kings. The commons of Yorkshire, for all their respect for the blood of the Percies, killed the fourth earl of Northumberland at Topcliffe in 1489 because he was too obviously the king's man; in 1536 at Wressle they would have killed his grandson for exactly the same reason.

It has been said with regard to the Pilgrimage of Grace: 'even if there had been no Reformation there must have been a rising in the North about this time.'[50] This is an overstatement. Religious issues were certainly not irrelevant in 1536, although popular concern often arose from an apparent threat to parish churches rather than the real threat to monasteries; this was especially the case in Cumberland and Westmorland. The dissolution of the monasteries must be seen as Aske saw it, in the context of a northern society in decline but carrying still a very heavy military responsibility.

It has been said that Aske exaggerated. In fact he probably understated northern England's economic, social and military predicament and the dire consequences of the dissolution of the monasteries. Thus in 1540, for example, the crown drew the enormous sum of £6,110 from land in the West Riding which a short time before had belonged to the church or other laymen.[51] The disaster for northern arms at the battle of Ancrum near Jeburgh in 1545 and its aftermath vindicates Aske's general analysis. After 1545 a standing army of around 4,000 men as well as foreign mercenaries were stationed on the northern frontier.[52] A detachment formed a permanent garrison for the castle that was at last being built (by government) at Lindisfarne seven and a half centuries after the first Viking attack. There had been nothing of this kind for more than a thousand years, since the last of the Roman legions was withdrawn from Hadrians Wall. The North had provided the men for its own defence. The year 1545 was the year in which a thousand years of northern military might, and northern society's capacity to sustain it, effectively came to an end.

MODERNITY AND THE PILGRIMAGE OF GRACE

The Pilgrimage of Grace was the protest of an ancient frontier society in decline, now seemingly stripped of its small but essential resources and faded symbols of significance in 1536. It was a claim not for separateness, but for recognition of its regional identity and continuing relevance. It demanded in the articles of Pontefract that parliaments should meet at Nottingham and York, and that 'no man upon subpoena is from Trent north to apeyr but at York.' York and not London must be the centre for justice in the North. But this was a rebellion that marked the end of a long era of importance and not a beginning. It would be the last great political initiative of northern society for more than 200 years.

The rebellion of 1536 (like the rebellion of the northern earls in 1569) has usually been described as reactionary and conservative: 'in essence it was a demonstration in favour of the old days and the old ways.'[53] This view emphasizes northern isolation and feudalism, a region standing outside the mainstream of national life. A recent judgment is more closely in accord with the facts: 'Neither rebellion (1536 and 1569) was notable for its feudal particularism or its provincial myopia but for its consciousness of national issues and national remedies.'[54] Nevertheless, it is important to distinguish between the two. The second rebellion was undoubtedly much more conservative than the first.

The charge that the Pilgrimage of Grace was conservative and reactionary is usually made on the grounds that it resisted the centralizing policy of a modernizing Tudor state and that it did so in defence of a still feudally ordered and relatively autonomous provincial society. The second proposition is by no means necessary to the first, and the very patchy support of the northern nobility scarcely suggests that they were leading a revolt to preserve a regional separateness which enshrined and protected their privileges.[55]

A cursory review of Tudor rebellions does indeed suggest that they might be regional reactions to a centralizing state. There were seven; they were all in the provinces; and six were directed against measures or policies of central government. The one that was not was Ket's rebellion of 1549 which arose out of local class conflict in East Anglia. It was in no sense provoked by central government, and its leaders did not look to central government for remedies. Here indeed was a highly feudal society in bitter conflict within itself.[56]

The other six provincial rebellions were directed against central government measures regarding either religion or taxation. There were two tax revolts, both in the later fifteenth century, one in the North in 1489 (in which the tax-gathering earl of Northumberland was assassinated), the other in Cornwall in 1497. They stood in a long and continuing tradition which saw levying taxes on local property and incomes as justified only when there were direct local benefits. This was a factor in the Peasants' Revolt of 1381: taxes were not securing the South-east from French attacks.[57] It would be at the heart of the ship-money crisis in the 1630s, for all the constitutional top-dressing: inland counties derived no direct benefit from the ship-money tax and so should not pay it.[58] In 1489 a tax was being raised for a Breton war and northern England saw no reason to pay for such a remote enterprise; in 1497 a tax was being raised for a war in Scotland, and Cornwall saw no reason for contributing to an equally remote cause.[59] The provincial revolts of 1489 and 1497 were not the outcome of a peculiarly Tudor policy.

The other four regional rebellions occurred after the breach with Rome in 1530. They were directed at least in part against some aspect of religious policy, as it affected monastic and other church property, ecclesiastical privileges, the liturgy, or the question of Protestant or Catholic succession to the throne. The four rebellions were the northern rising of 1536, the western rebellion of 1549, Wyatt's south-eastern rebellion of 1554, and the rebellion of the northern earls in 1569.

The most conservative of these provincial rebellions was undoubtedly the south-western rising of June 1549, a priest-led revolt to retain the Latin mass.[60] The other rebellions, though triggered by local issues and supported within a regional frame, confronted some of the wider implications of religious policy and change. Wyatt's rebellion was concerned to safeguard the stability of social structures built on the Tudor Reformation and to keep England out of international conflicts that the queen's Spanish marriage might entail. The Pilgrimage of Grace confronted among other wider issues a centuries-old dilemma of national defence now aggravated by the loss of monastic wealth. The rebellion of the northern earls was concerned with the international implications of a Protestant queen and an uncertain succession. 'Centralization' is insufficient to explain these provincial revolts. Religious issues had to be there in some form and to some degree before they occurred.

Thus there was centralization which was entirely secular and directed towards bringing privileged perimeter areas within the orbit of central authority. This was invariably met not with protest but immense relief. This was so in the case of the Cheshire 'avowries' which were abolished in

1542: ancient sanctuaries which had promoted settlement and provided soldiers in an exposed frontier, now a gigantic irrelevance and major source of lawlessness.[61] No one lamented their passing. Likewise the Act of Union with Wales in 1536: it extinguished the historic privileges and immunities of the marcher lordships and so removed a principal source of disorder in the region. It also broke down the isolation of Wales and the borders and brought them into a wider political community. This curtailment of perimeter independence and privilege was widely welcomed in Wales at all levels of society.[62]

If modernity was the 'use' and the independence of Parliament, the Pilgrimage of Grace was indeed its friend. The arch-reactionaries were the first two Tudor kings. The 'use' expressed and promoted the flexibility in social relations and freedom of choice which are the hallmark of a post-feudal society (see chapter 6). The Tudors opposed it not out of any ideological commitment to feudalism as a social system but because it lost them money. The Pilgrimage of Grace was from its outset dedicated to the repeal of the Statute of Uses, and this undoubtedly largely accounts for massive gentry support. The northern gentry were on the side of modernity too.

The Statute of Uses, like the act for the dissolution of monasteries, had been passed by Parliament under duress. The twenty-five abbots who were lords spiritual did not put up much of a fight for the monasteries, although it is true that only two – the abbot of Selby and the abbot of St Mary's, York – were from the North, which at this stage was most affected. But other parliamentary bills initiated by the king and Thomas Cromwell had been strongly opposed. In its support of the independence of members of Parliament the Pilgrimage of Grace spoke up for the future. Sir Thomas Tempest in his Pontefract memorandum dealt with this matter at some length and bitterly condemned the king and his ministers who had gagged Parliament and 'dyvysed that men may not speke of the kynges vyceys'. The Pontefract articles demanded 'reformation for the election of knights of the shire and burgesses, and for the uses amonge the lordes in the parliament house after theyr aunciene custome'.

The Statute of Uses was only one measure by which the early Tudors revived and extended feudal relationships and obligations. Henry VII diligently searched out military tenures that were quietly falling into abeyance; Henry VIII revived, extended and exploited military tenures in a much more systematic way. The sale of monastic lands by knight-service tenures *in capite* greatly extended military tenancies especially in the

North. This extension of feudalism was buttressed by an act of Parliament in 1540 establishing the Court of Wards and another establishing the Court of Wards and Liveries in 1542. A Court of Augmentations for handling monastic estates had been established in 1536. There was thus a formidable central machinery for overseeing the affairs and enforcing the feudal obligations of England's landed estates. Never had feudalism in England been so ruthlessly applied – although sales resistance seems to have led to some reduction in the amount of land sold on strictly feudal terms.[63]

There was also some retreat in the Statute of Wills of 1540 which allowed military tenants to dispose of two-thirds of their land as they thought fit. The Pilgrimage of Grace had undoubtedly helped to bring this about. In any event the rebels had opposed the feudal revival from the start. And so it is curious that a leading legal historian like Holdsworth, while giving a full and fair account of the rebirth of feudalism under Henry VIII, describes the Pilgrimage of Grace which opposed it as the product of northern society 'where feudal relations and feudal ideas still survived'.[64] Holdsworth described the seven-year opposition that Parliament sustained against the measure to restrict 'uses' which Henry first introduced in 1529. Parliament, an assembly predominantly of landowners and their representatives, eventually succumbed to bullying and threats that inquiries would be made into their titles to their lands.[65] It was the East Riding landowner and lawyer of Gray's Inn, Robert Aske, supported principally by the gentry of Yorkshire, who continued the struggle by extra-parliamentary means after the landowners of England in Parliament had given up the fight.

THE END OF THE MILITARY ARISTOCRACY

The rebellion of the northern earls in 1569 and the treaty of Berwick concluded in 1586 finally undermined the military aristocracy of the North. The rebellion was a self-inflicted wound; the treaty solved 'the problem of the North' by promising, albeit somewhat obliquely and implicitly, the union of England's and Scotland's Crowns. The king of Scotland was henceforth an Elizabethan pensioner. The historic military structures of the North, which had stood firm for three centuries, were obsolescent after 1586.

The rebellion of the northern earls was not simply an assertion of regional and aristocratic self-interest: it was concerned with great issues of national concern. But it was more backward-looking than the Pilgrimage of Grace and drew its main support from the deeply traditionalist society beyond the Tees. The lawyer-led rebellion of 1536 was rooted in the sophisticated, London-connected society of eastern Yorkshire; the priest-inspired rebellion of 1569 found such strength as it mustered in the remoter, more insulated lands of ancient regalian power.

The rebellion of the northern earls was intended to restore the Catholic religion and ensure for England a Catholic queen. In his examination before his execution in 1572 the earl of Northumberland explained: 'Our first object in assembling was the reformation of religion and preservation of the person of the Queen of Scots, as next heir, failing issue of Her Majesty.'[66] There is no reason to doubt that this was the heart of it, but it was the business of earls to be concerned about the succession to the throne when it was in any way a problem. An unmarried Protestant queen on the edge of a largely hostile Catholic Europe was a problem of proper concern to England's nobility. And most of them were duly concerned. The difficulty is why, in the end, only two earls, both in northern England, actually rebelled.

There was in fact very little resolution among the northern earls (there was much more among their wives). Only two of the four actually rebelled: the earl of Derby failed to give any support; Henry Clifford, earl of Cumberland, did not stir; the earl of Northumberland was nervous and hesitant and had to be pushed into rebellion. Charles Neville, sixth earl of Westmorland, brought matters to a head at Brancepeth on 10 November, but this was only after he and Northumberland had been summoned by the queen to Windsor after news of the conspiracy was out. The rebellion of the North was engineered to save the Neville and Percy earls from arrest.[67]

This view trivializes a genuine attempt by the earls to confront major problems facing the late-Tudor state, however. They were addressing urgent national issues concerning succession to the throne and the possibility of invasion by Catholic powers, but by November 1569 they were doing so from a strictly delimited northern base. They were reasserting their own threatened power. When they posted a proclamation on the door of Staindrop church on 16 November they referred to the danger of invasion, and to the queen's upstart advisers who had not only established a new, heretical religion, but 'dailie go about to overthrow and put down the ancient nobilitie of this realme'. It was because they were daily put down by the new men at the centre that the ancient nobility in the North were now in revolt.

It is this secular explanation that has found favour among historians in recent years and was most strikingly expressed by Lawrence Stone: the rebellion of the earls, he wrote, was 'the last episode in 500 years of protest by the Highland Zone against the interference of London'.[68] Late-Tudor policy had pushed the northern aristocracy somewhat to one side. In particular, the earl of Northumberland had lost exclusive rights over the wardenships of the east and middle march. The Tudors were now seriously challenging the historic tradition of the relative autonomy of the North.

But equally they were challenging a second distinctive and deeply cherished northern tradition of even greater antiquity: the religious heritage of St Cuthbert and Bede, still kept alive in parish churches but symbolized above all in the cathedral at Durham. As in the Pilgrimage of Grace, centralization was not enough. It was the conjunction of 'interference' by the centre and the subversion of the traditional religious life that brought matters to the point of open revolt.

Initially the earls found very little support in the North. There is certainly no evidence of any automatic feudal reflex which brought out the tenantry, and some of the northern gentry like Bowes and his supporters stood out, with little reward, against the earls. (They did not get compensation afterwards for extensive damage to their property.) Only ten Northumberland gentry out of some ninety gentry families came forward to support the earl.[69] In Richmondshire, where the earl was keeper of Middleham castle and steward of Richmond, the commons were very reluctant to turn out – they would not do so for 8*d*. a day, but were more forthcoming for a shilling.[70] It was only when the rebellion assumed the character of a religious crusade and mass was celebrated in Durham cathedral and elsewhere that it rallied any measure of popular support.

It was perhaps an unnecessary and even an unintended rebellion: the original purpose of the conspirators had simply been to secure a Catholic succession by marrying the duke of Norfolk to Mary Queen of Scots – until the duke lost his nerve and surrendered himself to Elizabeth. But the punishment of the North which followed the collapse of the rebellion was ferocious. Neville, Clifford and Percy earls were excluded from the North; some 800 rebels were condemned to death although perhaps only half that number were executed.[71] This compares strikingly with 132 condemned and executed after the Pilgrimage of Grace. The fines imposed crippled the northern economy from Richmondshire through Durham where the rebellion had received strongest support. 'The north

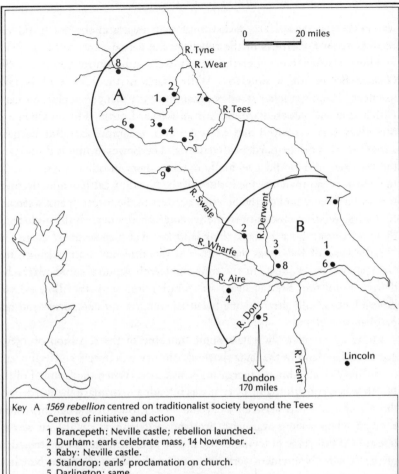

0   20 miles

R. Tyne
R. Wear
8
A 2
1 7
R. Tees
6 3
4
5
9
R. Swale
R. Derwent
7
2 B
R. Wharfe
3 1
8 6
R. Aire
4
R. Don
5
R. Trent
London
170 miles
Lincoln

Key A *1569 rebellion* centred on traditionalist society beyond the Tees

Centres of initiative and action

1 Brancepeth: Neville castle; rebellion launched.
2 Durham: earls celebrate mass, 14 November.
3 Raby: Neville castle.
4 Staindrop: earls' proclamation on church.
5 Darlington: same.
6 Barnard Castle: Bowes beseiged by rebels.
7 Hartlepool: rebels expect Spanish support troops.
8 Hexham: earls retreat, 16 December 1569.
9 Richmond: reluctant support for earls.

  B *1536 rebellion* centred on progressive 'Percy territory' in east Yorkshire

Centres of initiative and action

1 Beverley: rebel centre in October and again in January 1537.
2 York: 16 October triumphal entry by Sir Thomas Percy; Aske executed, July 1537.
3 Aughton: home of Robert Aske.
4 Pontefract: main centre for rebels' assembly; 'Pontefract articles', 4 December.
5 Doncaster: negotiations with king's representatives.
6 Hull: exemplary execution of Sir Robert Constable.
7 Bridlington: prior of Augustinian monastery implicated and executed.
8 Wressle: Percy castle.

MAP 8.1 Foci of the rebellions of 1536 and 1569

Source: author

was never the same . . . poverty was to persist and the north did not recover from the effects of the rebellion for perhaps two centuries.'[72]

The earls had gone, but the gentry were still securely in place. Sir George Bowes was a survivor. With estates in the middle of Neville territory, he nevertheless stood out magnificently in 1569 against the earls with a force he gathered around him in Barnard castle. His own house at Streatlam was destroyed and he was never recompensed. But he gave gallant service on the borders afterwards. The Bowes family had survived the Nevilles and would eventually outclass them in other ways. Indeed, their history summarizes the history of the North: wealth originally from service in France and on the Scottish borders in the fifteenth and sixteenth centuries; relative obscurity in the seventeenth century; in the eighteenth their fortunes reborn because their land lay over rich seams of coal. The Neville Rose of Raby was the mother of two fifteenth-century kings, but George Bowes, esquire, in the mid-eighteenth century could marry his daughter to the Scottish earl of Strathmore, and the Bowes-Lyon descendants would provide one twentieth-century queen-consort and one English queen.

Quite apart from the catastrophic outcome of the rebellion of 1569, northern England in the later sixteenth century was in serious decline and its military establishment increasingly insecure. When the Council of the North was reconstituted in 1537 it was intended to displace the wardens of the march (as it had between 1525 and 1527), but the wardenships were revived when serious war with Scotland began in 1542. There was no question at this stage of trying to use minor figures in the power structures of the North. Noblemen were now put on the Council of the North to help with its wider border obligations: the earls of Westmorland and Cumberland and Lord Dacre, all former wardens of the march.[73]

There were now two problems in filling top military command posts in the North: a serious shortage of noblemen of sufficient standing, and the unattractiveness of wardenship appointments starved of funds. Thomas Lord Dacre, who died in 1525, was wardern of the west march for thirteen years (1511–1524) without any pay. In 1525 he was put in the Fleet and ordered to recompense anyone in the borders who claimed to have suffered damage during his administration.[74] In the middle of the fifteenth century a wardenship still yielded handsome profits; a century later only very rich or frightened peers would take on the job. The earl of Cumberland was only prepared to be warden if he could reside at Skipton, eighty miles south of Carlisle; the earl of Westmorland if he could reside at Raby, ninety miles south of Berwick. The Tudors were expecting the northern nobility to subsidize northern defence on a very significant scale. In the reign of Henry VII the warden-general was paid £1,000 a year but his expenses were probably in excess of £3,000.[75]

Courtiers, sometimes relatives of the queen, often became wardens of the march in the later sixteenth century. This was undoubtedly encouraged as it counterbalanced the power of the northern earls. The governor of Berwick and warden of the east march in 1569 was, very conveniently (but also very provocatively), the queen's cousin, Henry Carey, first Lord Hunsdon, a southerner, formerly MP for Buckingham. (His salary as governor of Berwick was never paid.) He was zealous and effective in dealing with the rebellion of 1569.

After 1586 there is no doubt that the northern command posts were seen as of little account. Old Sir John Forster, warden of the middle march, now dominated Northumberland affairs. He spent thirty-five inglorious and incompetent years in office and was retained in spite of constant complaints. He was finally dismissed for gross negligence in 1595 at the age of ninety-four.[76]

It is over-simple to see northern rebellion in Tudor England as a response to a global policy of 'centralization', or some sort of generalized interference by London in the highland zone. It was much more selective. Some aspects of centralization the North warmly embraced. The main organ of centralization or 'interference' was the Council of the North, a massive intrusion into northern society, but the object of no serious and certainly no organized opposition at all. In the sixteenth century it remained highly regarded and valued at all levels of society even though it was especially vigorous and effective after 1537 in enforcing often unpopular government policies. But it was not long in trying to replace the wardens of the march or take military responsibility for frontier defence. It did not appoint wardens and the wardenships remained outside its jurisdiction. In short, this supremely sensitive area was outside its remit. The Council was dedicated to bringing justice to northern England and was seen to do so. In the reign of Elizabeth members of the Council were required 'faithfully and uprightly to the best of your power [to] cause justice to be duly and indifferently ministered to the Queen Majesty's subjects that should have cause to sue for the same'. This interference by the agency of London in the highland zone was not resisted even by the northern earls.

The measures of central government which disturbed northern England in the sixteenth century reached into the life of local communities to an unprecedented degree;[77] in this very loose and general sense they were an aspect of 'centralization'. But they caused trouble only when they cut across the two great traditions which were at the very heart of northern England's sense of identity: the powerful religious tradition which looked back to the age of St Cuthbert and Bede, and the military tradition of frontier defence which looked back to a long line of warrior-bishops and legendary wardens of the march. It was when the actions of government interfered in some way with these that northern England rose against the centre.

These government measures, discussed above, from the dissolution of the monasteries to the takeover of the Percy estates and the chronic underfunding of the wardens of the march, were seen at the time as weakening northern England, and undoubtedly did so. And yet they merely reinforced and confirmed the deep undertow of history which in economic and strategic terms was now set firmly against the North.

9

The Eclipse of the North

In 1603 the North became redundant. After five centuries its function was no longer to serve as a front-line of defence against the Scots. The four border counties were particularly affected, but the defensive system still entailed obligations as far south as the Humber and this was generally recognized and accepted throughout the sixteenth century. The east Yorkshire leaders of the Pilgrimage of Grace in 1536 made much of the need to maintain local resources for this continuing military role, and the gentry of the East Riding, 150 miles from Alnwick and 180 from Berwick-upon-Tweed, had always felt an overriding obligation to respond to the wardens of the march.[1] On the west of the Pennines the obligation extended in time of crisis as far south as Cheshire – as in 1513 when Sir John Stanley led his troop of Lancashire and Cheshire men to Flodden. The union of the English and Scottish Crowns in 1603 deprived northern England between Humber and Tweed of its great and heroic historic role.

The full effects of the North's redundancy were delayed until 1641 by the operations of the King's Council in the North. The Council gave protection to the small northern tenants which really made sense only when they were of crucial military significance. But 'redundancy' is the basic reason for the political decline of northern England in the seventeenth century; the result was isolation and backwardness. Major political and military initiatives no longer came from the North, as they had done down to the rebellion of the northern earls in 1569, and the great event of the century, the civil war, though engulfing the whole nation, was essentially an affair of London, East Anglia and the South-west. These were the three areas of greatest Puritan strength in early seventeenth-century England; and they were the principal source of political, military and ideological initiatives.

The 'great rebellion' was primarily an affair of the centre. The seven rebellions of Tudor England all originated in the provinces; the great rebellion originated in London and remained London-dominated throughout, although Cambridge was for a time, under a parliamentary ordinance of January 1644, an important administrative and financial centre for an eastern counties' army.[2] London was as decisive in 1660 in restoring the king as it had been in 1642 in opposing him.

The relegated seventeenth-century North is the polar antithesis of the pivotal North of the fourteenth century – a relegation reflected at all levels of public life. There were only three northern figures of national stature in the crowded political landscape of seventeenth-century England: Thomas Wentworth (earl of Strafford), Thomas Obsorne (earl of Danby), and George Savile (marquis of Halifax): three ambitious, avaricious and highly efficient south Yorkshire squires. Of these Wentworth was undoubtedly the most powerful and important, respected and feared, but he was kept in perimeter appointments (although his ambition was to be lord treasurer), as lord president of the King's Council in the North and additionally after 1633 as lord deputy of Ireland. He was called to the centre only in August 1639 when the king wrote to him privately and desperately to come over from Ireland to deal with a rapidly deteriorating situation.[3] At a different level the North's relegation appears in the low proportion of Yorkshiremen among 'civil servants' holding regular office at court or in central or regional administration, strikingly different from the fourteenth century when men of Howden-shire and Nottinghamshire dominated all the great departments of state.[4]

The initiatives came in the main from the gentry, but the picture in London is more complex. There merchants were initiators, and the 'middle sort of people' – craftsmen and apprentices – took political initiatives, too.[5] To a modest extent this was probably also true in industrial south-east Lancashire and the West Riding of Yorkshire, where on occasion, at the outset of the civil war, they pushed a hesitant gentry into decisive action. But the wealth, external relationships and Puritan connections of the gentry are the best indicators of a county's political and commercial energy and enterprise. Dorset is perhaps the most striking illustration: always a quite well-to-do county, it ranked around the middle out of thirty-nine counties in the early sixteenth century, but advanced steadily and was in the top third by 1636.[6] It was deeply involved in early colonizing ventures (through the Dorchester Company for settlement in

New England) and contributed some outstanding leaders to the Long Parliament on both sides of the developing conflict.[7] Men like Denzil Holles, member for Dorchester, one of the 'Five Members' whom Charles tried to arrest in 1642 for 'subverting fundamental laws', took the lead: they did not wait on events.

Indeed, the Five Members reflect quite accurately the geographical distribution of radical political energy. The king had identified them as foremost critics of his government, determined to deprive the monarch of his rightful powers. None was a northerner. Hampden's home county was Buckinghamshire, Haselrig's Leicestershire, Holles Dorsetshire, Pym Somerset (MP for Calne in Wiltshire) and Strode Devonshire. In northern England only south Yorkshire was at all comparable to the south-western and eastern counties as a source of political leaders of national standing. Wentworth had been a leader of parliamentary opposition to the king at an earlier stage (notably in the parliaments of 1625 and 1628), and Fairfax, although not a member of Parliament, would emerge as a military leader of national stature on the parliamentary side.

The north of England played an essentially supporting and reactive role in the civil war. It took its cue from initiatives in the South (although to talk of 'the myth of the royalist north', as some have done, is an absurdity).[8] The North produced a great parliamentary general in Fairfax, and the earl of Newcastle's 'popish army' was a formidable force for the king and certainly militarily significant down to July 1644. And the parliamentary attacks on Yorkshire's Thomas Wentworth, the earl of Strafford, and the Council of the North, was an important part of the prelude to rebellion. But the Yorkshireman was now 'court', not 'country', and the attack on him and the Council was not a centre–perimeter issue. It was an attack not on the importance and privilege of a region, but on the importance and privilege of a system.

The seventeenth century is dominated in retrospect by the great rebellion. But two other movements or events contributed to the century's historical importance: the overseas colonizing enterprise in the New World, and the Glorious Revolution of 1688. Northern England made an insignificant contribution to the first, and its involvement in the second curiously back-fired. When Dutch William decided, against all expectation and advice, to land his invasion army at Brixham in preference to Bridlington Bay, the political irrelevance of northern England was underscored. Yorkshire's earl of Danby, waiting confidently in the north for William's landing,[9] was contemptuously ignored.[10]

Of course 1688 was not 1399. Northern support for Bolingbroke had been crucial; for Prince William it would only have been an encumbrance. But although William treated it contemptuously it was not in fact contemptible. It had been growing steadily since the Restoration from a very limited geographical base in south Yorkshire and north Nottinghamshire and Derbyshire: a network of families and estates south of Doncaster and north of Mansfield flanked on the east by the great North road.

The men from this locality who were at the centre of events in 1687–9 were George Savile, marquis of Halifax, William Cavendish, earl of Devonshire, and Thomas Osborne, earl of Danby. Theirs was an uneasy alliance: they were personal and even political enemies, now in a fragile and mistrustful relationship. That some of the key men of 1688 had a collective power base in the North has been seen as 'largely an accident of history'.[11] This is not quite true. Power in south Yorkshire rose (slowly) after the Restoration on the grave of Yorkshire's political martyr, Thomas Wentworth, earl of Strafford, condemned to execution in 1641 by Parliament's Act of Attainder. High cavaliers from south Yorkshire who had Wentworth connections – notably Thomas Osborne and George Savile – had a slight edge on the thousands of cavaliers from elsewhere who besieged London in 1660 to reverse their fortunes. They became in time chief ministers of Charles II. And Strafford's home at Wentworth Woodhouse between Barnsley and Rotherham would lie at the heart of a growing northern power complex for more than a century. The Whig grandees of the eighteenth century who stood guardian to the Revolution Settlement were arrayed on their vast estates from Nottinghamshire and north Derbyshire through Yorkshire and finally, by the early nineteenth century, to Durham and Northumberland. A place of honour among them was occupied by Charles Watson-Wentworth, marquis of Rockingham, twice prime minister. His power base was the triangle formed by the racecourses at York and Doncaster and the ancestral home in Wentworth Park.

MILITARY REDUNDANCY

In the early seventeenth century the north of England turned in upon itself. It was increasingly isolated and backward and county communities of gentry were intensely insular. There were three principal reasons for this inward turning and decline: loss of military function in relation to Scotland; poverty; and Catholicism.

The King's Council of the North was the only major countervailing influence. It represented the centre and had done much since the mid-sixteenth century to bring the northern counties into line with the rest of the kingdom.[12] But it had no jurisdiction over Lancashire (or Cheshire); it met increasing opposition, especially in Yorkshire, from the county gentry whose separatist interests (for instance over taxation, especially ship-money, religious observance and Poor Law administration) were threatened;[13] and it ceased to exist after 1641 (although men in the North tried to have it revived at the Restoration).

The other great institution which had, historically, pulled northern counties towards the centre was the duchy of Lancaster. This was especially the case during the Hundred Years War when the duchy had pulled the gentry and yeomen of Lancashire and Derbyshire into the great affairs of the day and pitchforked many into top command posts of a far-flung imperial enterprise. These knights obtained vast administrative as well as military experience overseas and returned to live on substantial pensions and occupy important positions at home, like Sir Walter Ursewyk, knighted at Najera, head forester of the Blackburnshire chase. In 1419 eighty-six knights and gentlemen of Lancashire were annuitants of the duchy and of these thirty-four had been with Henry V at Agincourt. They were still the king-duke's right-hand men, available for royal service when the need arose.

By the seventeenth century the gentry of Lancashire were a rabble, and instead of tying the North to the centre the duchy had a contrary effect, isolating Lancashire from national institutions and the mainstream of national life. It kept Lancashire out of the jurisdiction of the King's Council in the North. It had even handled the dissolution of the monasteries in its area (with notable meanness) through its own bureaucracy instead of the Court of Augmentations, and duchy courts kept litigants from the king's courts in Westminster. Lancashire's gentry were immersed in local factions and feuds; they were not to be found in high offices of state. Their horizons did not extend beyond the limits of their local estates.[14]

Peace with Scotland meant that the north of England lost its political importance,[15] the gentry as military captains lost a source of income, and the yeomen of northern England lost security of tenure. The gentry had in large measure financed their purchase of monastic lands out of the profits of war. An unauthorized raid by Sir Robert Bowes in August 1542 cost £60,129 and the wider war against Scotland at this time £350,243.[16] Some of this expenditure was on fortifications, but exchequer costs were largely revenue for local military leaders. War with Scotland (and also with France) gave the gentry the lion's share of the monastic land market between 1542 and 1547.[17]

The landowners of northern England had for long enjoyed tax exemptions and immunities for their services in frontier defence. They lost their privileged tax position in 1610. Their exemption had been reaffirmed in 1581: the preamble to the act for fortifying the borders explained that northern landowners had been exempted from paying any of the subsidies voted by Elizabethan parliaments because the four border counties had borne the brunt of Scottish attacks.[18] The basis of this privilege had clearly been removed in 1603. (But in 1692, landowners in northern England largely recovered their tax privileges by the simple device of assessing their land for tax purposes at about one-fifth of its true value.[19] The now ancient history of the northern counties' contribution to frontier defence was still seen as justification for special treatment, although peace after 1603 in fact brought a significant rise in land values in border areas,[20] and with Parliament consisting largely of landowners it was disinclined to contest favours implicitiy claimed by the northern landed interest.)

The yeomen of northern England were unable to contrive any such recovery of lost privileges. Their eclipse in the seventeenth century is both a symptom and a cause of the decline of the North. Yeomen generally, in England fell from their fifteenth-century power and glory (as celebrated at the time by Sir John Fortescue and subsequently by many more).[21] This was part of the rise of the great landed estate of the eighteenth and nineteenth centuries and the reduction of small independent farmers to tenants-at-will. The land tax of 1692 was a principal factor in these developments, squeezing small landholders and forcing them out. But northern yeomen were especially vulnerable long before that. 'Yeomen' is not a tidy tenurial category: in the North they were less often freeholders, more commonly copyholders, tenants holding their land, hitherto very securely, by custom 'time out of mind.'[22] The principal reason for their decline was long prior to 1692, arising directly from the union of the English and Scottish crowns in 1603, and the two or three decades of relative peace that preceded it.

The Tudors had been quite clear that it was important to keep men and not sheep in a frontier zone, and a principal reason for reviving the Council of the North in 1530 was to safeguard the interests of customary tenants. That, indeed, was its essential brief. By the seventeenth century it functioned principally as a court of law, and its forty-two lawyer members, known as Judges at the court at York, handled around a thousand civil cases a year, most of them relating to customary tenures. The council had been specifically instructed to safeguard tenants against landlords who were 'extreme in taking gressoms'[23] (entrance fines charged when a tenant died and his son inherited); and the very low fixed rents were low indeed. In the south of England rents were usually as high as one-fifth of the value of the land; in the border areas as low as one-thirtieth or even one-hundredth.[24] The military role of the north of England had brought into being a highly privileged yeoman class.

These customary or 'tenant-right' tenures, which were widespread from Wensleydale and Swaledale up to the border, carried an obligation of military service which was in effect the major part of the rent. But these were not feudal knight-service tenures (which anyone who now held wanted to be rid of): tenant-right tenants insisted on their military obligations in border defence which were identified with their right to hold their lands (and pass them on to their heirs).

Remarkably, customary tenants in Wensleydale were insisting on their military obligations on the border in 1628. It was this that had always guaranteed their security, and they were now in conflict with the city of London which had received the Middleham lands from the crown in part-payment of debts. The city wished to curb their privileges and immunities, even to raise their rents and entry fines to an economic level, possibly to re-grant the land as leasehold, and most desirable of all, to make these copyhold tenants tenants-at-will.[25] The city lost and got rid of the land – just as James I had lost when, early in his reign, he relieved tenants on crown lands in border areas of their military service obligations and doubled their rents.[26] He had converted yeomen into tenants-at-will. But the outrage was enormous as tenants insisted on their military duties, and James countermanded the change.

But history was not on their side. A tenure secured by a military obligation that was now utterly irrelevant could not indefinitely survive. The Council of the North fought a long rearguard action. Wentworth acknowledged, when appointed lord president in 1628, that his essential purpose must be to protect the vulnerable from the proud and insolent: his fellow landowners in Yorkshire and the North. As Tawney emphasized, it was now only the prerogative courts that could possibly bridle the great landed proprietors and enforce the administration of unpopular statutes in the teeth of their opposition.[27] The 'grand remonstrance' presented to Charles I in December 1641 said that the lord president and the Council of the North (along with the Court of the Star Chamber) were 'so many forges of misery, oppression and violence'. There was not a single yeoman north of the Trent who would have agreed.

Long before 1640 the north of England was a demilitarized zone. There were no wardens of the march; tenant-right tenants with an obligation to keep a horse and weapons for border defence were clearly obsolete; the deputy-lieutenants who had responsibility for the county militia were militarily inexperienced and incompetent. In 1640, for the first time in six centuries, there was no one in northern England who had fought against the Scots. The only man of any military competence in the North was Thomas Fairfax of Denton, the future parliamentary general, and he had had to go to the Netherlands to learn his trade. This was part of the price for not having a standing army and for decades of peace with Scotland.

When the crisis (over the Laudian prayer book for Scotland) erupted in 1638, the vice-president of the Council of the North wrote to Secretary Coke that the commanders of the Yorkshire militia (there were thirty-seven greater gentry serving as deputy-lieutenants and many more lesser gentry serving as colonels under them) were so inefficient that eight or ten experts should be sent up from London to bring the trained bands to a reasonable standard of proficiency. By 1640 the military debacle in the North was total: two armies of occupation were quartered there, one from the south in Yorkshire, and one from Scotland in Northumberland and Newcastle-upon-Tyne.

In 1638 the gentry of Yorkshire refused to mobilize against the Scots (in 1640 citizens in Newcastle-upon-Tyne actually invited them in). The king had called the six northern counties to be brought to a state of readiness. Sir Edward Osborne of Kiveton, vice-president of the Council of the North, was the man mainly concerned with this operation (the lord president. Wentworth, was in Ireland). Sir William Savile of Thornhill refused point-blank to assemble with his troop of horse at York, and others made implausible excuses (Sir Hugh Cholmley refused to mobilize because he had caught a cold). Osborne was given larger powers early in 1639 as deputy-lieutenant-general but still met with widespread resistance. When an expeditionary force was needed for Scotland in 1640 the king's council of war decided that it should be drawn mainly from southern counties. It was thus that in 1640 there came to be quartered in Yorkshire an army of occupation from the South.

The contrast with 1513, the year of Flodden, is striking. The campaign of 1513 was also to be undertaken by the six northern counties, and they responded with enthusiasm. Seventy-year-old Sir Marmaduke Constable marched north with his East Riding contingent and distinguished himself in a battle in which ten Yorkshire knights were killed and eight West Riding gentlemen knighted for valour in the field. But in 1640 the north of England abdicated its historic role and its doing so led directly to civil war.

Of course the reasons for conflict in 1513 and 1640 were quite different. In 1513 the Scots were simply invaders supporting their allies, the French, but in 1640 there was some sympathy with the Scots on religious grounds. It was a group of Puritans in Newcastle-upon-Tyne who invited the army of the Scottish covenanters in in September 1640. But this is only a small part of the explanation. The events of 1638–40 suggest a formerly great military province in a state of demoralization and decline.

POVERTY AND CATHOLICISM

It was not only the loss of its historic military role that brought the north of England into decline, but also its increasing poverty (relative to southern and eastern England and especially London and the Home Counties), and its disproportionate Catholicism. Puritanism was the modernizing ideology of the age. Catholicism was strongly associated with social and economic conservatism and backwardness. There were northern pockets of Puritanism especially in the developing industrial regions of south-east Lancashire, north-east Cheshire, the West Riding of Yorkshire, and among the coal-miners of Tyneside, but England's Catholics were heavily concentrated in northern England, notably in Northumberland, but above all in Lancashire.

The Quakers, in their pioneering and excitable 'quaking' years, found their largest following in the north of England. Their founder, George Fox of Leicestershire, moved from the north Midlands in 1651 to preach in Yorkshire, and then went on to Durham and the Lakeland counties, where he found his strongest support. He was not well received by northern Puritan leaders, but by 1654 there were sixty towns or villages with 'settled meetings' in the six northern counties. They were overwhelmingly, although not exclusively, in the remotest backwaters of the land. Six were in industrially advanced south and west Yorkshire (in

Sheffield, Doncaster, Halifax, Bradford, Leeds and Wakefield), but twenty were in or around the north Yorkshire moors, the Yorkshire wolds, and in deepest Holderness (for instance at Ulrome, Skipsea, Granswick, Patrington and Cottam-on-Wolds). There were also six in the area of industrial enterprise in Lancashire, but twenty were in remote Furness, Westmorland and Cumberland (for instance at Brigham, Portinscale, Orton, Shap, Rampside and Pardshaw). The remaining eight were in Northumberland and county Durham. The North's contribution to Quaker leadership was James Nayler from Ardsley near Barnsley. His triumphal entry into Bristol in 1656 in the manner of Christ riding into Jerusalem, however, ended in personal tragedy (he was whipped and severely mutilated on a charge of blasphemy) and was a major set-back for the movement. Quakerism in northern England in the 1650s is not evidence of a burgeoning northern progressiveness, but of deep and continuing backwardness. If these quaking northerners had appeared half a century earlier, they would almost certainly have been executed as witches.

In terms of personal property assessed for tax in 1636 the northern counties were the poorest in England, with Cumberland the poorest of all. Close behind were Sussex, Shropshire, Staffordshire and Derbyshire. The richest were Middlesex and Hertfordshire.[28] The county which had experienced the steadiest and steepest long-term decline was Lincolnshire: among the wealthiest half-dozen counties in 1334, it was in the bottom third by 1636. The counties which were becoming richer had generally increased their proportion of urban wealth: Lincolnshire's proportion had remained fairly static (the wealth of Boston had actually declined). Among the northern counties only Yorkshire had been showing a marked increase in its proportion of urban wealth, some 12 per cent in the mid-fourteenth century, and by the mid-sixteenth century around 23 per cent. (But Berkshire's urban wealth rose from under 10 per cent to nearly 50 per cent over the same period.)[29] By the seventeenth century the urban wealth of Yorkshire was in the developing textile towns of the West Riding, notably Bradford, Halifax and Leeds.

The remoter rural areas of northern England were becoming miserably poor. Richmondshire in the seventeenth century was a pale shadow of its fifteenth-century glory. Poor squires were desperately trying to raise rents, contrasting sharply with the exuberant, well-to-do gentry two centuries earlier.[30] The decline in rural Northumberland was very similar;[31] although Newcastle itself experienced a remarkable development as London grew at a phenomenal rate and looked to Newcastle to supply its coal.[32] It was the gentry of south Yorkshire who were now the men of substance. Some were directly involved in the developing textile industry (like the Saviles in Halifax), but in any event their lands supplied wool, food, and cereals for beer for a growing market. (The Fairfax lands near Tadcaster were important for the production of beer which clothiers, unlike farmers, did not make or usually drink at home. They consumed their beer in public rather than private houses.)

The rise of the south Yorkshire gentry also owed much to the advantage they had taken of the West Riding monastic land sales in the 1540s. Many yeomen and lesser gentry bought monastic land, the aristocracy comparatively little.[33] In Yorkshire this major transfer of land resulted in 'a spectacular increase in the economic wealth of the squirearchy'.[34] The Lancashire gentry failed to rise, however. They gained little from the sale of monastic land sold relatively expensively by the duchy, and in the half century after 1590 their average income actually declined.[35] The Lancashire gentry (even as defined by the College of Heralds) were certainly numerous; they were also intensely conscious of rank, and markedly endogamous, compared for instance with the gentry of Essex and Hertfordshire. Only the gentry of neighbouring Cheshire were comparably clannish, insular, and inclined to marry almost exclusively within the county[36]

The Lancashire gentry were numerous but poor. Only 23 out of 774 gentry families (3 per cent) had incomes over £1,000 a year in 1640. In Yorkshire it was 73 out of 679, or 11 per cent. In all northern counties a large proportion of the gentry had less than £100 a year, many less than £10, such as Rowland Beckingham of Hornby in Lancashire, who had £8 a year. In Yorkshire, however, 15 (2 per cent) had over £2,000 a year. Sir Thomas Wentworth of Wentworth Woodhouse, five miles south of Barnsley, inherited an estate worth £4,000 a year in 1614; in 1628 it was worth £6,000 a year. In 1620 the house at Wentworth Woodhouse employed fifty servants and the cost of feeding the household was £1,500 a year.[37] This was wealth comparable to that of many aristocrats, and probably greater than that of the Stanley earls of Derby across the Pennines, who estimated their income in 1649 as £4,281 a year and not much more thirty years later.[38]

Two disabilities of the north of England in the seventeenth century were the loss of its historic military role and its relative poverty. A third disability was its Catholicism. Catholicism was associated with backwardness and conservatism, Puritanism with progress. The North also had its Puritans, but these were most commonly craftsmen, clothiers,

TABLE 9.1 Wealth of northern gentry in the early seventeenth century

County	Number of gentry families	Wealth over £1,000/year (no.)	(%)	Wealth under £1,000/year (no.)	(%)
Yorkshire	679	73	11	362	53
Lancashire	774	23	3	204	26
Northumberland	89	7	8	36	40
Lakeland Counties	180	7	4	41	23

Sources: J. T. Cliffe, *The Yorkshire Gentry. From the Reformation to the Civil War* (Athlone, 1969), pp. 29–31.

R. G. Blackwood, *The Lancashire Gentry and the Great Rebellion 1640–60* (Chetham Society, 1978), pp. 12–18.

S. J. Watts, *From Border to Middle Shire. Northumberland 1586–1625* (Leicester University Press, 1975), p. 63.

'urban yeomen'. Puritanism was most effective for 'progress' when it was the religion of merchant princes.[39] There were few merchant princes in the north of England: they were mostly in London.

By the early seventeenth century the great majority of Englishmen were neither Catholic nor Puritan. They had accepted the Elizabethan church settlement and were regular church-goers who seldom incurred the fine of twelve pence for non-attendance. But there was a minority of Puritans distinguished by their rejection of ecclesiastical hierarchy and the pride of place they gave to preaching in church services. There was also a minority of Catholics, some of whom (recusants) were openly defiant, refused church attendance, and paid their fines. Puritans were most heavily concentrated in East Anglia and London and to a lesser extent in the clothing areas of south-west England. The heaviest concentration of Catholics was in the isolated plain of south-west Lancashire. The Fylde, low-lying and remote, was probably the most intensely Catholic area of England.

Puritanism was urban and mercantile and its distribution was along trade networks. London and East Anglia were in close contact with Holland and gentlemen of this region quite often sent their sons to the University of Leyden (300 in the 1630s). Manchester and other textile towns of south-east Lancashire were in close contact with London. (Sir Nicholas Mosley, a Manchester merchant, became lord mayor of London in 1599.) Because of their Puritanism, Manchester and Bolton became known as 'the London of the North' and 'the Geneva of Lancashire' respectively. There were also eight or nine market towns in central and eastern Cheshire with close London connections and marked Puritan leanings.[40] Indeed Cheshire, unlike much of Lancashire, was widely disposed to Puritanism (except in the far West), and many of its gentry had wide trading contacts, notably Sir William Brereton, the future leader of a very effective local parliamentary army, patron of Puritan divines. His estates were at Handforth near Macclesfield; he knew Holland well; and he was involved in the Dorchester Company for trade and colonization in New England.

There were no Puritans in the Wirral, however, and in the Fylde there were only two small market towns (Poulton and Kirkham) and they were certainly not centres of Puritanism. These western areas were lost in mud-flats, moorland and sand-dunes. And even in the active industrial towns of the region, Wigan, Ormskirk and Preston, the weavers used flax and their contacts were not with London but Ireland. Their relations with a wider world did not bring in Puritan ideas and preachers; they fortified the Catholics.[41]

Taking England's population in 1640 as a whole, the Catholic element was very small indeed, probably less than 2 per cent. Even in Northumberland and Yorkshire, perhaps 4 per cent of households were Catholic, and in Durham 5 per cent. The highest proportion by far was in Lancashire, with probably between 18 and 20 per cent. (Only Monmouthshire was comparable.)[42] But among the gentry there were much higher proportions. Around a quarter of Yorkshire's gentry were Catholic;[43] and even in the Lake counties, where the population was generally Protestant, almost 20 per cent of the gentry were Catholic.[44] Proportions in the general population were also very high in some relatively small isolated communities. Some of the Pennine dales had a very high proportion: Coquetdale, Teesdale and Swaledale (although Redesdale, Weardale and Wharfedale had not). High concentrations were generally related to geographical isolation.

English Catholics in the seventeenth century were by no means invariably without entrepreneurial ability. Catholic gentry on Tyneside and in the West Riding of Yorkshire were much involved in the development of coal-mining (although this may be seen as a highly traditional industry carried on in highly traditional communities). One historian highly sympathetic to the Catholic position concedes that backward and isolated areas seem often to have attracted Catholic gentry at this time, and to have reinforced their conservatism. With the Fylde and

Amounderness particularly in mind, he concludes that the Catholic gentry were singularly unadventurous: 'Try as one may, one cannot quite escape from the prevailing notion that a choice of Catholicism must have corresponded to some more general sluggishness of spirit, and that in turn to some lack of stimulus in the regional environment.[45]

It was Puritanism that was more generally associated with energy, initiative and enterprise: in colonizing and trading ventures in America,[46] possibly in scientific research and discovery,[47] more certainly with political radicalism. These activities and interests overlapped; thus John Pym of Somerset was not only a revolutionary parliamentary leader but treasurer of the Dorset-based Providence Company for eight years (1630–8) and a man with a deeply informed interest in science. A similar overlap of interests was notable in the eastern counties: 'It is remarkable what a preponderant part East Anglia played in the great Puritan emigration and the Puritan revolution ten years later.'[48] Puritanism seems to have promoted independence of mind, individualism, rationality, and an emphasis on experience and experiment rather than authority (although in some circumstances it also produced intolerance, conformity and a collectivist spirit).[49] In south Yorkshire it produced a general hostility to all authority. As Wentworth complained in 1637: 'The very genius of that nation of people [the Puritans] leads them always to oppose civilly as well as ecclesiastically all that authority ever ordains for them.'[50]

THE CIVIL WAR: TAKING SIDES

The principal indication of the backwardness and deep-seated traditionalism of the north of England in the seventeenth century was its involvement in the civil war, mainly on the royalist side. The war was fought everywhere in a sea of neutrality, and in every county and major town there were divided loyalties. Nevertheless, it is quite possible to locate the two sides in an approximate way geographically, ideologically and economically. The war was fought between England's core and its northern and western perimeter. The perimeter was by definition remote and relatively isolated. It was also poorer, less Puritan, more Catholic, and less urbanized.

Some individual royalists were immensely rich and included merchants as well as landed aristocrats. Although cities were broadly associated with the parliamentarian cause, top mercantile wealth tended to be royalist. This was so even in the mainly parliamentarian cities of Norwich, Leeds

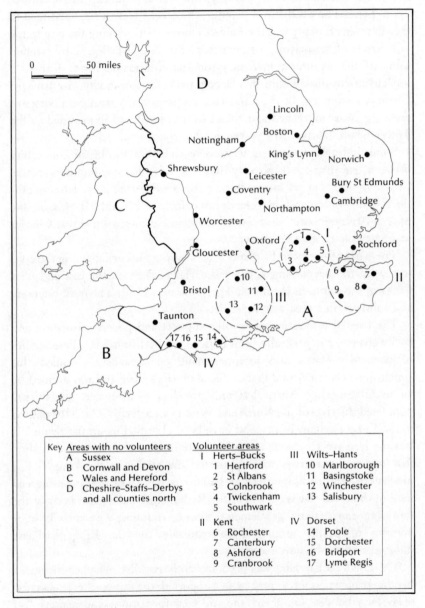

MAP 9.1 Thirty-four towns that raised volunteers for Parliament, June–September 1642
Source: adapted from A. Fletcher, *The Outbreak of the Civil War* (Arnold, 1981).

and Hull. Perhaps less surprisingly, this was also the case in Newcastle-upon-Tyne. The royalist commander, the earl of Newcastle, appointed in the summer of 1642, was soon able to move south leaving the city in the safe hands of its mayor and governor, Sir John Marley.[51] In London some of the wealthiest merchants on the aldermanic bench formed a nucleus of royalists within this largely parliamentarian city. Sir Richard Gurney, lord mayor in 1641 and 1642, a particularly strong supporter of the king, was impeached and found guilty, fined and imprisoned in the Tower where he died five years later.[52]

Some individual royalists were very rich, but the broad connection between royalism and poverty holds good: the communities where Charles found support and soldiers for his armies were poor. Monmouth-shire, Shropshire and Hereford came first to his aid. It was on the poverty-stricken outer perimeter of England at Shrewsbury that Charles was first able to raise an army.

The parts of northern England which supported Parliament in the civil war were the developing urban-industrial regions on the east and west flanks of the southern Pennines. There was also Hull. The most intensely and solid royalist area was Teesdale.

The overall association of royalist support and poverty, isolation and backwardness has generally been underlined by historians. Close studies of particular towns and localities have not seriously modified this conclusion. Gardiner said that by October 1642 'England was divided by an undulating line which left only the less wealthy and less thickly populated districts of the North and West to Charles.'[53] The MPs elected to the Long Parliament in 1640 have been classified in similar terms: 'It was the heart of England, in wealth, population and progressive quality' that returned members who supported the attack on the king.[54] The nineteenth-century biographer of Fairfax wrote: 'Nearly all commercial men in the great towns . . . were for Parliament; and a great body of the more ignorant country gentlemen in remote counties, who knew little or nothing of public affairs, were naturally for the King.'[55] These judgments were broadly correct.

The north of England was predominantly royalist, whether measured by the proportion of gentry who supported the king, the proportion of MPs who did so, or by the military formations and actions that occurred between 1642 and the battle of Marston Moor in July 1644. This royalism was prefigured in the petitioning movement regarding ecclesiastical organization and religious affairs that developed after December 1640. But there was no instant royalism in the north of

England in the summer of 1642. Northern England was not a region where great initiatives were taken on either side.

Even Sir Thomas Fairfax showed considerable hesitation in the West Riding on the parliamentary side. He had boldly and with some difficulty and even danger presented a petition to Charles on Heworth Moor in June 1642 and by September, although he was not an MP, was cast as a military leader in the West Riding for the parliamentary cause. In October he was making a neutrality pact with Yorkshire's royalists. Parliament refused to recognize the pact and the clothiers of Halifax called him to action on their behalf.

Yorkshire's potential royalists had also been holding back since Charles arrived in York in March expecting strong support. Only thirty-nine gentlemen came to his court. He was in Yorkshire to raise an army and secure the arsenal at Hull. He did neither. When he called the freeholders of Yorkshire to an assembly on Heworth Moor on 3 June – essentially a recruiting drive – he met with suspicion and hostility rather than support.[56] When he left Yorkshire for Nottingham it was still without an army. Active royalism in the north of England appeared only after the war had begun.

There was still widespread resentment among the gentry of the North against Yorkshire's first royalist, Thomas Wentworth, earl of Strafford. This caused distortions in the natural pattern of northern allegiance. Wentworth had curbed the gentry's pretensions and privileges, and while some had gained from his patronage, most had not. It was because they were the 'outs' rather than the 'ins' in the North, rather than in any national sense, that many Yorkshire gentry were at first against the king.

Sir John Hotham MP is a case in point: an East Riding squire who, on Parliament's instructions, took command of Hull and refused to let Charles in – in effect the first action of the civil war. In the factional strife of the region Hotham had failed to secure the patronage of Wentworth as lord president of the Council of the North and the hegemony of the East Riding of Yorkshire slipped from his grasp to Sir Thomas Metham. (Metham was an ardent royalist in 1642, in attendance on Charles in York, urging him on to his vain assault on Hull.) Eventually Hotham changed to support the royalist cause realizing that his true interests lay in a traditional hierarchical social order. Henry Bellasis, son of Lord Fauconberg, likewise deeply hostile to Wentworth, was another prominent Yorkshire MP who changed sides (somewhat earlier). Some 12 per cent of those MPs elected to the Long Parliament whose initial posture was against the king later changed sides.[57] In Yorkshire it was 30 per cent (four out of thirteen initially anti-royalist MPs). In 1640 there had been heightened resentment against Wentworth among the Yorkshire gentry as he tried to influence elections to the Long Parliament. But by 1642–3 these earlier 'distortions' in the pattern of Yorkshire's allegiance had been rectified. At least in terms of its MPs, 65 per cent of whom now supported the king, Yorkshire was clearly a royalist stronghold.

By the early stages of the civil war, 41 per cent of all England's MPs were royalists (as indicated by their later 'disablement' and exclusion). Three regions of England were significantly more royalist than this national average: the northern counties (Cumberland, Westmorland, Northumberland, Lancashire, Yorkshire and Cheshire), 61 per cent; the western counties of England (Hereford, Shropshire and Worcestershire), also 61 per cent; the South-west (Cornwall, Devon, Somerset, Dorset, Gloucestershire and Wiltshire), 50 per cent. Three regions were below: the Midlands (37 per cent); the South-east (27 per cent); and the eastern counties of Cambridgeshire, Essex, Hertfordshire, Huntingdonshire, Lincolnshire, Norfolk and Suffolk, (only 20 per cent). These groupings inevitably obscure some important exceptions: thus three 'mid-western' counties, Dorset, Wiltshire and Hampshire, were well below average in royalism (34 per cent of their MPs).[58]

The picture of northern royalism in terms of the region's 64 MPs is confirmed by an analysis of the region's 1,282 gentry who took an active part in the civil war. Table 9.2 summarizes the data for those counties for which information is available.

Only in the case of Cheshire do the data for MPs and for gentry point in opposite directions: 75 per cent of the small number of MPs were royalist, but only 46 per cent of the 255 active gentry. This second figure is a better reflection of the deeply and evenly divided conflict in Cheshire.

In all counties at least a significant minority, and sometimes a substantial majority of gentry remained neutral. Neutrality was generally related to poverty. In Lancashire, on the whole a very royalist county, two-thirds of the gentry, who were mostly quite poor, remained neutral;[59] in the Lake counties around 40 per cent did so,[60] and in Yorkshire about a third.[61]

The taking of sides at gentry level cannot be explained, except to a very minor degree, simply in terms of county factions. And at sub-gentry level it cannot be explained, except in quite rare instances, as pressure from landlords and other social superiors (so-called 'feudalism'). Nor can it be explained in any locality in terms of the army that arrived there first. The English civil war was about the way in which England should be

TABLE 9.2 Northern parliamentarian and royalist MPs and gentry 1642–3

	MPs		Gentry	
	Royalist	Parliamentarian	Royalist	Parliamentarian
Cumberland and Westmorland	7	3	77	21
Northumberland	5	5	—	—
Lancashire	7	7	272	138
Yorkshire	17	9	242	128
Cheshire	3	1	117	138
Shropshire	—	—	85	64
Total	39	25	793	489
Proportion (%)	61	39	61	39

Sources: D. Brunton and D. H. Pennington *Members of the Long Parliament* (Allen & Unwin, 1954).
J. S. Morrill, 'The northern gentry and the great rebellion', *Northern History*, 15 (1979),
pp. 66–87.

governed,[62] but no armies could have been raised to fight this war if the constitutional issues had not been transposed into religious terms. For local participants in the war, at all levels, this was a war of religion.[63] The men of northern England fought for the king in 1642 as they had fought for the northern earls in 1569, because the politics had been overlaid by religion and they were fighting a crusade.[64]

This was why Wentworth had to be executed in 1641. It was not because of his conduct of government, but because it was thought he would bring over an army of Irish Catholics. The conflict received its religious imprint after December 1640 when London's alderman Pennington initiated 'root and branch' petitions for the abolition of episcopacy. The initiative typically came from London, but the provinces took it up. A year later anti-popery petitions began in the counties around London (Essex, Suffolk and Buckinghamshire). Again there was a ripple-effect finally extending to counties on the perimeter. But all counties did not petition against episcopacy. Yorkshire, Durham, Northumberland, Cumberland and Westmorland did not, and some, including Lancashire, Cheshire and Northumberland, sent counter-petitions (to the king) in favour of episcopacy. It was in this protracted public debate about religion, extending over more than a year and a half, that the northern counties uncovered their underlying royalist stance.

What really calls for explanation in the north of England is not royalism but support for Parliament. Wentworth caused a limited and temporary deviation among the Yorkshire gentry, but a far more potent and lasting cause of deviation was Puritanism. It has been cogently argued in one close study of society at this time that Puritanism detached northern gentry from their natural allegiance: 'it is difficult to see how a parliamentary party could have developed within the Yorkshire gentry' without its powerful influence.[65]

Armies were raised for Parliament only in the very limited (but populous) areas of northern England, where Puritanism had become deeply entrenched and Puritan gentry were numerous. This was the position in the West Riding of Yorkshire where about a quarter of the gentry were Puritan – some seventy-five families. (In the remoter, poorer North Riding, by contrast, only some 10 per cent of gentry families were Puritan.) South-east Lancashire and eastern Cheshire were also Puritan strongholds. Sir Thomas Fairfax recruited his army from Yorkshire's Puritan areas; Sir William Brereton recruited his from Cheshire and Lancashire. Both armies were formidable. Indeed, Brereton had virtually conquered Cheshire by the end of 1643; after his victory at the battle of

Nantwich on 25 January 1644 he received a Roman triumph in the streets of London. Chester held out for the king until February 1646, but this was not a predominantly royalist county: Puritanism had a strong following among gentry, clergy, and the common people.[66]

Royalist armies in the north of England were far less exclusive. They embraced all shades of religious belief. Catholicism was not absolutely essential to royalist armies in the way that Puritanism was to parliamentary armies; indeed, some northern royalist armies had few Catholics, or even, for a time, none. The earl of Derby refused at first to recruit Catholics in Lancashire until they appealed over his head to the king, and there were few Catholics in Sir Philip Musgrave's Lakeland army: only seven officers, from the thirty-five Catholic gentry families in the area. There was probably more neutralism among Catholic gentry than among the gentry in general, except at the highest social levels,[67] but there is no doubt that dedication and commitment were enormously enhanced when Catholics were recruited in strength, and especially when they held top command posts.

And to a notable extent they did. Neither of the two principal royalist commanders in the North – the earl of Derby and the earl of Newcastle – was a Catholic, but very high status Catholic gentry were generally eager to fight. Royalist armies tended to be over-officered, and officers of field rank were disproportionately Catholic. The proportion of Catholic majors and colonels seems to have been directly proportional to military vigour. Only 5 per cent of officers of field rank in the Lakeland army were Catholics, and the army, insular and inactive, was practically useless. In Lancashire the proportion of Catholic officers of field rank was over 80 per cent (in Northumberland and Durham around 50, in Yorkshire about 30).[68] The (somewhat belated) inclusion of Catholics in the royalist army in Lancashire transformed the situation there: Charles had acceded to their appeal to take up arms in his cause and 'By consenting to their request the King received a measure of support which largely accounts for the length and bitterness of the war in Lancashire.'[69]

One region of northern England that did produce Catholic officers and men out of all proportion to the size of its population was the Tees valley on both the Yorkshire and Durham sides.[70] This was the very heart and soul of the northern royalist offensive, where the Catholic colonel Sir William Lambton raised his regiment of 'Newcastle's Lambs' – who put Hotham to flight at Piercebridge on 1 December 1642, and died almost to a man with their colonel at Marston Moor in July 1644, a remarkable re-enactment of the religious crusade fought by the men of Teesdale in 1569.

The northern royalist armies were volunteer armies, although it has often been claimed that they were feudal at least in the sense that landlords put pressure on their tenants to fight.[71] There is no truth in this.[72] The earl of Derby in particular has been accused of such feudalism, but in deeply divided Lancashire and Cheshire tenants could easily show their independence by fighting for parliamentary armies, and commonly did so (this helps to account for Brereton's success).[73] Tenants who went to fight for the king in 1642 appear to have done so quite independently.[74] William Cavendish, earl of Newcastle, has also been accused of feudalism in securing Newcastle-upon-Tyne for the king and raising his army of 'whitecoats' mainly in Northumberland and Durham. But William Cavendish of Welbeck and Bolsover, lord lieutenant of Nottinghamshire and Derbyshire, had only tenuous connections with the border counties and was a stranger there. His mother was a younger daughter of Lord Ogle of Bothal castle in Northumberland and had inherited very little land in the North.[75] When he marched to Newcastle-upon-Tyne with a force of 500 men they were not feudal tenants and retainers, they were the local militia of Durham county. His immortal whitecoats were not feudal retainers, either, but (very largely Catholic) volunteers. They were a professional army fighting for pay. But they were also fighting for a cause.

The cause, at bottom, was simply royalism. Religion, economics and geography were strongly associated with it but do not wholly explain it. Royalism in the north of England had a subterranean dimension; its explanation is primarily historical. Its roots were in the fifteenth century and its focal points were those castle towns of the North with either strong Lancastrian or Yorkist connections. In 1640, if they were parliamentary boroughs, they elected royalist MPs (for example Pontefract, Knaresborough, Ripon, Scarborough and Thirsk); in 1644 they held out militarily when the North had been defeated (Pontefract, Knaresborough, Sandal, Scarborough, Helmsley and Skipton). The second civil war of 1648 was not of their making, but when it occurred 'royalist groups appearing from nowhere'[76] seized Pontefract and Scarborough. Royalism in the north of England in the 1640s cannot be reduced wholly to religion or economics; or even to self-interest.

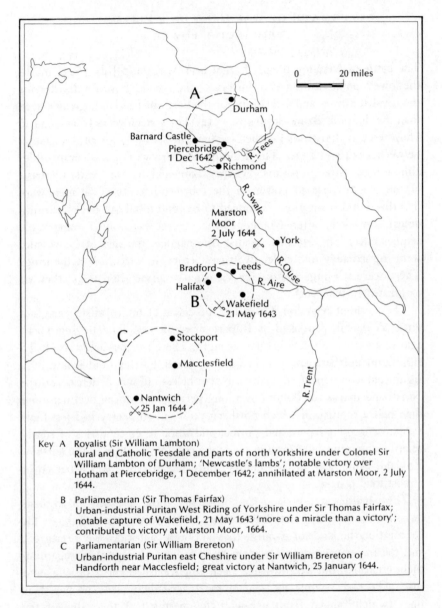

Key A Royalist (Sir William Lambton)
        Rural and Catholic Teesdale and parts of north Yorkshire under Colonel Sir
        William Lambton of Durham; 'Newcastle's lambs'; notable victory over
        Hotham at Piercebridge, 1 December 1642; annihilated at Marston Moor, 2 July
        1644.

     B Parliamentarian (Sir Thomas Fairfax)
        Urban-industrial Puritan West Riding of Yorkshire under Sir Thomas Fairfax;
        notable capture of Wakefield, 21 May 1643 'more of a miracle than a victory';
        contributed to victory at Marston Moor, 1664.

     C Parliamentarian (Sir William Brereton)
        Urban-industrial Puritan east Cheshire under Sir William Brereton of
        Handforth near Macclesfield; great victory at Nantwich, 25 January 1644.

MAP 9.2   Three areas of particular military commitment and potency in the
civil war

Source: author

AFTERMATH OF WAR: LONDON'S VICTORY AND
PROVINCIAL POWER

The battle of Marston Moor, fought near York on 2 July 1644, marks
the lowest point in the entire history of the North. It was a disaster for
the royalist armies and a calamity for the north of England, greater even
than the defeat at Bannockburn in 1314. The sixteen years from 1644 to
1660 were as disastrous for the North as the sixteen years of devastation
between 1314 and 1330. The drain on northern wealth was comparable,
although by different means. Whereas Bannockburn was really the basis
of the North's rise to power in the fourteenth century, as men were
mobilized and institutions fashioned to respond to all but overwhelming
defeat, however, after Marston Moor there was only a remarkable
acquiescence. The North's royalist commander, the earl of Newcastle,
went immediately into exile, five years before the execution of the king.
There were stirrings against the victorious regime after 1645: they all
originated in the South.

The battle of Marston Moor and the defeat of the royalists were in a
sense accidental, provoked by Rupert, after successfully relieving York,
against an army of much greater strength. The victorious army also had a
significant northern component fighting under Fairfax (and ironically a
significant component of Scots). Nevertheless, it was a defeat for the
North and marks the bottom of a long period of northern decline: more
than half a century in which northern yeomen and gentry had lost their
earlier sense of purpose and power, and some three centuries of steady
relative economic deterioration. A strong economic upturn in the north of
England came later in the century, but 1644 to 1660 was a period of
almost total eclipse.

The penalties imposed on Catholics, like those imposed on royalists
(whether Catholics or not) fell heavily on the northern counties. At the
Restoration the lands of royalists that had been confiscated were restored,
and the majority of royalists seem to have been successful in regaining
their estates.[77] But families had been impoverished for a decade, and
those who had 'voluntarily' sold or mortgaged their estates to pay their
fines (which ranged from one-tenth to one-third of the value of the
property) had no redress. The heir to the earl of Derby (who was executed
in 1651) was eventually allowed £500 a year to relieve his family's
distress: the value of the estate was around £5,000 a year. The
discriminatory tax of 10 per cent imposed in 1656 under the rule of

Cromwell's major-generals applied only to royalists. The tax was expected to raise only £1,100 a year in Lancashire where royalist gentry were deeply impoverished, but in Lincolnshire three times as much.[78]

The north of England remained remarkably quiescent. There were reports of an anti-government party forming in Northumberland and Durham after the imposition of the decimation tax, but northerners were involved in royalist conspiracies in only a minor and subsidiary way. Penruddock's four-day rising in Wiltshire in March 1655 should have been supported by an attack on York, but the northern conspirators failed even to achieve a preliminary rendezvous on Marston Moor.[79] Booth's rising in Cheshire in August 1659 was part of a nation-wide plan and occurred only because Sir George failed to receive the message which called the operation off.[80] The decisive influence in 1660 was precisely what it had been in 1640, 1642 and 1649: London. As Macaulay concluded: 'In truth it is no exaggeration to say that, but for the hostility of the City (of London), Charles the First would never have been vanquished, and that, without the help of the City, Charles the Second could scarcely have been restored.'[81]

The contrast with the thirteenth-century rebellion against King John is striking. Then the initiative came from the North and London's contribution was at a relatively late stage (although it proved to be of critical importance). The northern spearhead of revolt in the early thirteenth century was in eastern Yorkshire, one of England's richest regions, at the crest of a long period of steady economic growth. In the conflict of the early seventeenth century northern involvement came only in the wake of London's initiatives, and the principal contribution came no longer from east Yorkshire but from south Yorkshire and the West Riding. This developing urban-industrial region, along with south-east Lancashire and eastern Cheshire, was now the principal site of northern wealth, and the strongest northern initiatives, whether by gentry or 'the middle sort of people', originated there. The East Riding produced only the relatively lightweight Hotham; Brereton from east Cheshire and Fairfax from the West Riding were landed gentry in close touch with the new sources of wealth. But the nation's wealth was now heavily concentrated in East Anglia and London, and these were the regions that took the lead.

The seventeenth was indeed London's century. London's merchants and bankers, its aldermen, its preachers, and its citizens were in their different ways critically important in the events which led to the civil war and in the war itself. London's citizen army, a force of some 10,000 men, was formidable and twice saved the parliamentarians from defeat: in November 1642 when it repelled Prince Rupert's attack on London at Turnham Green, and in the following year when it relieved Worcester. The political pressure exerted by London's massed citizens was most apparent in the fortnight before Charles finally signed Strafford's death warrant on 10 May 1640, and again the week of 3 January to 10 January 1642 when London took the Five Members into its protection and forced the king and his family to leave the capital.

In the economic, religious and cultural life of the nation, London's influence was more subtly pervasive. Its sheer growth pulled in some 8,000 people a year and so established personal links with the capital throughout the kingdom.[82] England, it has been said, was 'Londonized' and the victory of Parliament over the crown confirmed and extended this process.[83] The period of Cromwell's rule saw a standardization of social life which culminated in the close moral supervision of community life under the major-generals. Legally and constitutionally, perimeter England was tidied up: the palatinate of Durham was formally abolished and for the first time in its history, in 1653, Durham sent MPs to Westminster (although the bishop was still able to resist this and parliamentary representation was not finally established until 1672 when the See was vacant). The commissioners for the propagation of the gospel in Wales and the four border counties carried London ideas and religion into the remotest and darkest corners of the land.[84]

In the short run the victory of Parliament over the crown was a victory for London and for the urban, mercantile, Puritan civilization of the South. But in the slightly longer term a victory for Parliament meant a victory for the county communities of England and the MPs who represented their interests. In 1660 the earl of Newcastle warned Charles II that he must first control London 'for so you master the whole of England', but a quarter of a century later James II knew that his real problem was not London but the power structures of the provinces. It was these he attempted to dominate through wholesale dismissals and replacements of lord lieutenants of counties, their deputies and justices of the peace as a means of controlling MPs;[85] in doing so he united the aristocracy and gentry of provincial England and provoked the essentially aristocratic Glorious Revolution of 1688.

The resurgence of northern England had begun. It did not have to wait on the industrial revolution. The Restoration itself had started the process by giving political opportunities to northern cavaliers especially when they had Wentworth connections. Thomas Osborne, later earl of Danby and duke of Leeds, was the son of Sir Edward Osborne of Kiveton in south Yorkshire who had been Wentworth's highly trusted deputy-lord-president of the Council of the North. George Savile, the future earl of Halifax, was Wentworth's nephew. Wentworths, Saviles and Osbornes were near-neighbours in south Yorkshire, although the Savile home at Thornhill was destroyed in the second civil war and the family moved to Rufford in Nottinghamshire. There was often tension between Saviles and Osbornes, but Sir George Savile was godfather to a daughter of Osborne (later earl of Danby). The Wentworth connection is not the sole explanation of their rise to 'cabinet rank' in the reign of Charles II (Osborne secured the patronage of another Yorkshire neighbour, George Villiers, second duke of Buckingham). But the Wentworth connection is a thread which runs through the political fortunes of Yorkshire's eminent statesmen down through the eighteenth century.

The rebirth of the North was beginning without benefit of the industrial revolution. Even coal brought the North new wealth, power and importance over the century before the industrial revolution actually began. It revivified the wealth and power of northern landed society between the later seventeenth and mid-eighteenth centuries. When Sir James Lowther of Whitehaven died in 1755 the *Gentlemen's Magazine* said that he was the richest commoner not only in England but the whole of Great Britain. Three-quarters of his income from his Cumberland estates now came from coal. The profits of his mines had risen tenfold between 1706 and 1750.[86]

The situation in Cumberland was broadly replicated in Durham. There, in the North-east, the Lumleys (earls of Scarborough after 1690), greatest landowners in Weardale, were comparable to the Lowthers in the North-west. Coal made proportionately the biggest contribution to their fortunes in the seventy years before 1750. Comparatively speaking, it was of much less importance by 1850.[87] (Landowners generally in Durham could expect royalties at the rate of 25 per cent of the pit-head price of coal from the late seventeenth to the mid-eighteenth century, but only 6 per cent by 1850.)[88] Lumleys and Lowthers were only the foremost among northern landowners who were enriched by coal during the century before Watt invented the steam engine and Cort developed a process for smelting iron with coke.

The landed society of the provincial North was experiencing a renaissance of power and wealth because of the massively disproportionate growth of capital cities in the South. The Lumleys shipped their coal from Sunderland to an extraordinarily exuberant and expansive London; the Lowthers shipped theirs from Whitehaven to a no less exuberant and expansive Dublin – the second city in Britain, the tenth in Europe (it more than trebled its size between 1700 and 1800). The rebirth of the North came in the first instance not from Watt's steam engine but from enormous imbalances in the development of centre and circumference.

Three of the 'immortal seven' who signed the invitation of Prince William of Orange were northerners: Lord Lumley of County Durham, William Cavendish, earl of Devonshire (who became duke of Devonshire in 1694) and Yorkshire's Thomas Osborne, earl of Danby (who became duke of Leeds in 1694). A fourth northerner, George Savile, marquis of Halifax, who was not a signatory, nevertheless played a vital role in preparing for the revolution and was in effect ruler of England between the departure of James II and Prince William's arrival in London. Henry Booth, the second Lord Delamere, was also active in his native Cheshire in support of the revolution (he became earl of Warrington in 1692 and received a pension of £2,000 a year).

Historians have tended to belittle the importance of all the 'immortal seven' and especially of the three northerners.[89] Even Danby, the most eminent of the three, it is pointed out, was now an elderly, unemployed ex-prisoner who had not held office for the past nine years, five of which he had spent in the Tower.[90] Lumley's strategic control over London's coal supply was certainly not irrelevant to deposing one king of England and installing another,[91] but the northerners certainly overplayed their hand. Danby had asked for a commission as lieutenant-general of the five northern counties: a strong echo of traditional northern separatism. He would have emerged from the revolution as virtual viceroy of the North. William undoubtedly recognized the importance of northerners and of northern power, which is why he had no intention of increasing it.

But there were now more general circumstances making for a revival of the provinces and especially of the North. The seventeenth-century victory of Parliament was a victory for MPs who claimed and exercized a remarkable independence as spokesmen of almost self-governing local communities. The party machinery and discipline which would circumscribe their independence was far in the future. Their regional power was most clearly signalled not in northern support for William of Orange but in the land tax of 1692 when northern landowners regained their favoured treatment. It would reach its peak in 1779–80 in the Yorkshire Association's assault on the power of the king's ministers. The centre was a threat to regional independence and privilege, and from Burton Constable in Richmondshire Christopher Wyvill would mobilize the squirearchy of Yorkshire – and indeed of England – to counter it. Only the squires of Lancashire failed to lend any support.

10

Resurgence and Renewal

The eighteenth century saw a resurgence of northern England which came to fruition in the great provincial cities of the Victorian age. Its nature was essentially economic, but there was also a resurgence of the landed interest which culminated in the activities of The Revd Christopher Wyvill and the Yorkshire Association in the late 1770s. The Association gave leadership to a quasi-revolutionary national movement asserting provincial power against the centre. The economic take-off towards the end of the century was the wave of the future; the Yorkshire Association of landowners was profoundly reactionary and narrowly self-interested: it was the unacceptable face of English regionalism. These two very different and apparently unrelated processes, one economic, the other political, had this in common: both were in some measure regional readjustments to an over-dominant centre. Political and economic power were heavily concentrated at the centre in seventeenth-century England; the eighteenth century saw the imbalance very considerably redressed.

THE POWER AND PRIVILEGE OF THE SQUIREARCHY
1692–1780

The squirearchy of northern England, and more particularly of Yorkshire, 'revived' in the eighteenth century in the sense that it grew in wealth and self-confidence and was the source of major political initiatives of national importance. It certainly revived in the sense that it more than held its own against the great northern Whig aristocrats. The revival is most clearly marked at the beginning by the land tax of 1692 and at its peak by Dunning's parliamentary motion of 6 April 1780 deploring the increasing power of the crown.

There were five main reasons for the revival. First, the Wentworth connection that had found favour after the Restoration continued to exploit its special status, and between 1759 and 1783 Sir George Savile, member for Yorkshire, was indeed a power in the land. Second, the better-off gentry amassed great estates as taxation became too burdensome for smaller landowners and, particularly between 1690 and 1715, increasingly forced them to sell.[1] Third, there were no longer effective countervailing centres of power in the provinces which represented central authority and could check the, proud and insolent, like the Tudor and early Stuart King's Council in the North. Fourth, the squirearchy now made Parliament itself their principal instrument of power. The House of Commons was their crucial link with the centre. They stood as members of Parliament not only for counties, but to a greater extent and for longer periods than elsewhere in England, for important boroughs, notably Durham (Lambtons), Newcastle-upon-Tyne (Blacketts and Ridleys), and Chester (Grosvenors).[2] And they had the preponderant control over the rotten and nomination boroughs in the North.

But the fifth reason was probably the most important: coal. Landowners from Nottinghamshire and Derbyshire through south Yorkshire, but especially in Durham and in Cumberland, were enriched because they happened to be sitting on coal. The Bowes family, the Lumleys and the Lambtons especially prospered in Durham, as did the Lowthers in Cumberland.

The Lowthers are perhaps the most striking illustration of a rich gentry family exercising formidable regional power not simply as great northern landowners but as members of Parliament and patrons of parliamentary boroughs. They controlled nine parliamentary seats (not all of them in the North), and Sir James himself sat in the House of Commons for twenty-seven years (1757 to 1784) – and 'Sir James's ninepins' voted exactly as he said. He was a powerful and effective adversary of the duke of Portland who had political and property interests in the North-west.

The revival of northern England's power and influence was clearly signalled in the land tax of 1692. It was a triumph for the northern landed interest: a mercilessly disproportionate levy on London and the South-east. The rate was uniform throughout England: four shillings in the pound on income from land. The northern gentry drastically under-assessed their liabilities, however, and had sufficient political leverage for this to go unchallenged by the Parliament that had imposed the tax and defined the methods and machinery of assessment and collection.

Contemporaries were quite clear that the tax actually amounted to four shillings in the pound in the Midlands and the South, as intended, but to only one shilling in the pound in the border counties. They were almost certainly correct.[3] In Northamptonshire and Bedfordshire, where assessments had been accurate, landowners paid a fifth of their rents in tax; in the border counties, where the land had been notoriously undervalued, they paid roughly a twentieth.

In 1690 a land tax had been based on the assessments made for the collection of 'ship money'. These assessments, for a very politically sensitive tax, were made with great care and were recognized as accurate and equitable. But in, 1692 new assessments were made for the land tax. They were carried out under the direction of county commissioners who were local gentry, and although they amounted to an overall increase of 16 per cent, regional variations were immense. For London, Middlesex and Westminster, the assessment was up by 68 per cent, for Buckinghamshire by 49 per cent, but for Yorkshire it was up by only 10 per cent. In Cumberland and Westmorland it was actually down by 1 per cent, and by no less than 14 per cent in Lancashire. London and the home counties were paying much more than ever before not only relatively but absolutely.[4]

Contemporaries were fully aware of what had been done and they did not condone it. It is true, the border counties were poor, but in any event they would pay only in proportion to their wealth. Scottish border raids, of some relevance to tax matters in the reign of Elizabeth, were now more than a century in the past. An anonymous pamphleteer in the early eighteenth century castigated the land tax of 1692 as 'the most unequal tax that was ever imposed in any age on any nation' and estimated that where landowners in Kent and Essex paid four shillings, in Yorkshire they would pay fourteen pence and in Cornwall and Cumberland only nine pence.[5]

In 1695 the political commentator Charles D'Avenant examined the underpayment by northern counties (and also some other 'extremities': Cornwall and the Welsh borders) and ascribed it to particularism protected by heavy parliamentary representation (post-Tudor Cornwall was particularly well blessed with members of Parliament).[6] Rotten and nomination boroughs controlled by landowners – relatively numerous in Yorkshire although not elsewhere in the North – were also part of this picture. But it was quite clear that northern counties were evading their fiscal responsibilities.

By 1707 county quotas based on the 1692 assessments were used for collecting the tax. They showed that the four border counties, 10 per cent of the land of England, were paying 1.6 per cent of the land tax; Yorkshire, also 10 per cent, was paying 4.7 per cent of the tax; but Essex, 2.8 per cent of England, was paying 4.4 per cent.[7] This disproportionate payment by Essex is in fact part of a larger picture in which we see the home counties shouldering an ever growing proportion of direct taxation far beyond what was proportional to their increase in wealth.[8]

This is a curious sequel to the victory of London and England's 'inner core' in the seventeenth-century civil war. Christopher Hill said that the victory led to the dominance of London and the 'Londonizing' of England;[9] in fact what happened was that England was 'provincialized'. This was partly because the home counties, especially Middlesex, Essex and Surrey, were markedly deficient in aristocratic landowners and even greater gentry.[10] It was the landed interest that had the power in the eighteenth-century Parliament: it was well represented in the distant shires. The south-eastern counties were predominantly a region of well-to-do yeomen, freeholders and lesser gentry who did not have the same political weight.

A further curiosity was that wealth derived from land in London underpinned the power and independence of at least some northern landowners. It was land that they owned in the west end of London that did much to enrich the Portlands and Cavendishes and especially the Grosvenors. Indeed, in the sixteenth and seventeenth centuries the Grosveners were squires of very modest means at Eaton near Chester. Their great eighteenth-century wealth derived principally from the marriage of Thomas Grosvenor to Mary Davies of London in 1676. In due course she inherited her father's Ebury estate, on which Belgrave Square and Pimlico now stand.

The gentry of northern England were not everywhere prosperous, powerful or even very numerous (there were very few indeed in Westmorland and Cumberland) but then the North was not yet a region dominated by great aristocrats. The northern Whig aristocracy in the first half of the eighteenth century was concentrated in Nottinghamshire, Derbyshire, and south Yorkshire. The Cavendish dukes of Devonshire had their seat at Chatsworth in Derbyshire, the Cavendish-Bentinck dukes of Portland at Welbeck in Nottinghamshire. Thomas Pelham-Holles, duke of Newcastle, lived in Nottingham castle; he was a Sussex man but undoubtedly wielded great power in mid-eighteenth century Nottinghamshire. In south Yorkshire Charles Watson-Wentworth, who became second marquis of Rockingham in 1750 (and lord lieutenant of the North and East Ridings), was the true inheritor of the wealth and prestige of Thomas Wentworth, first earl of Strafford. His seat at Wentworth park and the Rockingham club at York, were centres of great political power. But in Lancashire the Stanley earls of Derby had never entirely recovered from the penalties they suffered after the seventeenth-century civil war. They were Whigs in a land of minor Tory squires who conceded them one county seat. At Raby the Vanes – courtiers who had purchased the castle and estates in 1626, barons Barnard since 1698 – were feeble successors to the great house of Neville. And everywhere the squires of northern England claimed 'independence' from interference by the king's ministers and the local aristocracy, for themselves and their counties, and to a striking extent were able to get it.

This was not an aristocratic century, at least before 1783, in England generally, and particularly in the North. The aristocracy was still quite small and remarkably stable: in approximately seventy years before Pitt's administration was formed in 1783 (since the accession of George I) 114 new peers had been created; in the sixty years after 1783 the number created was 243. The rate at which new peerages were created between 1714 and 1783 scarcely exceeded the rate at which peerages became extinct or the rate at which wealth and population had grown. In 1714 there were 171 lay peers in the House of Lords, in 1783 there were 196, but in 1870 there were 470. The great age of the aristocracy in England, and especially in northern England, when aristocratic power was palpable and all-pervasive, was 1783 to 1911.

In the middle of the eighteenth century the control of rotten boroughs in northern England was overwhelmingly in the hands of the northern squirearchy, as distinct from the aristocracy. Northern England was not a region with numerous rotten boroughs. Namier estimated a total of 192 borough seats in the hands of private patrons, with only twenty-five (12 per cent) of these in the seven counties of northern England.[11] They were in thirteen boroughs. Nowhere in the North could compare with the swath of rotten boroughs across southern England: Lewes, Chichester, Steyning, Horsham, Petersfield, Weymouth, Plympton, Fowey and Truro. There were none in Northumberland, Durham, Cheshire or Cumberland, two in Lancashire and two in Westmorland. Yorkshire, however, had its 'fair share' with nine. These Yorkshire boroughs had seventeen seats in the hands of private patrons: roughly 10 per cent of the national total of such seats.

In the country at large, aristocratic and commoner patrons were almost evenly balanced both in their numbers and the number of seats they controlled. Namier estimated that 51 peers controlled 101 seats and 55 commoners controlled 91. But in northern counties in general, and even in Yorkshire, commoner patrons and their seats far outweighed the number of aristocratic patrons and the seats that they controlled.

In Yorkshire three aristocrats were the private patrons of four boroughs: the duke of Newcastle controlled two (Aldborough and Boroughbridge), the duke of Devonshire one (Knaresborough) and the marquis of Rockingham one (Malton). But the other five nomination boroughs in Yorkshire (Pontefract, Richmond, Northallerton, Ripon and Thirsk) were controlled by five commoners. In terms of seats, the three aristocrats controlled eight, the five commoners nine.

In the seven northern counties taken together, three aristocrats controlled four boroughs (eight seats) and nine commoners controlled nine boroughs (seventeen seats). Thus taking all northern seats in private hands together, the aristocracy controlled 32 per cent, the squirearchy 68 per cent. Whether we look at the situation in terms of the number of boroughs, the number of seats or the number of patrons, northern England's rotten and nomination boroughs were overwhelmingly under the control or influence of the squirearchy as distinct from the aristocracy, and this to a far greater extent than in England as a whole.

There is a certain unreality in the distinction between the landed gentry and the landed aristocracy; together they constituted the ruling class of eighteenth-century England. The distinction does not correspond in any precise way with social or economic differences. Nevertheless, the nobility in the eighteenth century was a clearly defined status group, the lay members of the House of Lords, as they had been since the sixteenth century.[12] Namier says that the division was 'no longer justified by the economic and social structure of the country' but concedes that the eighteenth century attached great importance to it.[13] Peerages were coveted (and so were promotions up the ranks of the peerage), they carried great social weight, and they gave access to privileges, offices (and advantageous marriages). Moreover the interests of the squirearchy and the aristocracy were not in all respects identical, if only because the latter were on average significantly richer and able to absorb more easily the expenses involved in a political career. The squirearchy was much more bothered about taxation. The Yorkshire Association was essentially a gentry, and not an aristocratic, affair. Sir George Savile, member for Yorkshire, supported it, but the marquis of Rockingham's attitude was highly ambiguous (see below).

The distinction between the aristocracy and squirearchy was both well understood and highly sensitive. No politically ambitious squire in northern England could afford to appear subservient to aristocratic influence. When Sir George Savile first stood for election as a member for Yorkshire in 1753 his youthful friend, the marquis of Rockingham (then twenty-three years of age) made the grievous error of openly supporting him. Savile withdrew. (He got in at a by-election in 1759.) The aristocracy had to treat the gentry with great circumspection to secure their political ends. The duke of Northumberland knew that if he was to contrive the return of his son as MP for the county he must avoid any appearance of dictating to the gentry. In 1774 he said that if the gentlemen of Northumberland 'would do him the honour to support his son, he would coincide with the sense of the county in the choice of the other member'.[14] The gentry in fact were firmly in the saddle north of the Humber, and even in Nottingham the duke of Newcastle's nominee in the election of 1754 was rudely challenged by Mr Plumptre, a Nottinghamshire squire.[15]

The 'independence' of the squirearchy was recognized as a fact and a right. It was the standing and independence of Sir George Savile that would be a real help to the marquis of Rockingham in Yorkshire, rather than the other way round.[16] Rockingham wrote to the duke of Newcastle in 1761 about 'the clamour that was raised personally against me, as desiring to dictate to the county' and affirmed that it was in no sense his purpose to undermine 'the principles and independency of Yorkshire gentlemen'.[17]

The great Whig aristocracy that would begin to dominate northern England and play a prominent role on the national stage from the end of the century was still far in the future. It would be recruited in large measure from the powerful squirearchy that served a long political apprenticeship in the middle of the century. But in 1760 the Grey family that would furnish the prime minister to preside over parliamentary reform in 1832 lived in deep obscurity in the old pele tower at Howick, in the shadow of the great Percy castle at Alnwick. The brother of Sir Henry, the current occupant of the tower, made his way in life as a professional soldier in Europe and America, entered the peerage as Baron Grey of Howick in 1801 and was promoted Earl Grey and Viscount Howick in 1806. His son Charles was MP for Northumberland for twenty years, from 1786 to 1807 when he succeeded to the title. He would be prime minister in the years of constitutional crisis, 1830 to 1832 (although he yearned to be reading his Tacitus in the pele tower at Howick). Even the Lowthers in 1760 would wait a quarter of a century before they entered the peerage (It was in fact a re-entry: an earlier peerage was now extinct.) Sir James was twenty-four years of age in 1760 and had been MP for Cumberland since 1757; he would enter the peerage as Earl Lonsdale in 1784. The Grosvenors would enter the peerage as Viscounts Belgrave and Earls Grosvenor in the same year. In 1760 they had held both parliamentary seats in Chester for forty-five years. They would eventually become dukes of Westminster in 1874. In 1760 the Lambtons of County Durham had represented the city of Durham for twenty-six years and would do so for another forty-three. John George Lambton became a baron in 1828 and the first earl of Durham in 1833. He would be deeply involved in the Reform Bill crisis, and as governor-general of the North American provinces would produce his famous report on the Canadian constitution in 1839. The powerful new aristocracy of the border counties had no medieval heritage: they were the product of the eighteenth-century revival of the northern squires. And the principal underpinning of that was the value that accrued automatically to land which lay over coal.

CHRISTOPHER WYVILL AND THE YORKSHIRE
ASSOCIATION 1779–80

The 'independence', claimed by the northern squirearchy was not only independence of the region's aristocrats, it was also independence of the king's ministers. The gentry who were MPs for the northern counties saw themselves as guardians of semi-independent domains. Sir George Savile, MP for Yorkshire for a quarter of a century, was not only independent in his dealings with the marquis of Rockingham, but in all matters relating to Yorkshire affairs. Sir James Lowther was notoriously inclined to speak of Cumberland in the House of Commons as if it were a separate state. MPs looked with deep suspicion on ministerial powers which they saw increasing at the expense of the regional interests. A major 'interest' of the northern counties was their favoured treatment in the land tax of 1692. When this was threatened, Sir George Savile had no doubt that he should take action in Parliament to defend it.

William III's war with France was the reason for the tax in the first place; George III's war with America seemed to be a reason to increase it. The simplest way to increase its yield was to equalize it, so that northern counties paid as much in proportion to their wealth as the Midlands and the South. That is precisely what the gentlemen of Yorkshire mobilized themselves to prevent.

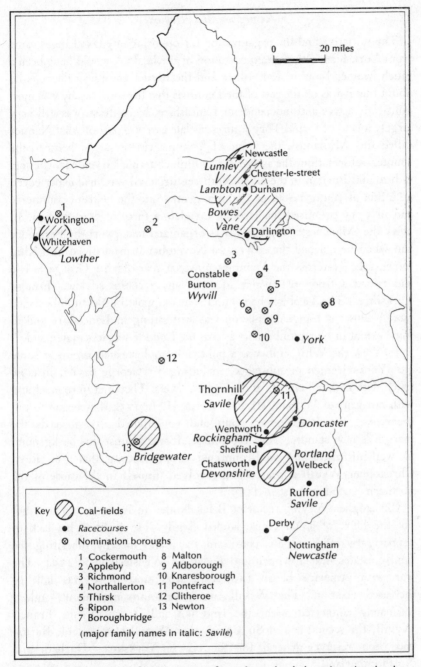

MAP 10.1 Elements of the power of northern landed society in the later
eighteenth century: rotten boroughs, racecourses and coal

Source: data taken from L. B. Namier, *The Structure of Politics at the Accession of George III*
(Macmillan, 1929).

The initiative and the organization for opposing any tax changes came from Yorkshire, although equalization of the land tax would have been a much heavier blow in Lancashire and the border counties. There is no doubt that it was on the east of the Pennines that the squirearchy was most politically active and independent. Lancashire, by contrast, was still very largely a land of torpid Tory squires: as late as 1760 part of what Namier called the 'Midlands', the home of 'genuine reactionaries, heirs to the counter-reformation, the authoritarian high church'.[18] Even Manchester, radical and Puritan in the seventeenth-century civil war, had experienced an influx of younger sons of Catholic gentry into the fields of commerce and in 1715 promised the Jacobite invaders a force of 20,000 men. In 1745 the 'Manchester regiment' was organized to support the Pretender and when he reached the city on 29 November it proclaimed him King James III.[19] (Across the Pennines nineteen-year-old Sir George Savile had raised a troop of cavalry to resist any Jacobite advance through Yorkshire.) The Jacobites had found some support in Northumberland, too. A sense of regional isolation was still strong in Lancashire and to some extent in Northumberland as coal for London was less in demand.[20]

In York the Whig club was a politically sophisticated group of some 130 Yorkshiremen of substance, including Sir George Savile, in close touch with national politics at the highest levels. They met in rooms hung with portraits of William III and George II. In 1754 they began to call themselves the Rockingham club and contributed £50 towards the marquis's new stand at York racecourse. It was against this background of well-informed and well-connected county society that The Revd Christopher Wyvill appeared and involved himself in the cause of the northern landed interest in 1779.

Christopher Wyvill, rector of Black Notley in Essex, was a son, but not the heir, of a Yorkshire landed family. He rectified his lack of property by marrying his cousin in 1773 and thereby inheriting the family estates near Leyburn and Bedale in Wensleydale in 1774. The war with America began two years later and there was talk of increased taxation. The Wyvills were well informed about, indeed intimately connected with, the land tax and its operations: Francis Wyvill, the second son of Sir Christopher Wyvill of Constable Burton had been receiver-general for the tax in Yorkshire, Durham and Northumberland.[21]

The Yorkshire Association of landowners was formed in 1779 ostensibly to petition Parliament about government extravagance. Wyvill became first its secretary and then its chairman, and from the start linked the issue of extravagance and the land tax together. Greater economy in government would obviate the need to raise taxes in general and the land tax in particular. Local newspapers, notably the *York Courant*, took up this theme: heavier government expenditure and increases in the land tax would be disastrous for the North.

The Association's primary concern was ostensibly with economy and efficiency in government, to be secured, for instance, by abolishing sinecures, and further, by reforming Parliament. It campaigned for an additional hundred MPs for the shires and more frequent elections, which would greatly enhance the political weight of county communities. But the essential purpose of the Association was clear in its demand that until such reforms were in place, no additional money should be spent 'beyond the produce of the present taxes'. In fact the whole issue of parliamentary reform was an afterthought. A subcommittee which drafted the first petition against waste and sinecures added the phrase: 'Whence the crown has acquired a great and unconstitutional influence, which, if not checked, may soon prove fatal to the Liberties of this Country.'[22] Henceforth the privileges of northern landowners would be protected by invoking Runnymede.

The marquis of Rockingham knew that parliamentary reform could be even more disastrous for the North than government sinecures, and that a 'corrupt' Parliament had secured and maintained northern landowners' high privileges. In a letter to Wyvill and his associates the marquis warned against undue enthusiasm for change, pointing out that Yorkshire was 'low rated to the Land Tax' because it sent thirty-two representatives to the House of Commons 'sixteen of which may be deemed to come from what are called Rotten Boroughs'.[23]

The Yorkshire Association assumed not only the mantle of Runnymede – the historical parallels were elaborated by the press – it explicitly modelled itself on the petitioning movement against episcopacy and tyranny in 1640.[24] But whereas in 1640 the initiative came from London and alderman Pennington, in 1779 it came from Yorkshire and The Revd Christopher Wyvill. The counties that were mobilized to support Yorkshire's campaign were more numerous (forty) than had supported Pennington. Yorkshire had stood aside from the petitioning movement that challenged tyranny then.

The seventeenth-century initiative was metropolitan: this eighteenth-century initiative was northern-provincial. This was an extra-parliamentary, quasi-revolutionary movement of very well-heeled Yorkshire country gentlemen. Wyvill remained a parson and was never an MP. The

Association's powerful spokesman in Parliament was Sir George Savile. The meeting in the York assembly rooms on 30 December 1779, which agreed to petition Parliament, was attended by 600 gentlemen whose total income was £800,000 – an average of £1,400 a year from land. The meeting had been called in the first place by a handful of north Yorkshire landowners worth £150,000 a year. This background of landed wealth was specified in some detail by Sir George Savile when he presented the petition, now signed by 9,000 Yorkshire freeholders, in Parliament in February 1780.

The culmination of the now nationally organized petitioning movement came on 6 April with Dunning's famous parliamentary motion that has echoed down the years: 'That it is the opinion of this committee that the influence of the crown has increased, is increasing, and ought to be diminished.' This, said Dunning, was the essential and fundamental point that the petitions from the counties had made. The real point was that the alleged increase in central power was at the expense of growing provincial autonomy. It was in these terms of high constitutional principle that the power and privilege of county communities of landed gentry were to be preserved.

It was a disgraceful episode. It was an expression of Yorkshire particularism in its most traditional form. In 1138, through the military mobilization of Archbishop Thurstan it inadvertently saved the nation; in 1780, through the political mobilization of Christopher Wyvill, it no less inadvertently cradled the cause of parliamentary reform.

REGIONAL IMBALANCES AND THE INDUSTRIAL REVOLUTION

In 1682 Ambrose Crowley moved craftsmen from his London ironworks to his new nail factory at Sunderland; in 1692 the new land tax gave highly favoured treatment to northern England; between 1685 and 1688 King James II felt constrained to dismiss twenty-eight of Cumberland's thirty-five justices of the peace.[25] The redeployment of industries related to shipbuilding to the North, the low tax levels secured by the north, and the independence shown by commissions of peace in the North, were all symptoms of profound readjustments between centre and perimeter that were taking place towards the end of the seventeenth century. The balance was being redressed in favour of the provinces. The very dominance of

London and the South-east, their sixteenth- and seventeenth-century overdevelopment, were driving out enterprise. The industrial revolution in the north of England in the eighteenth century was part of the process of correcting the regional imbalance.

It would be absurd to interpret the industrial revolution simply or even principally as the outcome of readjustments between centre and perimeter. But that is part of the explanation. Another major part of any explanation must be the growth of overseas markets and the enormous expansion of Britain's export trade. Both explanations shift attention from internal features of the north of England (and west Midlands) to aspects of the wider context. London and the Atlantic are the key to what was happening in Manchester.

The social and economic transformation that occurred in northern England in the course of the eighteenth century is most clearly indicated in the radically reordered hierarchy of England's cities. In the seventeenth century London's growth was indeed phenomenal: while England's population grew by 23 per cent, London grew by 188 per cent, and through its need for coal drew Newcastle-upon-Tyne in its wake. This continued a sixteenth-century trend when London and Newcastle-upon-Tyne prospered and expanded while urban England generally stagnated as real incomes fell. In the early sixteenth century Newcastle-upon-Tyne was England's ninth city in size (York was fourth); in 1600 it was fifth, but still smaller than York; by the year 1700 Newcastle-upon-Tyne had outstripped York and was exceeded only by London, Bristol and Norwich. In the eighteenth century, however, the two great success stories of the previous two centuries, London and Newcastle-upon-Tyne, failed to expand at the rate of the emerging commercial and industrial centres in the North, Manchester, Liverpool, Birmingham, Sheffield and Leeds. In 1801 both Manchester and Liverpool were twice as big as Newcastle-upon-Tyne which had fallen back to its early sixteenth-century position relative to other English cities: ninth.[26]

'During the eighteenth century the urban hierarchy of England was turned upside down.' Only Bristol and Newcastle-upon-Tyne remained in the seventeenth-century's 'top ten'. 'Many once-great centres were on their way to the pleasant obscurity of county rather than national fame: York, Exeter, Chester, Worcester, Salisbury.'[27] Liverpool and Manchester were the twin success stories now, moving to a position not only of national but international stature and significance. By 1850 they ranked seventh and ninth respectively in size among Europe's capitals: Liverpool was not as big as Paris, Constantinople, St Petersburg or

Berlin, but was closely matched with Naples and Vienna. Manchester was only a little behind.

In the eighteenth century London failed to maintain its percentage share of England's population (its share more than doubled in the previous century), and ten historic cities (including Norwich, Shrewsbury and Gloucester) lost a fifth of their share, but Birmingham, Manchester, Sheffield and Leeds together increased their share sixfold. In 1700 they had 0.53 per cent of England's population; in 1800 they had 3.0 per cent.

TABLE 10.1   Towns' shares (%) of total population 1600–1800

	1600	*1700*	*1800*
London	4.90	11.30	11.10
Ten historic towns[a]	1.70	2.10	1.70
Four new industrial cities[b]	0.26	0.53	3.00

[a] Norwich, York, Chester, Salisbury, Worcester, Exeter, Coventry, Shrewsbury, Cambridge, Gloucester
[b] Birmingham, Manchester, Leeds, Sheffield

Source: E. A. Wrigley, *People, Cities and Wealth* (Basil Blackwell, 1986) p. 166, table 7.3.

The hierarchy of England's counties (as measured by their wealth) also changed in a dramatic way in the century and a half (1693 to 1843) during which inter-regional power and wealth were redistributed away from the centre towards the provinces. Eight out of England's thirty-nine counties improved their rank order by ten places or more; all but one (Gloucestershire) were north of the Trent. Nine counties declined by at least ten places: all but one (Dorset) were in the South-east. Seven counties were static, their position remaining wholly unchanged (Middlesex at first place and Northumberland at thirty-seventh) or changing by no more than three places. These were either England's richest counties or its very poorest. The former bordered on London, the latter were on the outer perimeter. The biggest change of all was Lancashire, changing its rank by thirty-three from thirty-fifth to second, but Westmorland, by contrast had been thirty-eighth in 1693 and was thirty-ninth in 1843, Cumberland had been thirty-ninth and was now thirty-eighth, Northumberland had been thirty-seventh and was still thirty-seventh, and Cornwall, which had been thirty-first, was now thirty-fourth.[28] The

TABLE 10.2 Change in counties' rank order of wealth 1793–1843

Improvement by at least ten ranks		*Deterioration by at least ten ranks*		*Static: three ranks or fewer*	
Cheshire	+19	Beds	−21	Kent	+3
Derby	+16	Berks	−12	Middlesex	0
Durham	+23	Bucks	−21	Surrey	−1
Gloucester	+10	Dorset	−13	Cornwall	−3
Lancashire	+33	Essex	−12	Cumbd	+1
Notts	+10	Hunts	−13	Northd	0
Staffs	+25	Norfolk	−10	Westd	−1
Yorkshire	+14	Northants	−10		
		Suffolk	−13		

Source: E. J. Buckatzsch, 'The geographical distribution of wealth in England 1086–1843', *Economic History Review*, 3 (1950–1), pp. 180–202.

industrial revolution transformed northern England; it barely touched the outer perimeter.

Three preconditions have been claimed for the eighteenth-century economic 'take-off' (indeed, for any economic take-off): an innovation of sufficient importance and potency to constitute an economic 'leading sector'; change on a scale significant enough to be self-sustaining; a take-off period concentrated into a relatively short time-span (about twenty years). The leading sector in eighteenth-century England, it has been said, was cotton, and the take-off period was 1793 to 1802. Great emphasis has been placed on the transforming properties of leading sectors: 'The coming of a new leading sector thus often transformed the whole region where it took hold; as, for example, the cotton textile revolution transformed Manchester and Boston and the automobile industry transformed Detroit.'[29] But for all its undoubted importance, cotton has probably been given greater weight in these explanations than it can reasonably bear.

There are other strong contenders for the role of leading sector (or 'engine of change'), notably the greatly enlarged character of the export market, but none of this explains why the main site of the industrial revolution was the north of England. Even the location of iron, water power and coal in northern England, and a climate suitable for cotton manufacture in the north-west, do not quite explain it. (Industrially advanced Gloucestershire in particular had all the attributes required for revolutionary change, including easily accessible coal.) The circumstances which did much to promote an industrial revolution in the North were two major regional imbalances: one in wage levels, the other in fertility.

Inter-regional wage differentials help to explain the drift of ship-building from the South-east to the North-east in the eighteenth century. In the seventeenth century East Anglian ports, notably Ipswich and Woodbridge, had been major shipbuilding centres, but by the later eighteenth century the north-east coast from Hull to Newcastle-upon-Tyne was by far the largest seat of the industry. Scarborough reached its peak in the mid-eighteenth century, Sunderland grew strong in importance after its harbour was deepened in 1717, and Whitby and South Shields were important centres, too. The North-east built a majority of the big ships, over 200 tons, by 1790 and accounted for nearly twice the tonnage of East Anglia and London combined.[30]

Lower wages were not the sole reason for these developments in north-eastern England – there were ironworks and wood from the basins of Trent and Ouse – but wage levels in the North were certainly an attraction to developers. In 1704, according to Defoe, a labourer's wage in Kent and several other southern counties was between 7s. and 9s. a week, but it was only 4s. in Yorkshire and the bishopric of Durham. In 1768, according to Arthur Young (in his *Southern Tour*), agricultural wages were 10s. 9d. within twenty miles of London, but fell to 7s. 8d. at a distance of sixty miles; in northern counties (he reported two years later in his *Northern Tour*) wages ranged throughout the year between 4s. 11d. and 9s. 9d. but on average were about 7s. At 300 miles from London the average was only 5s. 8d.[31] Sixty years later the north–south difference would be reversed, even at a distance of 300 miles from London. When Cobbett wrote from South Shields and Sunderland in October 1832 it was in glowing terms about workmen with 24s. a week and rent-free houses.[32] Southern labourers had been burning ricks because they were refused 12s. a week. Throughout the eighteenth century, however, wage differentials were sufficient to encourage industrial development in the North.

That is principally why Ambrose Crowley set up his nail factory in Sunderland in 1682. He wrote at some length to his father in Stourbridge setting out his reasons for the Sunderland venture: costs generally were lower, and 'vitalls is above one-third cheaper than in the present naill country.' But above all labour was plentiful and cheap: 'The country is very poore and populous soe workmen must of necessity increase.'[33]

The second important regional difference was in population growth. The areas of England which were the principal site of the industrial revolution grew more rapidly in population in the early eighteenth century than the rest of the country; and this occurred in spite of net migration from north to south which continued until the early nineteenth century. The population increase did not arise from falling death rates but from rising birth rates; the dramatic fall in death rates came only after the population upsurge had passed its peak.[34] The consequence of this population growth was a larger domestic market, which stimulated industrial production and technical innovation. Later, the overseas market would be of crucial importance, but before the middle of the century the home market was the principal stimulus to development.[35]

Population growth and a significantly enlarged local market in the north-west of England seem to have been an important factor in the eighteenth-century economic take-off. And now, for the first time in England's history, population could continue to grow unchecked by an 'output barrier' in food production. Agricultural improvements were a pre-condition of continuing population growth and industrial advance. But population growth in the early eighteenth century (especially its disproportionate increase in the North-west) was a cause of the industrial revolution; in the nineteenth century it was a consequence.

A marked growth in population occurred before the mechanical inventions in the textile industry had appeared or made an impact. In the early years of the eighteenth century England's population had been stagnant, but between 1741 and 1751 it grew by almost 4 per cent. In the following decade there was an increase of 7 per cent, and during the last decade of the century by 11 per cent.[36] (This upward curve continued until it reached 18 per cent in the decade 1821–31 and then began to fall.) But there were marked regional differences in the sharing of the population increase: the north-west of England (essentially Lancashire, Cheshire, Staffordshire and the West and North Ridings of Yorkshire) had approximately 20 per cent of the population in 1701, but 28 per cent in 1831. By contrast the share of the North on the east of the Pennines (principally Lincolnshire, Nottinghamshire, the East Riding, Durham and Northumberland) actually fell, from 23 to 21 per cent. The share of London, Essex, Kent, Middlesex and Surrey taken together rose slightly, from 18 to 19 per cent, but the share of the southern counties fell as much as the North-west had risen, from 39 to 31 per cent.[37]

The marked growth of population from natural increase in the north-west of England was stimulated by the conditions of employment in rural textile industries. Fertility was particularly high in industrial villages around Manchester. Studies of births and deaths between 1690 and 1790 in 200 rural parishes, 100 north of a line from the Humber to the Severn and 100 to the south, have shown striking regional differences. Between 1690 and 1749 births exceeded burials by 21 per cent in the North, but only 11 per cent in the south. Between 1750 and 1794 the figure had increased to 39 per cent in the North and 30 per cent in the South. The records are not without their problems and are more reliable for the later than for the earlier period, but the superior 'vital indices' of the northern parishes seem generally to be well established and were particularly impressive (higher by 20 per cent) in the 1760s.[38]

In the textile areas of Lancashire and Yorkshire men married early and the wages of wives and children helped to balance family budgets. The textile industry was still mainly in villages: urban concentrations did not help natural increase, but rural conditions did. The north of England had other advantages which helped industrial development, notably its mineral resources. But regional differences in fertility, like differences in wage levels, were initially of crucial importance for economic take-off.

COTTON AND THE END OF ISOLATION

There can be no doubt about the importance of cotton in England's industrial revolution: it was the pace-setter, a new model, the paradigm of industrial change. It was eminently suitable for mass production for mass markets moreover at falling prices. And yet it scarcely qualifies as a 'leading sector', because its development was relatively late – it depended crucially on Arkwright's water-frame of the 1770s – and it did not have the widely pervasive effect throughout the economy that made its impact irreversible and decisive. But it certainly transformed Lancashire, principally by rescuing it from three centuries of isolation and self-absorption. Three centuries after the international connections afforded by the duchy's role in the Hundred Years War, Lancashire emerged again on to an international stage. Cotton rescued it from its long entombment by poverty, Stanleys, and Catholicism.

The contribution that cotton made to England's wealth increased very rapidly. In terms of 'value added' to raw materials by the process of manufacture, cotton accounted for less than half of 1 per cent of England's national income in 1770, but by 1800 it was around 5 per cent, and by 1812 it was 8 per cent and had outstripped the contribution made by the woollen industry. The cotton industry continued to grow (though at a decreasing rate after 1850) until 1914 and remained Britain's major textile industry.[39] This fact alone made Lancashire, and the Clyde, regions of great national importance and Manchester an international symbol of the new industrial age.

The rise of cotton was indeed spectacular, but the rise in England's exports after 1760 until the early nineteenth century was even more remarkable. Exports to Europe were especially strong and their value multiplied almost four fold between 1760 and 1820. They were considerable even without the cotton and iron components. It was this explosion of England's international trade that had important multiplier effects in the economy and tended to be self-reinforcing. Cotton was highly visible, but the less visible currents of international trade were the basis of sustained economic growth.

But cotton was nothing if not international, indeed its very emergence in England as a major industry depended on the increased productivity of upland soil in the southern United States of America to supply raw cotton cheap enough to be bought in bulk.[40] The international connections of cotton were important not simply for the economy of England and Lancashire. They shaped an outlook and fashioned a new, forward-looking northern society. Cotton revivified the civilization of the North in a way comparable to the international connections of monasticism in the age of Bede. It was more potent even than wool exports in the thirteenth century, which secured prosperity for eastern Yorkshire and an active place in a vigorous North Sea civilization. Lancashire was now an Atlantic state.

The cotton industry brought in to Lancashire – and especially to Manchester – a cosmopolitan community of Germans, Greeks, Armenians and Jews that immeasurably enriched its life, and the sons of Manchester cotton merchants often spent years in the Near East, India and China as representatives of their firms.[41] But it was not only or even primarily the marketing of manufactured cotton cloth and goods that linked Lancashire with the world: it was ensuring adequate and reliable cotton supplies.

By the middle of the nineteenth century Britain's cotton exports amounted in value to more than £30 million: India accounted for more than £5 million, America £4 million, the Hanseatic towns £3 million; Holland, Brazil, Turkey, China and Australia for more than £1 million each.[42] The American connection was ambiguous. America was increasingly a competitor, and Lancashire manufacturers wished to reduce their dependence on American supplies. They attempted to get cotton-growing established in India and in 1850 sent out a special agent to investigate the possibilities. The Manchester Chamber of Commerce induced Palmerston to send a mission with a similar purpose to the king of Dahomey, and an adviser was sent from Manchester to Egypt in 1851. The Cotton Supply Association was formed in Manchester in 1857 to encourage the production of cotton wherever appropriate throughout the world.[43]

The Clyde also became a major centre of the cotton industry, and the cotton interest established a network of connections linking Lancashire and Clydeside. This was an echo of the ancient kingdom of the North which extended from northern England to Dumbarton. (It would find a stronger echo later in party-political and trade union links.) Manchester was prized out of localism into a wider regional as well as international involvement. The chambers of commerce of Manchester, Liverpool, Blackburn and Glasgow collaborated in missions to find new sources of supply. In the age of Bede the kingdom of the North was defined by a network of monasteries; the emerging kingdom of cotton was defined by a network of chambers of commerce. There was increasingly a sense of common purpose from the Mersey to the Clyde.

Industrial Greatness

The nineteenth century was a triumphant age for the north of England. Its greatest triumph was Manchester: 'shock city' of the 1840s, international symbol of the new industrial age.[1] This was one of the four great epochs in the history of the North, comparable to the age of Bede and the period of military and political pre-eminence from the middle of the fourteenth to the later fifteenth centuries. But what is striking about the immense economic power of northern England in the nineteenth century is the extent to which it did not translate on a really significant scale into social and political weight.

It is true that the great provincial cities were a source of political movements and important ideological initiatives as well as the site of great industrial wealth: free-trade Manchester in the middle of the century and protectionist Birmingham at the end set the terms of the debate on the production and indeed the nature of wealth, on empire, and world peace; and there was a sense in which London, as a contributor to the *Cornhill Magazine* said in 1881, 'is now isolated in the midst of the agricultural south'. ('If Britain had now for the first time to choose a capital, its choice would naturally fall upon Manchester.')[2] And yet the north of England never quite achieved political significance commensurate with its powerful industrial base. Unlike bankers and merchant princes, industrialists had little connection with the landed elites and were little involved with the centre (the city and departments of state). Their ties and strength were in their localities, by which they were powerfully circumscribed; they were essentially and inherently provincial.[3] They made their wealth in the wrong way and had not quite enough of it – northern England in the nineteenth century never had more than a third of the non-landed millionaires. 'Manufacturers neither owned enough "top wealth" nor made it in a sufficiently acceptable way to be able to impose their will on the political system.'[4]

The north of England was the principal site of the industrial revolution and ordinary men and women and their children, at least after the 1820s, enjoyed its enormous benefits. That is why they migrated to the developing industrial towns from the countryside and came over in a deluge from Ireland. This great transformation and the steep rise in population and urban growth that accompanied it also brought social dislocation and conflict; in particular it made obsolete many traditional trades, notably handloom weaving. But the transformed industrial North was exhilarating, with a strong sense of the future. It was also in general remarkably tranquil. The principal site of class conflict was not in the industrial North but the agricultural South. The second half of the century was a time of striking social stability which falsified the confident predictions of doom and catastrophe that Engels and Leon Faucher had made in the 1840s. This has been variously explained in terms of the effects of religion, the aristocracy of labour, 'deference', 'the culture of the factory', and employer paternalism. The true explanation is quite simple: wealth. Class conflict was deferred to the twentieth century when international markets and industrial wealth in the North began to contract and working-class standards of living levelled off or actually fell.

The 1830s saw the beginnings of a major shift in the relationship between the state and the new industrial order. The deregulation and provincial autonomy of the eighteenth century which had been a precondition of take-off was now overtaken by its opposite, an ever more highly centralized state. A great deal of power remained located in the regions, especially in the countryside before 1888 with parsons and gentry who were justices of the peace. The only major encroachment on their powers before the County Councils Act of 1888 was the new Poor Law after 1834. But the changeover had begun in earnest in the 1830s, was strong by the 1860s (for instance in Lowe's 'revised code' and 'standards' for schools), received an historic boost in 1906 and 1945 and has now been with us for a century and a half. It was clearly signalled in the Factory Act of 1833 and even more strongly in the Poor Law Amendment Act of the following, year which established a central authority of three Poor Law commissioners. Jeremy Bentham and his lawyer-disciple Edwin Chadwick provided the ideology and the techniques for managing the social consequences of the rapid creation and rather less rapid diffusion of wealth. The ideology was utilitarianism, the key concept was inspectability, and its instrument a central bureaucracy.

Historians have sometimes lamented the passing of the Council of the North in the early seventeenth century. If it had survived it could have managed the industrial revolution from the outset and humanized its effects.[5] In fact it would have aborted it. It would have aborted the agricultural revolution too.

The industrial revolution depended crucially on an agricultural revolution to feed the swollen industrial population of the new towns. Well protected peasant farmers or a secure tenantry would have made this impossible. They would have obstructed the flexibility of land development which was essential for innovation and heightened efficiency.[6] By the later eighteenth century England was no longer a land of small freeholders and 'customary' (tenant-right) tenants, but was overwhelmingly a land of tenant farmers with no legal security or right to inherit. The Council of the North would have prevented any such development in the first place, but such circumstances were crucial if agricultural and industrial revolutions were ever to be born.

THE NEW GEOGRAPHICAL DISTRIBUTION OF WEALTH

In 1880, at the end of the industrial revolution's first century, Manchester had drawn level with London in wealth. The three richest provincial cities (in terms of income assessed for tax per head of population) were Manchester (£25), Liverpool (£20), and Newcastle-upon-Tyne (£13). Bristol, Birmingham and Nottingham were next in line: £10 a head; but Manchester in these terms was three times as rich as Hull, Leeds and Sheffield (each £8 a head) and six times as rich as Portsmouth (£4 a head). Manchester was almost exactly as rich as London – ten boroughs including the city – where incomes assessed for tax averaged £26 a head of total population, and significantly richer than London excluding the city (£15 a head). Some London boroughs, such as Greenwich (£4), Hackney (£4) and Lambeth (£9), were much poorer but Westminster was almost twice as rich (£45). The city itself (population 51,000, assessed income for tax purposes £41,237,000) was in a class of its own with an average of £808.[7]

It was not only northern taxpayers, the middle and upper classes, who were well off in 1880. (Incomes over £150 a year were liable to tax.) The industrial revolution was an immense success for everyone concerned, in terms of wages, profits, and the overall standard of life. The problem in the earlier years had been those who were left out, mainly small capitalists based in industrial villages engaged in obsolete trades as stockingers, handloom weavers and framework knitters. Progress in living standards was somewhat impeded in the first two decades of the century by the unproductive character of government spending in the Napoleonic wars – landlords and bondholders prospered – and the deflationary aftermath. But long before 1880 the increase in industrial production, which greatly exceeded the increase in population, had promoted significantly improved living standards for most of the nation, especially in the industrial – and indeed in the agricultural – North.

The early industrial revolution did not bring benefits equally to all sections of the community or to all parts of the country, and rapid urban growth produced problems of housing, sanitation and health and some increase in city mortality rates in the 1820s. Between 1780 and 1830, however, far more people were deriving substantial benefits from industrialization than were suffering hardships.[8] The strongly cyclical nature of trade also caused periodic set-backs: the vast railway-building enterprise from the mid century based on the heavy industries of the North did much to iron out their effects.[9] The very positive and hugely optimistic picture that Macaulay painted in 1830, based on the trends in vital statistics and the parliamentary Poor Law returns for 1825 and 1828, is undoubtedly substantially correct. And his basic point was the high levels of wealth and welfare in northern England compared well with the South.

In the *Edinburgh Review* in January 1830 Macaulay published a blistering review of Southey's *Colloquies* which lamented the passing of a bucolic age. In doing so he examined closely but in broad comparative perspective the benefits brought by industrialization in recent decades. He was clear that there was no record of 'any great nation, past or present, in which the working classes have been in a more comfortable situation than in England during the past thirty years'. The heavy poor rates necessary for the relief of distress in southern counties were unknown in the North, even in rural areas. In Sussex the rate was twenty shillings to every inhabitant, fifteen shillings in Kent and the eastern counties, but only eight shillings in Westmorland and the North Riding of Yorkshire, six shillings in Cumberland, five shillings in the West Riding and four shillings in Lancashire. The strong demand for labour in the urban North pushed up wages and reduced the need for relief in neighbouring agricultural areas. Moreover, compared with the previous century, mortality rates were greatly reduced, 'and this diminution has been greater in the manufacturing towns than anywhere else'. It was in southern England that Southey's rural idyll still lingered: 'Rose-bushes and poor rates, rather than steam-engines and independence.'[10]

William Cobbett would have agreed with Macaulay's picture. It was about this time that he finally reached the North after many years of rural rides in the South. In October 1832 he was in North Shields. On both sides of the Tyne he had observed high and general prosperity in both mining and agriculture: 'The working people seem to be very well off; their dwellings solid and clean, and their furniture good.' Cobbett explicitly contrasted this with the poverty in southern England: farm-workers, he said, 'are all well fed, and have no temptation to acts like those which sprang up out of the ill-treatment of labourers in the South'.[11] The pitmen near Sunderland were earning good wages: 'Theirs is not a life of ease, but it is not a life of hunger.' On top of their wage of twenty-four shillings a week they lived rent-free, their fuel cost them nothing and their doctor cost them nothing.[12] In the economically provoked 'swing' riots in the southern counties, labourers had recently been burning ricks in a vain attempt to obtain twelve shillings a week.

These regional differences in wages and living standards were not simply a feature of the early years of the industrial revolution; they persisted throughout the nineteenth century and beyond. In 1850 agricultural wages in the West Riding of Yorkshire were fourteen shillings a week, in Cumberland thirteen shillings, but in Suffolk and Gloucestershire they were only seven shillings.[13] Wiltshire labourers, said one investigator, were underfed and apathetic, lacking in the 'vigour and activity which mark the ploughmen of the northern counties'.[14] In Dorset in 1850 paupers were 16 per cent in the population, in Durham they made up 5 per cent.[15]

Similar north–south contrasts were evident at the end of the century. In 1886 women working in Lancashire textile mills earned 15*s*. 3*d*. a week, whereas in west country textile mills they earned 10*s*. 8*d*. In 1898, farm labourers earned twenty shillings a week in Durham and Northumberland fourteen shillings in Hampshire and in Berkshire thirteen shillings. 'Compared with other areas, and particularly with the rural south of England, the chief characteristic of labour in the industrial north was its high wages and long term prosperity.'[16] Over the period 1850 to 1914 there was 'a very gradual reduction in spatial differentials and a remarkable constancy in the relative position of different areas'.[17]

The northern counties in late Victorian England were also distinguished by their high level of trade union membership. Trade unionists were still a very small proportion of England's workers, and they were essentially apolitical. Unionism was a minority movement, associated before the 1890s not with oppressed and underpaid workers but with the high-wage economy of nothern England. The well-paid skilled workers of the northern counties joined unions not to fight for high wages but because they had got them already. They organized themselves to safeguard skill and regional differentials.[18] This elite unionism, often explicitly committed to a free market philosophy, did not depress but further promoted the high industrial productivity on which rising wage rates were based.

Trade unionism was a massively northern phenomenon. It was not particularly strong in the west Midlands; its strength was beyond Trent. Expressed in terms of population, trade unionists were 4.5 per cent of England in 1892, but they were 11 per cent of Northumberland and Durham, 8.6 per cent of Lancashire, and more than 5 per cent of the East and West Ridings of Yorkshire, Nottinghamshire, Leicestershire and Derbyshire. (In Warwickshire they amounted to only 4.2 per cent, in London 3.5 per cent.) But in sixteen counties trade unionists amounted to less than one per cent of the population: they were all in the South, South-west and South-east except Westmorland. In Dorset, Cornwall, Surrey, Berkshire, Bedfordshire, Buckinghamshire and Sussex they were less than half of 1 per cent. There was an obvious correlation between areas where unions were strong and wages were high, but the unions had not secured the high wages, they were exclusive associations which arose to protect them.

In spite of the ups and downs associated with trade cycles and the cotton famine of the 1860s, the prosperity of cotton operatives in Manchester, like that of workers generally in northern England, was on a strong upward curve throughout the nineteenth century. The French observer Leon Faucher was profoundly in error when he presented the workers of Manchester in 1844 as demoralized by the evils of industrialization and enduring extreme poverty. The member of the Manchester Atheneum who translated and wrote a preface to his book was able to present a formidable array of statistics, for instance on deposits in mutual aid and friendly societies, which refuted Faucher's contentions.[19] Curiously a book by Faucher's compatriot, Monsieur Tougan – Baronowski, *Les Crises industrielle en Engleterre*, depicted Lancashire cotton operatives of 1860 as enjoying high wages, with deposits in savings banks, and often buying their own homes. 'The Lancashire workers were the head of the English working class.'[20]

For all its nineteenth-century prosperity Manchester never achieved 'top wealth' comparable with London or even with Glasgow. Between 1809 and 1914 Manchester produced one cotton millionaire; Paisley produced thirteen.[21] Forty men died between 1809 and 1914 leaving fortunes in excess of two million pounds: four were landowners, twenty were Londoners, four were Clydesiders. None was a Manchester man.[22]

The industries at the heart of the industrial revolution, based preponderantly in northern England, were cotton, wool, iron and steel, shipbuilding, engineering and coal; between 1809 and 1914 they produced 73 of England's 316 non-landed millionaires: 23 per cent. The largest number of millionaires (24) were cotton manufacturers, but banking and merchant banking produced 51.

London lost its overall superiority in the number of millionaires for a period of twenty years, 1880 to 1899. During that time twenty-one of the forty-six millionaires who died were London-based, twenty-three elsewhere (sixteen in the North). But London was again comfortably superior to the rest of England in the number of millionaires who died between 1900 and 1914 (see table 11.1). And the greatest personal wealth in northern Britain was not in manufacturing centres but in the great *entrepôts*: Liverpool, Glasgow and Leeds.

TABLE 11.1   England's millionaires 1809–1914[a]

	1809–58 (no.)	(%)	1859–79 (no.)	(%)	1880–99 (no.)	(%)	1900–14 (no.)	(%)
London	5	63	16	66	21	45	40	67
North[b]	1	12	6	25	16	35	13	22
Rest of England	2	25	2	9	9	20	6	11

[a] The numbers and percentages in this table correspond to millionaires who died between these dates.

[b] Manchester, Merseyside, Yorkshire, Tyneside, Ribble, Teesside.

Source: W. D. Rubinstein, 'Wealth, elites and the class structure of modern Britain', *Past & Present*, 76 (1977), pp. 99–126.

CAPITALIST RADICALS IN THE EARLY NINETEENTH CENTURY

Northern industrial society in the nineteenth century was a battlefield. This was its unfailing excitement: a region of intemperate language on

public platforms, theatrical gestures, drilling by moonlight on the moors.
But the protagonists have commonly been wrongly identified. They were
not the new wage-earning proletariat arrayed against factory employers,
but northern industrial society in its entirety arrayed against the ruling
class. Northern England fought the ruling class for a century and
defeated it. The ruling class was not mill-owners; it was landowners.[23]
Mill-owners, mill-workers, obsolescent handloom workers and nonconformist parsons, with a good deal of help in the end from the Liberal
party, defeated the landowners and the Anglican church.

This was the essential conflict of the age. It was against an external
enemy; it was not within the new industrial order itself. Inner tensions
certainly arose, to some extent over the factory legislation of the 1830s
and 1840s; but this should not be overstated. The reduction of working
hours was a possible threat to employers' profits but a certain threat to
employees' wages, and had moreover the strong support of the Anglican
church. The real bone of contention was safety aspects of industrial
legislation. It is doubtless true, as one historian has said, that 'When we
look at the mid-Victorian city, we see not only consensus and stability but
unresolved ideological conflict: a stable culture in a state of inner
tension.'[24] But it was the twentieth century that saw effective mobilization
for class conflict, perhaps at its most menacing between 1911 and 1914.
All this came later, however. There were those in mid-Victorian England
who thought latent class conflict would become manifest in new working-
class political alignments when the secret ballot was introduced. As it
happened, the Ballot Act of 1872 was a supreme non-event.[25]

What is remarkable about nineteenth-century northern England is not
that the new factory-employed working class did not have a revolution,
but that the new class of mill-owners did not have one, perhaps in alliance
with the workers themselves. Instead they fought a long war of attrition
and were touchingly pleased by quite minor and partial victories like the
Reform Act of 1832. It was not Wesleyan Methodism that kept the
workers from revolution but it undoubtedly helped to keep their often
desperate employers from the barricades.

The new working class was in general remarkably quiet. This was
indeed an age of transformation, especially in northern society, and has
commonly been described in terms of social disintegration and working-
class disorder. Change occurred 'with unexampled rapidity' said Lecky:
'It was in many respects a movement of disintegration, breaking ties of
sympathy between class and class, and destroying the habits of discipline
and subordination that once extended through the whole community.'[26]

And yet the northern counties were the most orderly in England. In terms of criminals brought for trial in the five years 1834 to 1838, the six northern counties were 40 per cent below the average rate for the whole of England.[27] Crime rates in the mining communities of northern England were strikingly low, while in some of the southern agricultural counties they were strikingly high. The highest rates were in a cluster of counties around London – Middlesex, Hertfordshire, Essex and Kent – and a second cluster in the old manufacturing region of the South-west – Gloucestershire, Warwickshire and Somerset. In Yorkshire the crime rate was 40 per cent below the national average, in Gloucestershire it was 40 per cent above. If crime rates are an index of social disintegration, then disintegration was clearly most extensive in those regions of England formerly prosperous but now largely excluded from the new industrial age.

The cotton operatives in the new Manchester mills had a very high reputation for orderly and responsible conduct – almost as high as that of 'Rochdale man', respectable, self-improving, chapel-going, teetotal, with his deposit in the friendly society and his stake in the co-op. A correspondent with the *Morning Chronicle* (5 November 1849) claimed that 'The cotton mills of Manchester abound with hard-headed, studious, thoughtful men, who pass brooding, meditating lives.' He was writing to endorse a special report on Manchester's working class that had appeared in this newspaper a few weeks before. The self-discipline of mill-hands had been emphasized: 'Speaking generally, the exceedingly quiet and inoffensive character of the Manchester mill population cannot be too highly estimated. "After ten o'clock", says Sir Charles Shaw, the late head of the police, "the streets are as quiet as those of a country town".'[28]

On the strictly political front the Manchester cotton operative was, throughout the nineteenth century, the despair of radical reformers. A Blackburn newspaper man who had written on industrial affairs over many decades said of the Lancashire workman in 1868: 'The uttermost flight of his fancy never carries him to the shore of revolution. His intellect is not so volatile as to be led captive by subversive theories.'[29]

The significant cause of turbulence in the north of England in the first half of the nineteenth century was not the new industrial working class inside the new industrial order, but the small-scale pre-industrial capitalists who had been left out or were trying to get in. Most of them were handloom weavers although stockingers, framework-knitters and stuff weavers were of a similar status. They were not 'working class'. Engels, looking back in 1844, was quite clear about this: 'he (the weaver) was no proletarian, he had a stake in the country'. He was, said Engels, of the same status and general character as the yeoman.[30] Some of these yeomen-capitalists in fact got in to the new order with spectacular success, including Peel, and Strutt, whose descendant would become the first mill-owner peer, Lord Belper, in 1856.[31] At a more modest level, William Radcliffe, who described the late-eighteenth century system in his *Origin of Power Loom Weaving*, published in 1828, got in too. But many had an exiguous connection with the new power-based system and no long-term future in it. This last generation had been born around 1780, had no successors, and by 1850 were mostly dead. With their passing, a principal source of turbulence in the early nineteenth century was removed.

In the later eighteenth century handloom weavers commonly had thirty to fifty acres of land, a farmhouse and a loom-shed; they owned their own machinery and had bought or rented their farms. Whatever assistance they might need they employed, working in their own time, in their own way. They owned everything except the raw materials. They negotiated with suppliers of yarn. Earnings from the loom more than paid the rent of the land which they farmed, but these earnings gradually fell. In 1795, a weaver could expect to make 33 shillings, a week from his loom, in 1814 the sum had fallen to 24 shillings and in 1819 it was only 9 shillings. There were also weavers with little or no land and these probably became the majority, but at the end of the eighteenth century the *Manchester Mercury* was still carrying advertisements of small farms with loom-houses suitable for weavers.[32] William Radcliffe was one of some fifty such yeomen-weavers near Mellor in 1770. Fifteen years later he had £11,000 invested in his business and credit of £5,000 from the bank.[33]

It was these now sometimes precariously placed yeomen-weavers who responded after 1815 to the radical ideas and movements which originated among the independent small masters, small capitalists too, in the west end of London and especially the borough of Westminster. They were active in the Hampden clubs and the principal element in the 'blanketeers' and Peterloo. Hampden clubs, the blanketeers and Peterloo were all London-based or inspired. Bamford, the Lancashire radical, refused to support the march of the blanketeers from Manchester in March 1817 because the London connection was so strong.

A dozen episodes of conflict and highly vocal reform movements give a strong impression of instability within the new industrial society beyond the Trent between 1810 and 1850: from Luddites, the Pentridge rising, the Hampden clubs, the blanketeers and Peterloo, to the Reform Bill agitation, an anti-Poor Law movement, grandiose trade unionism in the 1830s, the 'plug riots of 1842, the Chartists, the Anti-Corn Law League and the Northumberland and Durham miners' strike of 1844. In this catalogue of conflict only 'plug' and the miners' strike were wholly northern and wholly working class, the rest were either London-based or capitalist-led or both. In some cases 'capitalists' were pre-industrial, obsolescent and poor, but in the case of the Reform Bill agitation, the anti-Poor Law movement and the Anti-Corn Law League they were well established and rich. The object of attack in all these movement and incidents except the miners' strike and 'plug' was not the new industrial employers but the old ruling class.

This was pre-eminently the case at Peterloo. Peterloo is deeply imbued with symbolic significance: symbolic of the conflict at the heart of the new industrial order, a landmark in the making of the modern working class.[34] But in fact Peterloo exemplifies above all the power and authority of the old order, High Tory and High Church, confronting the emergence of the new.

The new working class was not particularly interested or widely involved in the meeting to be held on St Peter's Field, Manchester on 16 August 1819. It was the middle of the day on Monday and the working class was actually at work, as it had been during the somewhat melodramatic rehearsals for an orderly assembly at the scene. The meeting was not to be about workers' rights or conditions of employment or even the iniquities of employers. It would be, as usual, about the iniquities of bankers, the burdens of taxation, the corruption of government, and the need for annual parliaments. These were subjects of immense fascination for capitalism both old-style and new; they were not of compelling interest to the factory-employed, wage-earning working class.

And yet cotton spinners in 1819 were in acute distress. Their wages had been falling and in the previous year they had been out on strike. The southern gentleman who had been invited to address the gathering on St Peter's Field was wholly ignorant of their affairs. The agenda for this radical meeting had conceivably some bearing on their problems in the very long term, but it had no relevance whatsoever to their immediate plight. Here was a radical meeting in the heart of a major and patently troubled industrial region in the aftermath of widespread strikes, which did not even raise the issue of the illegality of trade unions. This meeting was not simply irrelevant to the new working class: it was an affront to it.

The notice announcing the meeting appeared over eight signatures, most of them of handloom weavers.[35] The chair would be taken, the notice said, by H. Hunt, Esq. Hunt was a gentleman-farmer from Wiltshire, generally known for his eloquence as 'Orator' Hunt. The meeting was part of a London-initiated programme, the last in a series of four which had been held in Birmingham, Leeds, and London in July. It was no different from the meeting at Smithfield in London in either its militancy or its agenda, although it was certainly a good deal bigger and probably looked more menacing.

The meeting was held under the surveillance of a committee of the Lancashire and Cheshire magistrates, responsible for law and order in Manchester on 16 August 1819. The committee was a microcosm of England's ruling class: William Hulton and Thomas Tatton, both large landowners, James Norris, a barrister, and William Hay and Charles Wickstead Ethelston, both Anglican parsons. These were the men who ordered the Manchester yeomanry into action when they feared they had a revolution on their hands.

Among members of the capitalist class who were killed was John Lees. He had been involved in the preparatory drilling on the moors and had come down to the meeting from his father's spinning factory at Oldham. (Their workforce had been out on strike the previous year.) Among the capitalists who were arrested were Joseph Johnson, a Manchester brush manufacturer, and John Knight, a cotton manufacturer. Johnson was still a relatively young man of thirty, joint proprietor of the *Manchester Observer*; Knight was a man of fifty-six who had been prominent in the Hampden club movement. He was a cotton manufacturer of long standing and as long ago as 1801 had insured his stock with the Royal Exchange Fire Insurance Company for £1,500.[36] Another cotton manufacturer who had come along to hear Orator Hunt was John Edward Taylor. He was not arrested. He would found the *Manchester Guardian* in 1821.

When a declaration of protest against Peterloo was organized in Manchester, seventy-one cotton manufacturers attached their signatures.[37] This does not mean that what was at least a significant minority of Manchester's cotton manufacturers necessarily approved of the meeting and its aims, but they certainly disapproved of the way it had been handled by the ruling class. Peterloo was a protest by manufacturers against the old political order which excluded them. It has been quite correctly described as 'a rehearsal for 1832'.[38]

Chartism, which flourished intermittently between 1838 and 1848, was the last phase in the protest of mainly obsolescent pre-industrial capitalists, now twenty years older than when they had drilled on the moors in preparation for Peterloo. Its leaders in the North tended to be weavers like William Rider, a Leeds stuff weaver, John Skevington, a Loughborough stocking weaver, and Ben Rushton, a Halifax handloom weaver.[39] But established businessmen of substance were Chartists too; indeed, no less than fourteen Chartists were elected town councillors in Leeds in the 1840s – wool manufacturers, printers, grocers and the like – all with the necessary qualification of owning property worth at least £1,000.[40] It was a movement with significant support in a number of urban centres, notably Glasgow and Birmingham, but with essentially the same bipolar structure as the Hampden club movement, originating among the small capitalist class of west London, and finding support among similar men, as well as hard-pressed handloom weavers and stockingers, in the North.

The *Northern Star* in Leeds took up the chartist cause. This was something of an afterthought: the newspapers had been founded to support the opposition to the new Poor Law before the charter was even produced.[41] For a year (1842–3) the headquarters of the Chartist movement were in Manchester, but both headquarters and the *Northern Star* had moved to London by 1844. The Chartists' last demonstration ended in fiasco on Kennington Common in 1848. It would have been no more successful in Manchester: there was not a sufficiently broad base of support. There was no revolutionary fervour among the cotton operatives of Manchester for the six points of the charter.[42] It had not been their movement from the start.

This is the difficulty with E. P. Thompson's early nineteenth-century founder-members of the working class: they invariably turn out on close inspection to be capitalists, sometimes in difficulty because they are obsolescent and failing capitalists, but by no means necessarily so. Two have been singled out as of particular importance: Samuel Bamford and Gravener Henson. Their working-class credentials are not impressive. Bamford's father was a senior manager with the Poor Law administration in Manchester, manager of the cotton mill which was run by the Manchester workhouse before being promoted workhouse governor. Samuel attended Manchester grammar school and would probably have proceeded to Oxford, but his father decided that this could lead only to his becoming a parson. He set up in business as a silk weaver with his wife. He was arrested for his involvement in Peterloo, but enrolled as a special constable to curb possible Chartist excesses in 1848.

Gravener Henson was a Nottingham man, supposed by many to have

been 'General Ludd'. Henson was not a labourer, but an independent
master who experienced the usual ups and downs of small capitalists at
that time. By 1812 he was a master point-net maker in the Nottingham
lace industry and employed eleven journeymen. He became a manufacturer
of bobbinet in 1823. Henson had no notion of promoting greater equality
of rewards in industry and his efforts for working-class betterment were
directed towards maintaining the differentials of skilled workers. He
remained aloof from the Chartist movement but supported the campaign
against the new Poor Law of 1834.[43]

Bamford was born in 1788; the Chartist weaver Ben Rushton of
Halifax in 1785; Gravener Henson also in 1785. By 1848 they were old
men in their sixties. Henson died in 1852, although Bamford lived on for
another twenty years. They had no successors. With the passing of this
last generation of men, who had started out and often remained as hand
weavers, born around 1780, there ended half a century of aggravated
turbulence in the North.

NORTHERN QUIESCENCE AND SOUTHERN CLASS CONFLICT
IN THE LATER NINETEENTH CENTURY

On census Sunday, 30 March 1851, the number of people attending
public worship throughout England amounted to 41 per cent of the total
population. In Lancashire, Durham and Northumberland it was 27 per
cent, in London 21 per cent, but in Bedfordshire it was 57 per cent, the
highest rate of attendance in England, and 51 per cent in Huntingdon.[44]
If religion was indeed consolation, then clearly the people in the industrial
regions of the North had less need of it in the mid-nineteenth century than
most.

Between 1841 and 1851 the number of Wesleyan Methodists fell by 7
per cent, while the population of England continued on a strong upward
curve; in the three years 1851 to 1853 the number of Wesleyan
Methodists declined even more steeply, by a further 8.4 per cent. This
reversed the increase which had been uninterrupted between 1801 and
1841 (a remarkable 38 per cent growth 1811–21). The expansion in the
number of Wesleyan Methodists would never again exceed the rate of
population growth until the decade 1921–31.[45] In the meantime the West
Riding of Yorkshire was losing its preponderant regional share of the
Wesleyan church membership: between 1801 and 1901 it contracted
from 17.03 per cent to 12.9 per cent.[46] But primitive Methodism,

strongly concentrated in southern and especially eastern agricultural counties, never declined in total numbers, or grew less strongly than the general population, at any time in the nineteenth century. In the 1830s and mid-1870s growth was particularly strong: primitive Methodists actually doubled their total numbers between 1831 and 1841.[47] If Wesleyan Methodism was the 'chiliasm of despair',[48] then despair after 1840 was clearly a diminishing feature of the mining and industrial areas which were the chief support of the Wesleyan church, although it was never far from the agricultural counties of southern and eastern England throughout the nineteenth century and beyond.

The second half of the nineteenth century was notable for relative industrial peace in northern England. There was a powerful resurgence of class conflict in the agricultural South. In the factory society of northern England, it has been said, this period 'witnessed a degree of social calm perhaps unique in English industrial society'.[49] Forty years after he had predicted revolution in 1844, Engels conceded that he had been seriously in error. In an article for *Commonweal* (1 March 1885) he recognized the industrial peace that had in fact generally prevailed and highlighted especially the very comfortable situation of skilled workers and the excellent relations they enjoyed with their employers.[50] The revolution may not have been finally averted, but it had been indefinitely postponed.

The most distinctive and successful working-class movement of the second half of the nineteenth century was not a movement of opposition to capitalist industrial society but an expression of its deepest values: the co-operative movement inaugurated in 1844 by the Rochdale Pioneers. It was a vast commercial and manufacturing enterprise by 1870, hugely profitable and rich, and directly involving a third of Rochdale's adult population. Apart from its building society activities and dealings in real property, its retail shops were making an annual profit of more than £30,000 and its cotton factory at Mitchell Hey was worth £109,000.[51] It was not a deferential working-class institution, was courted by the Liberal party, and could take an independent political line, but it was an integral part of northern industrial society, an embodiment of its central values, and made a major contribution to its later nineteenth-century stability and peace.

Some historians have followed Engels in ascribing comparative industrial peace after 1850 principally to the influence of an 'aristocracy of labour'. A growing sector of skilled workers and foremen, it is said, were 'class traitors', bosses' men.[52] This is not a very strong argument if only because the chronology does not fit: a numerous aristocracy of labour had existed long before the mid-nineteenth-century era of peace.[53]

The principal reason for relative industrial peace after 1850 was undoubtedly the growth of industrial wealth in which the working class shared. There were other contributory circumstances, of which increasing residential segregation by 'class' was probably of particular importance. Nineteenth-century London was the most highly segregated city in England and arguably had the weakest class consciousness: the one followed from the other.[54] Residential segregation came later in the north but upper-class enclaves like Headingly and Victoria Park, Manchester, removed opulent employers to an unprovocative distance and promoted peace rather than conflict.[55] The significance of employer-housing and 'employers' villages' in producing a compliant workforce has been overstated: it was always a minority provision.[56] Much more important for social harmony were segregated working-class suburbs of owner-occupied houses, made possible by the proliferation of terminating building societies.[57]

Residential segregation by social class moderated the politics of envy, but high wages did so much more effectively. In the second half of the nineteenth century wages were good (they probably rose overall by as much as 50 per cent between 1850 and 1870), standards of living were improving, and employer paternalism provided an increment of welfare over and above the basic wage and cushioned periods of recession. There was, it has been claimed, 'a mighty reassertion of employer paternalism after the 1840s',[58] but paternalism could not in itself ensure industrial peace. It was ineffectual when wages were seriously threatened and experienced a sustained decline.[59] But it was effective 'in the margin', both in northern industry and on northern rural estates.

The second half of the nineteenth century was by no means an era of wholly unclouded northern peace. Brickmakers in Manchester, Stockport, Ashton and Oldham organized particularly violent opposition to changes in production methods between 1859 and 1867, when more than forty 'outrages' occurred involving assault and the destruction of new machines. But this underlines the fact that obsolescence was a very common cause of conflict in the industrializing North: the brickmakers were traditional, pre-industrial craftsmen who made bricks by hand, resisting the making of bricks by machine.[60]

The riots by cotton operatives at Stalybridge in 1863 occurred in the very special circumstances of the 'cotton famine' which brought the industry to a halt between 1861 and 1865. In general the situation was accepted with remarkable stoicism, and although some employers gave generously to augment the inadequate resources of the Poor Law authorities, many, said the *Times*, were sitting 'as still as their machinery and as cold as their own boilers'. It was the contemptuous and capricious behaviour of relief committees that provoked the disturbances at Stalybridge in 1863, which were settled only when a company of hussars from Manchester was brought in.[61] But what is really remarkable is not that this riot occurred but that over a period of some four years of very real suffering, others did not.

There were strikes by weavers in 1878 when considerable violence was shown to employers in Blackburn. The particularly bitter strike at the Manningham mills in Bradford in the early months of 1891 was a milestone in the history of working-class politics, an important prelude to the founding of the Independent Labour Party (ILP). But a spinners' strike in 1892 was presented by the *Manchester Guardian* as no more than a domestic dispute: 'the struggle is evidently not in the eyes of the operatives . . . a struggle of class against class . . . This is simply a difference of opinion between two partners in an industry as to the best remedy for an admitted evil.'[62]

Strikes in later Victorian England were often 'prosperity strikes' for higher wages and shorter hours, a greater share of generally increasing wealth, like the strike of 9,000 Tyneside engineers in 1871, but quite unlike the 'desperation strikes' of thirty years earlier – the violent 'plug' riots which swept through Lancashire and into Yorkshire in July 1842: riots against rising food prices and falling wages, in which desperate workers pulled the plugs out of boilers and brought industry to a halt.[63] The different circumstances of the later part of the century promoted generally better industrial relations, but the mining industry in Lancashire was never really at peace. This was a poor coal-field; owners had to trim wages to survive; they could not afford the lavish paternalism that was often highly effective in maintaining industrial peace in other regions, including the richer coal-fields of Nottinghamshire and Derbyshire and the North-east.[64]

'Classes' in the industrial north of England were still unformed, without sharp definition, even after the mid-century, which is one simple reason for the absence of class war. In the agricultural South, by contrast, classes had achieved a striking precision: landowners, tenant-farmers and labourers were tidily stacked in three impermeable layers.[65] In urban-industrial England there was greater social complexity and fluidity.[66] Employers were not sharply differentiated from wage-earners (together they formed the 'industrious class') and might easily fall back into their ranks. Workers and employers had a strong sense of interdependence, of a common fate in a shared enterprise. They sat together not only in nonconformist chapels but on radical platforms, and the two powerful ideologies which they shared, Methodism and Adam Smith's free market economics, united them against a protectionist and Anglican ruling class.[67]

Even a second-generation industrialist with large, well established mills and great wealth like John Fielden of Todmorden was in many respects, in outlook and way of life, like one of his workmen. Indeed, he had worked in his father's mill as a child for as many hours as other children and knew their problems at first hand. He stood as an MP for Oldham only when the famous radical William Cobbett agreed to do so. The radicalism of this great northern industrialist was quite typical and not abnormal. Oldham, one historian has claimed, was a prime site of class conflict before 1850,[68] and yet the mill-owners James Halliday and John Halliwell and the hat manufacturer William Knott were to the fore in the town's radical politics. A more convincing view of Oldham is that 'class collaboration rather than class war, between working and middle class groups, was the key to radical success in the town.'[69] Radical working-class politics in Oldham, as in Greenwich and Woolwich, was directed against privilege rather than wealth: against the privilege of a landed aristocracy, not the wealth of hard-working, risk-taking entrepreneurs.[70]

A northern contributor to the *Fortnightly Review* in 1868 wrote of the great respect that northern workers had for enterprising employers: 'The people worship courage and pluck and will follow the lead of a man who exhibits these qualities without stopping to investigate his opinions.'[71] Their fortunes were bound up together. Perhaps the most remarkable manifestation of this sense of interdependence was the willingness of miners' trade unions in the North-east and elsewhere in the 1870s to accept sliding scales whereby wages were tied to the selling price of coal. They even opposed the notion of a minimum wage on the grounds that it would be a breach of economic principles and weaken the entire mining enterprise.[72]

The fluidity of class lines and the instability of capitalist enterprise even in mid-Victorian northern England are most clearly reflected in the local politics of small industrial towns. Bolton and Rochdale do not exemplify 'bourgeois hegemony' or even the rule of an 'urban squirearchy', but recruitment to a remarkably 'open elite'.[73] Haslams and Arrowsmiths in

Bolton, and Brights and Heapes in Rochdale, were rich and firmly established in local industry and politics, but they were a small rather than important part of the picture. Both social leadership and political leadership were 'open-ended' and the self-improving found a ready acceptance in both.[74]

James Barlow, who was mayor of Bolton in 1867 and 1869, is not unrepresentative of the new municipal power elite, of the economic uncertainties of mid-nineteenth-century industrial capitalists, and of the ambiguities of 'class'. He was undoubtedly a capitalist. The son of a handloom weaver, he established himself as a small weaving manufacturer. After the business failed he became a quilt manufacturer in 1846, but it was not until thirty years later that he was really quite firmly established as part-owner of five cotton mills with a workforce of 2,000.[75]

The ambiguities of class are even more strikingly exemplified in the changing fortunes and many-sided political involvements of Alderman Thomas Livsey of Rochdale, whose funeral in 1863 was attended by an estimated 40,000 people including the mayor, the entire town council and the board of guardians. What class was this son of a blacksmith, a leading Chartist, who was also heavily involved in the Anti-Corn Law League? He was never rich; his career as a capitalist was chaotic. He was by turns iron-founder, cotton spinner and railway agent. But he saw himself as a radical, a disciple of 'Billy' Cobbett.[76] Although in a more minor key than Fielden of Todmorden, he led a very successful campaign against the implementation of the new Poor Law. He did not command a great army of mill-workers and had no resources for paternalistic benevolence. The undoubted power that this not overly successful capitalist exercised over working-class people arose from their shared perceptions and experiences.

Industrial employers and workers in northern England would develop a much stronger sense of their separate interests and identities by the end of the century, and some coal owners in the North-east already saw even conciliatory unions as an intolerable threat – the former pit-boy Joseph Love dismissed any worker who even contemplated joining one. In the 1860s and 1870s, however, there was still quite commonly a sense of partnership in a common enterprise. Mill-owners were risk-takers, still often quite precariously placed, and their workforce applauded their hard work and audacity.

Hatred ran through the countryside of southern and eastern England throughout the nineteenth century. It erupted into open and indeed violent conflict in the early 1830s and again in the mid-1870s. It was in rural Lincolnshire in April 1830 that Cobbett felt that there was revolution in the air.[77]

The root causes of the riots which occurred in the name of the anonymous and probably mythical 'Captain Swing' were the low wages and chronic insecurity of farm workers in the South. Some of the smaller farmers supported them. There would be a recrudescence of class warfare in the southern and eastern countryside in the 1870s (but now without any small-farmer support), more open, union-organized, with less reluctant validation by the primitive Methodist church. It would even get as far north as east Yorkshire, although generally the northern counties remained impressively immune until conflict developed in south-west Lancashire, around Ormskirk in 1913 (not because wages were low but because hours were long).[78]

The south and east were regions where the numerous villages (compared with England beyond the Tees) were transit camps: unstable, shifting populations of day-labourers who lived highly precarious lives spent, as a report from Berkshire said in 1849, 'in the majority of cases, in constant oscillation between their homes and the workhouse'.[79] There was pervasive fear and constant humiliation in the village. One labourer explained why agricultural workers did not form 'combinations' to keep up their wages: 'We are too much in their (the farmers') power for that. If any man complains they call him saucy, and discharge him at once. The employers all understand each other, and wont employ him again until he has learnt better manners, or is punished enough for his impudence.'[80] This was the desperate Victorian South.

The swing rioters destroyed threshing machines and burnt property. There were a few cases of incendiarism in Yorkshire and Cumberland, but the vast majority of incidents were in Norfolk, Berkshire, Kent, Hampshire and Wiltshire.[81] Attacks on the property of aristocrats and squires, as distinct from tenant-farmers, were disproportionately clustered along the London highways which carried stage-coaches and continental ideas from the channel ports.[82]

The conflict in the countryside after 1872 was again heavily concentrated in southern and eastern counties, extending over a slightly wider area than the 'swing' disturbances, with Norfolk as its main focus.[83] This was a 'modern', union-led movement to secure better wages and conditions; it was sustained by the primitive Methodist church. The union leaders – Joseph Arch, a Warwickshire man, Josiah Mills and George Edwards, both Norfolk labourers – were all primitive Methodists. Primitive Methodism, the religion of the desperate rural poor, had been established as a separate denomination in 1811. It was never particularly strong in northern England outside east Yorkshire. Its members were heavily concentrated in the pinched eastern counties; numbers had quadrupled in Norfolk in the early 1830s, the period of the 'swing riots'. It was now less politically conservative than in the heyday of its founder, George Bourne.

The rural areas of northern England were as little involved in the conflicts of the 1870s as they had been in those of the 1830s. Farm workers there were still much better paid. There was also a much higher proportion of workers who 'lived in', or occupied cottages not in separate village communities but around the home-farm. In the South it had been the larger villages that had been the principal source of swing disturbances:[84] they contained a sufficient number of like-situated people to develop a sense of class solidarity. There were comparatively few such contexts of class formation in the North. The scarcity of villages had struck Cobbett when he first travelled north and he made statistical comparisons between Northumberland and Suffolk and Durham and Dorset.[85] The northern 'hind' had relatively secure terms of employment (usually hired for a year), he lived on close terms with his employer, and he was much more isolated from his fellows than farm workers in the South.[86]

The region of rural class conflict in the nineteenth century was the region of small landed estates; the region of great landed estates which were often subsidized by profits from coal lay beyond Trent. (Thus 9 per cent of the land of Essex, 10 per cent of Surrey and 12 per cent of Kent was in estates of 10,000 acres or more, compared with 40 per cent in Nottinghamshire and 50 per cent in Northumberland.)[87] Liberal politicians in the late nineteenth century like Shaw-Lefevre attacked the formation of big estates for their social effects, not because they promoted social conflict, but because they did not. They were highly effective benevolent despotisms.[88] They could afford lavish paternalistic services and in hard times might significantly reduce rents, as after 1815 when duke of Northumberland reduced rents by 25 per cent. In the eastern counties estates had to pay and the pressure on tenant-farmers was transmitted to their labour force.

Neither large-estate paternalism nor delayed class formation is sufficient to explain the impressive immunity of virtually the whole of northern rural society from class war, however. The main reason was the persistent difference in wage levels between the North and the South. Although the gap narrowed somewhat between 1850, when wages were roughly double in the North, and the end of the century, when they were only one-third higher, this difference, when combined with considerations already mentioned, was enough to account for class war in the East and the South and relative peace north of the Trent.

THE ESSENTIAL CONFLICT: THE LANDED INTEREST
AND THE INDUSTRIAL NORTH

In the nineteenth century northern England beyond the Trent was a region of spectacular industrial and urban growth; it was a region of no less spectacular aristocratic landed estates. The 'dukeries' were so called because this coal-mining area of Nottinghamshire became encrusted with dukes. A great northern aristocracy had formerly been powerful and rich because of the signal contribution they made to frontier defence; the new landed aristocracy was rich because it drew mineral royalties from coal.

The obligations of land was a serious legal, fiscal, moral and political issue throughout the nineteenth century. The 'land problem' in England was not primarily a problem of the relationship between landlords and tenants, but of the balance of power between landowners and industrial society. Symbolic rather than substantial,[89] it was about the immorality of 'privilege' and unearned wealth. There had been a genuine uncertainty about the obligations of land since the Long Parliament abolished feudal tenures in 1645. Perhaps freehold property had no formal, or indeed, any obligation at all? This was a revolutionary concept which would have been incomprehensible to even the greatest medieval tenant-in-chief.

Throughout the Middle Ages there was only one landowner: the king. Everyone else with land was a tenant. Some had greater security, power and prestige than others, but all paid what was tantamount to 'rent'. Between the seventeenth and the nineteenth century landholders became landowners. This was a social change of tremendous proportions. In the reign of James I those who held land 'in-chief' of the king petitioned that their feudal incidents be commuted to an annual rent. Nobody, even by the early seventeenth century, had any notion that any land whatsoever was 'rent-free'. And indeed the total product of late-Tudor feudal incidents amounted to a third of the kingdom's revenues (although the net amount, after paying various commissions and expenses, was very substantially less).[90]

The rise of England's aristocratic landed society began around 1690. It had reached formidable and unprecedented proportions of wealth, power and privilege as it confronted the emergent industrial society in the early nineteenth century, and was disproportionately powerful and highly visible in the North. Clumber Park, the Nottinghamshire seat of the duke of Newcastle, had achieved an unenviable significance in the 'demonology' of radicalism as a symbol of landed power. Beyond the Tees, coal-rich landed heiresses could be traded in for impecunious Scottish and Irish peers. George Bowes set the precedent in the mid-eighteenth century by marrying his daughter to the earl of Strathmore. The Vanes, who had bought Raby and the Neville estates in Durham married off their daughter, the Lady Frances Anne Vane-Tempest, to the formidable Lord Castlereagh's brother and heir, the middle-aged widower, the third marquess of Londonderry, in 1819. Londonderry shared his brother's political and social outlook. This marriage was a singular misfortune for the relationship between the landed interest and industrial society in the North. It promoted a Liberal opposition to the landed interest at all levels of north-eastern industrial society of quite unusual virulence and tenacity.[91]

There were three main aspects of landed powers. The first was the social and economic influence that came from the ownership and management of an estate of between 10,000 and 200,000 acres, which now had no 'customary tenants' with heritable lands and secure tenancies, but only tenants-at-will who could be required to leave at the end of the year. The second was influence at the centre through the control of parliamentary constituencies, notably nomination boroughs (but also membership of a still powerful House of Lords). And finally, there was power, remarkable in its extent and independence in local government throughout the provinces. This local power extended into non-incorporated boroughs (like Manchester at the time of Peterloo) which were growing apace in the industrial North. Power in local government stemmed from the lord lieutenant of the shire, invariably a great landowner who proposed other landowners as justices of the peace. The JPs were royal appointments answerable to no one and they ruled England. As large landowners consolidated their estates by buying out smaller ones, the number of available landowners for the commission of peace diminished and Anglican parsons were increasingly made JPs. They were often substantial landowners, too, after the commutation of tithes, and by 1832 were a quarter of all magistrates.[92] This formidable alliance of landowners and the Anglican church constituted the ruling class. It was buttressed by outrageous fiscal exemptions and privileges which were tackled with effect only by Harcourt's budget of 1894, which drew a personal protest from the queen. The landowner–Anglican church hegemony was virtually unchallenged until 1832 and its power not seriously diminished for another fifty years. The County Councils Act of 1888, which established elected councils to do what had mostly been done by JPs, was a major landmark in the downfall of the ruling class.

As northern England grew in industrial might, it was increasingly the site of great aristocratic landed estates. The size of estates generally in England had been increasing since the later seventeenth century.[93] Landowners were now disinclined to dismember their estates in their 'last wills' in favour of younger and bastard sons, as they had been inclined to do in the later Middle Ages.[94] In the early fifteenth century 'big estates' of around 8–10,000 acres probably occupied only 10 per cent of England's land; by the late nineteenth century 25 per cent.[95] Beyond the Trent, the duke of Northumberland had an estate of 186,000 acres, the duke of Devonshire 198,000 acres, the duke of Portland 183,000 acres, the Earl Fitzwilliam of Wentworth House in south Yorkshire 115,000 acres.[96] Three of the most aristocratic counties in England in terms of estate ownership were Cheshire, Nottinghamshire and Northumberland; three of the least were Cambridgeshire, Essex and Berkshire.

The 'great estates' which covered a quarter of England's area included those of rich commoners. The big estates owned by peers of the realm occupied 17 per cent of England's area.[97] Thirty-seven peers owned 30 per cent of the land of Nottinghamshire, Derbyshire, Cheshire and Northumberland, while at the opposite extreme seventeen peers owned 10 per cent of all the land in Cambridgeshire, Essex, Middlesex and Berkshire. This profoundly bourgeois corner of eastern England had a similarly minuscule representation among the knightly class in 1436 (see chapter 7). Cambridgeshire had only one knight in 1436, Cheshire had twelve. In 1874 Cambridgeshire had only one peer with a seat and land in the county, Cheshire again had twelve.

Landowners had a preponderant share of 'top wealth' until the last twenty years of the nineteenth century. In the fifty years 1809–58, 190 millionaires died, of whom 181 (94 per cent) were landowners. In the following twenty years there was no significant change – 80 per cent of the milionaires who died were landowners – but in the last twenty years of the century only 40 per cent owned land, and between 1900 and 1914 the figure dropped to 30 per cent. Only 22 of the 97 millionaires who died in the last twenty years of the century were manufacturers. A successful industrialist who died at this time left about £100,000. When John

Bright, whose wealth came from the family textile mill in Rochdale, died in 1889, he left £86,000.[98]

The great wealth, the fiscal privileges and the administrative powers enjoyed by the landowners of England were well understood by nineteenth-century opponents of the ruling class. It was relevant and effective in argument to set them in historical perspective, and radical and Liberal politicians often became excellent medievalists. Cobden's scholarship, it is true, was a little sketchy when, in 1835, he attacked the lords of Clumber, Belvoir and Woburn in highly intemperate language, arguing that their powers in local government were far greater than those of their medieval predecessors.[99] Cobden's serious error was in overstating the powers of their medieval counterparts, however. Fifty years later Brodrick was still making similar charges but grounding his comparisons in far deeper erudition. The landowners of his day, maintained Brodrick, had less circumscribed power than 'either Saxon or Norman lord, in the fulness of his power, ever had the right of exercising'.[100] Harcourt deployed an impressive medieval scholarship and grasp of the principles of feudal taxation in the parliamentary debates on his budget of 1894. These historical comparisons were not merely a rhetorical device; they pin-pointed with some precision the enormous and still rising wealth, power and privilege of Victorian landed society.

The mobilization of northern industrial society against the landed interest began with the Wesleyan church and the lead-mining prospectors of upper Swaledale in the mid-eighteenth century, extending through extra-parliamentary pressure-group politics in the first half of the nineteenth century, and culminating in the Anti-Corn Law League. It was continued over the next sixty years through a more effective and responsive intra-parliamentary party organization and the expert services of a long line of Liberal chancellors of the exchequer from Gladstone to Lloyd George. There are six principal milestones on the long march to victory: the Reform Act of 1832; the Municipal Reform Act of 1835 (in the long run, although at the time it was a calamitous defeat); the repeal of the Corn Laws in 1846; the County Councils' Act of 1888; Harcourt's budget of 1894; and Lloyd George's budget of 1909. But final victory over the ruling class came from an unexpected quarter: the Great War of 1914–18.

Wesleyan Methodism was a major offensive by industrial developers against the Anglican, landed ruling class. In its beginnings it was essentially a frontier church: its strongest support in the mid-eighteenth century was at the interface between industrial entrepreneurs and the landed interest. Lead-miners in the upper Pennine dales, tin-miners in Cornwall and coal-miners in Northumberland were among the new church's earliest and most fervent adherents. They confronted the landed interest very directly, and so did the urban-yeomen industrialists of frontier towns like Bradford and Manchester. The latter were still, when Wesley found Manchester so strongly supportive, the part-farmers and part-manufacturers that Manning has described as the 'middling sorts' of the mid-seventeenth century: highly independent entrepreneurs, but as part-farmers often in conflict with gentry landlords.[101] No less than 62 per cent of the members of the Manchester Wesleyan circuit in 1759 were manufacturers.[102] These manufacturers were not insulated from the Anglican, landed ruling class in an urban-industrial enclave: they were involved in it and directly confronted it.

The Wesleyan church always had an important metropolitan base and, indeed, in numerical terms, this grew from about 4 per cent of all members at the time of Wesley's death in 1791 to 8 per cent in 1901.[103] But Wesley always devoted much of his time and effort to England's wilder perimeters, and that is where his church was strong. It was, however, industrial workers in perimeter zones, rather than farm workers, who turned to the Wesleyan church. They were lead-miners, tin-miners and coal-miners who, in the eighteenth century, worked in self-regulating work teams which negotiated the terms on which they extracted minerals from the land with the landowner's agent. Tin-miners in Cornwall were organized under 'adventurers' and were not paid wages but received a share of the profits. Lead-mining and coal-mining were similar small-team, profit sharing, somewhat swashbuckling enterprises.

Conflict between lead-miners and landowners was endemic in Swaledale. Lead miners had a relationship with landowners at two levels, both of which were negotiated on terms usually patently favourable to landowners. First, in the eighteenth century miners were often proprietors, lessees, members of companies which took land on a twenty-one-year lease, developed the minerals, and paid the landowner, the lessor, an agreed 'duty' or royalty which was between 12 per cent and a remarkable 25 per cent of the lead produced (usually 20 per cent). There was often a rent to be paid as well, with an agreement to double it if the mines were profitable. Miners as lessees/proprietors were less common in the nineteenth century when more capital for mining development was needed; but six of the ten members of the company which leased land in 1801 and developed the Lane End mine were miners, and as late as 1820 most and perhaps all of the twelve men who leased the land and developed the First Chance mine on Crackpot moor were miners.[104]

The second level of involvement was as 'ore winners' engaged for a few weeks or months by the agents of absentee landowners, like the earl of Pontefract, who were not leasing but developing their own minefields. Ore winners usually formed partnerships of six or eight men who bargained terms with the landowner's agent which were again highly variable, ranging from 6s. to 60s. for a measure of lead.[105]

Bargaining was on the basis of the estimated richness of particular fields and veins of lead. There was abundant scope in this bargaining process for misrepresentation and deceit. For this reason there were those who advocated fixed and uniform rates both for royalties and extracting the ore, but fixed rates would certainly have meant that the poorer and less obviously profitable fields and veins of ore would not be tried and developed.[106] The negotiation of rates within a very wide range often resulted in a deep sense of grievance. Only the man who owned the land and the mineral rights had nothing whatsoever to lose, and for no risk and negligible effort his gains could be huge.

Already deep in conflict with landowners and land agents the miners came down from the hills on Sunday to the Anglican churches at Grinton, Muker, Richmond and Marske to find most of the pews privately owned by the local gentry, commonly locked and usually unoccupied. As members of these Anglican congregations they quite literally 'went to the wall'. These were highly independent, non-deferential, eternally optimistic men who delighted in telling their stories of outwitting parson and squire. When Jacob Rowell was established as an itinerant preacher at Barnard Castle by Wesley in 1747, the lead-miners of the upper dales responded to his call with high enthusiasm, not out of despair but defiance.[107]

This is the real significance of Wesleyanism, with its roots in the frontiers of early industrial England, standing against an aristocratic and Anglican ruling class. Wesleyanism would become much more proletarian, but to see it as an essentially working-class religion growing in strength out of conflict with industrial employers, is wholly to misconceive its character. It was not about opposition to industrialists, but about opposition to landowners. It was at its most characteristic when it helped to bring together all classes of industrial society in opposition to landowners, as in the anti-Corn Law movement, where its influence was immense. (At one meeting of the Anti-Corn Law League no fewer than 700 nonconformist ministers sat on the platform.)[108] It was a similar unifying force in the anti-Poor Law movement, also directed against a landowning class seen to be failing once again in its obligations (see below). Northern industrialists were also to the fore in this movement, but the Methodist minister, J. R. Stephens, a great orator, was a power in the land.

The political pressure groups formed towards the middle of the nineteenth century met with varying success. They included both industrial workers and industrial employers and were quite explicitly directed against the power and privilege of the landowning ruling class. There were three: the political 'unions' (of the working and middle classes) founded in 1830 to support the Reform Bill; the anti-Poor Law movement; and the Anti-Corn Law League.

Political unions were formed in 1830 in many northern towns, notably Leeds, Manchester and Gateshead, but the most influential was undoubtedly the Birmingham Political Union founded by the banker, Thomas Attwood. They were far less interested in giving more people the vote than in giving industrial regions more power. The Birmingham union stated its objectives: 'The great agricultural interests of all kinds are well represented there (in the House of Commons). The landed interest, the church, the law, the monied interest – all these have engrossed, as it were, the House of Commons into their own hands.'[109] It was this political imbalance in favour of the landed interest that had to be rectified. The political unions were important in keeping Grey and his colleagues committed to the Reform Bill during the crises of 1832, and the outcome was certainly a gain for industrial England. Out of forty-one newly enfranchised English boroughs, twenty-four (59 per cent) were in industrial areas of the North; six (15 per cent) were in the industrial west Midlands; five (12 per cent) were London boroughs; the remaining six were Chatham, Devonport, Stroud, Frome, Cheltenham and Brighton. Of the fifty-six wholly disenfranchised boroughs, losing both members, only five were in northern England; of the thirty boroughs losing one member, only four were in the North. This was a significant redistribution of parliamentary seats in favour of the industrial Midlands and especially the North. Nevertheless rural England was still over-represented. The twelve rural counties of southern England still returned 174 members whereas three great industrial counties with exactly the same population, Lancashire, the West Riding of Yorkshire and Middlesex, returned only 58.[110]

The Municipal Reform Act of 1835 was a major triumph in the long run for the industrial society of northern England: it insulated urban

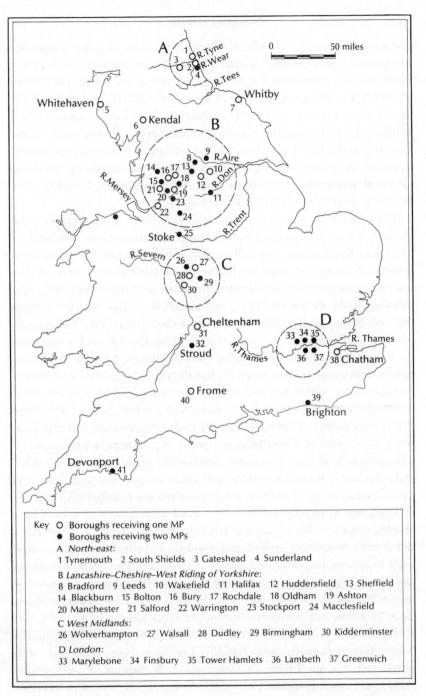

Key ○ Boroughs receiving one MP
     ● Boroughs receiving two MPs
A *North-east*:
1 Tynemouth   2 South Shields   3 Gateshead   4 Sunderland

B *Lancashire–Cheshire–West Riding of Yorkshire*:
8 Bradford   9 Leeds   10 Wakefield   11 Halifax   12 Huddersfield   13 Sheffield
14 Blackburn   15 Bolton   16 Bury   17 Rochdale   18 Oldham   19 Ashton
20 Manchester   21 Salford   22 Warrington   23 Stockport   24 Macclesfield

C *West Midlands*:
26 Wolverhampton   27 Walsall   28 Dudley   29 Birmingham   30 Kidderminster

D *London*:
33 Marylebone   34 Finsbury   35 Tower Hamlets   36 Lambeth   37 Greenwich

MAP 11.1   Boroughs enfranchised in 1832
Source: author

communities from the rule of the ruling class. In his pamphlet, *Incorporate Your Borough*, Cobden saw the issue in precisely these terms. In its original provisions the Municipal Reform Act was an outrageous affront to the industrial North and provoked renewed opposition to the landed interest which culminated in the Anti-Corn Law League. The act designated 178 boroughs for incorporation. Only 28 were north of the Humber and Mersey and they did not include Manchester, Bradford, Sheffield or Middlesborough. They did include northern towns of medieval importance and strong Anglican connections, however, like Beverley, Ripon, Clitheroe and Richmond.

The act made provision for securing incorporation by application to the Privy Council, and Manchester was incorporated in 1838, Sheffield in 1843 and Bradford in 1847. By 1880, sixty more boroughs had been incorporated, half of them in the North. But landowners were able to obstruct incorporation for decades: the duke of Northumberland, as a member of the House of Lords, had vetoed Alnwick's incorporation in the first place; the Lowther earls of Lonsdale controlled Whitehaven, which did not achieve incorporation until 1894; the duke of Portland was the lord of the manor of the mining town of Mansfield and prevented the town's incorporation until 1891.[111] But ratepayers' republics were slowly multiplying in which law and order were maintained by a police force under the authority of the town council's watch committee and not by the magistrates calling in the hussars. In Rochdale before 1867 three times as many adult men had a vote in municipal as in parliamentary elections.[112] The spread of ratepayers' republics outside the jurisdiction of the landed and Anglican ruling class undoubtedly made a significant contribution to overall social peace in nothern England in the later nineteenth century.

There was strong opposition in northern England to the new Poor Law of 1834 on a number of counts. Like the Factory Act of 1833 it was a Benthamite measure of centralization and the industrial North organized itself to oppose the power of London.[113] Northern Poor Law authorities saw themselves as efficient (that, they said, was why the poor rate was low in the North) and the authority of the new Poor Law commissioners, three 'briefless barristers', was simply unwarranted interference.[114] But all perimeter areas were aggrieved by centralization; the difference in the North was industrial concentration. The new Poor Law had been introduced into the House of Commons as 'a measure of agricultural relief', an economic measure to reduce the burden of rates in rural areas. Landed society, strongly represented in both houses of Parliament, was prepared to accept some reduction of magistrates' powers on these terms.[115] But the wealth of landlords, the radicals had always said, had been achieved at the expense of the monasteries in the sixteenth century: when they took over monastic lands they took over monastic obligations to the poor. They were now evading burdens which were properly theirs and shifting them on to the industrial (and industrious) class.

The Anti-Corn Law League was the culmination of northern extra-parliamentary pressure-group politics directed against the landed ruling class. The repeal of the Corn Laws which protected their interests in 1846 was by no means their final defeat, but thereafter the attack was generally conducted by less public, intra-parliamentary, means. The League was more exclusively northern, less bipolar, than the Hampden club movement, the Reform Bill support movement, or Chartism. Its originators and principal supporters throughout were Lancashire businessmen. The richest of the five founder members in 1838 was Thomas Potter, a leading cotton merchant, who was later knighted and became Manchester's first mayor, but the most public figures were the two members of Parliament, Cobden and Bright. (Neither was member for Manchester, which in 1841 preferred to adopt a Suffolk squire; Cobden became member for Salford in 1841, Bright for Durham in 1843.) The League moved its headquarters from Manchester to impressive offices in Fleet Street in 1843 but soon moved them back.

The campaign was conducted with typically highly coloured abuse: landed aristocrats were swindlers and parasites; feudalism was one of the milder terms in general use. The Leaguers were attacking not only the Corn Laws which protected the landed interest, but 'feudal tyranny'. And when the Corn Laws were repealed the *Daily News* said: 'Much more is repealed than the old corn laws. The pseudo-feudalism is abolished which entailed so many evils with so little of the romance of its chivalric prototype.'[116] The *Daily News* was quite wrong. Pseudo-feudalism was still in good heart more than half a century later when Queen Victoria died.

The Corn Laws would have been repealed in 1846 if there had never been an Anti-Corn Law League. After the repeal, Peel paid tribute to Cobden's parliamentary speeches but made no reference to the activities of the League. But in northern England repeal was generally seen as a victory achieved by the League. It was not a victory achieved only on behalf of industrial employers, but of the entire industrial community. Flags were hoisted on factories and bells rang throughout Lancashire and both workers and employers danced in the streets.

The power of landowners at the centre and in the provinces was little affected by the repeal of the Corn Laws in 1846. Cobdenite Liberals saw this quite clearly and spent considerable effort attacking the common law rule of primogeniture which finally ceased to be the law of the land in 1925. This was an irrelevance to the build up of great estates: all that mattered was the freedom to make a 'last will'. Much more important than primogeniture was the fiscal position of property in land. Gladstone, Goschen, Harcourt and Lloyd George slowly and haltingly curtailed some of the privileges of land that had been confirmed and consolidated in the late eighteenth century by Pitt. Pitt's Legacy Act of 1780, which gave land exemption from inheritance duties, was a source of deep resentment until Gladstone made (relatively minor) adjustments in 1853.

Pitt also froze the land tax which had been levied since 1692 at its early eighteenth century level. In consequence, land in England contributed 5 per cent of the national revenues by 1870; in France, by contrast, land contributed 18 per cent, in Belgium 20 per cent.[117] Goschen publicized such comparative statistics. (In England in 1600 the land tax (gross) had probably amounted to 30 per cent of national revenues.) The first really significant measure of adjustment was the estate duties imposed by Harcourt's budget of 1894. The landed aristocracy (and the queen) were incensed by the budget, but industrial England, strongly represented in the Liberal party, felt that it was more than a century overdue.

At the beginning of the twentieth century the mining interest and the landed interest stood opposed, as they had in a relatively simple and direct manner in upper Swaledale more than a century before. The conflict between Sir Arthur Markham, a major colliery owner in north Nottinghamshire, and the landed aristocrats of the dukeries, epitomizes the essential conflict of the nineteenth century. Sir Arthur was encircled by dukes – of Portland, Newcastle, Rutland and Devonshire, as well as Earl Manvers and Lord Savile. Sir Arthur owned and operated collieries. He did not own land, and his companies, he estimated, paid the duke of Devonshire some £8,000 a year in mineral royalties. Sir Arthur was enormously popular in north Nottinghamshire, and the mining town of Mansfield elected him Liberal MP in 1906 and again in 1910. Lloyd George used him as adviser on the royalties' clauses in his budget of 1909.[118] The mining community of Nottinghamshire was not ranged against Sir Arthur Markham, who clearly worked for his wealth; it was bitterly opposed to the great landed aristocrats who apparently did nothing for theirs.

DEFICITS IN AN INDUSTRIAL CIVILIZATION

By the end of the nineteenth century the industrial north of England was losing the economic parity it had achieved with London, and the majority of millionaires who died in the early twentieth century were London millionaires. Always symbolism without substance, Manchester after the middle of the century no longer supported the 'Manchester school', although it had never done so with any conviction anyway. In 1841, in the middle of the Anti-Corn Law campaign, it adopted the southern landowner Milner Gibson as its MP in preference to Richard Cobden. In 1857, a year after building the Free Trade Hall on the sacred site of Peterloo, it did not re-elect its MP John Bright, the principal architect of free trade. The strongest critic of the Manchester school and John Bright (stronger even than Mathew Arnold) was the *Manchester Guardian*. Manchester after the mid-century had ceased to be the 'shock-city' of the future, a major source of political and ideological initiatives: 'At the end of Victorian England, London, the London of the Jubilees, of the Empire, of the great political movements, was in the ascendant.'[119]

Five of the nineteenth century's nineteen prime ministers had come out of the North, somewhat concentrated in the earlier part of the century (only one had come out of the North in the previous century): the duke of Portland, Earl Grey, Peel, the earl of Derby, and Gladstone. They were educated at either Eton or Harrow and King's College, Cambridge or Christ Church, Oxford. Only Peel had a significant part of his family background in industry; Gladstone of Liverpool had a background in West Indian sugar and slaves. Three of the five were out of Lancashire – the earl of Derby, Peel and Gladstone – none was from Yorkshire. This must be reckoned a significant Lancastrian achievement, and not only numerically: the quality was abnormally high.

The intellectual aspects of this northern industrial civilization were extremely uneven and in some respects quite abysmal. Its redeeming features in the world of the mind and the arts were invariably associated not with manufacturing industry but banking and commerce. By the middle of the century there were, indeed, vigorous literary and philosophical societies, atheneums, statistical societies and a high quality provincial press, and shortly after the mid-century there were free libraries and, in Manchester', an embrionic university, Owen's college, and the Hallé. Virtually the only industrial manufacturers connected with any of these enterprises were the two brothers Greg, sons of the great

cotton spinner, reluctant and not very successful second-generation
industrialists with a profound distaste for the mills they inherited, who
were founder members of the Manchester statistical society in 1833.

Merchants and bankers lived by different values and rhythms of life:
they rose later, they had more leisure, they were often closely connected
with and married into the gentry. They were proud that they were not
involved in actually manufacturing cloth and they put little or no capital
into it.[120] They were, in fact, no great loss to industry. But they put
money into the arts. They were greatly assisted in their schemes by the
nonconformist clergy. William Roscoe, a Liverpool banker, was the
outstanding cultural leader of Lancashire for half a century after 1780. He
was the leader of a vry self-consciously aristocratic mercantile community
and when he pusblished his *Life of Lorenzo de Medici called the Magnificent*
in 1796 it was one great merchant prince paying tribute to another.[121]

Although the Gregs were founder members of the statistical society,
and the Bolton industrialist Edmund Ashworth became involved, the
society was overwhelmingly an enterprise run by merchants and bankers.
Even Dr James Kay (later Sir James Kay-Shuttleworth), a medical man,
had served his apprenticeship in Fenton's bank in Rochdale. Men
connected with Heywood's bank were the backbone of the society.[122]

At the level of basic literacy the effects of industrialization and
urbanization were catastrophic. In Halifax between 1800 and 1835
literacy 'plummeted to a level not far off what it had been two hundred
years before'.[123] In 1856 the average illiteracy rate for the whole of
England (as indicated by brides and grooms making a mark instead of
signing their names in marriage registers) was 35 per cent; in the urban-
industrial quadrilateral enclosed by Manchester, Bolton, Rochdale and
Oldham, it was 60 per cent. In the West Riding of Yorkshire it was also
60 per cent, and in Oldham the illiteracy rate was 63 per cent. In
Rothbury in Northumberland, however, it was only 3 per cent.[124]

There were three areas of England which had especially high illiteracy
rates (around 60 per cent): Lancashire–Cheshire and the West Riding of
Yorkshire; Cornwall; and a cluster of counties immediately to the north
and east of London: Cambridgeshire, Huntingdonshire, Bedfordshire,
Essex, Hertfordshire, Norfolk and Suffolk. There were also three
regions which had especially low illiteracy rates (around 25 per cent): the
rural North (except for rural Lancashire) including the East and North
Ridings of Yorkshire, Northumberland, Cumberland and Westmorland;
Hampshire; and London and Middlesex with two adjacent counties to the
south, Surrey and Kent.

The cluster of eastern counties around Bedfordshire and Cambridge-shire are precisely those non-gentry, non-aristocratic counties with small and relatively poor landed estates which were the areas of highest church attendance and the principal site of bitter class conflict between labourers and their employers throughout the nineteenth century. By contrast the northern counties of ancient landed wealth and a well-to-do gentry class, the East and North Ridings of Yorkshire and Northumberland, had remarkably low illiteracy rates, especially in old market towns such as Beverley, Bedale, Leyburn and Richmond (around 15 or 16 per cent) and even somewhat lower in Alnwick, Berwick, and Bellingham in Northumberland. But in Halstead in Essex, like Wigan in Lancashire, the illiteracy rate was 61 per cent.

At one pole of intellectual civilization we have in the nineteenth century the new industrial towns in the North along with the non-gentry counties of the East; at the other pole we have the counties of historic landed wealth, Hampshire, the East and North Ridings of Yorkshire, and Northumberland. This geographical pattern of basic literacy is broadly replicated at the level of intellectual distinction in literature, science, the professions and the arts. London was pre-eminent in England (but outclassed by Edinburgh) in terms of people who by the 1880s had earned a place in directories of eminence. Conan Doyle made a close analysis of this intellectual elite and published it in the *Nineteenth Century* in 1888.[125] (There was one person eminent in literature, science, the law, engineering, politics, 'and other intellectual walks of life' for every 30,000 of England's population.) Hampshire was the most distinguished county with one eminent person to every 13,000 of population; Northumberland had produced engineers of genius and partly for this reason had one eminent man to every 22,000 of population; but in Lancashire it was one in 74,000 and in Derbyshire one in 75,000. Even Cornwall (one in 45,000) did better than that.

For nine centuries landed wealth had been associated with monasteries and military defence; after the sixteenth century it was associated with privilege. The new industrial society of the nineteenth century faced in an acute form the problem of the post-sixteenth-century redundancy of a landed military class. But for a millennium – indeed since the age of Bede – landed wealth was also associated with intellectual productivity. It was still the principal correlate of intellectual achievement in the nineteenth century. Mercantile wealth came a poor second. Industrial wealth in the nineteenth century was no help at all.

12

Economic Decline and Radical Ferment

The twentieth century saw the north of England fall quite abruptly from its late-Victorian eminence. The North was the site of three closely related processes: industrial decline, class conflict, and the rise of the Labour party. In fact the Labour party has been the north of England's great twentieth-century triumph – albeit one it shares with London – one of the great, historic political initiatives. At the outset, it is true, northern industrial society rallied to the emerging Labour party only slowly, and with great reluctance, but finally became its principal base. In the 1980s the concentration of Labour support in the northern counties saved the party from virtual extinction.

By 1980 class conflict had been superseded by a wide-ranging attack on the exercise of power by a highly centralized state. The North played an important if overambitious part in this as it rediscovered great strength in the new-found political importance of coal. This regional power was not in the hands of landowners or industrialists as in the past, but in those of the National Union of Mineworkers (NUM). In 1688 Lord Lumley was a northern revolutionary who could starve London of coal; in 1984 Arthur Scargill, president of the union, was a northern revolutionary who could starve the entire nation.

CLASS CONFLICT AND ECONOMIC DECLINE

In the inter-war years northern England was the principal site of capitalism in crisis: the land of mass unemployment, designated depressed or, more tactfully, 'special' areas, strikes, the 'means test' for extended benefit for the long-term unemployed, and carefully staged 'hunger marches' to London, echoing the 'blanketeers'. The rest of England also experienced large-scale unemployment, but Jarrow was 'the town that died'. And when Scotland, south Wales, west Cumberland and Tyneside were designated 'special areas' at the end of 1934, production generally was up by 10 per cent on 1929 and the standard of living was up by 10 per cent; while wage rates had fallen by 3 per cent, the cost of living had fallen by thirteen.[1] But much of northern England had been left behind.

There were about 900 strikes a year in Britain between the wars, heavily concentrated in the industrial North, especially in the West Riding of Yorkshire. (There had been 1,607 strikes in 1920, but there were never more than 1,000 again until 1937, when the total was 1,129.) Between 1911 and 1947 there were 244 strikes in the West Riding of Yorkshire, a number exceeded only by south Wales, which had 247. There were 213 in Lancashire and Cheshire, 132 in Northumberland and Durham; in the south-west of England there were 7, in the eastern counties 13; even in the industrial east Midlands only 69. This rank order of propensity to strike is the same when measured in more sophisticated ways, by strikers as a proportion of working population or, allowing for type of industry, by standardized strike ratios.[2]

Even the general strike of 1926, for all its generality, had a very strong northern flavour because the mining industry was at its centre. The mine-owners had stated their intention to reduce miners' wages and increase their hours of work after a temporary government subsidy they had received came to an end. The miners replied: 'Not a penny off the pay, not a minute on the day' and were thereupon locked out. The general council of the Trades Union Congress called a wide range of workers out in the miners' support (an impressive contrast with the political Scargill strike 1984–5). The general strike of 1926 was a sympathy strike, a great gesture of generosity to help miners to secure a living wage. This was straightforward class war: the profits of mine-owners in conflict with the wage-levels of their employees. And at the heart of this class war were the coal-fields of the North.

When the level of strikes rose to even greater height after the Second World War the northern bias had gone. The reason may be simple: northern industry had been decimated. Between 1954 and 1979 there were never fewer than 2,000 strikes a year, in 1969 there were more than 3,000 and in 1970 almost 4,000.[3] But their geographical spread was now much more diffuse. The coal-mining industry was far less strike-prone after the mid-1950s until the two great strikes of 1972 and 1974. Strikes in the docks and shipbuilding also declined, but motor vehicle manufacturing, with major centres outside the North, was exceedingly strike-prone.[4] Even the miners' strike of 1972 experienced its high point not in the North but at the Saltley coke works near Birmingham. In the great northern conurbations at this time, days lost in strikes were significantly below the national average. This was particularly the case in Manchester and in west Yorkshire. Tyneside was around the national average, and only Merseyside was significantly above.[5]

Economic decline, class conflict and class-based politics occurred with singular abruptness and proceeded with remarkable speed in northern England between 1900 and 1910. One historian has described the political change in these years in apocalyptic terms as 'a leap from one kind of consciousness to another'.[6] This is perhaps an overstatement. But the north of England in the early twentieth century was not in any simple and straightforward way merely an extension of its high Victorian past.

The experience of the coal industry is not untypical. It enjoyed a boom period in the last two decades of the nineteenth century. The labour force expanded rapidly, rising by 70 per cent between 1881 and 1901, wages were high and rose steadily up to 1900, the wholesale price of coal consistently increased after 1850 and moved steeply upwards after 1883. But the rapidly expanding labour force was recruited easily from the vast national pool of unskilled labour, especially from rural areas, and there was little investment in new machinery. Productivity (measured by output per man) declined by 23 per cent between 1881 and 1911. The easier seams of coal were becoming exhausted. Miners' wages fell sharply between 1900 and 1905. They were still significantly below the 1900 level in 1911 and had not recovered in real terms by 1913.[7]

In the last twenty years of the nineteenth century the cost of living was actually falling and wages were rising; real wages rose by 32 per cent in these two decades. Between 1900 and 1914 wages overall were at best static.[8] Between 1902 and 1909 the cost of living rose by 5 per cent, and between 1909 and 1913 by 9 per cent. Wages in many sectors of industry caught up with the first rise, but often lagged behind the second: 'they rose unevenly, especially for the man who needed the rise most, the general worker'.[9]

In 1885 Friedrich Engels acknowledged England's general prosperity. Industrial progress over recent decades had been 'colossal and unparalleled', but he predicted economic contraction with consequences for working-class standards of life which would lead to the rebirth of socialism. The basic reason for the colossal progress, said Engels, was the international market; this would also be the reason for the forthcoming collapse.

International markets had enormously expanded; for Britain, with rising competition from America and Germany, they would now rapidly contract.[10] Both his prediction and diagnosis were substantially correct. Modern economic historians have similarly placed great emphasis on the international context in interpreting the economic acceleration in the late-eighteenth century and economic decline in the twentieth.[11] It was a major factor in the decline before 1914, and even more important in the period between the wars: 'when world trade collapsed in the inter-war period of the twentieth century the British rate of growth and of capital formation fell to pre-industrial levels.'[12]

The state of the economy was not the only reason for the upsurge of class conflict and the rise of class-based politics in the twentieth century, but it was the principal one.[13] Another reason was that by 1900 the class of industrial capitalists and the class of industrial workers were much more clearly formed and distinctly positioned: capitalists were richer, more established, secure and self-confident (and educated differently) than fifty or even thirty years before, but workers were also more secure and self-confident and aware of their separate interests. Capitalists were more distant from their employees as they formed limited companies which superseded family firms. The working classes were also drawing apart, and they were ever less inclined to be patronized as they established their own distinctive and valued patterns of life. The rise and change in management of working men's clubs is a case in point. They were established in the 1860s under middle-class leadership and with middle-class financial support, the intention being that the middle class should civilize the working class. The working class members first successfully asserted themselves in 1886 by insisting that the consumption of alcohol be allowed in the clubs; by the mid 1880s they had democratized the governing council and based finances on club affiliation fees instead of the subscriptions of middle-class patrons.[14] The classes were defining themselves, consolidating their positions, drawing apart. The scene was set for overt conflict when late-Victorian rising prosperity came abruptly to a halt.

Class war erupted in 1910. The home secretary, Winston Churchill, sent two warships and 7,000 troops to Liverpool in the summer of 1911, where the port employers had locked out their entire workforce, with whom they were in dispute. Liverpool was under seige. There was a national railway strike, and the miners struck for a minimum wage to protect underground workers assigned to poor seams where they found it impossible to earn a living wage. Five million working days were lost on average each year between 1898 and 1908; in the year 1912 it was forty million.

By the middle of the twentieth century the distinction between the economically depressed (and socialist-voting) North and the relatively prosperous (and Conservative-voting) South was evident in any regional breakdown of social characteristics. Moser and Scott made such a breakdown for the 1950s, focusing on 157 towns throughout England and Wales with a population in excess of 50,000. When these towns were compared on the basis of some sixty social and economic variables, they fell into two distinct clusters: one, with lower life expectancies, proportion of children at school beyond the statutory leaving age, number of adults in administrative and professional employment and the like, was above a line from the Wash to Bristol, the other was below. At one extreme were Bootle, Wigan and Barnsley in Lancashire and Yorkshire, at the other Coulsdon, Beckenham, Epsom and Esher in Middlesex and Surrey. It was a ring of suburban towns around London that was singularly well blessed in relation to the North. In Epsom and Coulsdon a child at the age of one could expect to live to the age of seventy-three; in Wigan the child would be fortunate to make it to sixty-seven.[15]

The two clusters of towns differed significantly overall in their class composition and political orientation. At one extreme there were towns with only around 8 per cent of their workers in professional and administrative employment, like Warrington, Bootle and St Helens, and at the other were towns with 40 per cent or more, like Coulsdon, Beckenham and Southgate. Less than 25 per cent of the electorate in towns like Southgate and Esher voted for the Labour party in 1955 while the figure was more than 70 per cent in Mansfield and Barnsley.

The two sets of towns overlapped to a modest extent: in the North there were Southport and Harrogate, as well blessed as any town in the South, while Dagenham, Barking and West Ham were similar to Barnsley, Dewsbury and Bootle. (Dagenham had only 8 per cent of its workers in professional and administrative employment, and over 70 per cent of the electorate voted for the Labour party.) But the polar extremities were much more starkly impressive than the relatively small overlap.

After the Second World War Merseyside was added to England's two previously designated depressed areas, Tyneside and west Cumberland. They were re-styled 'development areas'. In the 1960s refinements were made to the classification of assisted areas and the levels of subsidy they would receive. A category of 'intermediate area' was created. By the early 1970s the Midlands and the South (except parts of Cornwall) were unassisted, but virtually the whole of northern England was a vast, subsidized, special zone. This – as well as high redundancy payments for steelworkers and miners – was the pacification of the North.

A NORTHERN INITIATIVE: BRADFORD AND
THE LABOUR PARTY

The Labour party was born in Bradford in 1893.[16] It was a generally unwelcome child in the north of England, even in industrial working-class areas, and never widely or warmly embraced until after 1918. It was not fathered by trade unionism – indeed, it was born in Bradford precisely because trade unions there were demonstrably underdeveloped and other means were patently needed to protect a highly vulnerable working class. This had been abundantly clear in the fierce and violent strike at the Manningham mills which extended over the first five months of 1891. An early victim of suddenly contracting overseas trade, brought about by America's recently imposed McKinley Tariff, the wool worsted factories in Bradford were reducing wages by up to a third. The work-force at the Manningham mills staged a desperate and tenacious strike to protect their wages. It was not union initiated, organized or led and received no union financial support. Unionism in wool worsted manufacturing had not developed with advancing technology and the changing character of the work-force; Bradford's unions were still the old craft unions. A political party to represent and protect the interests of labour was pioneered in Bradford not because trade unions there were strong but precisely because they were so miserably weak.

The business of a political party was to represent an 'interest': its job was defence. (When the Labour party was formally established in 1900 with whips and a parliamentary leader, it modestly but accurately styled itself the LRC: the Labour Representation Committee.) This political representation and defence of an interest was well understood in Bradford. In the wake of the Manningham mills strike, towards the end of 1891, a Bradford 'labour union' was set up with 3,000 paying members to sponsor candidates in local and parliamentary elections who would represent the interests of the working class. It sponsored Alderman Ben Tillett in the parliamentary election for Bradford West in the following year. Tillett had a background in trade union activity (in the London docks) but he was not standing in any sense as a trade union nominee. He had no national party behind him, only a local committee scarcely a year old. He lost, perhaps not altogether surprisingly, to the Liberal candidate, a Bradford mill-owner. This is usually presented as a 'near-miss'. In fact he was easily defeated by the Conservative candidate as well. But that is not of the first importance: Bradford and Tillett had created the prototype of the Labour party.

The model was adopted at a national meeting held in Bradford and chaired by Keir Hardie at the beginning of 1893. Representatives from 120 labour organizations met and launched the Labour Party. (It would not be in the true sense a parliamentary party until 1900 and would not have the title 'Labour party' until 1906, but at this stage it called itself the Independent Labour Party [ILP].) This was not, perhaps, the most important political event in the nineteenth century, as some have claimed, but undoubtedly 'On any reckoning, it was a great turning point.'[17]

This is the judgment of hindsight. It was by no means apparent in the general election of 1895. The ILP sponsored twenty-eight candidates who stood in carefully selected working-class constituencies, sixteen in the industrial north of England, seven in Scotland mostly in or near Glasgow, and two in London (West Ham and Fulham). For the ILP the election was a rout. Not a single candidate was elected, and their share of the vote was usually derisory, around 10 per cent.

Ben Tillett was again comfortably defeated in Bradford West. The *Labour Annual* published an inquest in which Parliament was seen quite clearly and explicitly as representing 'interests'. In the new Parliament 155 MPs represented the landowners' interest, 138 represented the manufacturers' interest, 181 represented the lawyers' interest, but not one represented the interest of men who earned their living by their labour. And yet 'Most – I might say all – of these representatives of monopoly and privilege', said the *Labour Annual*, had been returned to power by 'the direct vote of the labouring classes themselves'.[18]

It was the catastrophe of the general election of 1895 that turned the ILP towards the trade unions for support.[19] The Trades Union Congress had agreed in principle in 1893 to raise a political fund to support parliamentary candidates; it also resolved (by a small majority) that no financial assistance would be given to any candidate who did not support the objective of public ownership and control of the means of production, distribution and exchange. This was a serious disability which the Labour party accepted in return for financial support: an alien, metropolitan notion imposed on the northern working class, and which some Labour MPs, once they were elected, quite explicitly renounced. Three Derbyshire miners elected to Parliament in 1910 were particularly unhappy with these policy objectives and tended to identify with the Liberal party; one of them, J. G. Hancock, was expelled from the party in 1914. It is perhaps significant that since 1911 MPs had been paid and ideological conformity was less easily enforced.

Theoretical socialism was certainly far from the minds of the men in Bradford who in effect launched the Labour party between 1891 and 1893; indeed, they were the despair of theoreticians who came up from the South. William Morris had lectured to a packed audience in Bradford in 1884 but concluded from this encounter that 'they are mostly a sad set of philistines there, and it will be long before we do anything with them.' But theirs was the initiative that a few years later brought the Labour party to life.

The survival of the Labour party was far from certain in 1900; a little more so by 1906 when it had thirty MPs; and assured perhaps of a modest small-party future by 1914 when it had forty. The reason for this slow and uncertain start of a party that arose from northern working-class initiatives was that it had powerful working-class opponents in the North. Three great northern institutions found socialism, with its collectivist thrust, highly uncongenial: nonconformity, trade unions, and Lancashire. Moreover, the class conflict to which northern working-class society was clearly committed after the turn of the century could perhaps be more effectively fought through the Liberal party. This was the instinct of many miners who still saw the landed interest as a major class enemy: the Liberal party was a tried and tested instrument for the curtailment of landowners' powers. For many workers in the North, especially in Nottinghamshire, Derbyshire, Yorkshire and Durham, the natural party for their class-based politics was the Liberal party. 'By 1910 the change to class politics was substantially complete. That from Liberalism to Labour had not really begun. Nor were there any signs that it must begin.'[20]

The semi-skilled and unskilled workers were becoming unionized in the later nineteenth century, and this 'new unionism, has often been seen as a major contribution to the rise of the Labour party. The successful London dock strike of 1889 (led by Ben Tillett) – a 'prosperity strike', unlike the desperation strike at Manningham mills a year later – demonstrated the power of the new form of unionism (as well as organizing unskilled workers it was based not on the crafts that men exercised but on the industries that employed them). In the 1892 preface to his *Condition of the Working Class in England* Engels placed great weight on the new unionism as promoting the cause of socialism: 'we now see these new unions taking the lead of the working-class movement generally.' The new unionism was perhaps not quite as new as Engels thought, but it was certainly less tied to the Liberal party than the old.[21] Engels gave it a precise geographical base in the east end of London. It was there that the future of socialism lay: 'the revival of the East End of London remains one of the greatest and most fruitful facts of this *fin de siecle*, and glad and proud I am to have lived to see it.'

There was no emphasis on the socialist possibilities and potential of Manchester now, and indeed they were exceedingly slight. Whatever might be happening in the east end of London, there was in the northern working class an enormous reluctance to embrace the Labour party which Bradford had initiated. While the ILP attempted to establish itself in the 1890s, the great northern coal and cotton unions 'were strongly hostile to independent labour representation'.[22] The triumph of Labour came in the end from three circumstances which lay outside the North: the Taff Vale judgment of 1901; the 1914–18 war, which transformed the outlook of a generation; and major post-war electoral support from working-class London. In the end the triumphant Labour party was not primarily a northern but a bipolar accomplishment.

THE NORTHERN WORKING CLASS AND THE LABOUR PARTY BEFORE 1914

By 1914 the north of England had all but rejected the Labour party it had initiated in 1893. The last general election before the outbreak of the European war was in December 1910, a time when northern industrial society was moving rapidly into a particularly menacing phase of conflict between capital and labour. The northern counties were convulsed as class war teetered to the verge of civil war. In the seven northern counties of England there were 154 parliamentary seats; in the general election 21 were won by Labour candidates: 13.6 per cent. In 1945, by contrast, 128 were won by Labour: 74 per cent.[23]

The northern working class gave its support to the Liberal party to quite an astonishing extent. It is true that the Liberal party curtailed the wealth and power of landowners, and miners in particular approved of this, but it was nevertheless the bosses' party.[24] It was not a matter of deference: the working class was often openly and fiercely in opposition to employers on the industrial front, but they still voted strongly for the

Liberal party down to 1914. Liberalism accorded with some of their deepest values; socialism did not.

In 1910 half of the forty Labour MPs sat for mining constituencies throughout Britain, and sixteen had been sponsored by the miners' federation. These, statistics give a wholly misleading impression of strong support among, miners for the Labour party. It was still the case as late as 1914 that 'if a Liberal candidate was in the field it was rare for the Labour man, even if he himself were a miner or miners' official, to poll as much as half of the mining vote in the constituency.'[25]

Part of the problem for the Labour party was nonconformity. This was a highly individualistic form of religious practice de-emphasizing the church hierarchy, promoting initiative among rank-and-file members in the conduct of church affairs, and encouraging spontaneous and unprogrammed communion between worshippers and their God. It was not a humble religion; it was reserved and aloof. Personal enterprise and advancement were favoured rather than equality, partnership and joint endeavour. Highly congruent with Liberalism, it was a disaster for the Labour party.

Primitive Methodism, trade unionism and class conflict were closely associated in the rural counties of eastern England in the later nineteenth century, and here, too, the instrument for political action was not the emerging Labour Party but that of the Liberals. It is true that in the crisis years in the 1870s a Labour party was not yet on the horizon, but the leader of the first national union of agricultural workers, Joseph Arch, was at the height of his career when the ILP was being established. An ardent primitive Methodist, he became Liberal MP for North-West Norfolk in 1885 and again held the seat for ten years 1892 to 1902. He showed no inclination to support the new party and when he retired his Liberal friends subscribed to buy an annuity on which he lived until his death in 1919. For Arch the Liberal party was an effective instrument in a singularly bitter class war waged against farmers who sacked labourers and evicted them from their homes simply on suspicion of having voted Liberal.[26]

There was the same close relationship between Methodism, liberalism and trade unionism on the northern coal-fields. The unions were usually led by Methodists and this helps to explain their political orientation. Under this Liberal–nonconformist leadership 'the mining unions were slow to accept an independent political stance and were the last to affiliate themselves to the Labour Party.'[27]

John Wilson, the general secretary of the Durham miners' association at the end of the nineteenth century is a good example of this style of leadership. Indeed, in his background, outlook and career he is strikingly like his contemporary, Joseph Arch. Wilson was a Methodist and became Liberal MP for mid-Durham. He had no interest in the emerging Labour party and spoke out strongly against socialism. But he had no difficulty in becoming leader of his union and securing election to Parliament in a mining constituency.

After 1906 there was some shift in attitude among miners' leaders in the North-east and they even invited socialist speakers to address union rallies, but they were in danger of moving ahead of their members. This was the case with W. House, the president of the Durham miners' association in 1910. He stood for Parliament not as a Liberal but as a Labour candidate; and solidly mining constituencies consistently failed to elect him. In January 1910 he stood for Bishop Auckland in a three-cornered fight and came bottom of the poll: the Liberal candidate was elected with a comfortable majority, the Conservative candidate came second, House came third with 25 per cent of the vote. House stood again in December 1910 and now obtained 33 per cent of the vote, but the Liberal candidate was successful again. In 1913 he stood for Houghton-le-Spring, a constituency with an even higher proportion of miners. The Liberal candidate was elected comfortably, the Conservative candidate came second. The president of the Durham miners' association obtained 25 per cent of the vote.[28]

Neither union leaders nor the rank-and-file in Yorkshire showed much enthusiasm for the early Labour party and the outcome of the parliamentary election in the mining constituency of Holmfirth in 1910 illustrates a general situation: the Liberal candidate easily topped the poll and the Labour candidate obtained only 14 per cent of the vote. In Nottinghamshire and Derbyshire the miners' unions were rich and respectable (as were the union leaders) and actively hostile to the Labour party. In 1909 the Nottinghamshire miners' association lent the Nottingham corporation £100,000 and by 1914 the Derbyshire miners' association had invested over £100,000 in the Chesterfield and Ilkeston corporations. They were not only averse to radical politics but to strike action which might deplete union funds.

When a ballot was first held in 1906 for affiliation to the Labour party, only 13 per cent of the Nottinghamshire miners voted in favour and the same percentage in Derbyshire. Overall the miners' federation of Great Britain to which these unions belonged rejected affiliation: 47 per cent in favour, 53 per cent against. Two years later affiliation was just accepted:

55 per cent of miners were in favour. The Nottinghamshire miners had now advanced to 33 per cent in favour, the Derbyshire miners to 26 per cent.[29]

The cotton unions were pushed into reluctant affiliation with the Labour party by the Taff Vale judgment of 1901, which made union funds highly vulnerable to legal action by employers. When legal action was taken against the weavers they put pressure on the united textile factory workers' association, to which they belonged, to affiliate with what was then (1902) the labour representation committee. This was essentially an opportunistic move: it reflected no change in political principle.[30] In a ballot held in 1902 a large majority of union members were in favour of affiliation: 81 per cent.[31] 'But the cotton workers still remained among Labour's more moderate adherents.'[32] They had made a pragmatic move of self-defence, but they had not been converted to socialism. 'The Lancashire unions, and especially the textile ones, fought to keep socialism out of union affairs . . . the ILP succeeding in the region only on the unions' terms.'[33] The success was in fact negligible by 1914.

Nonconformity was a big difficulty for the early Labour party, as were the northern trade unions, but Lancashire was the biggest difficulty of all. When, after 1918, the northern industrial counties turned massively to Labour, Lancashire lagged – and still lags – significantly behind. In the mid-1960s while 60 per cent of electors in the North-east supported the Labour party, only 50 per cent did so in Lancashire and Cheshire.[34]

In the early twentieth century Lancashire was not Liberal but impressively Conservative. Even the miners were Conservative. In Wigan, it is true, the Labour candidate was elected in January 1910, but the Conservative regained the seat in December; in other mining constituencies like Newton and Leigh there was never any serious challenge to the Conservatives.[35] The cotton workers voted overwhelmingly for affiliation with the Labour party and overwhelmingly for Conservative candidates in parliamentary elections. (When there was a shift in 1906 it was towards the Liberals.) The Lancashire miners were Conservative-voting and, in spite of relatively low wages, notably non-militant. While Yorkshire miners had twice as many strikes as the national average of miners' strikes in the decades after 1911, Lancashire had only half the national average.[36]

During the twenty-five years 1885 to 1910 a majority of all the electors in Lancashire (51 per cent) voted for Conservative and Unionist parliamentary candidates; in Yorkshire, the North-east, the east Midlands and East Anglia, only a minority (albeit a large minority, around 45 per cent) did so.[37] In terms of MPs elected, Lancashire's record of Conservative victories is impressive. In the High Peak, Lancashire and Cheshire there were sixty-six constituencies returning seventy-one MPs: in 1886 fifty-nine (83 per cent) were Conservatives, in 1895 sixty (84 per cent), and in 1900 fifty-six (80 per cent): 'This is by any standards a strong Tory tradition.'[38] But there was a marked change in 1906 when only sixteen (22 per cent) were Conservative, although there was some recovery in 1910 to thirty-two (45 per cent). The shift was mainly in urban working-class areas in the south-east of the region. The strong nonconformity of this area, strikingly different from the Catholicism of Wigan and the mining districts, seems belatedly to have asserted itself.

Lancashire remains nevertheless an anomaly which has perplexed political scientists. The orientation of the cotton towns was particularly difficult to explain: 'Considering that Nonconformity was quite strong in the area . . . the Conservatism of the cotton workers is puzzling.'[39] But the cotton workers significantly shifted their political ground in 1906 in a way which was congruent with their religious values and traditions – not to support the Labour party to which their union was affiliated, but the Liberals. There was now considerable industrial conflict in the cotton towns as international trade was depressed; the answer for northern workers still seemed to be the Liberal rather than the Labour party.

But political outlook and change in Lancashire, while clearly influenced by religion – Catholicism in the west and nonconformity in the east – seems to be anchored in older traditions: they suggest the primacy of region. Always an isolated and insular county, Lancashire never quite got into step with the rest of the North. It moved towards alignment belatedly, as so often in the past; and still never quite got into place in the end.

Indeed, the alignment has slipped in the years since the end of the Second World War. In terms of the percentage of its MPs who were Labour, Lancashire was not far behind Yorkshire and the North-east in the inter-war years, with 33 per cent of its MPs Labour, compared with 42 per cent and 56 per cent respectively. But in the years 1955 to 1970, 35 per cent of Lancashire's MPs were Labour, 56 per cent of Yorkshire's (including the mainly rural and Conservative North and East Ridings) and no less than 76 per cent in the North-east.[40] And yet their 'class' composition in terms of manual workers is much the same: about 70 per cent in Lancashire and Yorkshire, around 75 per cent in the North-east. Lancashire's political representatives have been as much out of line with the county's class base as they are with the rest of the north of England.

THE NORTH OF ENGLAND 1920–90:
A BASE FOR THE LABOUR PARTY AND FOR RENEWED
ATTACK ON THE CENTRE

During the past seventy years England's political landscape has been transformed by the rise of the Labour party to an established position as one of the two parties of government, and in the past twenty years by the rising attack on an over-extended centre. The north of England, in spite of de-industrialization and economic decline, has made a highly significant contribution to both these developments. Indeed, as Labour party support has diminished in the past decade, northern electoral geography has grown in importance. The significant contribution to the attack on the centre was made possible after 1970 by growing regional power based on the politically strategic importance of coal.

The Labour party rose in the inter-war years on continuing and heightened class conflict which reached its climax in the general election of 1945, with a major and decisive shift from conservatism to socialism in London's working-class boroughs, and with the radicalization of the generation that went to war in 1914. The London contribution was of particular importance. The much vaunted 'new unionism' in late nineteenth-century working-class London had not in fact produced any Labour MPs. Keir Hardie had been elected for West Ham in 1892 but lost the seat in the debacle of 1895, and by 1914 there were only three Labour MPs in the county of London's sixty parliamentary seats. After the war the Labour party gained great strength from the bipolar structure of support based on London and the North.

The war made a major contribution to the fortunes of the Labour party. It had taken young men out of familiar contexts and communities; it also meant life in an intensely class-based army, as well as military experience. After 1918 (as indeed after 1945) young men had had enough of class and the old ways. They were restless: they were also self-confident. In his book, *The Classic Slum*, Robert Roberts described the sense of release and awakening in the working-class community in Salford in which he was then growing up. Before 1914, said Roberts, working-class men in the area who came into contact with socialist ideas 'showed either indifference or, more often, hostility'. The local Hyndman Hall which brought socialist speakers and even 'Marxist ranters' to the district 'had about as much political impact on the neighbourhood as the nearby gasworks'. But now, after the war, men were changing their minds: 'Poor families, dyed-in-the-wool Tories, who had voted Conservative since getting the franchise, were now talking not "Liberal" but "Labour".' After the 1924 general election there was popular rejoicing in Salford: 'on the night of that triumph, our constituency returned its first Labour MP, simple socialists like my mother wept for joy and we, the young, felt ourselves the heralds of a new age.'[41]

The changes occurring in working-class London after 1918 were at least as important for the Labour party as those occurring in Salford and throughout the industrial North. Support for the Labour party had previously come overwhelmingly from northern England. The pre-war geographical bias to the North is shown not only in the distribution of Labour MPs but of those who bought shares in the ILP publication founded by Keir Hardie, the *Labour Leader*. Between 1904 and 1910 shareholders were 66 per cent in Yorkshire, Lancashire, Cheshire and the North-east, 10 per cent in London.[42] This geographical imbalance in support for the Labour party changed markedly after 1920.

The London-based theoretical socialism of Hyndman's Social Democratic Federation, which was founded in 1881, and of the Fabians, founded in 1884, had never been of much interest in northern England. The pragmatic, atheoretical ILP, by contrast, had found relatively little support in London, so that by 1895, 188 (62 per cent) of its 300 branches were in Yorkshire, Lancashire and the north-east, while 29 (10 per cent) were in London. In 1906 7 per cent of the Labour party's 30 MPs came from London constituencies, and 73 per cent came from Yorkshire, Lancashire, Cheshire and the North-east.

The change in London was dramatic between 1910 and 1945. Whereas only 5 per cent of London's sixty seats were held by Labour MPs in 1910, 77 per cent were held by Labour in 1945.[43] In the north of England (Lancashire, Cheshire, Yorkshire and all counties north) 13.6 per cent of all parliamentary seats were held by Labour in 1910, 74 per cent in 1945. In terms of the proportion of MPs who were Labour. London had achieved parity with the North.

The London zone had also achieved parity in terms of its absolute contribution to the Labour party. By 1945 London and the boroughs immediately adjacent to it presented a block of London-and-district Labour MPs of approximately the same size as the block from Lancashire, Cheshire and Yorkshire: eighty-nine compared with ninety-seven. The London zone contributed 23 per cent of all Labour MPs, Lancashire, Cheshire and Yorkshire contributed 24 per cent (see table 12.1). This was the bipolar structure of support that brought the Labour

TABLE 12.1 Regional distribution of Labour MPs 1906–45

General Election	London Area	Lancs Cheshire Yorks	County Durham	England Elsewhere	Scotland and Wales	Total
1906	4 (13%)	20 (67%)	2 (6%)	1 (3%)	3 (10%)	30
1923	37 (19%)	43 (22%)	10 (5%)	53 (27%)	54 (27%)	197
1929	54 (18%)	78 (27%)	18 (5%)	78 (27%)	61 (22%)	289
1945	89 (23%)	97 (24%)	19 (5%)	62 (16%)	126 (32%)	393

Source: F. W. S. Craig, *British Electoral Facts 1885–1975* (Macmillan, 1976).

party triumphantly to power and kept it there in the post-war period of reconstruction, centralization and reform.

The London pole was not simply of numerical importance: it made a vital qualitative contribution to the Labour party. Labour's progress in London in the inter-war years was exemplified by its success in local government.[44] C. R. Attlee became mayor of Stepney and Herbert Morrison became mayor of Hackney. Both Attlee and Morrison, prime minister and deputy prime minister in 1945, sat for London constituencies. Their political careers had been essentially London-based.

The Labour party rose in the twentieth century as a class-based party. By 1945 there was a tidy alignment between class and the two parties of government: two-thirds of the working class (manual, workers) supported the Labour party and two-thirds of the middle class supported the Tory party.[45] Class conflict was simpler and more straightforward after 1918 than before 1914 because the great landowners were of far less weight and the Liberal party in consequence of far less relevance: the conflict was now straightforwardly between industrial workers and industrial employers. Industrial capitalists were at last 'hegemonic'.

The great landowners were declining in wealth and political power. The agricultural depression of the later nineteenth century drastically reduced the value of their estates. Thus the vast agricultural properties of the earls of Scarborough in Lincolnshire lost 31 per cent of their value in the years 1879 to 1889, in Yorkshire 22 per cent, and in Durham 16 per cent. The decade 1908 to 1918 in particular was a watershed in their fortunes. The measures taken by Asquith's Liberal government after 1908 and the financial burdens of the war of 1914–18 saw the eclipse of the landowning class. The clauses relating to land values duties and mineral royalties in Lloyd George's budget of 1909, and the Parliament Act of 1911, which radically curtailed the power of the House of Lords, precipitated its decline. Between 1918 and 1920 many landowners were forced to sell up; in the space of two years England changed hands, probably on the same scale as after 1066.[46] After 1920 the formidable Victorian and Edwardian structure of English landed society was largely dismantled; serious power was now in the hands of industrialists. With the decline of landowners' wealth and power the Liberal party lost much of its point and the working class could give their undivided support to the Labour party and their undivided attention to attacking industrial employers.

The Labour party thus attracted increasing working class support, but throughout the inter-war years this was still too geographically diffuse, too thinly spread and diluted, to be electorally effective. It had achieved increased geographical concentration, notably in the industrial North by 1945, and this became still more pronounced after 1955.[47] This geographical concentration, in spite of a shrinking working-class base, saved the party from extinction after 1979. In 1931 the Labour party gained 31 per cent of the total vote but won only 52 seats; in 1983 it gained only 27.6 per cent of the total vote but won 209 seats: 'The increasing geographical concentration of Labour strength saved the Labour party from parliamentary rout.'[48]

Class conflict reached its peak in the general election of 1945, which was essentially an act of class war. The level of class support for the two parties of government remained unimpaired for the next twenty years, but after the mid-1960s class was of diminishing importance. And, indeed, radical politics in the post-war decades were less about opposing class interests than nuclear defence: the radicals now were the professional and educated middle classes involved in the campaign for nuclear disarmament in which manual workers took virtually no part. They were once again the despair of revolutionaries from the upper class.[49]

By 1983 a split had occurred between each class and its 'natural' party. In 1966, 69 per cent of all manual workers supported the Labour party; in 1983, 43 per cent. In 1959, 67 per cent of non-manual workers supported the Conservative party; in 1983, 55 per cent.[50] The decline in working-class support for Labour may be attributed in part to a reduction in the number of manual workers in the electorate: down by 13 per cent (from 47 to 34 per cent) between 1964 and 1983. In northern England the shrinkage in the number of manual workers was 10 per cent, but total support for the Labour party in the north declined by almost twice as much, down by 18 per cent from 55 per cent in the mid-1960s to 37 per cent in 1983.[51] The drop in the level of working-class support was not simply the decline in the size of the class base.

As the overall level of class support declines, its regional concentration becomes of paramount importance. The industrial north of England was never more important to the Labour party. There is no process of convergence between North and South even in terms of class, for the class of manual workers is contracting much more slowly in the North than in the South, and the gap between the North and the South therefore actually grows wider. Between 1964 and 1983 northern manual workers declined by 10 per cent, southern manual workers by 15 per cent.[52] As the size of the manual work-force shrinks and class declines in influence, working-class concentration in the North increases in party-political significance.

'Class' may still be with us but its edges have indubitably been blunted. One of the problems in examining class is its crude operational definition in terms of manual and non-manual occupations. This is not a good guide even to levels of income and status, even less to levels of power and wealth. But the power dimension is fundamental – power over one's own life, a measure of independence, as well as power over others. There is no doubt that class has been considerably eroded in these terms: the bulk of the English population has enjoyed an enormous access of power since 1909 and especially since 1945. Statutory entitlement to pensions and various welfare benefits, savings, redundancy payments, home ownership and the like have transformed the conditions of the industrial working class even while the heavy industries on which they depended have gone into decline. Property, though grossly unequal, was never so well spread in the North since the fifteenth century. It is this spread of power, which affords some protection against the caprice of the rich and insolent, that has reduced the importance of class and the sharpness of class conflict. The north of England was important as a major site of class conflict from 1910 to 1945 and even down to 1966; in the 1970s and 1980s it has been an important base for a renewed attack on the centre.

The essential conflict of the later twentieth century is not against a dominant 'class' but against a dominant and over-extended centre. During the past twenty years trade unions have not been fighting capitalists who were reducing wages – capitalists have been only too eager to increase them – they have been fighting the prices and incomes board and centrally imposed 'pay norms'. Since 1979 the government has been fighting an over-extended centre, too. The unions attack the centre out of pragmatic concern for better conditions for workers; the government curtails it on principle. But in any event we have an unlikely alliance of trade unions and Conservative governments to curtail the power of the centre.

The attack on the power of the centre arrived on cue, 150 years after the latest phase of centralization began with the Factory Act, the Poor Law Amendment Act, and the enthronement of the principle of inspectability, in the early 1830s. The management of the industrial revolution and its social consequences led to steadily increasing central power and highly effective machinery of government when the Trevelyan-Northcote report on the civil service was implemented in the 1870s. The welfare legislation of the Liberal government after 1906 and especially of the Labour government after 1945 resulted in an enormously powerful centre. The nationalization of basic industries, albeit in the form of quasi-governmental institutions (the public corporations), saw central power reach a crescendo. Even by 1950 a quarter of all people in work were employed by government or quasi-governmental agencies. Margaret Thatcher, prime minister in 1979, was a latter-day Caracalla taking draconian steps against a century and a half of the build up of formidable central power.

The principal measure for reducing the power of the centre in the 1980s was the privatization of nationalized industries. Privatization is the precise equivalent of 'bastard feudalism' in the fourtheenth and fifteenth centuries – the 'age of the perimeter' (see chapter 7). It has the same long-term implications for the greater decentralization of power.

Trade union action in the past twenty years has often been taken using the rhetoric of class war: this was especially the case in the miners' strike of 1984–5. This is entirely bogus. When the crescendo of union action came in the 'winter of discontent' in 1979 it was not against capitalists but against the government's 5 per cent pay norm. The miners' strikes of 1972, 1974 and 1984–5 were attacks not on a 'class' but on a government.

The post-war mining industry had been contracting, and by 1970 miners' pay was relatively low and mining areas were depressed areas. The strike of 1972 was a traditional strike for better pay. In the course of it miners discovered, somewhat to their surprise, that they now had great power. The strikes of 1974 and especially of 1984–5 were not about pay but about power; they did not arise out of industrial and regional weakness, but out of reborn industrial and regional strength.

In 1947 when the coal industry was nationalized, it produced 150 million tonnes of coal for British industry, of which 18 per cent (27 million tonnes) went for generating electricity. By 1970–1 the National Coal Board produced 112 million tonnes of coal for British industry of which 61 per cent (74.7 million tonnes) went to the Central Electricity Generating Board (CEGB).[53] The huge increase in the industrial use of electricity and the massive dependence of industry on centrally generated electricity had enormously and unwittingly increased the strategic and political power of its monopolistic supplier of coal. This power had a strong regional dimension. It was clearly signalled when the miners' president, Arthur Scargill, moved the union's headquarters from London to Sheffield, but it was highly visible in the great concentration of coal-fired power stations beyond the Trent: 'A vast programme of building had

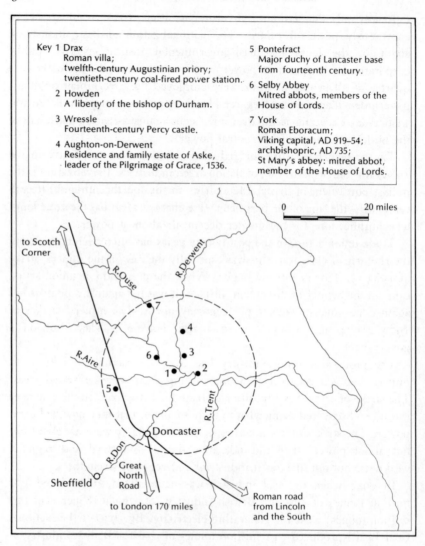

Key 1 Drax
   Roman villa;
   twelfth-century Augustinian priory;
   twentieth-century coal-fired power station.

   2 Howden
   A 'liberty' of the bishop of Durham.

   3 Wressle
   Fourteenth-century Percy castle.

   4 Aughton-on-Derwent
   Residence and family estate of Aske,
   leader of the Pilgrimage of Grace, 1536.

   5 Pontefract
   Major duchy of Lancaster base
   from fourteenth century.

   6 Selby Abbey
   Mitred abbots, members of the
   House of Lords.

   7 York
   Roman Eboracum;
   Viking capital, AD 919–54;
   archbishopric, AD 735;
   St Mary's abbey: mitred abbot,
   member of the House of Lords.

0   20 miles

to Scotch
Corner

R. Ouse

R. Derwent

R. Aire

R. Trent

R. Don

Doncaster

Great
North
Road

Sheffield

to London 170 miles

Roman road
from Lincoln
and the South

MAP 12.1   Drax: 2,000 years of power and wealth at the confluence of the rivers
Ouse, Aire, Derwent and Don
Source: author

produced a line of huge power stations tethered like anchored battleships
along the eastern flank of the Yorkshire coal-field, with an arc along the
river Trent farther south in Nottingham. Coal came to account for 80 per
cent of the CEGB's normal output.'[54] It was from this powerful regional
base that the North made its latest attempt to dominate the centre.

It was an attempt that should never in any case have been made: in essence a demand that the entire English people should maintain at enormous cost worked-out coal-mines that could no longer, by a very large margin, pay their way. This was 'regional sectionalism' of a more outrageous order even than that of Christopher Wyvill's Yorkshire Association in 1779–80, and the West Riding's opposition to paying 'ship-money' towards maintaining the nation's coastal defences (not least those of Hull and the Humber) in the sixteenth century. But it did not fail out of northern weakness: unity among all miners beyond Trent, by no means unattainable, would almost certainly have won the day. The strike failed from the egregious folly, the stupendous conceit, and at bottom the profound contempt for the rank-and-file on the part of those who led it.

Notes

CHAPTER I   TWO NORTHERN MILLENNIUMS

1 G. W. S. Barrow, 'Northern English society in the twelfth and thirteenth centuries', *Northern History*, 4 (1969), pp. 1–28.
2 P. Johnson, *The Offshore Islanders* (Weidenfeld and Nicolson), (1972), p. 430.
3 T. B. Macaulay, *The History of England from the Accession of James II* (Macmillan, 1913), pp. 374–6.
4 See F. Haverfield, *The Romanization of Roman Britain* (Clarendon Press, 1912).
5 C. Fox, *The Personality of Britain: Its Influence on Inhabitant and Invader in Prehistoric and Historic Times* (University of Wales Press, 1932), p. 35.
6 E.g. L. Stone, *The Crisis of the Aristocracy* (Clarendon Press, 1965), p. 251, explaining the rising of the northern earls in 1569.
7 Johnson, *Offshore Islanders*, p. 430.
8 See K. Berrill, 'International trade and the rate of economic growth', *Economic History Review*, 12 (1960), pp. 351–9.
9 Johnson, *Offshore Islanders*, p. 430.
10 J. Le Patourel, 'Is northern history a subject?', *Northern History*, 12 (1976), pp. 1–15.
11 See S. T. Gibson, 'The escheatries 1327–41', *English Historical Review*, 36 (1921), pp. 218–25.
12 Le Patourel, *Northern History*, 1976, pp. 1–15, esp. p. 11.
13 See G. J. Turner, 'The justices of the forest south of Trent', *English Historical Review*, 18 (1903), pp. 112–16.
14 See A. D. H. Leadman, 'The battle of Myton', *Yorkshire Archaeological and Topographical Journal*, 8 (1884), pp. 115–22.
15 A. J. P. Taylor, 'Manchester', *Encounter*, 8 (1957), pp. 3–13.
16 For these confident predictions see W. A. Abram, 'Social condition and

political prospects of the Lancashire workmen', *Fortnightly Review*, 10 (1868), pp. 426–41.

17 For a recent revaluation of Cheshire's wealth see P. H. W. Booth, *The Financial Administration of the Lordship and County of Chester 1272–1377* (Chetham Society, 1981).

18 See G. Barraclough, *The Earldom and County Palatine of Chester* (Basil Blackwell, 1953).

19 See H. R. Loyn, *The Vikings in Britain* (Batsford, 1977), pp. 65, 113.

20 A. Conan Doyle, 'The geographical distribution of British intellect', *Nineteenth Century*, 24 (1888), pp. 184–95, and Havelock Ellis, *A Study of British Genius* (Hurst and Blackett, 1904).

21 R. Schofield, 'The geographical distribution of wealth in England 1334–1649', *Economic History Review*, 18 (1965), pp. 483–510.

22 See G. T. Lapsley, 'The problem of the north', in *Crown, Community and Parliament in the Later Middle Ages*, ed. G. T. Lapsley (Basil Blackwell, 1951), pp. 375–405.

23 See F. M. Stenton, 'Norman London', in *Preparatory to Anglo-Saxon England*, ed. D. M. Stenton (Clarendon Press, 1970), pp. 23–47.

24 See P. J. Cain and A. G. Hopkins, 'Gentlemanly capitalism and British expansion overseas. I. The old colonial system 1688–1850', *Economic History Review*, 39 (1986), pp. 501–25.

25 See J. Le Patourel, 'The Plantagenet dominions', *History*, 50 (1965), pp. 289–308.

26 Johnson, *Offshore Islanders*, p. 100.

27 M. McKisack, *The Parliamentary Representation of the English Boroughs During the Middle Ages* (Oxford University Press, 1932), p. 16.

28 D. Read, *The English Provinces c.1760–1960* (Arnold, 1964).

29 W. D. Rubinstein, *Men of Property* (Croom Helm, 1981), pp. 102–5.

30 See A. L. Rowse, *Tudor Cornwall* (Macmillan, 1969), p. 136.

31 See D. L. Keir, 'The case of ship-money', *Law Quarterly Review*, 52 (1936), pp. 546–74.

32 See E. Searle and R. Burghart, 'The defense of England and the peasants' revolt', *Viator*, 3 (1972), pp. 365–88.

33 See J. A. F. Thompson, *The Transformation of Medieval England 1370–1529* (Longman, 1983), pp. 26, 384–5.

34 See R. Hilton, *Bond Men and Free* (Temple Smith, 1973), p. 162, and A. Harding, 'The revolt against the justices', in *The English Rising of 1381*, ed. R. H. Hilton and T. H. Aston (Cambridge University Press, 1984), pp. 165–93.

35 See R. L. Storey, *The End of the House of Lancaster* (Barrie & Rockliff, 1966), p. 67.

36 See W. E. Wightman, *The Lacy Family 1066–1194* (Clarendon Press, 1966), pp. 19–29.

37 See S. Wood, *English Monasteries and their Patrons in the Thirteenth Century* (Oxford University Press, 1955), pp. 122–9.

38 Cf. B. D. Hill, *English Cistercian Monasteries and their Patrons in the Twelfth Century* (University of Illinois Press, 1968), pp. 36, 41.

39 See R. H. C. Davis, *King Stephen 1135–1154* (Longmans, 1967), pp. 111–13, 129.

40 Cf. W. A. Morris, 'The office of sheriff in the early Norman period', *English Historical Review*, 33 (1918), pp. 147–75.

41 P. Borsay, *The English Urban Renaissance. Culture and Society in the Provincial Town 1660–1770* (Clarendon Press, 1989), pp. 117–20, 329–31.

42 I. R. Christie, 'The Yorkshire association 1780–4: a study in political organization', *Historical Journal*, 3 (1960), pp. 144–61.

43 For a close examination of this first phase of centralization see W. C. Lubenow, *The Politics of Government Growth. Early Victorian Attitudes towards State Intervention 1833–1848* (David and Charles, 1971).

44 D. Roberts, *Victorian Origins of the British Welfare State* (Yale University Press, 1960), pp. 169–70, 327–33.

45 Cf. ibid., p. 316.

46 See O. MacDonagh, 'The nineteenth-century revolution in government; a re-appraisal', *Historical Journal*, 1 (1958), pp. 52–67, and H. Parriss, 'The nineteenth-century revolution in government: a re-appraisal re-appraised', *Historical Journal*, 3 (1960), pp. 17–37.

47 M. Abramovitz and V. F. Eliasberg, *The Growth of Public Employment in Great Britain* (Princeton University Press, 1957), p. 25, table 1.

CHAPTER 2   UNDER ROMAN RULE AD 43–410

1 Cf. D. J. Breeze, *The Northern Frontiers of Roman Britain* (Batsford, 1982), pp. 164–5.

2 W. S. Hanson, *Agricola and the Conquest of the North* (Batsford, 1987), p. 107.

3 Breeze, *Northern Frontiers*, p. 33.

4 B. Dobson, 'Agricola's life and career', in *Agricola's Campaigns in Scotland*, ed. J. Kenworthy (Edinburgh University Press, 1981), pp. 1–13, esp. p. 8.

5 Breeze, *Northern Frontiers*, p. 161.

6 See J. N. Dore and J. P. Gillam, *The Roman Fort at South Shields* (Society of Antiquaries of Newcastle-upon-Tyne, 1979), p. 64.

7 Breeze, *Northern Frontiers*, p. 166.

8 D. J. Breeze and B. Dobson, *Hadrian's Wall* (Penguin Books, 1987), p. 127.

9 See S.Johnson, *Later Roman Britain* (Routledge and Kegan Paul, 1980), pp. 54–8.

10 See chapter 4, and G. Jobey, 'Note on some population problems in the area between the two Roman walls', *Archaeologia Aeliana*, 2 (1974), pp. 17–26, and 'Homesteads and settlements of the frontier area' in *Rural Settlement in Roman Britain*, ed. C. Thomas (Council for British Archaeology, 1966), pp. 1–14.

11 Breeze, *Northern Frontiers*, p. 83.

12 R. G. Collingwood and J. N. L. Myres, *Roman Britain and the English Settlements* (Clarendon Press, 1937), pp. 156–8.

13 P. Salway, *The Frontier People of Roman Britain* (Cambridge University Press, 1965), p. 2, and *Roman Britain* (Clarendon Press, 1981), p. 222.

14 J. P. Gillam and J. C. Mann, 'The northern British frontier from Antonius Pius to Caracalla', *Archaelogia Aeliana*, 48 (1970), pp. 1–44, esp. p. 42.

15 Collingwood and Myres, *Roman Britain*, p. 277.

16 Salway, *Roman Britain*, p. 313.

17 Cf. D. E. Eichholz, 'Constantius Chlorus' invasion of Britain', *Journal of Roman Studies*, 43 (1953), pp. 41–6.

18 Cf. Salway, *Frontier People*, p. 5.

19 Ibid., p. 66.

20 Johnson, *Later Roman Britain*, p. 102, and Salway, *Frontier People*, p. 200.

21 See Johnson, *Later Roman Britain*, pp. 93–4.

22 A revised version of the paper is the basis of F. Haverfield, *The Romanization of Roman Britain* (Clarendon Press, 1912).

23 Ibid., p. 20.

24 A. L. F. Rivet, 'Social and economic aspects', in *The Roman Villa in Britain*, ed. A. L. F. Rivet (Routiedge and Kegan Paul, 1969), pp. 173–216, esp. p. 194.

25 Salway, *Frontier People*, p. 196.

26 Rivet, 'Social and economic aspects', p. 102.

27 J. Walcher, *The Towns of Roman Britain* (Batsford, 1975), p. 4.

28 See Collingwood and Myres, *Roman Britain*, p. 198, and Walcher, *Towns of Roman Britain*, p. 59.

29 Salway, *Frontier People*, p. 67.

30 See M. Todd, *Roman Britain* (Harvester Press, 1981), p. 200.

31 Cf. M. P. Charlesworth, *The Lost Province* (University Press Cardiff, 1949), p. 5.

32 Salway, *Frontier People*, p. 7, and Salway, *Roman Britain*, p. 5.

33 The enumeration of monasteries and vlllas respectively are in *Oxford Studies in Social and Legal History*, ed. P. Vinogradoff (Clarendon Press, 1909), pp. 1–303 and *The Roman Villa in Britain*, ed. Rivet, pp. 173–216.

34 See H. Ramm, *The Parisi* (Duckworth, 1978), p. 106.

35 D. J. Smith, 'Regional aspects of the winged corridor villa in Britain' in

Studies in the Romano-British Villa, ed. M. Todd (Leicester University Press, 1978), pp. 117–47.

36 See Ramm, *Parisi*.

37 S. Piggott, 'Native economies and the Roman occupation of north Britain', in *Roman and Native in North Britain*, ed. I. A. Richmond (Nelson, 1958), pp. 1–27, esp. p. 22.

38 Rivet, 'Social and economic aspects', pp. 196–7.

39 P. Salway, 'The Roman fenland', in *Rural Settlement in Roman Britain*, ed. C. Thomas (Council for British Archaeology, 1966), pp. 26–7.

40 See W. H. Manning, 'Economic influences on land use in the military areas of the highland zone during the Roman period', in *The Effects of Man on the Landscape: the Highland Zone*, ed. J. G. Evans, S. Limbrey and H. Cleere (Council for British Archaeology, 1975), pp. 112–16.

41 See J. K. St Joseph, 'Air reconnaissance of southern Britain', *Journal of Roman Studies*, 43 (1953), pp. 81–97, and C. E. Stevens, 'The social and economic aspects of rural settlement', in *Rural Settlement in Roman Britain*, ed. Thomas, pp. 108–28.

42 P. Brewis, 'Roman Rudchester', *Archaeologia Aeliana*, 1 (1925), pp. 93–120.

43 See M. P. Charlesworth, *Trade Routes and Commerce of the Roman Empire* (Cambridge University Press, 1926), pp. 214–15, Charlesworth, *Lost Province*, p. 41, and Salway, *Roman Britain*, p. 360.

44 See L. C. West, *Roman Britain: The Objects of Trade* (Basil Blackwell, 1931), p. 15, Johnson, *Later Roman Britain*, p. 21, and I. A. Richmond, *Roman Britain* (Penguin Books, 1963), p. 163.

45 Anonymous, 'The origins of London', *Cornhill Magazine*, 43 (1881), pp. 169–82.

46 H. J. Hewitt, *The Organization of War under Edward III* (Manchester University Press, 1966), p. 55.

47 See Salway, *Frontier People*, p. 3.

48 R. B. Hartley, 'Roman York and the northern military command in the third century AD', in *Soldier and Civilian in Roman Yorkshire*, ed. K. M. Butler (Leicester University Press, 1971), pp. 55–69.

49 See I. Richmond, *Roman Archaeology and Art* (Faber, 1969), pp. 621–79.

50 J. C. Mann, 'The administration of Roman Britain', *Antiquity*, 35 (1961), pp. 316–20.

51 Salway, *Roman Britain*, p. 523.

52 R. W. Davies, '*Singulares* and Roman Britain', *Britannia*, 7 (1976), pp. 134–51.

53 Breeze and Dobson, *Hadrian's Wall*, pp. 111–12.

54 K. A. Steer, 'Roman and native in north Britain: the Severon reorganization', in *Roman and Native in North Britain*, ed. I. A. Richmond, (Nelson, 1958), pp. 91–111.

55 E.g. I. A. Richmond, 'Roman and native in the fourth century AD and after', in ibid., pp. 112–30.

56 Salway, *Roman Britain*, pp. 385–6.

57 M. Rostovtzeff, *The Social and Economic History of the Roman Empire* (Clarendon Press, 1957), p. 417.

58 J. Wacher, *Roman Britain* (Dent, 1978), p. 102, and I. Richmond, *Roman Archaeology and Art* (Faber, 1969), pp. 62–79.

59 Todd, *Roman Britain*, p. 200.

60 Ibid., pp. 196–7.

61 Collingwood and Myres, *Roman Britain*, p. 203.

62 Ibid., p. 204.

63 Wacher, *Roman Britain*, p. 102, and Todd, *Roman Britain*, p. 188.

64 See Salway, *Frontier People*, pp. 196–7.

65 Ibid., p. 3.

CHAPTER 3   THE LOST KINGDOM

1 J. A. Tuck, 'The emergence of a northern nobility 1250–1400', *Northern History*, 12 (1986), pp. 1–17.

2 G. W. S. Barrow, *The Anglo-Saxon Era in Scottish History* (Clarendon Press, 1980), p. 7.

3 Bede, *A History of the English Church and People*, tr. Leo Sherley-Price (Penguin Books, 1968), p. 83.

4 J. le Patourel, 'Is northern history a subject?', *Northern History*, 12 (1976), pp. 1–15.

5 See W. E. Kapelle, *The Norman Conquest of the North* (Croom Helm, 1979), p. 121.

6 See C. Fox, *The Personality of Britain: Its Influence on Inhabitant and Invader in Prehistoric and Early Historic Times* (University of Wales, 1932), pp. 35 and 62.

7 See A. P. Smyth, *Scandinavian York and Dublin* (Templekieran Press, 1974), p. 15.

8 P. Hunter Blair, *An Introduction to Anglo-Saxon England* (Cambridge University Press, 1956), p. 162.

9 S. J. Crawford, *Anglo-Saxon Influence on Western Christendom 600–800* (Oxford University Press, 1933), p. 104.

10 W. Levison, *England and the Continent in the Eighth Century* (Clarendon Press, 1946), p. 51.

11 P. Hunter Blair, *The World of Bede* (Secker & Warburg, 1970), pp. 6–7.

12 Bede, *A History of the English Church and People*, p. 332.

13 D. C. Douglas (ed.), *English Historical Documents*, (12 vols, Eyre & Spottiswoode, 1955), vol. 1, p. 778.

14 See W. Page, 'Some remarks on the Northumbrian palatinates and regalities', *Archaeologia*, 51 (1888), pp. 143–55.

15 See D. M. Wilson, 'Scandinavian settlement in the north and west of the British Isles', *Transactions of the Royal Historical Society*, 26 (1976), pp. 95–113.

16 F. M. Stenton, 'The Danes in England', in *Preparatory to Anglo-Saxon England*, ed. D. M. Stenton (Clarendon Press, 1970), pp. 156–65.

17 D. M. Stenton, *English Society in the Early Middle Ages* (Penguin Books, 1951), pp. 130–1.

18 F. M. Stenton, *Anglo-Saxon England* (Clarendon Press, 1971), p. 506.

19 Cf. H. R. Loyn, *The Vikings in Britain* (Batsford, 1977), pp. 132–3: 'It has long been an axiom of medieval studies that where one finds a wealthy church there is also a dependent peasantry.'

20 See C. Mahany and D. Roffe, 'Stamford: the development of an Anglo-Scandinavian borough', in *Anglo-Norman Studies*, vol. V, ed. R. A. Brown (10 vols, Boydell Press, 1982), pp. 197–219.

21 Smyth, *Scandinavian York and Dublin*, p. 86.

22 Stenton, 'The Danes in England', pp. 162–4.

23 A. L. Binns, *The Viking Century in East Yorkshire* (East Yorkshire Local History Society, 1963), p. 11.

24 Kapelle, *The Norman Conquest of the North*, p. 13.

25 Page, *Archaeologia* (1888), pp. 143–55.

26 B. Wilkinson, 'Northumbrian separatism in 1065 and 1066', *Bulletin of the John Rylands Library*, 23 (1938), 504–26.

27 Page, *Archaeologia* (1888), p. 148. See also G. P. Lapsley, *The County Palatine of Durham* (Longmans, Green & Co., 1900), p. 27.

28 Stenton, 'The Danes in England', p. 162.

29 Ibid., p. 162, and Loyn, *The Vikings in Britain*, p. 89.

30 E. A. Freeman, *The History of the Norman Conquest* (Clarendon Press, 1869), vol. 3, pp. 58–9.

31 F. W. Brooks, *Domesday Book in the East Riding* (East Yorkshire Local History Society, 1986), p. 55.

32 Wilkinson, 'Northumbrian separatism in 1065 and 1066', p. 504.

33 For a discussion of this revolutionary step see Kapelle, *The Norman Conquest of the North*, p. 87.

34 Freeman, *The History of the Norman Conquest*, pp. 421–2.

35 See G. W. S. Barrow, 'The beginnings of feudalism in Scotland', *Bulletin of the Institute of Historical Research*, 29 (1956), pp. 1–27.

36 See G. W. S. Barrow, *The Anglo-Norman Era in Scottish History* (Clarendon Press, 1980), pp. 99, 107, 116.

37 See R. L. G. Ritchie, *The Normans in Scotland* (Edinburgh University Press, 1954), pp. 230–1.

38 See D. Nicholl, *Thurstan: Archbishop of York 1114–1140* (Stonegate Press, 1964).

39 G. T. Lapsley, The County Palatine of Durham p. 302.

40 See J. H. Ramsay, *The Foundations of England* (Oxford University Press, 1898), vol. 2, pp. 367–71 for comment on the very unwarlike and unresistant North in the face of Scottish incursions.

41 Ritchie, *The Normans in Scotland*, p. 319.

CHAPTER 4   A FRONTIER PROVINCE

1 F. W. Maitland, 'Northumbrian tenures', *English Historical Review*, 5 (1890), pp. 625–32.

2 F. M. Powicke, 'Distraint of knighthood and military obligation under Henry III', *Speculum*, 25 (1950), pp. 457–70 and N. Denholm-Young, *The Country Gentry in the Fourteenth Century* (Clarendon Press, 1969), p. 4 7.

3 C. M. Fraser, *A History of Antony Bek* (Clarendon Press, 1957), p. 186.

4 H. C. Hunter Blair, 'Baronys and knights of Northumberland 1166–1260', *Archaeologia Aeliana*, 30 (1952), pp. 1–54.

5 J. H. Ramsay, *The Foundations of England* (2 vols, Oxford University Press, 1898), vol. 2, p. 367.

6 W. Stubbs, *The Constitutional History of England* (3 vols, Clarendon Press, 1880), vol. 2, p. 305.

7 G. H. Tupling, *South Lancashire in the Reign of Edward II* (Chetham Society, 1949), pp. xxviii–xxix.

8 T. E. Morris, 'Mounted infantry in medieval warfare', *Transactions of the Royal Historical Society*, 8 (1914), pp. 77–102.

9 S. Armitage-Smith, *John of Gaunt* (Constable, 1904), p. 295.

10 F. W. Brook, *The Council of the North* (Historical Association, 1966), p. 7.

11 H. M. Chew, 'Scutage', *History*, 14 (1930), pp. 236–9.

12 H. M. Chew, *Ecclesiastical Tenants-in-Chief and Knight Service* (Oxford University Press, 1932), p. 4.

13 N. B. Lewis, 'The last medieval summons of the English feudal levy 13 June 1385', *English Historical Review*, 73 (1958), pp. 1–26.

14 J. H. Round, 'Introduction', *The Great Roll of the Pipe 1185–1186* (1914), p. xviii.

15 A. D. H. Leadman, 'The battle of Myton', *Yorkshire Archaeological and Topographical Journal*, 8 (1884), pp. 115–22.

16 N. B. Lewis, 'The organization of indentured retinues in fourteenth-century England', *Transactions of the Royal Historical Society*, 27 (1945), pp. 29–39.

17 J. E. Morris, *The Welsh Wars of Edward I* (Clarendon Press, 1901), p. 45.

18 R. Nicholson, *Edward III and the Scots* (Oxford University Press, 1965), pp. 248–50.

19 Ibid., p. 250.

20 Lewis, 'The last medieval summons of the English feudal levy 13 June 1385', pp. 1–26.

21 M. Prestwich, *War, Politics and Finance under Edward I* (Faber, 1972), p. 91.

22 P. W. Smith, *A Study of the Lists of Military and Parliamentary Summons in the Reign of Edward I* (Ann Arbor, 1967), p. 436.

23 G. T. Lapsley, *The County Palatine of Durham* (Longmans, Green & Co., 1900), p. 27.

24 R. R. Davies, *Conquest, Co-existence and Change: Wales 1066–1415* (Clarendon Press, 1987), pp. 64, 93, 284.

25 R. R. Davies, *Lordship and Society in the March of Wales 1282–1400* Clarendon Press, 1978), p. 228.

26 R. L. Storey, *Thomas Langley and the Bishopric of Durham 1406–1437* (Society for Promoting Christian Knowledge, 1961), p. 52.

27 T. B. Pugh and C. D. Ross, 'The English baronage and the income tax of 1436', *Bulletin of the Institute of Historical Research*, 26 (1953), pp. 1–28.

28 C. M. Fraser, 'Prerogative and the bishop of Durham 1267–1376', *English Historical Review*, 74 (1959), pp. 467–76.

29 Lapsley, *County Palatine*, p. 27.

30 M. Chibnall, *Anglo-Norman England 1066–1166* (Basil Blackwell, 1986), p. 13.

31 H. M. Cam, *Liberties and Communities in Medieval England* (Cambridge University Press, 1944), p. 207, and H. M. Jewell, *English Local Administration in the Middle Ages* (David & Charles, 1972), p. 66.

32 Storey, *Thomas Langley*, pp. 226–44.

33 See W. J. Corbett, 'The development of the duchy of Normandy and the Norman conquest of England', *Cambridge Medieval History*, 5 (1926), pp. 481–520, and J. F. A. Mason, 'The honour of Richmond', *English Historical Review*, 78 (1963), pp. 703–4.

34 W. E. Rhodes, 'Edmund, earl of Lancaster', *English Historical Review*, 10 (1895), pp. 21–40.

35 K. Fowler, *The King's Lieutenant: Henry Grosmont First Duke of Lancaster* (Elek, 1969), p. 226.

36 K. B. McFarlane, 'History of the duchy of Lancaster', *English Historical Review*, 70 (1955), pp. 107–11.

37 R. Somerville, *History of the Duchy of Lancaster* (Chancellor and Council of the Duchy of Lancaster, 1953), p. 161.

38 C. T. Clay, *Early English Charters: The Honour of Richmond* (12 vols, Yorkshire Archaeological Society, 1935), vol. 4, part 2, p. vii.

39 W. E. Rhodes, 'Edmund, earl of Lancaster', *English Historical Review*, 10 (1895), pp. 21–40.

40 Fowler, *The King's Lieutenant*, p. 226.

41 W. Farrer, 'Feudal baronage', in *Victoria County History: County of*

Lancaster ed. W. Farrer (8 vols, Archibald Constable & Co., 1908), vol. 2, pp. 291–375.

42 For a statement of this view with reference to the border counties see G. W. S. Barrow, 'Northern English society in the twelfth and thirteenth centuries', *Northern History*, 4 (1969), pp. 1–28. For the total of 'barons' (and any definition is very arbitrary) see S. Painter, *Studies in the History of the English Feudal Baronage* (John Hopkins Press, 1943), p. 16.

43 Corbett, 'The development of the duchy of Normandy', pp. 481–520.

44 R. H. Hilton, *A Medieval Society* (Weidenfeld and Nicolson, 1966), p. 58.

45 Lapsley, *County Palatine*, pp. 292–3.

46 Corbett, 'The development of the duchy of Normandy', p. 513.

47 The average baronial income may have been about £200 a year at the beginning of the thirteenth century and £600 a year at the end: see S. Painter, *Studies in the History of the English Feudal Baronage* (Johns Hopkins University Press, 1943), p. 133.

48 See F. R. H. Boulay, *The Lordship of Canterbury* (Nelson, 1966), pp. 93, 99.

49 R. F. Treharne, 'The knights in the period of reform and rebellion 1258–67: a critical phase in the rise of a new class', *Bulletin of the Institute of Historical Research*, 21 (1946–8), pp. 1–12, D. A. Carpenter, 'Was there a crisis of the knightly class in the thirteenth century?' *English Historical Review*, 95 (1980), pp. 721–52; and S. Harvey, 'The knight and the knights fee in England', *Past & Present*, 49 (1970), pp. 3–43.

50 M. M. Postan, 'Medieval agrarian society in its prime: England', *Cambridge Economic History of Europe*, 7 vols, (Cambridge University Press, 1966) vol. 1, pp. 548–632.

51 E. King, 'Large and small landowners in thirteenth-century England', *Past & Present*, 47 (1970), pp. 26–50.

52 G. H. Tupling, *South Lancashire in the Reign of Edward II* (Chetham Society, 1949).

53 N. Denholm-Young, *Collected Papers on Medieval Subjects* (Basil Blackwell, 1946), p. 61.

54 S. K. Mitchell, *Studies in Taxation under John and Henry III* (Yale University Press, 1914), p. 248.

55 Morris, *Welsh Wars*, p. 45.

56 Denholm-Young, *Collected Papers*, pp. 61–2.

57 Ibid., p. 62.

58 Morris, *Welsh Wars*, p. 36. (Morris did not include Richmond's sixty-four knights fees.)

59 H. C. Hunter Blair, 'Knights of Northumberland 1278 and 1324', *Archaeologia Aeliana*, 27 (1949), pp. 122–75.

60 N. Denholm-Young, *The Country Gentry of the Fourteenth Century* (Clarendon Press, 1969), pp. 16–18.

61 H. C. Hunter Blair, 'Baronys and knights in Northumberland 1166–1260', pp. 1–54.

62 J. F. Willard, 'Taxes upon movables in the reign of Edward II', *English Historical Review*, 29 (1914), pp. 317–22, and 'Taxes upon movables in the reign of Edward III', *English Historical Review*, 30 (1915), pp. 69–74.

63 F. W. Maitland, 'Northumbrian tenures', *English Historical Review*, 5 (1890), pp. 625–32.

64 E. A. Kosminsky, *Studies in the Agrarian History of England in the Thirteenth Century* (Basil Blackwell, 1956), pp. 194–5, table 8.

65 Calculated frorh J. C. Russell, *British Medieval Population* (University of New Mexico Press, 1948), p. 132, table 6.4.

66 G. W. S. Barrow, 'Scottish rulers and the religious orders 1070–1153', *Transactions of the Royal Historical Society*, (5th series) 3 (1952), pp. 77–100.

67 G. W. S. Barrow, *The Kingdom of the Scots* (Edward Arnold, 1973), p. 295.

68 G. W. S. Barrow, 'The beginnings of feudalism in Scotland', *Bulletin of the Institute of Historical Research*, 29 (1956), pp. 1–27.

69 I. B. Cowan and D. E. Easson, *Medieval Religious Houses – Scotland* (Longman, 1976), pp. 55–107.

70 D. Knowles and R. N. Hadcock, *Medieval Religious Houses: England and Wales* (Longmans, Green & Co., 1953), pp. 58–181.

71 Cowan and Easson, *Medieval Religious Houses – Scotland*, pp. 116–25.

72 P. Dixon, 'Towerhouses, pelehouses and border society', *Archaeological Journal*, 136 (1979), pp. 240–52.

73 C. J. Tabraham, *Smailholm Tower* (Her Majesty's Stationery Office, 1985), p. 4.

CHAPTER 5   FROM POWER TO REBELLION

1 See A. J. Pollard, 'The tyranny of Richard III', *Journal of Medieval Studies*, 3 (1977) pp. 147–65.

2 M. Chibnall, *Anglo-Norman England 1066–1166* (Basil Blackwell, 1986), pp. 134–6.

3 J. C. Russell, *British Medieval Population* (University of New Mexico Press, 1948) pp. 53–4, 132.

4 See D. Nicholl, *Thurstan Archbishop of York* (Stonegate Press, 1964), pp. 113, 115.

5 See A. R. Bridbury, *Economic Growth, England in the Later Middle Ages* (Allen & Unwin, 1962), pp. 112–13: cf. J. W. F. Hill, *Medieval Lincoln* (Cambridge University Press, 1965), pp. 272–3, and J. N. Bartlett, 'The expansion and decline of York in the later middle ages'. *Economic History Review*, 12 (1959–60), pp. 17–33.

6 These calculations are based on data in R. S. Schofield, 'The geographical distribution of wealth in England 1334–1649', *Economic History Review*, 18 (1965), pp. 483–510.

7 H. C. Darby, *Domesday England* (Cambridge University Press, 1977), p. 359. Of course these estimates are approximate: 'We must be under no illusion about the precarious nature of these county totals' (p. 277).

8 Calculated from J. F. Willard, 'Taxes upon movables in the reign of Edward III', *English Historical Review*, 30 (1915), pp. 68–75.

9 J. Beddoe and J. Hambley, 'The ethnology of West Yorkshire', *Yorkshire Archaeological and Topographical Journal*, 19 (1907), pp. 31–60.

10 F. W. Brooks, *Domesday Book and the East Riding* (East Yorkshire Local History Society, 1986), p. 53.

11 Willard, 'Taxes upon movables in the reign of Edward III', pp. 68–75.

12 For a perhaps somewhat overstated view of England's wealth at this time see P. H. Sawyer, 'The wealth of England in the eleventh century', *Transactions of the Royal Historical Society*, 15 (1965), pp. 145–64.

13 H. J. Hewitt, *Medieval Cheshire* (Chetham Society, 1929), p. 124.

14 See R. Allen Brown 'Royal castle-building in England 1154–1216', *English Historical Review*, 70 (1955), pp. 353–98.

15 Chibnall, *Anglo-Norman England 1066–1166*, p. 134.

16 W. E. Kapelle, *The Norman Conquest of the North* (Croom Helm, 1979), pp. 219, 225, 234.

17 M. Beresford, *New Towns in the Middle Ages* (Lutterworth Press, 1967), p. 469.

18 C. Stephenson, *Borough and Town* (Mediaeval Academy of America, 1933). The king modelled Hartlepool and Alnwick on the same legal basis as Newcastle-upon-Tyne; the bishop of Durham did likewise at Gateshead, Wearmouth and Norham.

19 Ibid.

20 See Allen Brown, *English Historical Review* (1955), pp. 353–98.

21 See M. McKisack, *The Parliamentary Representation of the English Boroughs during the Middle Ages* (Oxford Univerity Press, 1932).

22 At the Shrewsbury parliament of September 1283, when Edward I wanted nation-wide support to pronounce sentence on David of Wales, twenty specified towns sent burgesses; eight (40 per cent) were northern: York, Scarborough, Newcastle-upon-Tyne, Carlisle, Lincoln, Grimsby, Chester and Nottingham.

23 See M. Beresford, *The Lost Villages of England* (Alan Sutton, 1983).

24 Ibid., p. 29.

25 See R. B. Dobson, 'The risings in York, Beverley and Scarborough 1380–81', in *The English Risings of 1381*, ed. R. H. Hilton and T. H. Aston (Cambridge University Press, 1984).

26 R. Hilton, *Bond Men Made Free* (Temple Smith, 1973), p. 174.

27 See H. Heaton, *The Yorkshire Woollen and Worsted Industries* (Clarendon, 1920).

28 C. M. Fraser, 'The pattern of trade in the north-east of England 1265–1350', *Northern History*, 4 (1969), pp. 44–66.

29 See T. H. Lloyd, *The English Wool Trade in the Middle Ages* (Cambridge University Press, 1977).

30 H. Zins, *England and the Baltic in the Elizabethan Era* (Manchester University Press, 1972), pp. 8–17.

32 T. H. Lloyd, *Alien Merchants in England in the High Middle Ages* (Harvester Press, 1982), pp. 143–4.

32 See McKisack, *The Parliamentary Representation of the English Boroughs.*

33 J. C. Holt, *The Northerners. A Study in the Reign of King John* (Clarendon, 1961), pp. 31–2.

34 S. Painter, *The Reign of King John* (Johns Hopkins, 1949), pp. 286–8.

35 Also strong East Anglian connections: Holt convincingly argues that he was a northerner. See Holt, *The Northerners*, pp. 62–3.

36 The quotas amounted to 1,187 knights for 24 of the committee: the mayor of London did not have a quota of knights. See C. R. Cheney, 'The twenty-five barons of magna carta', *Bulletin of the John Rylands Library*, 50 (1968), pp. 280–307.

37 The knights fee was not a standard size, probably ranging between 120 and 200 acres and commonly around 180 acres: see S. Harvey, 'The knight and the knights fee in England', in *Peasants, Knights and Heretics*, ed. R. Hilton (Cambridge University Press, 1976). See also A. L. Poole, *From Domesday Book to Magna Carta* (Clarendon, 1955), pp. 14–15. Poole's estimates, while emphasizing wide variability, would make a knights fee significantly larger: the quite common but by no means universal five-hide fee would be 600 acres; the quite common ten-carucate fee in Yorkshire would be 1,000 acres. (One hide in Domesday was 120 acres; one carucate in a late twelfth-century assessment was 100 acres.) Of course this larger multiplier would mean an even bigger gap between those with few fees and those with many. It is relevant to point out that Parliament in 1431 defined an income from land of £20 a year as the equivalent of a knights fee; but an income from an acre at this time is generally reckoned as 6*d*. (see J. P. Cooper, 'The social distribution of land and men in England 1436–1700', *Economic History Review*, 20 (1967), pp. 419–40) which makes a knights fee about 800 acres. This suggests that the larger estimate of the size of a knights fee (perhaps around 500 acres) rather than the smaller estimate (around 180 acres) may be the better one.

38 S. Painter, *Studies in the History of the English Feudal Baronage* (Johns Hopkins, 1943), p. 16.

39 Painter, *The Reign of King John*, p. 19.

40 Holt, *The Northerners*, p. 23.

41 B. English, *The Lords of Holderness 1086–1260* (Oxford University Press, 1979), p. 152.

42 T. F. T. Plucknett, *Legislation of Edward I* (Clarendon, 1949), p. 89: 'A tenant holding lands of many different lords is never at the mercy of any one of them.'

43 English, *Lords of Holderness*, p. 165.

44 Ibid., p. 163.

45 Holt, *The Northerners*, p. 44.

46 This is Holt's view; it is also Painter's. Both point to willing service earlier in the reign and to the large number of rebel barons, including northerners, who in fact followed John to Poitou. See Painter, *The Reign of King John*, p. 214.

47 Holt, *The Northerners*, p. 34.

48 Ibid., p. 20.

49 M. J. Vine, 'Two Yorkshire rebels: Peter de Brus and Richard de Percy', *Yorkshire Archaeological Journal*, 47 (1975), pp. 69–79.

50 See Painter, *Studies in the History of the English Feudal Baronage*, pp. 224–5.

51 Poole, *From Domesday Book to Magna Carta*, p. 478.

52 Painter, *The Reign of King John*, pp. 253–5.

53 W. Stubbs, *Walter of Coventry*, vol. II, p. lxxv.

54 For the significance of the developing tax system for the structure of power in the shires and for some particulars of these tax assessors see S. K. Mitchell, *Taxation in Medieval England* (Yale University Press, 1951), pp. 6–7, 75–83.

55 Holt, *The Northerners*, p. 197.

56 Painter, *The Reign of King John*, p. 298.

57 Holt, *The Northerners*, p. 42.

58 This is Painter's estimate based on a sample of 1,173 writs issued to individual sheriffs: see *The Reign of King John*, p. 298.

CHAPTER 6   WAR ON TWO FRONTS 1296–1453

1 J. A. Tuck, 'Richard II and the border magnates', *Northern History*, 3 (1968), pp. 27–52.

2 J. Le Patourel, 'The Plantagenet dominions', *History*, 50 (1965), pp. 289–308.

3 J. Le Patourel, 'Is northern history a subject?', *Northern History*, 12 (1976), pp. 1–15.

4 G. W. S. Barrow, 'Northern English society in the twelfth and thirteenth centuries', *Northern History*, 4 (1969), pp. 1–28.

5 J. W. Sherborne, 'Indentured retinues and English expeditions to France, 1369–1380'. *English Historical Review*, 79 (1964), pp. 718–46.

6 H. J. Hewitt, *The Organization of War under Edward III* (Manchester University Press, 1966), p. 33.

7 See J. M. W. Bean, 'Henry IV and the Percies', *History*, 44 (1959), pp. 212–27.

8 R. L. Storey, *Thomas Langley and the Bishopric of Durham 1406–1437* (Society for Promoting Christian Knowledge, 1961), p. 4.

9 B. C. Keeney, 'Military service and the development of nationalism in England, 1272–1327', *Speculum*, 22 (1947), pp. 534–9.

10 Cf. H. A. Hicks, 'Edward IV, the duke of Somerset and Lancastrian loyalism in the north', *Northern History*, 20 (1984), pp. 23–37.

11 G. W. S. Barrow, *The Kingdom of the Scots* (Arnold, 1973), p. 161.

12 C. Hunter Blair, 'Baronys and knights in Northumberland 1166–1260', *Archaeologia Aeliana*, 30 (1952), pp. 1–54.

13 W. Stubbs, *The Constitutional History of England* (3 vols, Clarendon Press, 1880), vol. 2, p. 305.

14 M. Prestwich, 'Colonial Scotland: the English in Scotland under Edward I', in *Scotland and England 1286–1815*, ed. Roger A. Mason (John Donald, 1987). pp. 1–16.

15 A. Goodman, 'The Anglo-Scottish marches in the fifteenth century: a frontier society?', in *Scotland and England 1286–1815*, ed. Roger A. Mason (John Donald, 1987), pp. 18–33.

16 B. Wilkinson, 'The Sherburn indenture and the attack on the Despensers, 1321', *English Historical Review*, 63 (1948), pp. 1–28.

17 See J. S. Roskell, *The Knights of the Shire for the County Palatine of Lancaster 1377–1460* (Chetham Society, 1937).

18 G. A. Holmes, *The Estates of the Higher Nobility in the Fourteenth Century* (Cambridge University Press, 1957), p. 40.

19 J. M. W. Bean, 'The Percies and their estates in Scotland', *Archaeologia Aeliana*, 35 (1957), pp. 91–9.

20 J. A. Tuck, 'War and society in the medieval north', *Northern History*, 21 (1985), pp. 33–52.

21 R. Nicholson, *Edward III and the Scots* (Oxford University Press, 1965).

22 H. J. Hewitt, *Medieval Cheshire* (Chetham Society, 1929). p. 159.

23 J. E. Morris, *Bannockburn* (Cambridge University Press, 1914), p. 40.

24 J. E. Morris. 'Mounted infantry in medieval warfare', *Transactions of the Royal Historical Society*, 8 (1914), pp. 77–102.

25 R. L. Storey, 'The north of England', in *Fifteenth-century England 1399–1509*, ed. S. B. Chrimes, C. D. Ross and R. A. Griffiths (Manchester University Press, 1972), pp. 129–44, esp. p. 130.

26 R. Fieldhouse and B. Jennings, *A History of Richmond and Swaledale* (Phillimore, 1978), p. 55, and J. Scammell, 'Robert I and the north of England', *English Historical Review*, 73 (1958), pp. 385–403.

27 Storey, *Thomas Langley*, p. 105.

28 J. M. W. Bean, *The Estates of the Percy Family 1416–1537* (Oxford University Press, 1958), p. 83.

29 K. B. McFarlane, *The Nobility of Later Medieval England* (Clarendon Press, 1973), p. 22.

30 D. M. Broome, 'Exchequer migrations to York in the thirteenth and fourteenth centuries', in *Essays in Medieval History Presented to Thomas Frederick Tout*, ed. A. G. Little and F. M. Powicke (Manchester University Press, 1925), pp. 291–300.

31 T. F. Tout, *Chapters in the Administrative History of Mediaeval England* (6 vols, Manchester University Press, 1928), vol. 3, pp. 56–60.

32 G. L. Harriss, 'The formation of parliament, 1272–1377', in *The English Parliament in the Middle Ages*, ed. R. G. Davies and J. H. Denton (Manchester University Press, 1981), pp. 29–60.

33 Nicholson, *Edward III and the Scots*, p. 42.

34 J. E. Powell and K. Wallis, *The House of Lords in the Middle Ages* (Weidenfeld and Nicolson, 1968), p. 226.

35 F. M. Stenton, 'The changing feudalism of the middle ages', *History*, 19 (1934–5), pp. 289–301.

36 Ibid., p. 297.

37 M. Prestwich, *War, Politics and Finance under Edward I* (Faber, 1972), p. 88.

38 Ibid., p. 285.

39 See W. Farrer, 'Feudal baronage', in *Victoria County History: County of Lancaster* ed. W. Farrer (8 vols, Archibald Constable's, Co., 1908) pp. 291–375.

40 J. L. Grassi, *The Clerical Dynasties from Howdenshire, Nottinghamshire and Lindsey in the Royal Administration 1280–1340* (Oxford University D. Phil. thesis. 1959), p. 11.

41 M. M. Postan, *Essays on Medieval Agriculture and General Problems of the Medieval Economy* (Cambridge University Press, 1978), p. 57.

42 E. B. Fryde, 'Loans to the English crown 1328–31', *English Historical Review*, 70 (1955), pp. 198–211.

43 L. H. Butler, 'Archbishop Melton, his neighbours and his kinsmen, 1317–1340' *Journal of Ecclesiastical History*, 2 (1951), pp. 54–67.

44 R. Horrox, *The De La Poles of Hull* (East Yorkshire Local History Society, 1983), p. 16.

45 Roskell, *Knights of the Shire*, p. 23.

46 H. Nicolas, *History of the Battle Agincourt* (Johnson & Co., 1832), p. 385.

47 P. H. W. Booth, *The Financial Administration of the Lordship and County of Chester 1272–1377* (Chetham Society, 1981), p. 136.

48 Nicolas, *Agincourt*, p. 385.

49 Storey, *Thomas Langley*, p. 153.

50 J. S. Roskell, *The Commons in the Parliament of 1422* (Manchester University Press, 1954), pp. 93–5.

51 A. E. Prince, 'The payment of army wages in Edward III's reign', *Speculum*, 19 (1944), pp. 137–60.
52 N. B. Lewis, 'The organization of indentured retinues in fourteenth-century England', *Transactions of the Royal Historical Society*, 27 (1945), pp. 29–39.
53 S. L. Waugh, 'Tenure to contract: lordship and clientage in thirteenth-century England', *English Historical Review*, 101 (1986), pp. 811–39.
54 See Prestwich, *War, Politics and Finance*, p. 67.
55 A. Z. Freeman, 'The king's penny: the headquarters paymasters under Edward I 1295–1397', *The Journal of British Studies*, 6 (1906), pp. 1–22.
56 Nicolson, *Edward III and the Scots*, p. 15.
57 R. L. Storey, *The End of the House of Lancaster* (Barrie & Rockliff, 1966), pp. 108–109.
58 R. R. Reid, 'The office of warden of the marches; its origin and early history', *English Historical Review*, 32 (1917), pp. 479–96.
59 R. L. Storey, 'The wardens of the marches of England towards Scotland 1377–1489', *English Historical Review*, 72 (1957), pp. 593–615.
60 G. H. Tupling, *South Lancashire in the Reign of Edward II* (Chetham Society, 1949), pp. xxxv, 15.
61 C. H. Hunter Blair, 'Wardens and deputy wardens of the marches of England towards Scotland in Northumberland', *Archaeologia Aeliana*, 28 (1950), pp. 18–77.
62 Reid, 'The office of Warden of the marches', pp. 479–96.
63 G. T. Lapsley, *The County Palatine of Durham* (Longmans, Green & Co., 1900), pp. 307–8.
64 J. A. Tuck, 'War and society in the medieval north', pp. 33–52.
65 C. G. Cruickshank, *Elizabeth's Army* (Clarendon Press, 1966), pp. 208–9.
66 F. H. Mares, *The Memoirs of Robert Carey* (Clarendon Press, 1972), p. 22.
67 E. Carleton Williams, *My Lord of Bedford 1389–1435* (Longmans, 1963), pp. 12–13. 27.
68 J. M. W. Bean, 'Henry IV and the Percies', pp. 212–27.
69 J. M. W. Bean, *The Estates of the Percy Family 1416–1537* pp. 106–7.
70 H. C. Hunter Blair, 'Knights of the march of Northumberland 1278 and 1324', *Archaeologia Aeliana*, 27 (1949), pp. 122–75.
71 J. F. Willard, 'The taxes upon morables in the reign of Edward II', *English Historical Review*, 29 (1914), pp. 317–22.
72 J. F. Willard, 'The taxes upon morables in the reign of Edward III', *English Historical Review*, 30 (1915), pp. 69–74.
73 A. Steel, *The Receipts of the Exchequer 1377–1485* (Cambridge University Press, 1954), p. 271.
74 Tuck, 'War and society in the medieval north', pp. 33–55.
75 A. J. Pollard, 'The northern retainers of Richard Nevill earl of Salisbury',

Northern History, 11 (1976), pp. 52–69. For the weakness of geographically dispersed retainers, see C. Carpenter, 'The Beauchamp affinity: study
of bastard feudalism at work', *English Historical Review*, 95 (1980),
pp. 514–32.

76 M. Weiss, 'A power in the north? The Percies in the fifteenth century', *The
Historical Journal*, 19 (1976), pp. 501–9.

77 Storey, *End of the House of Lancaster*, p. 115.

78 C. M. Fraser, 'The pattern of trade in north-east England, 1265–1350',
Northern History, 4 (1969), pp. 44–66.

79 R. A. Donkin, 'Changes in the early middle ages', in *A New Historical
Geography of England*, ed. H. C. Darby (Cambridge University Press,
1973), pp. 75–135 esp. pp. 132–4.

80 B. Waites, 'Medieval assessments and agricultural prosperity in north-east
Yorkshire, 1292–1342', *Yorkshire Archaeological Journal*, 44 (1972), pp.
134–45.

81 I. Kershaw, *Bolton Priory: The Economy of a Northern Monastery 1286–
1325* (Oxford University Press, 1973), p. 17.

82 I. Kershaw, 'A note on the Scots in the West Riding, 1318–1319', *Northern
History*, 17 (1981), pp. 231–9.

83 J. Scammell, 'Robert I and the north of England', *English Historical
Review*, 73 (1958), pp. 385–403.

84 R. B. Dobson, *Durham Priory 1400–1450* (Cambridge University Press,
1973), p. 274.

85 Bean, *Estates of the Percy Family*, p. 35.

86 Butler, *Journal of Ecclesiastical History* (1951), pp. 54–67.

87 Prestwich, *War, Politics and Finance*, p. 175 and Nicolson, *Edward III and
the Scots*, p. 38.

88 Morris, 'Mounted infantry in medieval warfare', pp. 77–102.

89 Prestwich, *War, Politics and Finance*, p. 175 and Nicholson, *Edward III
and the Scots*, pp. 33–8.

90 Willard, 'The taxes upon movables in the reign of Edward III', pp. 69–74.

91 A. E. Prince, 'The strength of English armies in the reign of Edward III',
English Historical Review, 46 (1931), pp. 353–71.

92 R. A. Hilton, *A Medieval Society: The West Midlands at the End of the
Thirteenth Century* (Weidenfeld and Nicolson, 1966), p. 166.

93 Prestwich, *War, Politics and Finance*, p. 286.

94 K. B. McFarlane, *The Nobility of Late Medieval England* (Clarendon Press,
1973), p. 23.

95 K. B. McFarlane, *England in the Fifteenth Century* (Hambledon Press,
1981), p. 147.

96 McFarlane, *Nobility of Late Medieval England*, p. 21.

97 D. Hay, 'The division of spoils in war in the fourteenth century',
Transactions of the Royal Historical Society, 4 (1954), pp. 91–109.

98 A. D. Carr, 'Welshmen and the hundred years war', *Welsh History Review*, 4 (1968–9), pp. 21–46.
99 McFarlane, *Nobility in Late Medieval England*, p. 22.
100 S. M. Wright, *The Derbyshire Gentry in the Fifteenth Century* (Derbyshire Record Society, 1983), pp. 8–9.
101 C. T. Allmond, 'The Lancastrian land settlement in Normandy, 1417–50', *Economic History Review*, 21 (1968), pp. 461–79.
102 Poston, *Essays on Medieval Agriculture*, pp. 75–6.
103 Booth, *Financial Administration*, p. 135.
104 P. H. W. Booth, 'Taxation and public order: Cheshire in 1353', *Northern History*, 12 (1976), pp. 16–31.
105 J. G. Bellamy, 'The northern rebellions in the later years of Richard II', *Bulletin of the John Rylands Library*, 47 (1964–5), pp. 254–74.
106 Lapsley, *County Palatine*, p. 67.
107 J. Scammell, 'The origins and limitations of the liberty of Durham', *English Historical Review*, 81 (1966), pp. 449–71.
108 C. M. Fraser, *A History of Antony Bek* (Clarendon Press, 1957), pp. 185–6.
109 J. Bellamy, *Crime and Public Order in England in the Late Middle Ages* (Routledge and Kegan Paul, 1973), pp. 48–9.
110 Storey, *Thomas Langley*, p. 133.
111 Dobson, *Durham Priory*, pp. 197–201.
112 Wright, *Derbyshire Gentry*, p. 84.
113 P. McNiven, 'The Cheshire rising of 1400', *Bulletin of the John Rylands Library*, 52 (1969–70), pp. 375–96.

CHAPTER 7   TO A GOLDEN AGE 1351–1485

1 P. M. Kendall, *Warwick the Kingmaker* (Allen & Unwin, 1957), p. 97.
2 R. L. Storey, *The End of the House of Lancaster* (Barrie & Rockliff, 1966), p. 193.
3 See K. B. McFarlane, 'The wars of the roses', *Proceedings of the British Academy*, 50 (1965), pp. 87–119.
4 C. D. Ross, *Edward IV* (Methuen, 1974), p. 33.
5 See D. A. L. Morgan, 'The king's affinity and the polity of Yorkist England', *Transactions of the Royal Historical Society*, 23 (1973), pp. 1–25.
6 See H. G. Richardson and G. O. Sayles, *The Governance of Medieval England* (Edinburgh University Press, 1963), p. 85.
7 C. Carpenter, 'The Beauchamp affinity: a study of bastard feudalism at work', *English Historical Review*, 95 (1980), pp. 514–32.
8 McFarlane, 'The wars of the roses', p. 115.

9 See G. L. Harriss, 'Introduction' in *England in the Fifteenth Century*, K. B. McFarlane (Hambledon Press, 1981), pp. ix–xxvii.

10 McFarlane, *England in the Fifteenth Century*, pp. 18–20.

11 H. M. Cam, 'The decline and fall of English feudalism', *History*, 25 (1941), pp. 216–33.

12 See N. Williams, *Thomas Howard, Fourth Duke of Norfolk* (Barrie & Rocklift, 1964), p. 104.

13 G. H. Tupling, *South Lancashire in the Reign of Edward II* (Chetham Society, 1949), p. lx. Cf. J. Bellamy, *Crime and Public Order in England in the Later Middle Ages* (Routledge and Kegan Paul, 1973), p. 10.

14 S. Armitage-Smith, *John of Gaunt* (Constable, 1904), p. 206.

15 Tupling, *South Lancashire*, p. lx.

16 Armitage-Smith, *John of Gaunt*, p. 206.

17 R. Barber, *Edward, Prince of Wales and Aquitaine* (Allen Lane, 1978), p. 77.

18 M. G. A. Vale, *English Gascony 1399–1453* (Oxford University Press, 1970), p. 1.

19 Ross, *Edward IV*, p. 15. For an examination of the complexities of London's attitudes and politics see M. I. Peake, 'London and the wars of the roses', *Bulletin of the Institute of Historical Research*, 4 (1926–7), pp. 45–7.

20 C. M. Barron, 'The quarrel of Richard II with London 1392–7', in *The Reign of Richard II*, ed. F. R. H. Du Boulay and C. M. Barron (Athlone Press, 1971), pp. 173–201.

21 R. R. Davies, 'Richard II and the Principality of Chester, 1397–9', in *Reign of Richard II*, pp. 256–79.

22 J. L. Kirby, 'The financing of Calais under Henry V', *Bulletin of the Institute of Historical Research*, 23 (1950), pp. 165–97.

23 G. L. Harriss, 'The struggle for Calais: an aspect of the rivalry between Lancaster and York', *English Historical Review*, 75 (1960), pp. 30–53.

24 E. Carleton Williams, *My Lord of Bedford 1389–1435* (Longmans, 1963), p. 96.

25 R. A. Newhall, *The English Conquest of Normandy 1416–1424* (Russell & Russell, 1924), pp. xv, 173.

26 R. R. Davies, *Lordship and Society in the March of Wales 1282–1400* (Clarendon Press, 1978), p. 188.

27 Ibid., p. 39.

28 K. Fowler, *The King's Lieutenant: Henry Grosmont, First Duke of Lancaster 1310–1361.* (Elek, 1969), p. 226.

29 Armitage-Smith, *John of Gaunt*, p. 218.

30 See C. Plummer (ed.), *The Governance of England by Sir John Fortescue* (Oxford University Press, 1885), pp. 211–15, and J. L. Kirby, 'The issues of the exchequer and Lord Cromwell's estimates of 1433', *Bulletin of the Institute of Historical Research*, 24 (1951), pp. 121–51.

31 McFarlane, *'The wars of the roses'*, p. 98.

32 Ibid., p. 98.

33 G. M. Trevelyan, *History of England* (Longmans, 1928), p. 258.

34 Ross, *Edward IV*, p. 16.

35 R. A. Griffiths, 'Local rivalries and national politics: the Percies, the Nevilles and the duke of Exeter, 1422–55', *Speculum*, 43 (1968), pp. 589–632.

36 J. M. W. Bean, 'Henry IV and the Percies', *History*, 44 (1959), pp. 212–27.

37 See T. B. Pugh, 'The magnates, knights and gentry', in *Fifteenth Century England*, ed. S. B. Chrimes, C. D. Ross and R. A. Griffiths (Manchester University Press, 1972), pp. 87–128, J. T. Rosenthal, 'The estates and finances of Richard, duke of York 1411–1460', in *Studies in Medieval and Renaissance History*, ed. W. M. Browsky (University of Nebraska Press, 1965), pp. 117–204, C. D. Ross, *The Estates and Finances of Richard Beauchamp Earl of Warwick* (Oxford University Press, 1956); and T. B. Pugh and C. D. Ross, 'The English baronage and the income tax of 1436', *Bulletin of the Institute of Historical Research*, 26 (1953), pp. 1–28.

38 Ross, *Edward IV*, p. 38.

39 H. A. Hicks, 'Edward IV, the duke of Somerset and Lancastrian loyalism in the north', *Northern History*, 20 (1984), pp. 23–37.

40 Ross, *Edward IV*, p. 203.

41 See A. J. Pollard, 'The tyranny of Richard III', *Journal of Medieval Studies*, 3 (1977), pp. 147–65.

42 J. Hatcher, *Plague, Population and the English Economy 1348–1530* (Macmillan, 1977), pp. 38–40.

43 Ross, *Edward IV*, p. 338.

44 See C. D. Ross, *Richard III* (Eyre Methuen, 1981), p. 8.

45 See M. Hicks, 'Richard, duke of Gloucester and the north' in *Richard III and the North*, ed. Rosemary Horrox (Centre for Regional and Local History, University of Hull, 1986), pp. 11–26.

46 See M. Jones, 'Richard III and the Stanleys' in *Richard III and the North*, pp. 27–50.

47 Ross, *Edward IV*, p. 200.

48 R. Horrox, 'Richard III and the East Riding' in *Richard III and the North*, pp. 82–107 esp. p. 91.

49 Ross, *Edward IV*, p. 201.

50 See J. R. Lander, *The Wars of the Roses* (Secker & Warburg, 1965), p. 224.

51 Williams, *Thomas Howard Fourth Duke of Norfolk*, p. 104.

52 Ross, *Edward IV*, p. 202, and Ross, *Richard III*, p. 26.

53 M. Postan, 'The fifteenth century', *Economic History Review*, 9 (1938–9), pp. 160–7.

54 E. H. Phelps Brown and S. V. Hopkins, 'Seven centuries of the prices of

consumables, compared with builders' wages', *Economica*, 23 (1956), pp. 296–314.

55 R. B. Dobson, *Durham Priory 1400–1450* (Cambridge University Press, 1973), p. 252.

56 I. Kershaw, *Bolton Priory. The Economy of a Northern Monastery 1286–1325* (Oxford University Press, 1973), pp. 182–3.

57 Rosenthal, 'The estates and finances of Richard, duke of York *1411–1460*', p. 148.

58 Ibid., p. 151.

59 J. M. W. Bean, *The Estates of the Percy Family 1416–1527* (Oxford University Press, 1958), pp. 27–35.

60 See H. Belloc, *The Servile State* (Liberty Classics Indianapolis, 1977), p. 78.

61 H. L. Gray, 'Incomes from land in England in 1436', *English Historical Review*, 49 (1934), pp. 607–39.

62 J. Fortescue, *De Laudibus Legum Angliae*, tr. A. Amos (Cambridge University Press, 1825), p. 104.

63 A. J. Pollard, 'The Richmondshire community of gentry during the wars of the roses', in *Patronage, Pedigree and Power*, ed. C. D. Ross (Alan Sutton, 1979), pp. 37–59.

64 A. J. Pollard, 'Richard Clervaux of Croft: a North Riding squire of the fifteenth century', *Yorkshire Archaeological Journal*, 50 (1978), pp. 151–69.

65 T. H. Lloyd, *The English Wool Trade in the Middle Ages* (Cambridge University Press, 1977), p. 316.

66 J. W. F. Hill, *Medieval Lincoln* (Cambridge University Press, 1965), pp. 272–3.

67 J. N. Bartlett, 'The expansion and decline of York in the later middle ages', *Economic History Review*, 12 (1959–60), pp. 17–33.

68 D. M. Palliser, 'A crisis in English towns? the case of York 1460–1640', *Northern History*, 14 (1978), pp. 108–25.

69 H. Heaton, *The Yorkshire Woollen and Worsted Industries* (Clarendon Press, 1920), p. 44.

70 R. B. Dobson, 'Urban decline in late medieval England', *Transactions of the Royal Historical Society*, 27 (1977), pp. 1–22.

71 A. R. Bridbury, *Economic Growth. England in the Later Middle Ages* (Allen & Unwin, 1962), pp. 112–13.

72 R. S. Schofield, 'The geographical distribution of wealth in England 1334–1649', *Economic History Review*, 18 (1965), pp. 483–510.

73 J. H. Ramsay, 'The strength of English armies in the middle ages', *English Historical Review*, 29 (1914), pp. 221–7, and A. E. Prince, 'The strength of English armies in the reign of Edward III', *English Historical Review*, 46 (1931), pp. 353–71. There were probably 16,000 men in the Crécy

campaign, around 8,000 in the Harfleur-Agincourt campaign: see A. H. Burne, *The Agincourt War* (Eyre & Spottiswoode, 1956), p. 48.

74 Phelps Brown and Hopkins, 'Seven centuries of prices of consumables', p. 306.

75 Prince, 'The strength of English armies in the reign of Edward III', pp. 353–71.

76 J. W. Sherburne, 'Indentured retinues and English expeditions to France, 1369–1380', *English Historical Review*, 79 (1964), pp. 718–46.

77 N. Denholm-Young, *The Country Gentry of the Fourteenth Century* (Clarendon Press, 1969), p. 16.

78 H. Nicholas, *History of the Battle of Agincourt* (Johnson & Co., 1832), pp. 333–70, and Newhall, *Conquest of Normandy*, p. 193.

79 Gray, 'Incomes from land in England in 1436', pp. 607–39.

80 Ibid.

81 See also J. P. Cooper, 'The social distribution of land and men in England, 1436–1700', *Economic History Review*, 20 (1967), pp. 419–440, esp. p. 422. Cooper combines two lists, of 1434 and 1429–36, and concludes that there were between 180 and 190 knights, but allowing for those serving in France at the time, something in excess of 200.

82 See M. J. Bennett, 'A county community: social cohesion among the Cheshire gentry, 1400–1425', *Northern History*, 8 (1973), pp. 24–44.

83 See J. S. Roskell, *The Knights of the Shire for the County Palatine of Lancaster 1377–1460* (Chetham Society, 1937), p. 23.

84 Gray, 'Incomes from land in England in 1436', pp. 607–39.

85 H. C. Hunter Blair, 'Knights of Northumberland 1278 and 1324', *Archaeologia Aeliana*, 17 (1949), pp. 122–75.

86 E. Powell, 'Lords by creation', *The Listener* (8 September 1955), pp. 363–5.

87 F. M. Stenton, 'The changing feudalism of the middle ages', *History*, 19 (1934–5), pp. 289–301.

88 See T. F. T. Plucknett, *Legislation of Edward I* (Clarendon Press, 1949), p. 108, and G. A. Holmes, *The Estates of the Higher Nobility in the Fourteenth Century* (Cambridge University Press, 1957), p. 83.

89 See J. R. Lander, 'Attainder and forfeiture 1453 to 1509', *The Historical Journal*, 4 (1961), pp. 119–51.

90 Nicolas, *Battle of Agincourt*, pp. 170–1.

91 R. Somerville, *History of the Duchy of Lancaster* (Chancellor and Council of the Duchy of Lancaster, 1953), pp. 162–4.

92 Bean, *Estates of the Percy Family*, p. 91, and Pugh, 'Magnates, knights and gentry', in *Fifteenth Century England*, p. 103.

93 Ross, *Estates and Finances of Richard Beauchamp*, p. 16.

94 K. B. McFarlane, 'History of the duchy of Lancaster', *English Historical Review*, 70 (1955), pp. 107–111.

95 Somerville, *Duchy of Lancaster*, p. 188.

96 Bean, *Estates of the Percy Family*, p. 134.

97 Armitage-Smith, *John of Gaunt*, pp. 229, 440–6.

98 See Bellamy, *Crime and Public Order*, pp. 71–2, and Storey, *End of the House of Lancaster*, pp. 55–7.

99 See W. T. Waugh, 'The Lollard Knights', *Scottish Historical Review*, 11 (1913), pp. 55–92.

CHAPTER 8   THE TUDOR CHALLENGE

1 See C. G. Cruickshank, *Elizabeth's Army* (Clarendon Press, 1966), p. 208.

2 See J. S. Watts, *From Border to Middle Shire. Northumberland 1586–1625* (Leicester University Press, 1975), p. 59.

3 R. S. Schofield, 'The geographical distribution of wealth in England, 1334–1649', *Economic History Review*, 18 (1965), pp. 483–510.

4 Ibid., p. 509.

5 Ibid., p. 507.

6 A. R. Bridbury, *Economic Growth. England in the Later Middle Ages* (Allen & Unwin, 1962), p. 111.

7 H. Heaton, *The Yorkshire Woollen and Worsted Industries* (Clarendon Press, 1920), p. 44.

8 R. G. Wilson, *Gentlemen Merchants. The Merchant Community of Leeds 1700–1830* (Manchester University Press, 1971), pp. 10–11.

9 H. Zins, *England and the Baltic in the Elizabethan Era* Manchester University Press, 1972), p. 105.

10 Schofield, *Economic History Review* (1965) pp. 483–510, and E. J. Buckatzsch, 'The geographical distribution of wealth in England 1086–1843', pp. 180–202.

11 E. H. Phelps Brown and S. V. Hopkins, 'Seven centuries of the prices of consumables, compared with builders' wages', *Economica*, 23 (1956), pp. 296–314.

12 L. Stone, 'Patriarchy and paternalism in Tudor England: the earl of Arundel and the peasants' revolt of 1549', *Journal of British Studies*, 13 (1973), pp. 19–23.

13 See D. Loades, *The Tudor Court* (Batsford, 1986), pp. 193–202.

14 J. G. Russell, *The Field of Cloth of Gold* (Routledge and Kegan Paul, 1969), pp. 191–204.

15 See A. Fletcher, *Tudor Rebellions* (Longman, 1983), pp. 37, 109–10.

16 See G. R. Elton, *Reform and Reformation. England 1509–1558* (Arnold, 1977), pp. 200–206, and D. Lindsay Keir, *The Constitutional History of Modern Britain 1485–1937* (Black, 1943), p. 304.

17 See R. B. Smith, *Land and Politics in the England of Henry VIII. The West Riding of Yorkshire 1530–46* (Clarendon Press, 1970), p. 139.

18 See N. Williams, *Thomas Howard Fourth Duke of Norfolk* (Barrie & Rockliff, 1964), pp. 65, 104.

19 G. Scott Thomson, *Lords Lieutenant in the Sixteenth Century* (Longman, 1923), p. 52.

20 See J. M. W. Bean, *The Estates of the Percy Family 1416–1537* (Oxford University Press, 1958), pp. 151–7.

21 See M. E. James. 'The murder at Cockledge 28 April 1489', *Durham University Journal*, 26 (1965), pp. 80–7, and M. A. Hicks, 'The Yorkshire rebellion of 1489 reconsidered', *Northern History*, 22 (1986), pp. 39–62.

22 H. Miller, *Henry VIII and the English Nobility* (Basil Blackwell, 1986), p. 35.

23 Holinshed, *Chronicles*, quoted in G. T. Lapsley, *The County Palatine of Durham* (Longmans, Green & Co., 1900), p. 299.

24 Cf. H. A. Hicks, 'Dynastic change and northern society: the career of the fourth earl of Northumberland 1470–89', *Northern History*, 14 (1978), pp. 78–107.

25 C. Haigh, *Reformation and Resistance in Tudor Lancashire* (Cambridge University Press, 1975), p. 105.

26 B. Coward, *The Stanleys: Lords Stanley and Earls of Derby 1385–1672* (Chetham Society, 1983), p. 116.

27 Ibid., pp. 96–7.

28 See S. T. Bindoff, *The House of Commons 1509–1558* (Secker & Warburg, 1982), pp. 238–53, P. W. Hasler, *The House of Commons 1558–1603* (Secker & Warburg, 1981), pp. 280–95, and J. E. Neale, *The Elizabethan House of Commons* (Jonathan Cape, 1949), pp. 189–229.

29 Neale, *Elizabethan House of Commons*, p. 229.

30 D. Mitchell, *Richard III, Middleham and King's Council of the North* (Silver Boar, 1984), pp. 8–10.

31 Elton, *Reform and Reformation*, p. 272.

32 G. T. Lapsley, 'The problem of the north', in *Crown, Community and Parliament in the Later Middle Ages*, ed. G. T. Lapsley (Basil Blackwell, 1951), pp. 375–405, esp. p. 389.

33 Elton, *Reform and Reformation*, p. 347.

34 R. R. Reid, *The King's Council in the North* (Longmans, Green & Co., 1921), pp. 58, 508.

35 R. H. Tawney, *The Agrarian Problem in the Sixteenth Century* (Longmans, 1912), pp. 318, 323–4.

36 See Fletcher, *Tudor Rebellions*, pp. 106–7.

37 Elton, *Reform and Reformation*, p. 268.

38 Fletcher, *Tudor Rebellions*, p. 109.

39 For a feudal class-conflict thesis see M. E. James, 'The first earl of Cumberland (1493–1542) and the decline of northern feudalism', *Northern History*, 1 (1966), pp. 43–69; for its rebuttal see R. W. Hoyle, 'The first earl of Cumberland: a reputation re-assessed', *Northern History*, 22 (1986), pp. 63–94.

40 R. H. Tawney, *The Agrarian Problem in the Sixteenth Century* (Longmans, 1912), p. 318.

41 Haigh, *Reformation and Resistance*, p. 136.

42 See P. Williams, 'Rebellion and revolution in early modern England' in *War and Society* ed. M. R. D. Foot (Paul Elek, 1973), pp. 39–40.

43 See A. Savine, 'English monasteries on the eve of the dissolution' in *Oxford Studies in Social and Legal History*, ed. P. Vinogradoff (Clarendon Press, 1909), pp. 1–303, and P. Hughes, *The Reformation in England* (Hollis and Carter, 1952), vol. I, p. 296.

44 Hughes, *Reformation*, p, 296.

45 See W. S. Holdsworth, *A History of English Law* (17 vols, Methuen, 1924), vol. 4, p. 464, and J. T. Hurstfield, 'The revival of feudalism in early Tudor England', *History*, 37 (1952), pp. 131–45.

46 See J. A. Youings, 'The terms of the disposal of the Devon monastic lands 1536–58', *English Historical Review*, 69 (1954), pp. 18–38.

47 I. D. Thornley, 'The destruction of sanctuary' in *Tudor Studies*, ed. R. W. Seton-Watson (Russell & Russell, 1924), pp. 182–207.

48 Bean, *Percy Estates*, p. 154.

49 J. C. Cox, 'William Stapleton and the Pilgrimage of Grace', *Transactions of the East Riding Antiquarian Society*, 10 (1902), pp. 80–106.

50 Reid, *King's Council in the North*, p. 144.

51 See Fletcher, *Tudor Rebellions*, p. 39, quoting R. B. Smith, *A Study of Landed Income and Social Structure in the West Riding of Yorkshire 1535–46* (Ph. D. Leeds University, 1962).

52 See M. L. Bush, 'The problem of the far north; a study of the crisis of 1537 and its consequences', *Northern History*, 6 (1971), pp. 40–63.

53 J. D. Mackie, *The Earlier Tudors* (Clarendon Press, 1952), p. 385.

54 B. W. Beckingsale, 'The characteristics of the Tudor north', *Northern History*, 4 (1969), pp. 67–83.

55 Elton, *Reform and Reformation*, pp. 265–6.

56 See D. MacCulloch, 'Ket's rebellion in context', *Past & Present*, 84 (1979), pp. 36–59.

57 See E. Searle and R. Burghart, 'The defense of England and the peasants' revolt', *Viator*, 3 (1972), pp. 365–88.

58 See D. L. Keir, 'The case of ship-money', *Law Quarterly Review*, 52 (1936), pp. 546–74.

59 See A. L. Rowse, *Tudor Cornwall* (Macmillan, 1969), p. 121.

60 Ibid., p. 264.

61 R. Stewart-Brown, 'The avowries of Cheshire', *English Historical Review*, 29 (1914), pp. 41–55.

62 Elton, *Reform and Reformation*, p. 204.

63 See J. Hurstfield, 'The Greenwich tenures in the reign of Edward IV', *Law Quarterly Review*, 65 (1949), pp.72–81, but compare H. J. Habakkuk, 'The market for monastic property 1539–1603', *Economic History Review*, 10 (1957–8), pp. 362–80.

64 Holdsworth, *History of English Law*, vol. 4, p. 39.

65 Ibid., pp. 453, 461, 464.

66 See Fletcher, *Tudor Rebellions*, p. 129.

67 Cf. Haigh, *Reformation and Resistance*, p. 252.

68 L. Stone, *The Crisis of the Aristocracy* (Clarendon Press, 1965), p. 251.

69 Watts, *Border to Middle Shire*, pp. 56–7.

70 R. Fieldhouse and B. Jennings. *A History of Richmond and Swaledale* (Phillimore, 1978), p. 90.

71 See H. B. McCall, 'The rising of the north: a new light upon one aspect of it', *Yorkshire Archaeological Journal*, 15 (1905), pp. 74–87.

72 Williams, *Fourth Duke of Norfolk*, pp. 174–5.

73 H. Miller, *Henry VIII and the Nobility* (Basil Blackwell, 1986), p. 196.

74 Ibid., p. 190.

75 Bean, *Percy Estates*, p. 107.

76 Watts, *Border to Middle Shire*, p. 95.

77 P. Williams, *The Tudor Regime* (Oxford University Press, 1979), p. 321.

CHAPTER 9 THE ECLIPSE OF THE NORTH

1 See A. E. Goodman, 'Responses to requests in Yorkshire for military service under Henry V', *Northern History*, 17 (1981), pp. 240–52.

2 Penry Williams has properly emphasized the overriding importance of London. 'All Tudor revolts found it difficult to transcend regional boundaries', but the seventeenth-century revolution was essentially London-based. 'The role of London makes seventeenth-century politics quite different from the rural and provincial protests of the sixteenth'. See P. Williams, 'Rebellion and revolution in early modern England', in *War and Society*, ed. M. R. D. Foot (Paul Elek, 1973).

3 See C. V. Wedgwood *Thomas Wentworth First Earl of Strafford 1593–1641* (Jonathan Cape, 1961), p. 119. Wentworth certainly wanted the presidency of the Council of the North and he was interested in Ireland but he was immensely ambitious and as lord president 'was very far from the political dominance for which he longed'.

4 In the reign of Charles I from 1625 to 1642, out of a sample of 194 regular civil servants, only three came from Yorkshire and three from Nottingham-

shire, but seven came from Warwickshire, eight from Worcestershire and nine from Suffolk. See G. E. Aylmer, *The King's Servants. The Civil Service of Charles I 1625–1642* (Routledge and Kegan Paul, 1961), p. 270, pp. 267–8 table 19.

5 See B. Manning, *The English People and the English Revolution 1640–1649* (Heinemann, 1976) p. 197.

6 One estimate places Dorset twentieth in 1503. See E. J. Buckatzsch, 'The geographical distribution of wealth in England 1086–1843', *Economic History Review* 3 (1950–1), pp. 180–202. Another perhaps more realistically places it sixteenth in 1513. See R. S. Schofield, 'The geographical distribution of wealth in England, 1334–1649', *Economic History Review*, 18 (1965), pp. 483–510.

7 M. F. Keeler, *The Long Parliament 1640–1641* (American Philosophical Society, 1954), p. 44.

8 E.g. C. B. Phillips, 'The royalist north', *Northern History*, 14 (1978), pp. 169–92.

9 See A. Browning, *Thomas Osborne, Earl of Danby and Duke of Leeds 1632–1712* (Jackson, 1951). p. 388.

10 For a vigorous statement of this view see J. P. Kenyon, *The Nobility and the Revolution of 1688* (University of Hull Publications), p. 12.

11 D. Hosford, *Nottingham, Nobles, and the North* (Anchor Books, 1976), p. 31.

12 For a very positive view of these integrative functions of the Council see G. T. Lapsley, 'The problem of the north', *American Historical Review*, 5 (1900), pp. 440–60.

13 See R. R. Reid, *The King's Council in the North* (Longmans, Green & Co., 1921), pp. 413, 435.

14 See J. B. Watson, 'The Lancashire gentry and public service 1529–1558', *Transactions of the Lancashire and Cheshire Antiquarian Society*, 73 (1966), pp. 11–59.

15 Compare R. R. Reid, 'The political influence of the "north parts" under the late Tudors' in *Tudor Studies*, ed. R. W. Seton-Watson (Russell and Russell, 1970), pp. 208–30.

16 F. C. Dietz, *English Government Finance* (Urbana, 1920), p. 147.

17 See H. J. Habakkuk, 'The market for monastic property, 1539–1603', *Economic History Review*, 10 (1957–8), pp. 362–80.

18 J. S. Watts, *From Border to Middle Shire. Northumberland, 1586–1625* (Leicester University Press, 1975), p. 30.

19 The county commissioners entrusted with the assessment were the local landed gentry. See W. R. Ward, *The English Land Tax in the Eighteenth Century* (Oxford University Press, 1953), pp. 7–10, and H. J. Habakkuk, 'English landownership 1680–1740', *Economic History Review*, 10 (1940), pp. 2–17.

20 In some border areas land values rose sixfold between 1603 and 1676. See 'Roger North in the north', in *English Historical Documents 1660–1714*, ed. A. Browning (Eyre & Spottiswoode, 1953), pp. 446–51. Lord Grey of Werke's estate was worth about £1,000 per annum in 1603, between £7,000 and £8,000 in 1676.

21 See John Fortescue, *De Landibus Legum Angliae*, tr. A. Amos (Cambridge University Press, 1825), pp. 104–5, G. Shaw Lefevre, *Agrarian Tenures* (Cassell, 1893), p. 6; and H. Belloc, *The Servile State* (Indianapolis Liberty Classics, 1977), p. 78.

22 R. H. Tawney, *The Agrarian Problem in the Sixteenth Century* (Longmans, 1912), p. 26. Tawney estimated that 91 per cent of landholders in Northumberland were copyholders, 77 per cent in southern counties, only 54 per cent in East Anglia.

23 Reid, *The King's Council in the North*, p. 19.

24 See P. Dixon, 'Towerhouses, pelehouses and border society' *Archaeological Journal*, 136 (1979), pp. 240–52.

25 See R. Fieldhouse and B. Jennings, *A History of Richmond and Swaledale* (Phillimore, 1978), p. 121.

26 See M. Campbell, *The English Yeoman* (Yale University Press, 1942), pp. 148–50.

27 Tawney, *The Agrarian Problem in the Sixteenth Century* p. 394.

28 See E. J. Buckatzsch, 'The geographical distribution of wealth in England 1086–1843', pp. 180–202.

29 A. R. Bridbury, *Economic Growth: England in the Later Middle Ages* (Allen & Unwin, 1962), p. 79, pp. 111–13.

30 As described by A. J. Pollard. 'The Richmondshire community of gentry during the wars of the roses' in *Patronage, Pedigree and Power*, ed. Charles Ross (Alan Sutton, 1974), pp. 37–59, and 'Richard Clervaux of Croft: a north riding squire of the fifteenth century', *Yorkshire Archaeological Journal*, 50 (1978), pp. 151–69.

31 See J. S. Watts, *From Border to Middle Shire: Northumberland 1586–1625* (Leicester University Press, 1975), p. 39.

32 E. A. Wrigley, *People, Cities and Wealth* (Basil Blackwell, 1987), p. 159, p. 160, table 7.1.

33 R. B. Smith, *Land and Politics in the England of Henry VIII: The West Riding of Yorkshire 1530–46* (Clarendon, 1970), p. 241.

34 T. J. Cliffe, *The Yorkshire Gentry. From the Reformation to the Civil War* (Athlone Press, 1969), p. 15.

35 R. G. Blackwood, *The Lancashire Gentry and the Great Rebellion 1640–60* (Chetham Society, 1978), p. 19.

36 G. P. Higgins, 'The government of early Stuart Cheshire', *Northern History*, 12 (1976), pp. 32–52.

37 J. P. Cooper, 'The fortune of Thomas Wentworth, earl of Strafford', *Economic History Review*, 11 (1958), pp. 227–48.

38 B. Coward, *The Stanleys. Lords Stanley and Earls of Derby 1385–1672* (Chetham Society, 1983). p. 79.

39 Robert Ashton, 'Puritanism and progress', *Economic History Review*, 17 (1964–5), pp. 579–87.

40 See R. C. Richardson, *Puritanism in North-West England* (Manchester University Press, 1972).

41 See C. Haigh, *Reformation and Resistance in Tudor Lancashire*. (Manchester University Press, 1975), p. 325.

42 J. Bossy, *The English Catholic Community 1570–1850* (Darton, Longman and Todd, 1975), p. 405.

43 Cliffe, *The Yorkshire Gentry*, p. 262.

44 Phillips, *Northern History*, 14 (1978).

45 Bossy, *The English Catholic Community*, p. 102.

46 See A. P. Newton, *The Colonizing Activities of the English Puritans* (Yale University Press, 1914), pp. 49, 77–9.

47 See C. Hill, *Intellectual Origins of the English Revolution* (Clarendon, 1965), pp. 108, 119; but contrast H. F. Kearmy, 'Puritanism, capitalism and the scientific revolution', *Past & Present*, 28 (1964), pp. 81–101.

48 Newton, *Colonizing Activities*, p. 78.

49 M. Walzer, 'Puritanism as a revolutionary ideology', *History and Theory*, 3 (1964), pp. 59–90.

50 Quoted Cliffe, *Yorkshire Gentry*, p. 361.

51 R. Howell, *Newcastle-Upon-Tyne and the Puritan Revolution* (Clarendon, 1967), p. 145.

52 V. Pearl, *London and the Outbreak of the Puritan Revolution* (Oxford University Press, 1961), p. 158.

53 S. R. Gardiner, *History of the Great Civil War* (Longmans, Green & Co., 1901), vol. I, p. 33.

54 R. N. Kershaw, 'The elections for the long parliament, 1640', *English Historical Review*, 33 (1923), pp. 496–508.

55 C. R. Markham, *A Life of the Great Lord Fairfax* (Macmillan, 1870), p. 51.

56 See J. L. Malcolm, 'A king in search of soldiers: Charles I in 1642', *Historical Journal*, 21 (1978), pp. 251–73.

57 See M. F. Keeler, *The Long Parliament 1640–1641* (American Philosophical Society, 1954), pp. 11–12.

58 Calculated from D. Brunton and D. H. Pennington, *Members of the Long Parliament* (Allen & Unwin, 1954), p. 187.

59 Blackwood, *Lancashire Gentry*, p. 38.

60 Phillips, 'The royalist north', pp. 169–92.

61 Cliffe, *The Yorkshire Gentry*, p. 336.

62 The 'primacy of constitutional issues' has been properly emphasized in P. Zagorin, *The Court and the Country* (Routledge and Kegan Paul, 1969), p. 331.

63 Compare A. Fletcher, *The Outbreak of the Civil War* (Arnold, 1981), pp. 417–18: 'There is a real sense in which the English civil war was a war of religion', and J. S. Morrill, *The Revolt of the Provinces* (Allen & Unwin, 1976), pp. 46–7.

64 See F. Walker, *Historical Geography of South west Lancashire before the Industrial Revolution* (Chetham Society, 1939). This study de-emphasizes economic and class conflict issues and sees religion as central.

65 Cliffe, *Yorkshire Gentry*, p. 361.

66 See R. N. Dore, *The Civil War in Cheshire* (Cheshire Community Council, 1966).

67 See Keith Lindley, 'The part played by Catholics' in *Politics, Religion and the English Civil War*, ed. B. Manning (Arnold, 1973).

68 See P. R. Newman, 'Catholic royalists of northern England 1642–1645', *Northern History*, 15 (1979), pp. 88–95.

69 G. H. Tupling, 'The causes of the civil war in Lancashire', *Transactions of the Lancashire and Cheshire Antiquarian Society*, 65 (1955), pp. 1–32.

70 See P. R. Newman, *The Royalist Army in Northern England 1642–5* (2 vols, D. Phil. thesis University of York, 1978), vol. I, p. 94.

71 E.g. C. Hill, 'Some recent interpretations of the civil war', *History*, 41 (1956). pp. 66–87.

72 See K. Hatton, *The Royalist War Effort 1642–1646* (Longman, 1982), pp. 19–28, and Newman, *The Royalist Army*, vol. I, p. 62.

73 Dove, *The Civil War in Cheshire*, p. 19.

74 See M. D. G. Wanklyn and P. Young, 'A king in search of soldiers: Charles I in 1642: a rejoinder', *Historical Journal*, 24 (1981), pp. 147–54.

75 See G. Trease, *Portrait of a Cavalier: William Cavendish. First Duke of Newcastle* (Macmillan, 1979).

76 I. Roots, *The Great Rebellion* (Batsford, 1966), p. 127.

77 J. Thirsk, 'The restoration land settlement', *Journal of Modern History*, 26 (1954), pp. 315–28.

78 D. W. Rannie, 'Cromwell's major-generals', *English Historical Review*, 10 (1895), pp. 471–506.

79 See A. H. Woolrych, *Penruddock's Rising* (George Philip & Sons, 1955).

80 See D. Underdown, *Royalist Conspiracy. in England 1649–1660* (Yale University Press, 1960).

81 T. B. Macaulay, *The History of England* (6 vols, Macmillan, 1913), vol. I, p. 344.

82 See E. A. Wrigley, 'A simple model of London's importance in changing English society and economy 1650–1750', *Past & Present*, 37 (1967), pp. 44–70.

83 The 'Londonizing' thesis has been strongly advanced by Christopher Hill in various publications: see *Reformation to Industrial Revolution* (Penguin Books, 1969), p. 137, and *Change and Continuity in Seventeenth Century England* (Weidenfeld & Nicolson, 1974), pp. 4, 38.

84 T. E. C. Hill, 'Puritans and "the dark corners of the land" ', *Transactions of the Royal Historical Society*, 13 (1963), pp. 77–102.

85 See L. K. Glassey, *Politics and the Appointment of Justices of the Peace 1675–1720*. (Oxford University Press, 1979), pp. 84, 91, and J. R. Jones, *The Revolution of 1688 in England* (Weidenfield & Nicholson, 1972), pp. 128–75.

86 J. V. Beckett, *Coal and Tobacco. The Lowthers and the Economic Development of West Cumberland 1660–1760* (Cambridge University Press, 1981), pp. 13, 80, 218.

87 T. W. Beastall, *A North Country Estate. The Lumleys and Sandersons as landowners, 1600–1900* (Phillimore, 1975), p. 55.

88 Ibid., pp. 13–14.

89 E.g. W. A. Speck, *Reluctant Revolutionaries. Englishmen and the Revolution of 1688* (Oxford University Press, 1988), p. 220.

90 Kenyon, *Nobility and the Revolution of 1688*, p. 9.

91 Beastall, *North Country Estate*, p. 11.

CHAPTER 10   RESURGENCE AND RENEWAL

1 H. J. Habakkuk, 'English landownership 1680–1740', *Economic History Review*, 10 (1940), pp. 2–17.

2 L. B. Namier, *The Structure of Politics at the Accession of George III* (Macmillan, 1929), pp. 108–22.

3 Habakkuk, 'English landownership 1680–1740', pp. 1–17, esp. p. 9.

4 W. K. Ward, *The English Land Tax in the Eighteenth Century* (Oxford University Press, 1953), pp. 7–8.

5 G. E. Mingay, *English Landed Society in the Eighteenth Century* (Routledge & Kegan Paul, 1963), p. 82.

6 Ward, *English Land Tax*, p. 9.

7 Calculated from A. Browning (ed.), *English Historical Documents 1660–1714* (Eyre & Spottiswoode, 1953), pp. 318–21.

8 Ward, *English Land Tax*, p. 9.

9 E.g. C. Hill, *Reformation to Industrial Revolution* (Penguin Books, 1969), p. 137.

10 See Mingay, *Landed Society*, pp. 20, 87–8, and Namier, *Structure of Politics*, p. 83.

11 Namier *Structure of Politics*, pp. 176–81.

12 Helen Miller, *Henry VIII and the Nobility* (Basil Blackwell, 1986), p. 2.

13 Namier, *Structure of Politics*, p. 181.

14 Ibid., p. 92.

15 J. D. Chambers, *Nottinghamshire in the Eighteenth Century* (Cass, 1966), pp. 32–4.

16 R. J. S. Hoffman, *The Marquis: A Study of Lord Rockingham, 1730–1782* (Fordham University Press, 1973), p. 27.

17 Namier, *Structure of Politics*, p. 91.

18 L. B. Namier, *England in the Age of the American Revolution* (Macmillan, 1929), p. 230.

19 W. Farrer (ed.), *Victoria County History: County of Lancaster* (8 vols, Archibald Constable's Co., 1908), vol. 2, pp. 245–6

20 B. Lenman, *The Jacobite Risings in Britain 1689–1746* (Eyre Methuen, 1980), p. 123.

21 Ward, *English Land Tax*, p. 55.

22 H. Butterfield, *George III, Lord North and the People 1779–80* (Bell, 1949), p. 200.

23 Ibid., p. 289.

24 H. Butterfield, 'The Yorkshire association and the crisis of 1779–80', *Transactions of the Royal Historical Society*, 29 (1947), pp. 69–91.

25 L. K. J. Glassey, *Politics and the Appointment of Justices of the Peace 1675–1720* (Oxford University Press. 1979), p. 85.

26 E. A. Wrigley, *People, Cities and Wealth* (Basil Blackwell, 1987), pp. 159, 160 table 7.1.

27 Ibid., p. 190.

28 E. J. Buckatzsch, 'The geographical distribution of wealth in England 1086–1843', *Economic History Review*, 3 (1950–1), pp. 180–202.

29 W. W. Rostow, 'Leading sectors and the take-off', in *The Economics of Take-Off into Sustained Growth*, ed. W. W. Rostow (Macmillan, 1963), pp. 1–21, esp. p. 6.

30 R. Davis, *The Rise of the English Shipping Industry* (Macmillan, 1962), pp. 62–5.

31 W. E. H. Lecky, *A History of England in the Eighteenth Century* (8 vols, Longman, Green & Co., 1879), vol. I, pp. 561–4.

32 William Cobbett, *Rural Rides* (2 vols, Everyman, 1973), vol. 2, pp. 290, 294.

33 M. W. Flinn, *Men of Iron: The Crowleys in the Early Iron Industry* (Edinburgh University Press, 1962), pp. 35–8.

34 P. and W. A. Cole, *British Economic Growth 1688–1959* (Cambridge University Press, 1964), p. 133.

35 D. E. C. Eversley, 'The homemarket and economic growth in England 1750–1780', in *Land, Labour and Population in the Industrial Revolution*, ed. E. L. Jones and G. E. Mingay (Arnold, 1967), pp. 206–59.

36 P. and H. J. Habakkuk, 'The take-off in Britain' in *Economics of Take-Off*, pp. 63–82.
37 Deane and Cole, *British Economic Growth*, p. 118 table 27.
38 J. T. Krause, 'Some aspects of population change, 1690–1790', in *Land, Labour and Population*, pp. 187–205.
39 Deane and Cole, *British Economic Growth*, pp. 184–6.
40 K. Berrill, 'International trade and the rate of economic growth', *Economic History Review*, 12 (1960), pp. 351–9.
41 A. J. P. Taylor, *'Manchester'*, *Encounter* 8 (1957), pp. 3–13.
42 Arthur Redford, *Manchester Merchants and Foreign Trade 1794–1858* (Manchester University Press, 1954), pp. 243–5.
43 Ibid., p. 224.

CHAPTER II   INDUSTRIAL GREATNESS

1 See A. Briggs, *Victorian Cities* (Odhams Press, 1963), pp. 83–135.
2 Anonymous, 'The origins of London', *Cornhill Magazine*, 43 (1881), pp. 169–82.
3 R. Gray, 'Bourgeois hegemony in Victorian Britain', in *Class, Hegemony and Party*, ed. J. Bloomfield (Lawrence and Wishart, 1977), pp. 19–41.
4 P. J. Cain and A. G. Hopkins, 'Gentlemanly capitalism and British expansion overseas. I. The old colonial system 1688–1850', *Economic History Review*, 39 (1986), pp. 501–25.
5 F. W. Brooks, *The Council of the North* (Historical Association, 1966), p. 31.
6 Cf. F. M. L. Thompson, 'The social distribution of landed property in England since the sixteenth century', *Economic History Review*, 19 (1966), pp. 505–17, esp. p. 516.
7 Calculated from data in W. D. Rubinstein, 'Wealth, elites and the class structure of modern Britain', *Past & Present*, 76 (1977), pp. 99–126.
8 For somewhat different emphases in interpreting the early years of the industrial revolution see T. S. Ashton, 'The standard of life of the workers in England 1790–1830' in *Capitalism and the Historians*, ed. F. A. Hayek (Routledge & Kegan Paul, 1954), pp. 127–59, and E. J. Hobsbawm, 'The British standard of living 1790–1850', *Economic History Review*, 10 (1957–8), pp. 46–61.
9 See G. Stedman Jones, 'Class struggle and the industrial revolution', *New Left Review*, 90 (1975), pp. 35–69.
10 T. B. Macaulay, 'Southey's Colloquies', *Edinburgh Review*, 50 (1830), pp. 528–65.
11 William Cobbett, *Rural Rides* (2 vols, Everyman, 1973), vol. 2, p. 290.
12 Ibid., p. 294.

13 J. Caird, *English Agriculture in 1850–51* (Frank Cass, 1968), p. 512.

14 Ibid., p. 85.

15 Ibid., p. 516.

16 E. H. Hunt, *Regional Wage Variations in Britain 1850–1914* (Clarendon Press, 1973), p. 39.

17 Ibid., p. 4.

18 Ibid., p. 339.

19 L. Faucher, *Manchester in 1844* tr by member of Manchester Atheneum (Frank Cass, 1969), pp. 108–10.

20 Quoted in W. O. Henderson, *The Lancashire Cotton Famine 1861–1865* (Manchester University Press, 1934), p. 3.

21 W. D. Rubinstein, *Men of Property* (Croom Helm, 1981), p. 83.

22 W. D. Rubinstein, 'The Victorian middle classes: wealth, occupation and geography', *Economic History Review*, 30 (1977), pp. 602–23.

23 For the curious view that the industrial bourgeoisie was 'hegemonic' and the landed aristocracy merely 'dignified' see Robert Gray, 'Bourgeois hegemony in Victorian Britain' in *Class, Hegemony and Party*, pp. 19–41.

24 T. R. Tholfsen, *Working Class Radicalism in Mid-Victorian England* (Croom Helm, 1976), p. 11.

25 W. D. Rubinstein, 'Wealth, elites and the class structure of modern Britain', *Past & Present*, 76 (1977), pp. 99–126.

26 W. E. H. Lecky, *A History of England in the Eighteenth Century* (8 vols, Longmans, Green & Co., 1879) vol. 2, p. 636.

27 R. W. Rawson, 'An inquiry into the statistics of crime in England and Wales', *Journal of the Statistical Society*, 2 (1839), pp. 316–44.

28 P. E. Razzell and R. W. Wainwright, *The Victorian Working Class* (Cass, 1973), p. 190.

29 W. A. Abram, 'Social condition and political prospect of the Lancashire workmen', *Fortnightly Review*, 10 (1868), pp. 426–41.

30 F. Engels, *The Condition of the Working Class in England* (Penguin Books, 1987), p. 31.

31 G. W. Daniels, *The Early English Cotton Industry* (Longman, Green & Co., 1920), p. 142.

32 Ibid., pp. 134–6.

33 Ibid., p. xxix. A recent study of handloom weavers emphasizes the part-time nature of handloom weaving, concedes that the weaver owned his own loom and promises and, especially at the 'fancy' end of the trade, might employ journeymen and apprentices, but insists nevertheless that he cannot be regarded as an 'independent manufacturer'. But the weaver certainly knew that going to work as a 'hand' in a factory was a massive reduction in independence and status and was extremely reluctant, however deep his distress, to do this. See D. Bythell, *The Handloom Weavers* (Cambridge University Press, 1969), pp. 38, 61, 253.

34 Thompson, *English Working Class*, pp. 734–8.

35 D. Read, *Peterloo* (Manchester University Press, 1958), p. 118.

36 J. Foster, *Class Struggle in the Industrial Revolution* (Weidenfeld and Nicholson, 1974), p. 315 n. 55.

37 Read, *Peterloo*, p. 175.

38 Thompson, *English Working Class*, p. 737.

39 Ibid., p. 325.

40 E. P. Hennock, *Fit and Proper Persons* (Arnold, 1973), p. 198.

41 See E. Glasgow, 'The establishment of the Northern Star newspaper', *History*, 39 (1954), pp. 54–67.

42 See D. Read, 'Chartism in Manchester' in *Chartist Studies*, ed. A. Briggs (Macmillan, 1959), pp. 29–64.

43 Roy A. Church and S. D. Chapman, 'Gravener Henson and the making of the English working class' in *Land, Labour and Population in the Industrial Revolution*, ed. E. L. Jones and G. E. Mingay (Arnold, 1967), pp. 131–61.

44 W. S. F. Pickering, 'The 1851 religious census – a useless experiment?' *British Journal of Sociology*, 18 (1967), pp. 382–407.

45 Calculated from Robert Currie, *Methodism Divided* (Faber, 1968), p. 87 table 1, p. 90 table 2, p. 95 table 3.

46 Ibid., p. 104.

47 Ibid., p. 87.

48 Thompson, *English Working Class*, p. 427.

49 P. Joyce, *Work, Society and Politics. The Culture of the Factory in Later Victorian England* (Harvester Press, 1980), p. 90.

50 Quoted by Engels in the preface to the 1892 publication of his book on the English working class. See Engels, *Working Class in England*, p. 42.

51 J. Garrard, *Leadership and Power in Victorian Industrial Towns 1830–80* (Manchester University Press, 1983), pp. 132–4.

52 Foster, *Class Struggle*, p. 229.

53 A. E. Musson, 'Class struggle and the labour aristocracy 1830–60', *Social History*, 3 (1967), pp. 335–56.

54 D. Cannadine. 'Residential differentiation in nineteenth-century towns: from shapes on the ground to shapes in society', in *The Structure of Nineteenth-century Cities*, eds. J. H. Johnson and C. G. Pooley (Croom Helm, 1982), pp. 235–51.

55 Cf. J. Foster, 'Nineteenth-century towns – a class dimension', in *The Study of Urban History*, ed. H. J. Dyos (Arnold, 1968), pp. 281–99.

56 See R. Dennis, *English Industrial Cities in the Nineteenth Century* (Cambridge University Press, 1984), p. 176.

57 Ibid., p. 177 and W. Ashworth, 'British industrial villages in the nineteenth century', *Economic History Review*, 3 (1950–1), pp. 378–87.

58 Joyce, *Work, Society and Politics*, p. 59.

59 See R. Moore, *Pitmen, Preachers and Politics. The Effects of Methodism in a Durham Mining Community* (Cambridge University Press, 1974), pp. 81–92.

60 R. Price, 'The other face of respectability: violence in the Manchester brick-making trade 1859–70', *Past & Present*, 66 (1975), pp. 110–32.

61 Henderson, *Cotton Famine*, p. 90.

62 See M. I. Watson, 'The cotton trade unions and labour representation in the later nineteenth century', *Northern History*, 20 (1984), pp. 207–16.

63 G. Rudé, *The Crowd in History* (Wiley, 1964), p. 184.

64 See R. Gregory, *The Miners and British Politics 1906–1914* (Oxford University Press, 1968), p. 57. For paternalism on the north-east coalfield in the later nineteenth century see Moore, *Pitmen, Preachers and Politics*, pp. 81–92.

65 See J. Obelkevich, *Religion and Rural Society. South Lindsey 1825–1875* (Clarendon Press, 1976), p. 23.

66 See R. S. Neale, 'Class and class consciousness in early nineteenth-century England: three classes or five?', *Victorian Studies*, 12 (1968), pp. 5–32.

67 For a critical examination of the view that such bourgeois ideologies were imposed by employers on employees see N. Abercrombie and B. S. Turner, 'The dominant ideology thesis', *British Journal of Sociology*, 29 (1978), pp. 149–70.

68 See Foster, *Class Struggle*. This conflict theme runs through the book.

69 D. S. Gadian, 'Class consciousness in Oldham and other north-west industrial towns 1830–1850', *Historical Journal*, 21 (1978), pp. 16–17 For a particularly strong emphasis on the identity of interests and outlook of workers and employers see a recent notable study of John Fielden: S. A. Weaver, *John Fielden and the Politics of Popular Radicalism 1832–1847* (Clarendon Press, 1987), pp. 15, 64–5, 297.

70 For industrial peace and radical politics in Woolwich and Greenwich see G. Crossick, *An Artisan Elite in Victorian Society: Kentish London 1840–1880* (Croom Helm, 1978), p. 230.

71 Abram, 'Social condition and political prospect', pp. 426–41.

72 Moore, *Pitmen, Preachers and Politics*, p. 37.

73 Garrard, *Leadership and Power*, p. 31.

74 Ibid., p. 33.

75 Ibid., p. 32.

76 Ibid., pp. 35, 127.

77 Cobbett, *Rural Rides*, vol. 2, p. 257.

78 See R. Groves, *Sharpen the Sickle. The History of the Farm Workers Union* (Porcupine Press, 1949), p. 140.

79 Razzell and Wainwright, *Victorian Working Class*, p. 3.

80 Ibid, p. 11.

81 E. J. Hobsbawm and G. Rude, *Captain Swing* (Lawrence and Wishart, 1969), pp. 199, 202, 304–5.

82 A Charlesworth, *Social Protest in a Rural Society* (Historical Geography Research series, 1979), pp. 43–4.

83 J. P. D. Dunbabin, 'The "revolt of the field": the agricultural labourers, movement in the 1870s', *Past & Present*, 26 (1963), pp. 68–97.

84 Hobsbawm and Rude, *Swing*, p. 180.

85 Cobbett, *Rural Rides*, vol. 2, p. 296.

86 *News Chronicle* accounts in Razzell and Wainwright, *Victorian Working Class*, pp. 62–4.

87 See F. M. L. Thompson, *English Landed Society in the Nineteenth Century* (Routledge and Kegan Paul, 1963).

88 G. Shaw-Lefevre, *Agrarian Tenures* (Cassell, 1893), p. 27.

89 Cf. F. M. L. Thompson, 'Land and politics in England in the nineteenth century', *Transactions of the Royal Historical Society*, 15 (1965), pp. 23–44.

90 J. Hurstfield, 'The profits of fiscal feudalism 1541–1602', *Economic History Review*, 8 (1955–6), pp. 53–61.

91 T. J. Nossiter, *Influence, Opinion and Political Idioms in Reformed England 1832–74* (Harvester Press, 1975), p. 29.

92 W. R. Ward, 'The tithe question in England in the early nineteenth century', *Journal of Ecclesiastical History*, 16 (1965), pp. 67–81.

93 See H. J. Habakkuk, 'English landownership 1680–1740', *Economic History Review*, 10 (1940), pp. 2–17, J. V. Beckett, 'The pattern of landownership in England and Wales 1660–1880', *Economic History Review*, 37 (1984), pp. 1–22; and G. E. Mingay, *English Landed Estates in the Eighteenth Century* (Routledge and Kegan Paul, 1963), p. 50.

94 K. B. McFarlane, *The Nobility in Later Medieval England* (Clarendon Press, 1973), pp. 69–73.

95 F. M. L. Thompson, 'The social distribution of landed property in England since the sixteenth century', pp. 505–17, but for criticism of this trend analysis see J. P. Cooper, 'The social distribution of land and men in England, 1436–1700', *Economic History Review*, 20 (1967), pp. 419–40.

96 A. S. Turberville, *The House of Lords in the Age of Reform 1784–1837* (Faber, 1958), p. 409.

97 Calculated from George C. Brodrick, *English Land and English Landlords* (Cassell, Petter and Galpin, 1881), pp. 173–87.

98 W. D. Rubinstein, 'Wealth, elites and the class structure of modern Britain', pp. 99–126.

99 Quoted D. Read, *The English Provinces c1760–1960* (Arnold, 1964), pp. 131–2.

100 See Brodrick, *English Land and English Landlords*, pp. 267–71.

101 B. Manning, *The English People and the English Revolution 1640–1649* (Heinemann, 1976), pp. 162, 215, 253.

102 C. D. Field, 'The social structure of English methodism: eighteenth – twentieth centuries', *British Journal of Sociology*, 28 (1977), pp. 199–225.

103 See Corrie, *Methodism Divided*, p. 144.

104 R. Fieldhouse and B. Jennings, *A History of Richmond and Swaledale* (Phillimore, 1978), p. 209.

105 B. Lee (ed.), *Lead Mining in Swaledale: From the Manuscript of Edward R. Fawcett* (Faust Publications, 1985), p. 33.

106 Ibid., pp. 11–12.

107 Fieldhouse and Jennings, *Richmond and Swaledale*, p. 347.

108 J. L. Hammond and B. Hammond, *The Bleak Age* (Penguin Books, 1947), pp. 200–1.

109 Read, *English Provinces*, p. 86.

110 Ibid., p. 85.

111 See J. E. Williams, 'Paternalism in local government in the nineteenth century', *Public Administration*, 33 (1955), pp. 439–46.

112 Garrard, *Leadership and Power*, p. 130.

113 N. Gash, *Aristocracy and People. Britain 1815–1865* (Arnold, 1965), p. 197.

114 See M. E. Rose, 'The anti-poor law movement in the north of England', *Northern History*, 1 (1966), pp. 70–91.

115 G. M. Trevelyan, *English Social History* (Longmans, Green & Co., 1946), p. 539.

116 Quoted N. McCord, *The Anti-Corn Law League 1838–1846* (Allen & Unwin, 1958), p. 215.

117 Brodrick, *English Land and English Landlords*, pp. 247–53.

118 Gregory, *Miners and British Politics*, p. 57.

119 A. Briggs, *Victorian Cities* (Odhams Press, 1963), p. 371.

120 See R. G. Wilson, *Gentlemen Merchants. The Merchant Community in Leeds 1700–1800* (Manchester University Press, 1971), p. 34.

121 C. P. Darcy, *The Encouragement of the Fine Arts in Lancashire 1760–1860* (Chetham Society, 1976), p. 4.

122 See T. S. Ashton, *Economic and Social Investigations in Manchester 1833–1933* (King & Son, 1934), pp. 11–12.

123 L. Stone, 'Literacy and education in England 1640–1900', *Past & Present*, 42 (1969), pp. 69–139, esp. p. 103.

124 W. B. Stephens, *Education, Literacy and Society 1830–70* (Manchester University Press, 1987), pp. 322–3.

125 A. Conan Doyle, 'The geographical distribution of British intellect', *Nineteenth Century*, 24 (1888), pp. 184–95.

CHAPTER 12 ECONOMIC DECLINE AND RADICAL FERMENT

1 A. J. P. Taylor, *English History 1914–1945* (Clarendon Press, 1985), pp. 351–2.
2 K. G. J. C. Knowles, *Strikes – A Study in Industrial Conflict* (Basil Blackwell, 1952), pp. 197, 207, 312.
3 M. Stephens, *Roots of Power* (Spa Books, 1986), p. 233.
4 R. Hyman, *Strikes* (Fontana. 1984), pp. 30–3.
5 See S. Fothergill and G. Gudgin, *Unequal Growth: Urban and Regional Employment Changes in the UK* (Heinemann, 1982), p. 101.
6 P. Joyce, *Work, Society and Politics. The Culture of the Factory in Later Victorian England* (Harvester Press, 1980), p. 332.
7 R. Gregory, *The Miners and British Politics 1906–1914* (Oxford University Press, 1968), pp. 180–1, and A. J. Taylor, 'Labour productivity and technological innovation in the British coal industry, 1850–1914', *Economic History Review*, 14 (1961), pp. 48–70.
8 A. L. Bowley, *The Change in the Distribution of the National Income 1880–1913* (Clarendon Press. 1920), p. 19.
9 E. H. Phelps Brown, *The Growth of British Industrial Relations* (Macmillan, 1959), p. 337.
10 In *Commonweal*, 1 March 1885 reprinted in the preface to Friedrich Engels, *The Condition of the Working Class in England* (Penguin Books, 1987).
11 K. Berrill, 'International trade and the rate of economic growth', *Economic History Review*, 12 (1960), pp. 351–59.
12 H. J. Habakkuk and P. Deane, 'The take-off' in *The Economics of Take-Off into Sustained Growth*, ed. W. W. Rostow (Macmillan, 1963), pp. 63–82.
13 Cf. R. C. K. Ensor, *England 1870–1914* (Clarendon Press, 1936), p. 501.
14 See R. N. Price, 'The working men's club movement and Victorian social reform ideology', *Victorian Studies*, 15 (1971), pp. 117–47.
15 See C. A. Moser and W. Scott, *British Towns* (Oliver and Boyd, 1961), p. 37 table 18.
16 See J. Reynolds and K. Laybourn, 'The emergence of the independent labour party in Bradford', *International Review of Social History*, 20 (1975), pp. 313–46.
17 Ensor, *England 1870–1914*, p. 222.
18 Joseph Edwards (ed.), *Labour Annual* (Clarion Company, 1906), p. 30.
19 See H. Pelling, *Popular Politics in Late Victorian Society* (Macmillan, 1968), pp. 20–30.
20 P. F. Clarke, *Lancashire and the New Liberalism* (Cambridge University Press, 1971), p. 406.
21 See A. E. P. Duffy, 'New unionism in Britain, 1889–1890: a reappraisal', *Economic History Review*, 14 (1961), pp. 306–19.

22 H. Pelling, *The Origins of the Labour Party 1880–1900* (Macmillan, 1954), p. 205.

23 David Butler, 'Electors and elected' in *Trends in British Society since 1900*, ed. A. H. Halsey (Macmillan, 1972), pp. 227–47, esp. pp. 240–1.

24 For some examination of this paradox see J. F. Glaser, 'English nonconformity and the decline of Liberalism', *American Historical Review*, 63 (1957–8), pp. 352–63.

25 Roy Gregory, *The Miners and British Politics 1906–1914* (Oxford University Press, 1968), p. 189.

26 See K. Groves, *Sharpen the Sickle* (Porcupine Press, 1949), p. 105.

27 Robert Moore, *Pitmen, Preachers and Politics. The Effects of Methodism in a Durham Mining Community* (Cambridge University Press, 1974), p. 36.

28 Gregory, *Miners and British Politics*, pp. 80–1, 97.

29 Ibid., p. 32 table 6.

30 H. A. Turner, *Trade Union Growth, Structure and Policy. A Comparative Study of the Cotton Unions* (Allen and Unwin, 1962), p. 360.

31 M. I. Watson, 'The cotton trade unions and labour representation in the late nineteenth century', *Northern History*, 20 (1984), pp. 207–16.

32 Turner, *Trade Union Growth*, p. 361.

33 Joyce, *Work, Community and Politics*, p. 332.

34 D. Butler and D. Stokes, *Political Change in Britain* (Penguin Books, 1971), p. 179 table 6.14.

35 See Gregory, *Miners and British Politics*, pp. 99–100, and H. Pelling, *Social Geography of British Elections 1885–1910* (Macmillan, 1967), p. 420.

36 Knowles, *Strikes*, p. 197.

37 Pelling, *Social Geography of British Elections*, p. 415 table 52.

38 Clarke, *Lancashire and the New Liberalism*, p. 10.

39 Pelling, *Social Geography of British Elections*, p. 259.

40 J. P. D. Dunbabin, 'British elections in the nineteenth and twentieth centuries: a regional approach', *English Historical Review*, 95 (1980), pp. 241–67,

41 Robert Roberts, *The Classic Slum* (Manchester University Press, 1971), pp. 14, 178, 179.

42 Calculated from data in D. Hopkin, 'The membership of the independent labour party 1904–10: a spatial and occupational analysis', *International Review of Social History*, 20 (1975), pp. 175–97.

43 See Halsey, *Trends in British Society*, pp. 240–1 table 8.2, and Dunbabin, 'British elections in the nineteenth and twentieth centuries', pp. 241–67.

44 See D. Read, *The English Provinces* (Arnold, 1964), pp. 205–6.

45 A. Heath, K. Jowell and J. Curtice, *How Britain Votes* (Pergamon Press, 1985), p. 29.

46 See M. F. L. Thompson, *English Landed Society in the Nineteenth Century* (Routledge & Kegan Paul, 1963), pp. 332–3.

47 Heath, Jowell and Curtice, *How Britain Votes*, p. 74.

48 Ibid., p. 75.

49 F. Parkin, *Middle Class Radicalism. The Social Bases of the British Campaign for Nuclear Disarmament* (Manchester University Press, 1968), p. 91.

50 Heath, Jowell and Curtice, *How Britain Votes*, p. 30, table 3.1.

51 Ibid., p. 75 table 6.1, and Butler and Stokes, *Political Change in Britain*, pp. 178–9 table 6.14.

52 Heath, Jowell and Curtice, *How Britain Votes*, p. 81 table 6.5.

53 See M. Adeney and J. Lloyd, *The Miners' Strike 1984–5. Loss Without Limit* (Routledge and Kegan Paul, 1986), p. 15.

54 Ibid., p. 15.

Index